The impact of violence on
the family

DATE DUF

The Impact of Violence
on the Family

RELATED TITLES OF INTEREST

THE IMPACT OF VIOLENCE ON THE FAMILY

Treatment Approaches for Therapists
and Other Professionals

Dean M. Busby, Editor

Syracuse University

NEW ENGLAND INSTITUTE OF TECHNOLOGY
LIBRARY
Allyn and Bacon

Boston • London • Toronto • Sydney • Tokyo • Singapore

Copyright © 1996 by Allyn & Bacon
A Simon & Schuster Company
Needham Heights, Massachusetts 02194

Library of Congress Cataloging-in-Publication Data

The impact of violence on the family : Treatment approaches for
  therapists and other professionals / Dean M. Busby, editor.
       p.   cm.
  Includes bibliographical references and index.
  ISBN 0-205-17570-8
       1. Family violence—Psychological aspects.   2. Victims of family
  violence—Rehabilitation.   3. Family psychotherapy.   I. Busby, Dean M.
RC569.5.F3I47   1996
616.85'82--dc20   95-40081
                                                                      CIP

Printed in the United States of America
10 9 8 7 6 5 4 3   00

CONTENTS

v

PREFACE

This book is designed to give therapists and other helping professionals a comprehensive overview of treatment approaches for violence in the family. A broad ecological viewpoint is used to explore the different types of violence family members may experience, including violence from people outside the home. The chapters focus on treatment issues and approaches that can be utilized by all helping professionals. The chapters are very diverse in form and content because some areas, such as abuse of the elderly, have received little attention in the literature, while other areas, such as adult survivors of sexual abuse, have received considerable research attention. Although much of the content was gleaned from existing research, each chapter contributes new ideas and strategies for dealing with the complicated problems that violence creates.

Each year it is becoming harder to keep abreast of the new books and journal articles devoted to the topic of interpersonal violence; literature on violence has erupted like the Malthusian population curve. It is heartening to see so much attention focused on a problem that causes severe suffering in families. Considering how late in this century family violence emerged as an important area of inquiry, it is surprising how rapidly information has accumulated. This speaks to both our fascination with and repulsion of the subject matter.

Although the literature is burgeoning, there are several reasons to remain pessimistic about our understanding of family violence. With all of the increased attention to the issue of violence, it is doubtful whether any significant decreases have occurred in prevalence rates. Probably the only clear issue that has emerged from the literature on violence is that most people will experience and/or inflict a significant amount of violence over the course of their lives.

It is unpleasant to face the fact that most of us are victims and/or perpetrators of violence, and that no matter how much energy is invested in the prevention and treatment of the problem of violence, it will probably never be eliminated from the human experience. Is it a lost cause?

Survivors of violence often perceive the world very differently than individuals who have not experienced violence. People and relationships are viewed with skepticism, new experiences are approached with tremendous trepidation, rage seems to emerge unpredictably, and feelings of hopelessness may recur uncontrollably. Any helping professional knows that an entire lifetime invested in attempting to prevent or ameliorate the effects of violence is well spent even if only one person escapes a severe beating, or if only one person heals from the scars of childhood trauma.

An additional reason to remain pessimistic about progress in the area of violence prevention is that the treatment literature has simply not kept pace with the nontreatment research. There are considerable gaps in what we know about successfully treating the antecedents and consequences of violence. In addition, the existing treatment literature is overly focused on the individual. Hence many of the approaches emphasize long-term individual treatment, ignore natural support systems, fail to address the impact of violence on the entire family, and seldom acknowledge the larger social problems that interfere with successful outcomes and contribute to increased violence.

THEMES

Making Violence the Primary Focus of Therapy

Although they may not be explicitly stated in each chapter, there are several consistent themes throughout this book. By writing a book on treatment approaches for violence, the authors adopt a philosophical stance that violence is worthy of *primary symptom focus*. Rather than assume that violence is the result of some underlying psychopathology or dysfunctional family processes, the authors in this book are assuming that violence can, and often should be, the primary focus of treatment. At the same time, because of the ecological focus of the writing, an additional theme here is that therapists must see beyond the individual.

An Ecological Perspective

It may seem like making violence a primary focus in therapy is somehow inconsistent with an ecological view. It is possible to focus on individual responsibility in the therapy room, while at the same time addressing how violence impacts other systems and exploring how other systems influence violent tendencies.

There are few problems in society that attract as many people to "help out" as does family violence. Often there are several therapists, police officers, child protective workers, family and criminal court lawyers and judges, social workers, school personnel, friends, and extended family members all trying to do their part to solve the problem. If the therapist acts in isolation, solely concerned with the process within the therapy room, it is likely that the clients will be receiving inadequate care.

Emphasizing Relationships in the Healing Process

Violence is an interpersonal process. The pain and damage that occurs when people resort to violence speaks to the breakdown of a relationship. Although the physical and psychological damage is often extreme, the most enduring damage is that perpetrators and victims learn to establish and maintain distorted and dissatisfying relationships. Even though the players in the relationship may change, the dissatisfaction and the emotional damage continues to accumulate over time. The ever-increasing amount of damage can stop only when dissatisfying relationships are improved or replaced by healthy ones.

Because the most enduring damage from violence is relational in nature, healing from trauma is best accomplished within healthy relationships. Healing relationships can take many forms, from the therapist–client relationship, to one between adult partners, or between a parent and a child. Professionals will have the greatest impact when they help clients develop healthy relationships that will endure beyond the end of therapy.

Empowering Survivors of Violence

The beginning point for therapy is to stop the violence and help the perpetrator and the victim place the responsibility for the violence with the perpetrator. Much of the energy in treatment, though, should focus on helping victims to become empowered so that they can see themselves as survivors with choices. In a family "the victim" is often more than one person.

Once a person has resorted to violence to solve problems, there is no guarantee that violence will not be used again. Even if violence never reoccurs, it is questionable whether someone who has had his or her physical safety threatened in a serious way will ever believe he or she is entirely safe with a violent family member. How would it feel to live for the rest of your life next door to someone who had sexually abused your child? Worse yet, how would it feel to be married to that person? In families, sometimes these are the difficult circumstances that survivors must face.

Many abuse survivors make the difficult choice to stay in a relationship with someone who has been violent. With the exception of survivors who are underage, it is usually not the therapist's responsibility to oppose or support these decisions. It is the therapist's job to help survivors gain sufficient confidence in and understanding of their own abilities to make decisions that promote long-term safety and satisfaction. More than anything else, this demands patience and continued support from the therapist.

Putting a priority on the victim(s) does not imply that perpetrators are left out of treatment. Almost all perpetrators were also victims. Nevertheless, if two individuals were arguing and one punched the other, the first priority would be to stop the hitting. If the person who was punched had a broken jaw, while the one who threw the punch had some unhealed wounds from previous fights, the physician would first treat the broken jaw and then deal with the perpetrator's unhealed wounds. Additionally when it was time for the patients to go home, the choice of whether to return to the same home and relationship would be the victim's. The physician's role is to provide the victim with adequate time and space to make the difficult decision without pressure.

A Focus on Resiliency and Strength

An additional theme throughout the chapters of this book is that people are resilient. Trauma of any form tends to exacerbate or amplify preexisting weaknesses in the individual, family, and social systems. These weaknesses are often called presenting problems by clients, or symptoms by therapists. At the same time, trauma creates a series of responses that help the individuals cope with intrusive memories, thoughts, and feelings. These responses, such as denial, numbing, compulsive behaviors, depression, addictions, and so on, can help the individual face the trauma but, simultaneously, may produce additional dysfunction in other areas. In this book, then, it is recognized that all symptoms can be seen as both a strength and a weakness. The helping professional has the difficult task of emphasizing the strength underlying any coping mechanism while at the same time helping family members adopt strategies that are more functional.

OVERVIEW OF THE BOOK

The book is divided into two main sections: intrafamilial violence and extrafamilial violence. *Intrafamilial* violence refers to violence that occurs between family members. *Extrafamilial* violence refers to violence that is inflicted on a family member from someone who is not legally a member of the family.

The identity of the perpetrator of the violence can have a profound impact on the consequences for the family. The issues are quite different when an unknown assailant physically assaults a family member than when a parent or a sibling is the perpetrator. On the one hand the perpetrator speaks to the ills of the larger society and the family can pull together against the outsider to help each other heal. However, in some instances, violence from outsiders exacerbates existing problems in the family. In other instances, violence from an outsider creates such a sense of uncertainty that previously stable relationships seem to hang by a thread. In both cases, assistance from a therapist can greatly enhance recovery.

On the other hand, violence within the family speaks to the problems that exist inside the individual and between family members. The violence is inflicted by people who purport to love the victims but the behaviors speak more about hate and anger. This confusion of love and hate creates a scenario where victims may have nowhere to look for support. Loyalty to the family may be strong, thereby increasing the tendency to deny problems. In addition, the victims may have genetically and behaviorally inherited violent tendencies that can further confuse the distinction between victim and perpetrator. Intrafamilial and extrafamilial violence demand different approaches and skills from the helping professional.

In this book, additional divisions are made between different types of perpetrators and victims within the family. There are unique therapeutic issues for violence that occurs between two adults, violence that is inflicted by parent to child, and violence that is inflicted by child to parent. Each of these areas is given attention in separate chapters.

Another important division in this book is that between different types of violence such as physical and sexual abuse. Although both types of abuse can have similar characteristics, there are important effects specific to each that deserve delineation. Writing separate chapters on physical and sexual abuse, however, should not be interpreted to mean that physical and sexual abuse usually occur independently.

It is hoped that the quantity of research on treatment strategies for violence will dramatically increase in the coming years. This book is intended to help those therapists and researchers who are struggling in a therapeutic area that is still in its infancy. It is also intended to assist professionals who have the courage to help clients leave the angry, painful world of violence for a better place.

ACKNOWLEDGMENTS

I gratefully acknowledge the contributions of Susan Crockett, the Dean of the College for Human Development at Syracuse University, for her encouragement and financial assistance with this project. Special research and summer grants were instrumental in bringing this work to completion. Deborah Banks gave invaluable assistance in the manuscript preparation and organization that is required in a multi-authored book. Colleen Busby was a constant source of encouragement and assistance with the editorial tasks of this book.

ABOUT THE EDITOR AND CONTRIBUTORS

Dean M. Busby is an assistant professor and the Director of Clinical Training and Research in the Marriage and Family Therapy Program at Syracuse University. He received his Ph.D. and M.S. degrees in Marriage and Family Therapy, with a minor in statistics, from Brigham Young University. He received his B.A. in Psychology, with a minor in Spanish, from the University of Utah. Professor Busby has presented workshops to national audiences in the area of family violence. He has published articles on family violence, premarital couples, assessment, and play therapy.

Susan V. Compton is a Marriage and Family Therapist at the Family and Children's Service in Ithaca, New York. Susan received her M.S. in Education from SUNY Binghamton. She is a doctoral candidate in the Marriage and Family Therapy Program at Syracuse University. She has conducted workshops on working with adolescents and their families from a contextual therapy perspective.

Steven M. Harris has four years of experience working with survivors of rape and sexual assault at Syracuse University's Counseling Center. He currently works as an Employee Assistance Professional with Crouse Irving Memorial Hospital in Syracuse, New York. Steven earned his M.A. from the Marriage and Family Therapy Program at Syracuse University where he is a doctoral candidate. He has published articles on ethics, counseling programs, and assessment.

Virginia Hullings Catalano is a counselor in the Alcohol/Drug Rehabilitation Unit of the Syracuse Community Health Center. She is completing her M.S. and Ph.D. degrees in Child and Family Studies at Syracuse University.

Jill R. Inman is a Marriage and Family Therapist in private practice in Syracuse, New York. She received her M.A. in Marriage and Family Therapy from Syracuse University. Jill is pursuing a dual doctorate in Anthropology and Marriage and Family Therapy. She has presented papers on violence in couple systems, intimate relationships, diversity issues in the classroom, and the effects of heterosexism and homophobia.

Kyle D. Killian is the Resident Coordinator of the International Living Center at Syracuse University. He is also an adjunct faculty member in the Human Services Department at Onondaga Community College. He earned his M.A. from the Marriage and Family Therapy program at Syracuse University where his is finishing his Ph.D. Kyle has published and presented papers on premarital sexual abuse, inhibited sexual desire, and interracial couples.

Sabine Krummel is currently the Director of Family Services, ARC Otsego, in Oneonta, New York. She earned her M.A. degree in Marriage and Family Therapy from Syracuse University. Sabine has received specialized training in medical family therapy, experiential family therapy, and working with the elderly.

Laurie B. Levine is a Family Therapist for Partners in Change, Inc., in Morristown, New Jersey. She earned her M.A. from Hofstra University and her Ph. D. from Syracuse University in Marriage and Family Therapy. Laurie has published in the area of social constructionism and premarital couples.

Joseph R. Norton is the Case Supervisor of the Child Protective Services Unit of the Department of Social Services in Seneca County, New York. He has been working in the child protective services area for more than ten years. Joseph earned his M.A. degree in Marriage and Family Therapy from Syracuse University and has received specialized training in sex therapy.

Jan Osborn is a licensed Marriage and Family Therapist specializing in the treatment of sexual abuse. She is an Assistant Professor at Northwestern University in the Department of Education and Social Policy. Jan has published and presented articles on incest and family therapy research.

Johanna Wilson is a Marriage and Family Therapist in private practice in Cortland, New York. She received her M.A. in Marriage and Family Therapy from Syracuse University. Johanna has also received specialized clinical training in working with problem adolescents and young children in family therapy.

1

PHYSICAL ABUSE OF WOMEN IN MARRIAGE

DEAN M. BUSBY, JILL R. INMAN

There are 13 steps…and he (father) hit me on every step…
—*A BATTERER'S RECOLLECTION OF HIS ABUSE*

…No matter what happens it doesn't warrant
my behavior anymore.
—*HIS THOUGHTS ON HIS ABUSE OF HIS WIFE*

That's what broke me, it's left me defeated…I don't
want to be that person, I can't be that person.
—*HIS FEELINGS ABOUT BEING A PERPETRATOR*

These statements from a batterer depict the intergenerational abuse he experienced from his father and the feelings he had about becoming a perpetrator. A feminist informed systems perspective is used to address treatment issues for married batterers, their spouses and children. To help those in violent relationships recover from the battering, the treatment context will include the batterer, his spouse, their families of origin, their children, and larger systems. A case study that utilizes video playback is examined in the context of a couple requesting therapy. Therapy assessment, goals, and treatment are examined for the different potential contexts of family members.

BACKGROUND

Some authors estimate that the number of intimate relationships with violent husbands ranges from 20 to 30 percent (Stark & Flitcraft, 1988; Straus & Gelles, 1986). Broken bones, miscarriages, broken families, and death are some of the consequences of battering in intimate relationships. Each year over one million women seek medical care due to battering. Victims also experience nightmares and somatic consequences, and children who witness abuse may be symptomatic, displaying a high number of somatic, psychological, and behavioral problems (Nadelson & Sauzier, 1989). School phobias, enuresis, stuttering, and problems with schoolwork are additional problems that result for children (Nadelson & Sauzier, 1989).

In addition to psychological scarring for victims, children, and batterers, there are broader societal repercussions of domestic violence. "The structural, cultural, and social characteristics of our society continue to perpetuate the victimization of women on all levels" (Williams-White, 1989). Violence within familial relationships reflects and helps maintain violence and oppression culturewide. Violent husbands not only contribute to maintaining the level of violence in society, but they reflect "a direct manifestation of socially learned sex-role behaviors" (Jennings, 1987, p. 195). The prevalence of battering crosses race, ethnicity, and socioeconomic status (Hotaling & Sugarman, 1986). Nontreatment of violence can lead to more violence (Walker, 1984). In systems that do not change, future generations may continue to resort to violence to solve problems. In addition, in many of those systems, violence may become more severe with time.

Systems theory conceptualizes wife abuse within the frame of family violence, and assumes that "violence is the outcome of the complex social interaction within the family system which exists as part of a larger social system" (Giles-Sims, 1983, p. 19). The current patterns of conflict resolution and violence are born of historical patterns in previous generations. Systems theory is concerned with *how* violence, or wife battering, becomes a pattern within a specific system. Within the frame of systems theory, many therapies have been utilized to help families in which husbands are violent. Brief solution-focused, cognitive/behavioral, feminist theory, and a variety of integrated models have all attempted to help families deal with violence.

HOW VIOLENCE EMERGES IN THERAPY

There are a number of directions therapists may follow when the issue of physical violence comes to the forefront, whether through the client's initial disclosure or the therapist's investigation. Sometimes the abused spouse will present to the therapist for issues dealing directly with the violence or she may present with other issues. Occasionally couples will come in for therapy regarding related issues, and some may present with the physical violence as the primary issue. Parents may bring their children in for therapy because of acting out, poor school performance, and other reactions to violence in the family system. A batterer may present because his wife is threatening to leave, or because he is concerned about the battering. The variety of ways in which people seek help gives therapists a number of accesses into the system.

Some therapists routinely assess new clients for physical violence with the Wife Abuse Inventory (Lewis, 1985, 1988) and the Index of Spouse Abuse

(Hudson and McIntosh, 1981). These screening techniques do not guarantee clients' forthrightness about battering. Neidig and Friedman (1984) suggest utilizing the Conflict Tactics Scale (Straus, 1979), Locus of Control Scale (Nowicki & Marshall, 1974), and a variation of the Holmes and Rahe Social Readjustment Rating Scale (Holmes & Rahe, 1967) for assessing methods of conflict resolution, how much control clients perceive they have over their life, and level of stress. Asking questions about how the couple fights, what happens when there is tension at home, and if forms of battering occur are also important when investigating violence in the system. When therapists realize physical violence exists, assessment of the danger level and other related variables—severity, length of time, determining the direct recipients of the violence, and history of family of origin—is recommended. Assessment is important regardless of which member of the family has come to the therapist. It provides information for the therapist regarding the level of danger family members perceive in the system and who the victims of the violence are. It may also bring to light substance abuse or any other issues that complicate or contribute to the violence. For clients, assessment may increase their awareness of the extent of the problem, and begin the sensitization process for the batterer.

Results of assessment may indicate particular strategies for treatment. Safety plans for the abused spouse and children are critical and need to be implemented with them and with the battering spouse, if he is available. Establishing a contract for nonviolence with the batterer is also an important first step in treatment, and separation may be warranted, depending on the abused spouse's wishes and the availability of resources. Some form of support system for the victim and children is also recommended. How these strategies are implemented will largely depend on who is coming to therapy and the therapist's theoretical premise regarding physical violence.

The primary goal of any therapy aimed at helping batterers and their families is to stop the violence. Some therapists conceptualize this goal to mean all members of the family participate in trying to stop the violence. Others may place emphasis on the batterer to stop his actions, while victims are counseled to find safety and regain control over their lives. As such, goals for particular members may differ, but, the combined actions of holding the batterer responsible for the abuse and helping the victim regain control and pursue safety are consistent across cases.

TREATMENT ACCESS THROUGH THE ABUSED SPOUSE

Much of the literature on spouse abuse has focused on the characteristics of victims. Walker (1984) suggests that abused women will have low self-esteem; adhere to gender-related stereotypes; suffer guilt, anger, fear, isolation from supports; have difficulty making decisions; and believe they are unable to act on their own behalf—"learned helplessness." These signs may indicate violence when therapists see an individual woman, couple, or family. From a feminist-informed perspective, it is important to validate the experiences of the battered spouses and support them, while holding the batterers responsible for the violence. As Bograd (1988, p. 15) states,

> When men's lives, values, and attitudes are taken as the norm, the experiences of women are often defined as inferior, distorted, or are rendered invisible. To counteract this, feminists believe that a basic step toward understanding the factors contributing to wife abuse is illuminating the experiences of women from their own frames of reference.

The primary goals of treatment with an abused spouse include helping her acknowledge the existence of the abuse, encouraging her to stop the battering by removing herself (or legally removing her husband) from the site, strengthening her coping abilities and sense of power, and helping her clarify the mixed emotions she experiences (Williams-White, 1989). "Victims of domestic violence must be helped to validate their sense of self-esteem and self-worth so that they feel able and competent to make decisions about their lives and carry their decisions through to action" (Williams-White, 1989, p. 51). Abused spouses have a relationship that is "marked by violence, yet at the same time interspersed with kindness and affection...which makes it all but impossible for the battered woman to take decisive action" (Williams-White, 1989, p. 50). This combination of love and hate in an intimate relationship creates uncertainty and ambivalence for abused spouses. Sensitivity to these responses is critical.

Throughout this process, the therapist must believe that the woman knows and will do what is in her best interests; by believing in the victim, she may be able to believe in herself. Assessment entails determining the extent of the abuse: the most recent episode, the most dangerous episode; how she currently copes with the abuse (i.e., escaping to family/friends, fighting back or being passive); the involvement of children; and legal intervention.

Implementing a safety plan is one of the first goals of treatment. It is necessary to discuss what options the abused spouse has available to her, such as finances, family and/or friends who can provide shelter, extra keys to any vehicles, and her willingness to involve the authorities during or directly after violent episodes. During this discussion, the therapist can explore how willing the client is to leave the batterer, temporarily or permanently, and also assess the client's perceptions of her husband's willingness for treatment. If the husband is willing to seek treatment, the therapist, depending on her or his theoretical philosophy, can provide therapeutic and group referrals or arrange for an individual session with the batterer. It is also a good opportunity to suggest that the client bring in anyone who will support her with implementation of the plan. Part of the safety plan might entail connecting the abused spouse and children with the area domestic violence shelter for potential housing. In addition to shelter, most domestic violence agencies have group programs and educational support that work well in conjunction with therapy. Timing of the referral is important; some clients respond better to additional social supports after a strong connection has been built with their therapist, while others want additional support right from the start. The therapist must be cautious about letting supportive persons usurp or disempower the client. Implementation of the plan must rest with the client for only she can help with another primary goal of treatment, regaining control and power in her life. This can be achieved through supporting the client regarding decisions she makes, being sensitive and understanding when the client experiences ambivalence, and placing her in positions of power in determining goals, both of the therapy and of her life. These suggestions can be carried out through helping the client recognize cognitive thoughts that undermine her feelings of power and trust in herself. From a feminist-informed perspective, these treatment goals can be achieved through reminding the victim she is not at fault, acknowledging domestic violence as a major social problem, and validating her experiences (Bograd, 1984; Yllo & Bograd, 1988).

Reminding the abused spouse of the choice her husband makes every time he batters her may help her overcome feelings of responsibility for the abuse. Feelings of ambivalence about staying in the relationship also need to be addressed. The process of a victim becoming a survivor can be lengthy. Although it may be difficult, when the abused spouse wishes to remain or return to her abusive husband, the therapist must communicate trust in the client's judgment and at the same time hold the battering reality in front of the victim to remind her of the potential impact of her decision. Supporting abused spouses in making what the therapist might consider unhealthy decisions is relevant to the transformation from victim to survivor.

The therapist can help the victim deconstruct the belief that she cannot survive or act for herself. This can be approached by discussing what was learned in the family of origin and previous relationships and by identifying the beliefs, their history, and their incongruence with her current life situation. Any woman surviving battering *is* a survivor, which stands against the idea of weakness. Identifying sources of personal strength for the victim can facilitate growth while at the same time the therapist is deconstructing the beliefs that hold her prisoner. The therapist can help the abused spouse identify times when she acted on behalf of herself in her marriage and other important relationships. This will begin to construct a story of strength.

As the abused spouse recovers from the battering and protects herself and her children, family work is helpful in bringing the violence out in the open and providing a forum for the victim to talk about it with her own family and her children (see the section on "when children are involved"). Couple therapy is not recommended unless the batterer is in treatment, does not exhibit extreme psychopathology, is following his nonviolence contract, and the abused spouse wants him present (see the couple presentation section).

Inherent in a system where males are battering family members is the potential for extreme forms of violence such as death or permanent physical injury to women and children. Sometimes familiy members retaliate against batterers by using extreme violence that can also lead to death or injury of the batterer. It is critical for the therapist to remember that battered women, children, and therapists may be at risk of death. Trusting the client's and therapist's instincts about their safety is vital during treatment, when issues will very likely become intensified.

THE BATTERER

Theoretical Frames

Batterer treatment commonly uses a combination of feminist-informed, cognitive, behavioral, and rational-emotive therapies. Each approach has particular strengths that are useful for the therapist. According to Bograd (1988, pp. 13–14), there are four common tenets of feminist theory regarding wife abuse:

1. The explanatory utility of the constructs of gender and power;
2. The analysis of the family as a historically situated social institution;
3. The crucial importance of understanding and validating women's experiences;
4. Employing scholarship for women.

The experience of a husband beating his wife is specific to the differential power base of gender. Historically, women have been viewed as not as powerful as men; thus, men beat women because economically and physically they have the power to do so. Feminist theorists view families within their context, which is an oppressive societal institution. Men's violence occurs within this frame.

Feminist therapists see psychotherapy as one system that exists within the patriarchal society; psychotherapy is one place that can perpetuate or challenge male domination. "The feminist insight that informs the profeminist approach to batterers [is that] wife beating is controlling behavior that serves to create and maintain an imbalance of power between the battering man and the battered woman" (Martin, 1981; Schechter, 1982; Adams, 1988).

The cognitive approach focuses on the cognition of the batterer. Cognition is based on an "analysis of perceptions of external or internally produced stimuli and inner dialogue of self-statements that convey attitudes and decisions" (Deschner, 1984, p. 68). This dialogue of self-statements does not necessarily have to have angry connotations for violence to erupt, but a "negative emotional response" results from the thoughts (Hamberger & Lohr, 1989, p. 60). Battering results from the man trying to escape or release tension resulting from the negative response. Cognition controls emotions because cognitive activity occurs before having an emotional response. To help men who batter, interventions attempt to alter the cognitive thoughts and subsequently, control the emotions that result in violence. Ellis (1976), a proponent of rational emotive therapy, suggests that violent rage is based on the conclusions people draw from irrational demands. By changing the irrational demands, violence and rage will be avoided. Deschner (1984) clarifies the behavioral piece in which, when the batterer resorts to physical violence, if the repercussions are positive (i.e., he gets his way), then his behavior is reinforced and he is more likely to attempt it again.

Group Treatment with Batterers

Treatment for battering men may utilize a combination of group treatment and individual therapy. EMERGE is one example of a group treatment agency specifically focused toward the treatment of battering men (Adams & McCormick, 1982). A team of male social workers who have experience with consciousness-raising groups lead unstructured groups because men originally learn dominating male behaviors in peer groups and the group format offers opportunities to learn and share self-help skills that can be used at home to prevent violence.

Characteristics of group programs vary. Some are short term (three to six months) and others require a longer commitment (one year). Meetings might be once or twice a week, and some groups are open-ended while others are closed. Gondolf (1987) suggests three general categories of psychoeducational groups: counseling groups under mental health services and clinics, groups as part of women's shelters, and self-help groups. The counseling groups tend to be more clinical and focus on psychological issues and anger management, while the self-help groups are more focused on addressing anti-sexist issues and socialization issues for batterers.

Criticism for batterer groups comes from some feminist theorists. Their concern is that groups may offer an environment that allows for collusion with the batterer, and that lessens their sense of responsibility for the battering, while minimizing the power and gender role aspects (Adams, 1988).

One additional criticism is that battering may be situation specific: men batter women, not other men. This means that men's groups do not prepare the batterer to handle interaction with his wife or significant other, nor do some discuss the issues of gender and power inherent in an intimate male–female relationship (Adams, 1988). Often it is only the spouse that is the target of the batterer's abuse (Schechter, 1982). The man may be able to successfully demonstrate his mastery of the goals of the group, but not use the new behaviors at home.

Although professionals in the domestic violence field express differences about the appropriateness and effectiveness of batterer groups, most concede that the group experience is important to the batterer's treatment. Group process lessens the sense of isolation batterers have, and also addresses denial in a context that allows power equals (peers) to challenge each other (Ganley,

1981). A primary component shared by all groups is helping the batterer recognize his responsibility for the violent behavior. Groups also provide batterers opportunities to practice communication skills and manage anger and conflict.

Assessment

Intake sessions or interviews are the most common forms of assessment used to determine the appropriate match between a program and a batterer. Potential group candidates are assessed on the frequency, intensity, and history of violence within their intimate relationship and family of origin (Beninati, 1989; Nosko & Wallace, 1988). The Conflict Tactics Scale is a popular instrument to measure conflict in families, and the Index of Spouse Abuse measures the severity of abuse, both physical and emotional (Gondolf, 1987). Some programs assess motivational factors. Batterers who are motivated to seek treatment as a result of a potential arrest or divorce are less appropriate for group treatment than men who are internally motivated to change (Farley & Magill, 1988). Most programs will screen for alcohol/drug abuse, criminal histories, and mental health. Those who have current drug/alcohol problems are not allowed into the group unless receiving conjoint treatment for the substance abuse, or are encouraged to reapply when maintaining a drug-free lifestyle. Beninati (1989) screens for those men who are violent in general and have criminal records, preferring men who batter only their wives. Anyone with chronic mental health problems is generally not accepted into treatment (Nosko & Wallace, 1988). The general areas of assessment for men in groups also applies for men entering therapy.

General Treatment Issues with Batterers

A peer group format emphasizes that battering is a socially learned behavior with its roots in the societal patriarchy rather than an individual or relationship pattern. Adams and McCormick (1982) suggest that a combination of didactic exercises and group discussion helps men take responsibility for their behaviors while understanding and challenging the social context within which battering occurs.

With the overt goal being to stop the violent tendencies of batterers, combined therapy and group treatment may work well for most batterers. Specific goals focus on the particulars of the batterer program. For example, development of better communication skills, the ability to handle anger and stress, and lessening gender stereotypes are all goals for programs that utilize these interventions. The attainment and maintenance of goals is measured by verbal feedback from group members, homework, contracts, journals, and rarely, periodic interviews with the battered women (Adams & McCormick, 1982; Edelson & Grusznski, 1986; Neidig & Friedman, 1984).

The focus of treatment will be different in the group context than it is in the individual or couple context. In therapy, formal learning may not be as emphasized. The batterer may process his experiences from the group experience and how they translate to his behavior with his spouse. Therapists can effectively monitor and coordinate the group treatment and the home experiences. Therapy also may be a place where, on a one to one basis, the therapist can re-emphasize the batterer's responsibility for the abuse and explore his family history to facilitate understanding of his abusiveness. Although nonviolence contracts begin with the idea of finding other ways to handle rage, it is important to continue discussing behavioral methods that can assist the batterer in managing his rage. This can occur in group work and/or individual therapy.

The process of treatment may include the following. When the batterer appears in therapy and/or in a group treatment program, the therapist begins "challenging the batterer's attempts to control his partner through the use of physical force, verbal and nonverbal intimidation, and psychological abuse" (Adams, 1988, p. 191) and develops a safety plan with the husband to protect his wife. Two additional early interventions include educating the batterer about the effects of his abuse and challenging his denial of responsibility. When the batterer is unwilling to take responsibility for the violence, it is questionable whether his good intentions will be sufficient for successful treatment.

One way of sensitizing the batterer to his abusive ways is through video playback (see the next section on couple treatment for further information). Therapy may bring to the surface issues of violence the batterer experienced in his family of origin, which can lead to identifying the vulnerabilities that contribute to his actions. This also can present an opportunity to involve family members. The family can serve to help the batterer process his grief and anger about any abuse he received and how he learned his violent behaviors, and the family can support the batterer's attempts at recovery. However, if members of the batterer's family of origin continue to deny his victimization and or emphasize the utility of violence as a control mechanism, it may be counterproductive to include them. Usually, though, there is at least one member of the family of origin who can be helpful to the batterer's recovery.

It is important for the batterer to avoid using previous family violence as an excuse for his own perpetration. Connecting the batterer's experiences and feelings about being abused to his partner's feelings can be effective, and this can be achieved through family-of-origin work. Awareness of the impact of his violence keeps the focus on the woman's damaging experience, and helps the man become aware of the damage to the relationship (i.e., erosion of trust, security, and closeness) (Adams, 1989). In addition, it is important for the man to recognize what benefits he receives from perpetrating abuse. Ellis (1970) and Novaco (1975) note that it is harder for men to continue their abusive behavior when it is seen as deliberate.

Their behavior and attitudes may be dealt with conjointly, or the therapist may focus on one and then the other. For safety reasons, initially focusing on behavior control may be prudent in order to help the batterer identify and eliminate all behaviors that are violent, controlling, and abusive, including those that oppress his partner (Adams, 1988, 1989). Modification of behavior can be promoted through substituting behaviors that are nonviolent and nonabusive, and contracting for legal repercussions if the batterer does not remain nonviolent. Homework can include control logs in which men track their abusive and controlling behaviors in order to recognize them and the attitudes and expectations leading to them.

An additional way of helping the batterer face his violence and recognize that it is deliberate is to explore exceptions to the violence. Pointing out instances when the batterer has decided to not be violent serves several purposes. First, it indirectly emphasizes that if he can choose to *not* be violent, his violence is a willful act that is not out of control. Second, it helps the batterer understand and expand existing strategies, which he already possesses, that impede his violent tendencies (Sheinberg, Goldner, Penn, & Walker, 1992).

As his violent behavior is eliminated, therapy and group treatment can focus on attitude change. Challenging and exposing the batterer's sexist and oppressive attitudes and beliefs regarding women in general and his partner in particular are important. When the battering man demonstrates that he accepts his lack of control over his partner's feelings, attitudes, and thoughts, he may be approaching the end of formal treatment. Some profeminist treatment programs have follow-up advocacy for men who complete the group experience. This is offered to consolidate the man's nonabuse and commitment. "Battering men are expected to develop a critical awareness of [patriarchal, oppressive] arrangements while continuing to take responsibility for their own participation in them" (Adams, 1989, p.14). In therapy, this transition may indicate his readiness for conjoint treatment.

COUPLE PRESENTATION

Debates about conjoint treatment of couples when there has been violence are common in the psychotherapy fields. Some professionals treat the couple together, while others do not see a batterer and his victim together at all. Concerns for the battered spouse's safety, the message sent to batterers when they are seen conjointly, and therapeutic contracts are some of the more pressing issues regarding conjoint treatment.

Gutsche and Murray (1991) itemize four risks of conjoint treatment:

1. It may jeopardize the safety of the wives and children (Bograd, 1984; Willbach, 1989).
2. With the batterer present, victims and their children run the risk of being abused when they return home because of some thing(s) they said at therapy.
3. Conjoint treatment may minimize the abuse (Bograd, 1984).

4. With a systems theory approach, therapists may view the battering as one of many issues. Appropriate attention and focus may not be placed on the importance and priority of stopping the violence.

The presence of the nonoffending spouse may diffuse the batterer's responsibility for the violence (Bograd, 1984; Willbach, 1989). The batterer may dodge responsibility for the abuse by noting that the therapist required his wife to attend. This can imply that the therapist sees the victim as part of the battering problem and, thus, is responsible for it.

Family systems theory has not fully captured the importance of power and gender issues when considering families in the larger societal context (James & MacKinnon, 1990). Many therapists work without considering the impact of a male-dominated society. By not weaving power and gender differences throughout the therapy process, wives in therapy with their batterers may feel that their reality of inferiority in the face of their husbands is not valued or considered during treatment.

Some clinicians will determine conjoint treatment to be inappropriate based on the following criteria (Gutsche & Murray, 1991; Jennings & Jennings, 1991):

1. The husband refuses to be nonviolent;
2. Either spouse has substance abuse issues and refuses to address them;
3. The husband is not motivated for himself (i.e., he is in therapy because of his spouse's threats to leave/divorce him or he is court ordered);
4. The level of violence (serious injury or threats of murder) is extreme;
5. The wife and/or husband does not want conjoint work.

These criteria consider the abused spouse and children's safety first. If there is any indication that the husband cannot or will not work at nonviolence, conjoint therapy is not recommended. Indications that may suggest the timeliness of conjoint work include: the violence having stopped, the man has taken responsibility for the abuse and his future behavior; the woman no longer fears her husband, she has restored her self-esteem and is becoming assertive regarding her rights; and both spouses agree to conjoint treatment (Pressman, 1989). Of course, the validity of either the batterer's or the victim's reports of violence are not always high. In some instances, either partner will have a considerable amount of investment in reporting that violence has ceased when it is still occurring. Therapists are often left to their own intuitive sense of whether clients are telling the truth.

As with individual treatment with batterers and their wives, a number of therapies have been adapted to conjoint treatment of couples with violent husbands. The more traditional approach has been the cognitive/behavioral systems theory as discussed by Steinfeld (1989). Neidig and Friedman (1984,

p. 9) list the following goals of treatment from a cognitive/behavioral theoretical perspective:

1. Accept personal responsibility for the violent behavior;
2. Contract for change;
3. Develop and use time out and other security techniques;
4. Understand the violent sequence;
5. Learn and master anger control skills;
6. Contain interpersonal conflict through the problem-solving process.

Feminist-informed therapy is an additional theoretical approach that has had a dramatic impact on wife-abuse cases. Yllo and Bograd (1988) and Adams (1988, 1989) offer extensive discussion of feminist theory and battering. More recently, Gutsche and Murray (1991) consider feminist theory with Michael White's narrative style, and Lipchik (1991) discusses conjoint treatment of domestic violence in the brief solution-focused therapy context.

Some of these therapies have been utilized not only in a conjoint couple-session format but in group format for couples. Neidig and Friedman (1984) and Guerney, Waldo, and Firestone (1987) are two good sources for couple group format. Guerney, Waldo, and Firestone (1987) prefer to utilize couple group treatment because abusive couples "1) are typically more socially isolated than other couples, 2) are appreciative of an opportunity to reduce their isolation, and 3) benefit from the reduction of isolation" (p. 39).

Regardless of the format, the primary goal with conjoint treatment is helping the batterer control his violence and helping the family recover. To illustrate conjoint treatment, the couple in the case study that follows was treated from a feminist-informed systems framework. After discovery of the violence, they were seen individually while the husband attended a batterer's group and the wife worked on self-esteem issues and identified support systems. Conjoint treatment ensued until termination.

CASE STUDY

For most couples, when there is has been violence the presenting issue will be something other than the abuse (Mack, 1989). As such, therapists need to develop effective, thorough assessment procedures to explore issues of violence and abuse. Mary and Mike[*] completed a demographic questionnaire and a few instruments to assess general couple functioning and whether substance abuse was an issue. The couple did not circle physical abuse under "concerns for therapy" or identify battering as the primary problem during the first session. They were both in their mid-thirties with no children. It was the first marriage for both of them, and Mike had his own business, with

---

[*]The names have been changed to protect client confidentiality.

which Mary assisted. She also worked part-time while coming for some of the therapy sessions.

During the first session, the couple defined problems with communication as their primary reason for wanting to enter therapy. The therapist explored goals for treatment by asking what signs of change would indicate improvement. The couple had previously been in conjoint therapy. Mary indicated dissatisfaction with the therapist because she did not "get what was going on." Another issue brought up by Mary was Mike's lying; both agreed that his lying was something that needed to be worked on. A second appointment was set up.

Thorough assessment is crucial, and part of the assessment needs to include seeing each partner separately for some part of the session. It is often only in this way that the abused spouse will feel safe enough to acknowledge the violence. Whether the couple presents initially for physical violence or if the abuse is discovered at some point during treatment, it is necessary to assess the extent of the violence and the danger. If the abuse is discovered later in treatment, assessment is still recommended. Important questions to ask are: how does the couple fight (a thorough step-by-step description of a typical fight sequence, or the most extreme fight); who gets angrier; and how often does hitting, pushing, and/or other abusive tactics occur. Harris (1986) offers an extensive list of assessment areas.

Between the clients' first and second visits, during a supervision session, it was agreed that there seemed to be an elephant in the room. Hypotheses ranged from an affair to excessive substance abuse. During the second session, the therapist explored these options with the couple. At one point, Mary answered a question with, "He gets angry." When asked what happens when Mike gets angry, she said, "He yells, that's all." What happens if Mike gets angrier? She acknowledged, "He gets violent." At this point, the goal of therapy became cessation of the violence. Mike concurred, but Mary struggled about this throughout therapy, indicating it was Mike's lying that was the real problem. Attempts at reframing the lying as an attempt at avoiding his anger did not register for her, and it was also suggested that once she and Mike could be sure he wouldn't hurt her, they would be better equipped to work on their communication problems. They contracted for a third session.

It is important to note that sometimes the wife is more reluctant to prioritize the violence than the batterer is. This reluctance can be due to feelings of shame, the victim's sense of responsibility for the violence, hopelessness that the violence will ever stop, a pattern of violence during the entire lifespan that makes it seem normative, or fear. Therapists can become easily frustrated with victims who are reluctant to prioritize the cessation of violence. It is easy to take a hierarchical stance and decide for her what will be the focus of therapy; it is more therapeutic to slowly explore how fear and violence permeate much of the woman's experience in the marriage. Therapy will not progress very far until the couple and therapist have reached a satisfactory contract regarding the presenting problem. This is especially difficult with wife abuse. Batterers will also downplay the extent and importance of the violence. Some potential avenues to take include making overt the extent to which the violence permeates the relationship; the kinds of damage battering incurs on the victim, the batterer, and other relatives; and wondering what a violence-free relationship would be like for them.

If battering is discovered during conjoint therapy, the therapist takes an active stance, prioritizing the battering as the primary problem and recommending group treatment for the man. If Mike had been unwilling to agree to the stated goal of nonviolence, couple therapy would have been terminated and Mary would have been offered supportive services.

On discovering the violence, the couple was seen individually with separate treatment goals. Mary's goal was to increase empowerment, pursue safety for herself, and work on her use of substances for coping. Mike's treatment goal was to cease the violence and work on honesty. In individual sessions, each spouse made it clear that they were not ready or willing to separate at that time. The therapist supported their decision while reminding Mary of the likelihood of continuing abuse.

When the couple arrived for their third session, the therapist asked to see them individually and suggested starting with Mary. This was to implement a safety plan with Mary and to explore and offer resources in case Mike decided they would not return.

During the session with Mike, a genogram was done to trace his history with violence. Mike indicated receiving severe abuse from his father that continued until he grew bigger than his Dad. Mike talked explicitly about the abuse he experienced and his feelings about his father. Some of his feelings were helplessness, fright, and anger. He recalled being pinned to the ground and beaten as a child and remarked that he had feelings of anger and disappointment about their relationship as an adult until the time his father died.

Therapy continued individually with Mary around empowerment and her occasional drug use. The goal of the fourth session with Mike was to confront him about his behavior and to sensitize him to Mary's experience when he was violent. This was done through the video playback of his previous session when Mike talked about his experience with his father's abuse.

Video playback has been used for training, education, and confronting clients in individual and group therapy (Berger, 1978). Paul (1966) was one of the first to use this technique on conjoint couples in therapy. More recently, Alger (1976) applied video playback to family therapy. Playback has been shown to be effective in precipitating crises in stuck systems, stimulating thought and feedback, and "confronting patients in crises" (Berger, 1978, p. 26).

Video playback was used to sensitize Mike to his wife's feelings of victimization and to help him face his feelings of becoming a batterer by showing the specific segment where he talked about his own abuse as a child and imposing the interpretation—"pretend you are listening to your wife, and she is talking about you and your battering"—on Mike. The tape was stopped at appropriate moments so he could express what he was feeling and thinking.

Mike speaking on the videotape:

M: I thought to myself, "I'll be safe when I get home for dinner. There are thirteen steps from the bottom floor to the floor with the bedrooms, and he [his father] hit me with a strap on every step."

The therapist pauses the tape.

T: And so, you thought you would be safe but you weren't.

M: Never was. Only time I was safe was when I went away to school. The threat was never there.

T: The only way you felt safe was to be away from him. Now think about Mary.

M: She probably feels the same way.

T: The threat to her is probably always there.

M: To alienate me.

T: The only way she can feel safe is to be away from you.

M: It's hard, it really is. I don't...I wish that there was some way that part of my upbringing could be eliminated...it's one of those things that was beat into me.

T: So bring that to your relationship with Mary right now. I'm wondering what it feels like for her when you get physical. Do you remember your father hitting you at those times when you are hitting Mary?

M: Yea, I was defenseless.

T: That must have felt pretty frightening.

M: It was, but I had done something wrong.

T: You yourself said it was never justified. (*Simultaneously with client.*)

M: Oh it was never...never justified. The thing that sets me off used to be the sharpness of the tongue, the agitatedness of her, but we both have reached a control point, we both walk away from it.

T: No matter what words you called your mother it never justified your father giving you three welts that were black and blue that you still carry today.

M: No.

T: That's what I think is part of what happens with you and Mary...no matter what words come out of her mouth it doesn't justify your hitting her or make it right.

M: Granted...I agree one-hundred percent.

T: At the same time there is recognition that this is what you learned when you were a child—your father modeled for you how to deal with your anger, and that was to hit.

M: Yea. The whole family was always in fear about what was going to happen to me, no matter what I did.

T: You would get hit.

M: Yea, a losing proposition all the way around.

At the beginning of the transcript, the client is still thinking of his own abuse. Time was spent during the previous session processing Mike's memories and feelings about his father's violence. A session with his mother could be effective in between the fourth session, when he discussed his own abuse, and the fifth session, when the focus was redirected to his perpetrated violence. Opportunities to bring in brothers and sisters who might help the client work through family of origin abuse and support him in nonviolence with his partner also could be timely. Without the physical presence of other family members or his wife, the systems approach is used by discussing the intergenerational aspect of violence in Mike's life and by discussing the reactions that Mary has to his anger.

The goal of the session was to redirect Mike's attention to how Mary felt about his violence toward her. The transcript demonstrates how the therapist parallels the batterer's personal abuse and the abuse he perpetrated on his wife. This began the process of helping Mike accept responsibility for the violence.

Prior to the fifth session, Mike and Mary had a fight, and Mike broke down instead of becoming violent. Mary confirmed this during her individual session. The therapist continued to press Mike to accept responsibility for the abuse by talking about the label "wife beater."

M: Why Dad, did you do these things to me…? Here I am in the same scenario, I'm not doing nothing wrong and still getting beat on?

T: Mike, I would switch that to why now, am I doing the same thing to Mary that Dad did to me when no matter what she's doing it's not wrong enough to warrant getting beat on?

M: That's probably what broke me today. I realized myself that no matter what happens it doesn't warrant that behavior anymore—it's just not right. I think that's what left me defeated more than anything else, because I…that's not an acceptable outlet anymore…go cry in a corner or something.

T: So now you're feeling like you've made a little movement. What is it like to hear me use the phrase "wife beater"?

M: It hurts. Hurts a lot. I'm not proud of that at all.

T: So there's some shame there too?

M: Definitely, a lot of shame. I don't *want* to be that person, I *can't* be that person.

It is clear that Mike is still struggling with taking responsibility; his behavior is changing, but his attitude is still that of being a victim, first of his father and then of Mary. Taking on the label "wife beater" challenges Mike to accept responsibility for the abuse. Using this label also allows the therapist to present Mike's recovery process as similar to people who recover from addiction—it is a long process that requires maintenance. As Mike more fully faced his responsibility for the abuse, the area batterers' group was added to his treatment program.

In the ideal therapy experience, the batterer's movement parallels the wife's growth. As the perpetrator moves from seeing himself as a powerless victim who has no control of his behavior to a responsible adult who can decide to not use violence, the victim is also moving from the victim stance to one where she sees herself as capable and responsible for the direction of her life.

Work with Mary continued to focus on helping her recognize and express her pain, accepting and understanding her ambivalence about the marriage, and strengthening her sense of self. Discussion ensued regarding family of origin issues and support systems. If individual therapy had continued, this would have been a good opportunity to bring in family and other persons Mary considered supportive.

After many individual sessions with each of them, both indicated a desire to return to a conjoint session. Mike demonstrated accepting responsibility for the violence and had consistently substituted other behaviors for the violence. Mary indicated having no fear about Mike's potential for violence, she was being more assertive regarding her own rights in their relationship, and both spouses requested conjoint therapy. Mike agreed to continue with the batterers' group.

The remainder of the therapy consisted of helping Mike and Mary's interactive patterns adjust to their individual work. Mike's changes were hard for Mary, and occasionally his attendance at the batterers' group was affected by her. Mary's ambivalence about the relationship was hard for Mike, and from time to time Mike would ask for Mary's trust when Mary wasn't ready to give it.

The end result of their pattern of escalation had changed, with either of them calling a time out or Mike breaking down, but the pattern itself continued to plague them. Mike's lying, which represented his attempts at avoiding conflict, appeared occasionally, and Mary's inability to trust him would be heightened during those times. Communication work also was incorporated into the therapy. Periodically a verbal assessment was done to find out if Mike's battering had returned. Each spouse indicated that the violence was not recurring.

Other issues related to the violence included Mike's attempts at avoiding his anger, and thus avoiding his potential for violence. Mike's ability to accept Mary's testing of his potential for violence was also an ongoing issue, and both were struggling to live with her continued ambivalence. Attention also was paid to discovering new methods of handling anger for both of them to promote better and more constructive fighting. During the most recent session, Mary was still ambivalent about trusting Mike, and

Mike was feeling very frustrated that he had made these changes and still might lose her.

As the risk of violence seemed to decrease, the couple initiated additional goals of treatment. Using other systems, such as the families of origin for each spouse, the area shelter for group support, and other professionals in the field, the therapist can widen the perspective on treating couples in which the husbands are violent.

More attention should be given to Mary's need to test Mike's change. Often spouses of batterers do not trust that their partners have changed. To prove that violence will not re-emerge after a period of progress in therapy, a common tactic is to repeatedly push the batterer to see if he will become violent. This is also a mechanism that allows the wife to vent anger and frustration from years of battering and domination. Therapists cannot overlook this process and the risks that are inherent in it. Often it is exaggerated by therapy because the partners feel that therapy is a safety mechanism that will somehow keep the violence from happening. During this testing phase, the possibility exists that the husband will become violent again. Therapists can help both partners pass through this stage by predicting that it will happen and letting them decide beforehand how they will act during a fight. They can also practice arguing in sessions to role-play how they will be different. Husbands can learn to monitor their rage and decide how to take time out. Wives can learn to express their frustration and pain in ways that are not demeaning or destructive to their husbands' self-esteem.

Throughout this stage of treatment the therapist should remember three points: First, it is not appropriate to imply to either partner that the batterer's violence is somehow caused by the woman's behaviors. Second, trying to get the wife to avoid testing her husband will be countertherapeutic; she may never feel safe if she is not sure that in the face of her worst behavior he still doesn't use violence. Third, just because her husband refrains from violence now does not mean he will refrain from violence in the future. She may never really know, or be able to trust, that he won't use violence again.

WHEN CHILDREN ARE INVOLVED

This section represents a brief consideration of children in abusive homes. In families with violent husbands, children are unavoidably affected. Treating children who are indirect victims of wife abuse, until recently, has been a neglected field. Battered women's shelters have and continue to provide groups for children of battered women.

"The damage to children is well documented and is evidenced by aggression in boys, withdrawal in girls, poor school achievement, isolation, low self-esteem, truancy, and the likelihood of boys growing up to be abusers" (Pressman, 1989, p. 26). Sometimes children's reactions to the spousal violence are what draws families into therapy. Weidman (1986, p. 212) says:

Children learn about the nature of interpersonal relationships and the roles of husband and wife, parent and child, and mother and father by watching their parents.... When children experience a home in which violence occurs between their parents or is directed against them, they will suffer psychological, emotional, and interpersonal damage.... These feelings and issues may best be addressed directly in conjoint family therapy as well as in children's groups.

The therapist, depending on her or his framework, may choose to see the batterer individually, the wife individually, and the wife and children together. Some clinicians choose to see the family conjointly from the first interview; others may not see the family together until safety issues, responsibility for the violence, and recovery for the victim is addressed. Weidman (1986) suggests that goals of therapy and group work for children can include exploring the roles children play in relation to the violence and their parents, promoting the appropriate expression of feelings, establishing safety plans conjointly with their parents, and discussing how they are affected by the violence. Group work also can offer children opportunities to develop their socialization skills.

CONCLUSIONS

Most families do not initially present violence as their primary problem. As a result, therapists must be willing and capable of exploring the role of violence in every family. Utilizing the variety of secondary systems available, such as other family members, friends, school personnel, and women's shelters to supplement treatment, can provide a fuller, more complete approach to treatment. Legal repercussions for batterers can also provide a societal response that communicates no tolerance for violence. Because families and agencies are part of the larger cultural system, violence can be perpetuated by agencies and therapists if they do not confront it. Addressing violence at the familial, societal, and cultural levels may promote a lessening of intergenerational violence. Further work needs to be done on treating victims, batterers, and the children of abusive relationships.

There is an inherent difficulty in treating batterers whose behaviors are reinforced in many ways: the media, television, and movies; our justice system; world relations. Protecting the victims of violence and helping batterers change are only part of the treatment process. In order for second order change to occur, the violence inherent in our very existence must be addressed. The risks involved in treating batterers and addressing the excessiveness of violence in the world include danger for those who confront and danger for those who live with the violence. The risks of not confronting violence are far greater. Current and future generations will pay the price if we ignore violence and the impact if has on our lives.

REFERENCES

Adams, D. (1988). Treatment models of men who batter. In K. Yllo & M. Bograd (Eds.), *Feminist perspectives on wife abuse* (pp. 176–199). Newbury Park, CA: Sage.

Adams, D. (1989). Feminist-based interventions for battering men. In P. L. Caesar & L. K. Hamberger (Eds.), *Treating men who batter: Theory, practice, and programs* (pp. 3–23). New York: Springer.

Adams, D. & McCormick, A. (1982). Men unlearning violence: A group approach based on the collective model. In M. Roy (Ed.), *The abusive partner* (pp. 170–197). New York: Van Norstrand Reinhold.

Alger, I. (1976). Integrating immediate video playback in family therapy. In P. Guerin (Ed.), *Family therapy: Theory and practice* (pp. 547–553). New York: Gardner.

Beninati, J. (1989). Pilot project for male batterers. *Social Work with Groups, 12,* 63–74.

Berger, M. (1978). Confrontation through videotape. In M. M. Berger (Ed.), *Videotape techniques in psychiatric training and treatment* (pp.19–36). New York: Brunner-Mazel.

Bograd, M. (1984). Family systems approaches to wife battering: A feminist critique. *American Journal of Orthopsychiatry, 54,* 558–568.

Bograd, M. (1988). Feminist perspectives on wife abuse: An introduction. In K. Yllo & M. Bograd (Eds.), *Feminist perspectives on wife abuse* (pp. 11–26). Newbury Park, CA: Sage.

Deschner, J. P. (1984). *The hitting habit.* New York: The Free Press.

Edelson, J. & Gruszunski, R. (1986). Treating men who batter: Four years of outcome data from the Domestic Abuse Project. *Journal of Social Service Research, 12,* 3–22.

Ellis, A. (1970). *The essence of rational psychotherapy: A comprehensive approach to treatment.* New York: Institute for Rational Living.

Ellis, A. (1976). Technique of handling anger in marriage. *Journal of Marriage and Family Counseling, 2,* 305–315.

Farley, D. & Magill, J. (1988). An evaluation of a group program for men who batter In a special issue on Violence: Prevention and Treatment in Groups. *Social Work with Groups, 11,* 53–65.

Ganley, A. (1981). Participant and trainer's manual for working with men who batter Unpublished manuscript. Washington D.C.: Center for Women Policy Studies.

Giles-Sims, J. (1983). *Wife battering: A systems theory approach.* New York: Guilford Press.

Gondolf, E. W. (1987). Evaluating programs for men who batter: Problems and prospects. *Journal of Family Violence, 2* (1), 95–108.

Guerney, B, Waldo, M., & Firestone, L. (1987). Wife-battering: A theoretical construct and case report. *The American Journal of Family Therapy, 15*(1), 31–43.

Gutsche, S. & Murray, M. (1991). The feminist meets the cybernetician: An integrated approach to spousal violence. *Journal of Strategic and Systemic Therapies, 10,* 76–91.

Hamberger, L. K. & Lohr, J. M. (1989). Proximal causes of spouse abuse: A theoretical analysis for cognitive-behavioral interventions. In P. L. Caesar & L. K. Hamberger (Eds.), *Treating men who batter: Theory, practice, and programs.* New York: Springer.

Harris, J. (1986). Counseling violent couples using Walker's model. *Psychotherapy, 23,* 613–621.

Holmes, T. H. & Rahe, R. H. (1967). The social readjustment rating scale. *Journal of Psychosomatic Research, 11,* 213–218.

Hotaling, G. T. & Sugarman, D. B. (1986). An analysis of risk markers in husband-to-wife violence: The current state of knowledge. *Violence and Victims, 1,* 101–124.

Hudson, W. W. & McIntosh, S. R. (1981). The assessment of spouse abuse: Two quantitative dimensions. *Journal of Marriage and the Family, 42,* 873–885.

James, K. & MacKinnon, L. (1990). The "incestuous family" revisited: A critical analysis of family therapy myths. *Journal of Marital and Family Therapy, 16,* 71–88.

Jennings, J. P. & Jennings, J. L. (1991). Multiple approaches to the treatment of violent couples. *The American Journal of Family Therapy, 19,* 351–362.

Jennings, J. (1987). History and issues in the treatment of battering men: A case for unstructured group therapy. *Journal of Family Violence, 2,* 193–213.

Lewis, B. Y. (1985). The Wife Abuse Inventory: A screening device for the identification of abused women. *Social Work, 30,* 32–35.

Lewis, B. Y. (1988). Psychosocial factors related to wife abuse. *Journal of Family Violence, 2,* 1–10.

Lipchik, E. (1991). Spouse abuse: Challenging the party line. *Networker, 15 (May/June),* 59–63.

Mack, R. N. (1989). Spouse abuse—A dyadic approach. In G. R. Weeks, *Treating couples: The intersystem model of the marriage council of Philadelphia.* New York: Brunner/Mazel.

Martin, D. (1981 rev.) *Battered wives.* San Francisco: Volcano Press.

Nadelson, C. C. & Sauzier, M. (1987). Intervention programs for individual victims and their families. In L. J. Dickstein and C. C. Nadelson (Eds.), *Family violence: Emerging issues of a national crisis* (pp. 155–178). Washington, D.C.: American Psychiatric Press.

Neidig, P. H. & Friedman, D. H. (1984). *Spouse abuse: A treatment program for couples.* Champaign, IL: Research Press.

Nosko, A. & Wallace, B. (1988). Group work with abusive men: A multidimensional model. In a special issue on Violence: Prevention and Treatment in Groups. *Social Work with Groups, 11,* 33–52

Novaco, R. (1975). *Anger control: The development and evaluation of an experimental program.* Lexington, MA: Lexington Books.

Nowicki, S., Jr., & Marshall, D. (1974). A Locus of Control Scale for college as well as non-college adults. *Journal of Personality Assessment, 38,* 136–137.

Paul, N. (1966). Effects of playback on family members of their own previously recorded conjoint therapy material. *Psychiatric Research Reports, 20,* 175–185.

Pressman, B. (1989). Wife-abused couples: The need for comprehensive theoretical perspectives and integrated treatment models. *Journal of Feminist Family Therapy, 1,* 23–43.

Schechter, S. (1982). *Women and male violence: The visions and struggles of the battered women's movement.* Boston: South End Press.

Sheinberg, M., Goldner, V., Penn, P., & Walker, G. (1992). Love and violence: Gender paradoxes in volatile attachments. Paper presented at the Annual Conference of the American Association for Marriage and Family Therapy, Miami Beach, October 16.

Stark, E. & Flitcraft, A. (1988). Violence among intimates: An epidemiological review. In V. B. Van Hasselt, R. L. Morrison, A. S. Bellack, & M. Hersen (Eds.), *Handbook of family violence* (pp. 293–317). New York: Plenum.

Steinfeld, G. J. (1989). Spouse abuse: An integrative-interactional model. *Journal of Family Violence, 4*(1), 1–23.

Straus, M. A. (1979). Measuring intrafamily conflict and violence: The Conflict Tactics Scale. *Journal of Marriage and the Family, 41,* 75–88.

Straus, M. A. & Gelles, R. (1986). Societal change and change in family violence from 1975 to 1986 as revealed by two national surveys. *Journal of Marriage and the Family, 48,* 465–479.

Walker, L. (1984). *The battered woman syndrome,* New York: Springer.

Weidman, A. (1986). Family therapy with violent couples. *The Journal of Contemporary Social Work, April,* 211–218.

Willbach, D. (1989). Ethics and family therapy: The case management of family violence. *Journal of Marital and Family Therapy, 15,* 43–52.

Williams-White, D. (1989). Self-help and advocacy: An alternative approach to helping battered women. In L. J. Dickstein and C. C. Nadelson (Eds.), *Family violence: Emerging issues of a national crisis,* (pp. 45–60). Washington, DC: American Psychiatric Press.

Yllo, K. & Bograd, M. (1988). *Feminist perspectives on wife abuse.* Newbury Park, CA: Sage.

2

SEXUAL ABUSE OF
WOMEN IN MARRIAGE

CLARK CHRISTENSEN

He would take out his knife and he would cut marks in my skin with it. He would tie me whenever we had sex to a bed or a chair or whatever. Sometimes he would force me to suck him and would stick his penis in my mouth all the time. Sometimes he would tie me around facing the other way and would have anal sex with me. He ripped my rectum so many times that the doctors in the emergency room used to laugh when I'd walk in. (Excerpted from Walker, 1979, pp. 121–122)

This woman's experiences may not represent the experiences of every victim of spousal sexual abuse, but they demonstrate what may occur. Given the possible extreme nature of the abuse this and other women face, it is critical that clinicians are aware of the existence and possible ramifications of spousal sexual abuse.

This chapter focuses on the treatment of spousal sexual abuse. Although much of the research on this subject has utilized the more legally useful term "marital rape," here the emphasis is on the broader issues of spousal sexual abuse and its treatment. While examining this topic from a systemic perspective, this chapter also incorporates feminist views and gender issues which are so powerfully woven into the fabric of domestic violence.

Victims of spousal sexual abuse face varying levels of abuse ranging from the extreme, as typified by the previous example, to less damaging forms. For instance, David Finkelhor and Kersti Yllo (1985, p. 39) in their book entitled *License to Rape: Sexual Abuse of Wives* recount the experience of Jessica, a wife of five years:

After their marriage, she decided that she didn't want to have sex any more: the excitement was gone. So they fell into a pattern of having sex rarely more than once a month…. It was an episode of forced sex that brought their relationship to its close. He had been gone for several days and came home drunk. As they were going to bed, he told her he wanted to have sex with her. She particularly did not like having sex with him when he was drunk, and so she told him she didn't want to. He insisted, pinning her down on the bed and holding her arms. "I was crying and saying, 'No, I don't want to do this.' I was not totally hysterical, but I was real clear. After he forcibly entered me, I just gave up and cried. It was not really possible to resist more. With my arms pinned down and him on top of me, there was just nothing I could do except hurt myself. If he was not going to stop because I did not want to do it, then there was no way I could have stopped it physically. So I just gritted my teeth and said to myself, 'It'll soon be over.' When he was done, he rolled over and went right to sleep."

Given the diversity of types of sexual abuse spouses may face, helping professionals must be sensitive to the needs of each client and have knowledge of the available treatment methods. It should be noted that while it is entirely possible that some men are sexually abused by their wives, the overwhelming majority of reported cases of spousal sexual abuse are of women abused by their husbands. As in the cases of premarital and extramarital sexual abuse (see Chapters 11 and 13 of this book, respectively), the apparent one-sidedness of this type of abuse has resulted in research which focuses almost entirely on women as victims and men as perpetrators. What little treatment literature is available is also written from this perspective, and generalizations to marital and family systems in which the male is the victim, or to same-sex couples, should be made with discretion.

Spousal sexual abuse has only become a subject of study in the recent past. A primary reason for this lack of interest has been traditional definitions of marital roles which view sexual-relations-on-demand as a right of marriage (Finkelhor & Yllo, 1985; Russell, 1990). One of the outcomes of the feminist movement has been the realization by social scientists and politicians that such expectations place women in a subjugatory position. While these traditional role definitions and marital expectations appear to be weakening, their influence is still with us. As late as April 1992, a jury in Columbia, South Carolina, acquitted a man charged with raping his wife. This case did not suffer from the usual lack of incriminating evidence; the husband had videotaped the event. The videotape showed the couple "having sex, with her hands and legs tied with rope, her mouth and eyes taped shut with duct tape. Her muffled screams were audible" (Pesce, 1992, p. 3A). The defense lawyer explained the acquittal on the basis that "the tape also showed there wasn't much resistance [from the woman]" (Pesce, 1992, p. 3A).

Although this case is anecdotal and may not fully represent the social changes that have occurred, it is clear that much of the time women are still seen as compliant unless they can prove otherwise. Also clear is the fact that even today men are given a free reign over couple sexuality, and that they tend to rule with impunity. The steps we have taken toward the disassembling of commonly held traditional beliefs, which hold women as their husbands' property, have resulted in the redefinition of forced sexual contact as deviant and worthy of social-scientific and clinical study (Finkelhor & Yllo, 1985; Russell, 1990).

To date there is no consensus as to what types of behavior should be included under the heading spousal sexual abuse. Legally the definition varies by state, but generally includes forced intercourse, sex obtained by threat, and in some states relations where one partner is unconscious or otherwise unable to consent. A small contingent is endeavoring to have these definitions enlarged to include any form of coerced sexual activity regardless of whether penetration took place or whether physical violence was used or threatened. Much of the literature and research that is available on this topic was generated for the sake of supporting these legislative changes (Russell, 1990). For the purposes of this chapter, *spousal sexual abuse* is defined as any sexual behavior forced on one spouse by another. This coercion may take many forms: physical violence, the use of greater physical size and strength to gain compliance, threats, or emotional intimidation or manipulation.

In considering the context of spousal sexual abuse, reference should be made to Chapter 1 of this book because spousal sexual abuse appears to be related to spousal physical abuse. For a more thorough understanding of the methods used to treat rape victims, a review of Chapter 13 on the treatment of sexual abuse by a non-family member may be helpful. Later portions of this chapter discuss similarities between spousal sexual abuse and these other forms of abuse.

WHAT IS KNOWN ABOUT SPOUSAL SEXUAL ABUSE

Spousal sexual abuse is one of the most recently acknowledged forms of domestic violence, and relative to other forms of domestic violence little research or writing on the subject has been done. There are, however, a few literature reviews available (Finkelhor & Yllo, 1985; Russell, 1990; Shields, Resick, & Hanneke, 1990).

Scope of the Problem

Studies examining the nature and prevalence of spousal sexual abuse can generally be categorized by the context in which the information was gathered. These categories include studies that sample the general population, studies exploring the prevalence of spousal sexual abuse in physically abusive relationships, and studies in which spousal rape is measured as a subsample of rape experiences.

In studies that sample the general population, the prevalence rates for marital sexual abuse range from 10% (Finkelhor & Yllo, 1985) to 14% (Russell, 1990). In samples from clinical populations, the figures range from 6% (Finkelhor & Yllo, 1982) to 10% (Lewis, 1984). The differences between these two groups may represent the fact that spousal sexual abuse goes under-reported in the clinical setting. Women who divulge instances of abuse to a researcher with the guarantee that she will remain anonymous may hesitate when the question is posed by a therapist or other helper who is seen as com-mitted to stopping abuse and/or abusive relationships. Another possible explanation may be a selectivity bias, with sexually abusive marriages tend-ing to either dissolve on introduction to an intervention system, or the abuse naturally occurring less frequently in marriages likely to come into contact with support systems. In either case, the practitioner should be sensitive to the fact that this type of abuse occurs frequently and may be present in the relationships they see.

Studies which examine marital rape in conjunction with spousal physical abuse or wife battering have also been conducted. The relationship between spousal physical abuse and spousal sexual abuse has been shown to be fairly strong. Studies examining this relationship have found that between 32% (Prescott & Letko, 1977) and 59% (Walker, 1984) of battered women are also victims of sexual abuse at the hands of their husbands. Other authors reported similar results (Frieze, 1983; Shields & Hanneke, 1983).

Another feature of spousal sexual abuse that has been examined is its relation to other forms of rape. Estimates of the percentage of rape attribut-able to spousal perpetration range from 9% (perpetrator a member of the family, including husbands—Koss, Dinero, & Seibel, 1988) to 20% (George & Winfield-Laird, 1986). As a portion of the total number of rapes experienced by women in the United States, these numbers may seem relatively small. To see more clearly the relative prevalence of sexual abuse committed by hus-bands, one investigator (Russell, 1990) has broken down the non-spousal rapes by relationship (i.e. stranger, acquaintance, friend, date, boyfriend, lover, and authority figure). The findings of this study, in terms of the prev-alence of spousal sexual abuse, was that, "however one analyzes this ques-tion, wife rape is clearly one of the most prevalent types of rape, and by some measures, it is the most prevalent form." (Russell, 1990, p. 68). Said slightly different: "One of the most common forms of sexual victimization for a woman is to be forced into having sex, or engaging in a sex act she objects to, by her husband." (Gelles & Cornell, 1985, p. 70).

There has been some research conducted to establish the severe nature of the consequences of spousal sexual abuse. Russell (1990) found that not only is rape by a spouse the most common form of rape, but it is also one of the more traumatic. Women raped by their husbands were traumatized as much as women raped by strangers, and more so than those raped by a date, friend, or lover.

Consequences

Finkelhor and Yllo (1985, p. 138) state: "When you are raped by a stranger you have to live with a frightening memory. When you are raped by your husband you have to live with your rapist." Although there is little information available as to the specific effects of spousal sexual abuse, there has been some research done which shows that women who experience spousal sexual abuse frequently suffer psychological side effects. Several authors have attempted to identify and label these effects.

Shields, Resick, and Hanneke (1990) found that women who had been physically and sexually assaulted by their husbands scored lower than non-victims on measures of self-concept, with battered-only women scoring higher than women who were both physically and sexually abused on some subscales. A similar pattern was found using measures of compulsive behaviors and fear. Raped women scored higher than nonabused women on all subscales, and in some cases the women who had been raped in their marriages scored significantly higher than women who had been physically battered but experienced no sexual abuse. In general the battered women were more likely to suffer from stress and stress-related problems than non-victims, but less than their counterparts who had been sexually abused and battered.

Finkelhor and Yllo (1985), citing self-reports of the effects of marital rape, report that women who have experienced marital rape suffered from sexual dysfunction, feelings of anger, betrayal, and humiliation. There may also be long-term consequences such as more frequent fearfulness and a general difficulty trusting others. Russell (1990) found a general mistrust of others and frequent sexual dysfunction, as well as an increase in negative feelings toward their husbands and men in general. In a global rating of trauma, of the women interviewed who had experienced spousal sexual abuse, Russell found that 34% suffered extreme trauma, 30% experienced considerable trauma, and 19% felt some trauma.

In addition to the individual psychological consequences of spousal sexual abuse, there are very real interpersonal consequences. These consequences may be quite different from those experienced by victims of sexual abuse by a stranger. When someone is raped by a stranger, the victim may develop a fear of strangers or of being alone at night, or other characteristics that may put her at risk for rape or which she associates with her past rape experience (Kilpatrick, Veronen, & Resick, 1978). The victim of marital rape develops a different set of fears. For this victim, it is intimate relationships that are to be feared. Relationships with men are viewed differently, with more hostility and less trust; sexual relationships can be particularly problematic. Women who have experienced this kind of abuse have an especially difficult time relating to their husbands (Finkelhor & Yllo, 1985). Given the way their trust has been treated, it is not difficult to understand why women would distrust an abuser.

In the context of therapy, these consequences inevitably will play themselves out in the dyadic relationship. There needs to be a careful assessment of the relationship and the damage that may have been caused by the abuse. The introduction of these extreme behaviors into the marriage changes meanings, rewrites scripts, and shifts the power in the relationship, causing severe and often irreparable damage.

Factors Associated with Spousal Sexual Abuse

Several factors have been found to be associated with the occurrence of spousal sexual abuse. The association with other forms of spousal violence has already been mentioned. Some studies have found that spousal sexual abuse rarely occurs in relationships where the woman is not also being physically abused (Frieze, 1983; Hanneke, Shields, & McCall, 1986). On the other hand, Finkelhor and Yllo (1985) describe one type of perpetrator who is not also a wife batterer. Referred to as "force-only rapists," these men use only the force necessary to obtain desired sexual relations. The amount of force actually used may vary from emotional coercion in the form of emotional manipulation and the intentional use of guilt, to more extreme forms such as choking, hitting, or threatening with a knife or gun. Otherwise, these relationships may be violence-free and relatively egalitarian. These authors also identify a second type of perpetrator who seems to be motivated by an obsession for perversion rather than a desire to hurt or dominate as is frequently the case in physically violent marriages. Finkelhor and Yllo further warn that "to characterize marital rape as the province of battered women alone is not to see its full scope" (1985, p. 60). Diana Russell echoes this view with results from her study which found "a large and significant group of women who experience both wife rape and wife beating," but also identified "a large group of women who experience wife beating but no rape, and a smaller but significant group of women who experience only wife rape…. Hence wife rape cannot and must not be subsumed under the battered woman rubric" (1990, p. 101).

There is convincing evidence to support the belief that a strong association exists between alcohol and drug abuse and the occurrence of physical abuse and rape (Russell, 1990). Russell also indicates that there is no reason to believe that should these men stop abusing drugs and alcohol their tyrannical and abusive behavior would change, although there may be a decrease in their violent behavior. Preliminary estimates place the percentage of spousal sexual abuse, which occurs at the hands of a husband who is drinking or drunk, at 24 to 29 percent. Russell states, however, that because respondents were not asked directly about the use of alcohol, the real figures may be much higher. (These figures represent the percentage of cases in which alcohol was mentioned in the course of describing an event of abuse or the abuser himself.) Further research in this area is still necessary.

Other factors, especially personality characteristics of the abuser, have been speculated as possibly being related to the incidence of spousal sexual abuse. Although some have suggested that men who abuse their wives do so out of a desperate need to establish some control in a situation in which they perceive themselves as hopelessly powerless (Groth & Gary, 1981), others have viewed abusers as tyrannical, violent men, who will do anything to maintain control over their property (Frieze, 1983).

TREATMENT OF SPOUSAL SEXUAL ABUSE

Given the frequency with which this type of abuse is inflicted on women in our society, there is a definite need for helping professionals to be aware of its existence (Bidwell & White, 1986; Bowker, 1983). Unfortunately, in terms of the literature and research available, treatment of spousal sexual abuse is an "unexplored frontier" (Shields, Resick, & Hanneke, 1990). There are at present only two published sources—Shields, Resick, and Hanneke (1990) and Weingourt (1985)—that discuss treatment methods and issues.

Attempts have been made to create an initial heuristic from which to begin to understand the dynamics of spousal sexual abuse and how it can be treated. However, efforts to do this by comparing and contrasting sexual abuse within marriage with other forms of abuse have had mixed results. Some, like Bidwell and White (1986), and Bowker (1983), point out the similarities between spousal sexual abuse and spousal physical abuse. These similarities include traditional gender roles of the perpetrators and the frequent occurrence of alcohol abuse in the perpetrator. Another strong associating link is that the vast majority of sexually abused wives are also beaten by their husbands. Bowker (1983) specifically examined whether sexual abuse of wives is typified by a distinct syndrome or whether this is merely an extension or exacerbation of the physical abuse syndrome. The results of the study showed little difference between violent couples where the wife was not sexually abused and violent couples where the wife was sexually abused. The central difference between these couples is that measures of marital satisfaction tend to be lower in couples where abuse is both physical and sexual in nature.

In contrast, the findings of Weingourt (1985) argue that spousal sexual abuse is distinct from spousal physical abuse, and must not be thought of as merely part of the spouse abuse picture. To further compound the problem, other researchers have found that, at least in terms of the psychological impact of the abuse on victims, spousal sexual abuse is more like extrafamilial rape than spousal physical abuse (Shields, Resick, & Hanneke, 1990). With as little research as is currently available on this type of abuse and its treatment, a general picture of the nature of the abuse is needed and future research will need to address this issue before more comprehensive treatment plans can be formulated. Until and unless spousal sexual abuse is identified as part of the wife-battering syndrome, clinicians are cautioned against generalizing from the spouse abuse literature (Bidwell & White, 1986).

Therapeutic Assessment

The nature of the assessment process varies depending on the circumstances under which the client presents for therapy. In general, clients come for treatment not with the sexual abuse as the issue, but with individual symptoms or relational difficulties. Assessment of the couple dyad may at times be possible, but assessment frequently involves only the victim of the abuse. Because of the frequency of this type of abuse and its elusive and secretive nature, it is important that questions regarding forced sexual contact are part of the initial clinical evaluation (Weingourt, 1985). This is especially true of clients presenting for treatment of physical or emotional abuse (Shields, Resick, & Hanneke, 1990). Because victims rarely view what has happened to them as "criminal," care should be taken that, at least during the assessment period, the term "rape" is not used. Some possible assessment questions might be, "Have you ever felt pushed into having sex when you did not want to?" or "Some wives find themselves forced to have unwanted sex, has this ever happened to you?"

Some personal and interpersonal consequences are seen in victims of sexual abuse, and these generally are present in victims of spousal sexual abuse as well. Watching for these cues alerts professionals that some abuse may have occurred, and indicate a more careful assessment. These symptoms may include such things as low self-esteem, sexual dysfunction, difficulty committing to relationships, fear and panic symptoms. Some manifestations more characteristic of spousal sexual abuse include parentified children (Bidwell & White, 1986), and distancing from men in general (Weingourt, 1985). Lee Bowker (1983) identifies some ways in which physically and sexually abused wives differed from their counterparts who were only physically abused. They experienced lower marital satisfaction; utilized more outside sources of aid, both formal and informal; their marriages were more likely to end in divorce; and if they remained together, had long-term problems with marital quality. Typical probing questions include: "I am wondering what might have happened in your past that would have taught you to be so careful in relationships with men" or "It seems like relationships with men are frightening for you, could you tell me what might happen that would be so scary?"

Another difference between these groups is that couples in which the husband rapes or otherwise sexually abuses the wife are less likely to have "honeymoon periods" or "make-up" periods after intermittent acts of abuse. For women who are subjected to physical abuse, these times are often somewhat healing respites in the cycle of abuse, with the perpetrator apologizing, buying his wife gifts, and helping out around the house. These make-up periods may also include rewarding sexual intimacy. Women who suffer sexual abuse in marriage are less likely to have these periods, and even when they do occur, they are less likely to have any interest in "making-up" sexually. This could help to explain why these marriages more often end in divorce and why they report lower marital quality. Querying about making-up is especially helpful when interviewing couples where physical abuse is also present or suspected, but it can be a good source of information even when there is no apparent physical abuse. Specific probes such as, "What happens after you have a fight, how do you make-up?" or "How consistent is your sex life?" may prove helpful in identifying make-up periods which may indicate the presence of sexual abuse.

Assessment of the client's safety should be an ongoing concern for the therapist if evidence of abuse is found. Information needs to be gathered concerning threats of death or harm in the past and present. Any following or stalking behavior by an angry husband should be considered a sign of danger. Although therapists can do little to actually prevent harm to clients, they should still be attentive to signs of danger, and should encourage clients to take whatever steps they can to ensure their safety. Some questions for a therapist to ask include:

How has your husband threatened you lately?

Where do you see yourself and this marriage in five years? Ten years?

Does your husband admit that this behavior is abusive?

Will he agree to seek therapy or at least join group therapy for spouse abuse perpetrators?

Do you want to remain in the marriage?

Does he know and approve of you being in therapy?

If there are signs that spousal sexual abuse has occurred, the therapist's first priority should be to help the client create and maintain a safe living environment, both physically and emotionally.

The manner in which identification and assessment of spousal sexual abuse begins varies widely. Cases where this type of treatment is necessary generally fit into one of four categories:

- Couples or families already in therapy for treatment of other problems.
- One marriage partner (usually the wife) is still involved in the abusive relationship and is fairly committed to maintaining it while presenting with other symptomatology.
- A marriage partner (again usually the wife) who presents specifically for treatment of marital abuse and is questioning the future of the relationship.
- A woman who has been the victim of marital abuse but who is no longer in the abusive relationship.

Each of these modalities has distinct implications for assessment and treatment. The remaining discussion of assessment and treatment is presented in such a way as to help the therapist deal with the various issues and difficulties that arise in these different types of cases.

Couples and Families

Because of the social and interpersonal consequences of spousal sexual abuse, for couples where the wife has been sexually abused by her mate, they experience a variety of problems for which they might seek treatment. These initial presenting problems may include sexual dysfunction, extreme conflict, and consideration of divorce, or a variety of problems in which a child is the identified patient.

Couples and families may also be participating in treatment when the identified patient is a wife or mother suffering from depression, anxiety, or somatic complaints. Given the high degree of association between physical and sexual abuse, a couple's presenting problem may be spousal physical abuse, especially in the case of referrals from other mental health professionals or the court system; however, a more likely scenario would be a couple seeking treatment for one of the previously mentioned difficulties and disclosing physical violence in response to probes by the therapist. Further probes may reveal that the abuse took both physical and sexual forms.

When the therapist has the opportunity to view interactions between spouses, special attention should be paid to levels of trust, intimacy, and fear that may be evident. Although inordinately high or low levels of these relationship traits do not necessarily mean that sexual abuse has occurred, these observations may indicate the need for a more detailed assessment. The types of questions a therapist might ask in order to assess a couple for the presence of possible sexual abuse might include the following: "Do you think that there are times when your wife is afraid of you?" "Do you think your wife trusts you?" "How would your husband describe your interest in sex?" Asking these circular questions, where one partner is asked to answer for the other, tends to allow clients to reveal only as much as they feel safe disclosing. This may reduce anxiety and provide more safety for the wife.

Wives Presenting with Nonabuse Symptoms

A second type of case, which has the potential to require assessment and treatment for spousal sexual abuse, is a wife who seeks therapy individually for relationship or intrapsychic difficulties. This type of case is relatively common to marriage and family therapists. Such a woman may be seeking therapy because she is experiencing the aftereffects of forced marital sexual activity. Symptoms presented for treatment may range from those commonly experienced by rape victims (i.e., panic attacks, memory flashbacks, chronic or acute feelings of anxiety, or sexual dysfunction) to those experienced by women who have been subjected to physical violence in the marital relationship (i.e., difficulties with self-esteem and self-confidence, feelings of having little or no control over life circumstances, but also experiencing feelings of responsibility for the violent episodes).

Much the same as women who have been physically abused in marriage, women who have been sexually abused are often deeply committed to their relationships and may find it very difficult to leave, even in the face of extreme violence. In connection with this loyalty to the relationship, therapists may find assessment difficult, with the woman sending mixed messages about the nature of the relationship and her wishes for the future of the relationship. Indeed, even obtaining disclosure of any abuse, whether physical or sexual, may be difficult or impossible because of the client's wish to protect her husband from social sanctions and to protect herself from her husband. Her hope may be that through therapy she can somehow indirectly stop the abuse by improving herself and the relationship. In these cases, assessment needs to focus on disclosure of the abuse and the questions to ask should reflect this focus: "Have you ever wanted to leave your husband?" "Has your husband ever done anything to you that would make you want to leave?" "Does your husband respect your wishes and opinions?" "Has your husband ever forced you to participate in unwanted sex?"

Any hesitation to discuss issues that could incriminate the client's partner can be a significant handicap to assessment and treatment efforts. If the therapist senses that such a hesitancy exists, the perceived reluctance and the observational reasons for its supposed existence should be addressed along with trust within the therapeutic relationship in order to avoid any collusion or attack–avoidance behaviors between the therapist and client that might inhibit therapy.

Wives Presenting for Treatment of Sexual Abuse

Women may also request therapy with the specific complaint that they are being sexually abused by their husbands. Although this type of case has a simpler assessment process than the three previously described, treatment of these cases is not necessarily any easier, and in fact may require extra care and patience. For these women, assessment issues need to focus more on the nature of the current relationship and what the future status of the relationship will be rather than on whether abuse has taken place. Women in this category may be in danger of increasing violence from their husbands as a result of husbands' perceptions that they are being either betrayed or abandoned. Assessment of the client's safety should be a special concern when she has presented specifically for treatment of sexual abuse. Therapists should be attentive to signs of danger and should encourage clients to take whatever steps they can to ensure their safety.

Some women may have had extensive experience with external support services like those provided to battered wives, and they may be very sensitive to victim-blaming statements. Because women who come to therapy already recognize the abusive nature of their husbands' behavior and are open to disclosing the abuse and discussing it, there is a good chance that these women have had extensive psychotherapy experience. If this is the case, then an important part of the assessment of these clients would involve discussing what those experiences were like, what kinds of things were helpful, and what things were not. This information does a great deal to help focus therapy on issues important to the individual client, and to avoid therapeutic styles and techniques that the client finds offensive.

Survivors of Spousal Sexual Abuse

Women who have been sexually abused by a husband and have terminated the relationship display yet another unique set of circumstances that require special attention for assessment and treatment. For these clients, safety is much less an issue than it would be for women who are currently involved in an abusive relationship. In this case, assessment needs to focus primarily on long-term consequences of abuse and how these can be healed. Issues to consider include trust in relationships, interest in sexuality, healthy self-concept and self-confidence, and degree of dependence. Other areas needing assessment are the amount of time that has passed since the abusive relationship ended, whether there has been more than one abusive relationship, and how the relationship ended, including the degree of closure or resolution the client feels about the relationship.

Although other possibilities exist for ways in which treatment may begin, their likelihood of occurring is extremely low. For instance, a man presenting himself for treatment because he sexually abuses his wife is highly improbable, regardless of whether the relationship is still intact. The vast majority of cases will fall within these four main categories. Another possible variation may be that a client passes through one or more of the classifications just described either before disclosure—as in the case of a woman who comes in for individual treatment of nonabuse difficulties and ends up in couples therapy—or during treatment a couple discloses abuse, but only the wife will continue treatment, and separation later occurs, reclassifying the client as a survivor of spousal sexual abuse.

Therapeutic Goals

In the words of Groth and Gary, "raped wives, then are silent victims and silence serves to perpetuate such victimization" (1981, p. 127). Because of the silent nature of marital sexual abuse, the assessment process and client disclosure of the abuse is often the initial therapeutic goal. As mentioned earlier, the assessment and treatment of spousal sexual abuse may not become a therapeutic goal itself until work has begun on other presenting problems. The assessment process helps the therapist ascertain whether the marriage is or has been sexually abusive.

Once the therapist identifies the abuse, the therapist then begins the process of labeling the husband's behavior as sexual abuse or rape (Shields, Resick, & Hanneke, 1990). This is true regardless of whether the victim is being seen alone or with the abusing partner. For victims to overcome the effects of abuse, they must learn to view the abuse as violence they cannot control and for which they are not responsible (Bidwell & White, 1986). Husbands, whether they are involved directly in the therapeutic process or not, typically fight the reframing of the abuse as "his fault," preferring instead that the abuse be seen as a shared responsibility or primarily the wife's fault. Such behavior makes acceptance of the reframe difficult for the client regardless of whether these defensive arguments are voiced in the therapy room or at home. A variety of rationalizations will be used to place the blame for the abuse anywhere but on the husband. He usually tries to blame his childhood, his wife's lack of respect, obedience, or sexual interest, or anything else that might seem remotely plausible. In some cases the husband may even claim his wife enjoys and encourages "rough" sex. The early sessions of therapy then, generally need to focus on assessing whether abuse has taken place, and once disclosure has been made, identifying the abuse as something that was done to her and for which she carries no blame.

After the disclosure and the recounting of what actually happened, it is important to explore with the victim her reactions to the abuse. Doing so can serve to help the victim see the degree to which forced sex has infiltrated her ways of being (Weingourt, 1985). A healthy introspection and assessment of the effects of abuse has the result of making the victim aware of the extent to which she has been affected. A common reaction people have to trauma is to downplay the negative effects. Minimization or exaggeration of the abuse and its consequences are probably both harmful, and the client's ability to deal effectively with the abuse requires a realistic appraisal of its impact and potential impact. Attempts to accomplish this goal encourages the client to discuss how the abuse has influenced her ability to form and maintain relationships, how the abuse has changed her views on sex and intimacy, and what lessons she has learned from the abuse.

Along with the elimination of any symptomatology that may have originally brought the client(s) in for treatment, a further therapeutic goal to pursue is the client's adoption of a balanced, though ambivalent, view of the marital relationship. Victims of spousal violence and the professionals who help them are often discouraged and dismayed by the victim's desire to return to the relationship. One of the goals of therapy should be to help the client explore both the pain she has suffered at the hands of her husband, and the ways in which the relationship has been rewarding for her. There are parts of the relationship other than the abuse, and some of these may be very rewarding for the client. If these issues are not acknowledged, the client may be confused by her desire to return and make poor decisions for herself, her children and even her marriage. A therapist might ask, "If you decided to leave the relationship, what sorts of things would you miss?" Another question might be, "We've said so much about the hurtful things your husband did to you, could you tell me some of the nice things he has done?" If the client decides to end the marriage, she may need help grieving for what she loses in addition to celebrating her freedom and the end of the abuse (Weingourt, 1985).

In cases where the client has weighed the costs and benefits of staying in the abusive relationship and feels that leaving might be the best alternative, there are practical considerations to be dealt with. As wife abuse advocates have experienced, a painful and unrewarding relationship is not always easy to leave. Women often feel that by leaving their husbands they are selfishly denying their children a father. These feelings may be accompanied by feelings of personal failure at not being able to make the marriage work. Wives who have been full-time mothers often have few marketable job skills, offering little hope of financial independence should they choose to leave. These feelings and fears must be discussed in the therapeutic setting if the client's best interests are to be fully considered. In cases where the client presents for therapy after having left the relationship, these issues still need to be addressed in order to prevent an unwise or hasty return to the abusive relationship.

The therapeutic goals just described may be applied whether the client is an individual or a couple. If the husband is involved in therapy, then the therapist must be careful to prevent his presence from contaminating his wife's open and honest discussion of her thoughts and feelings. If this can be done, the husband can benefit greatly from seeing the pain and suffering he has caused his wife. However, the husband's inclusion in the therapy must be predicated on the condition that the wife is committed to continuing the relationship, that the abuse has stopped, and that the wife in private sessions confirms that his presence is not a hindrance to her openness.

Treatment Strategies

One of the essential subtleties the therapist must master in order to do effective therapy with victims of marital sexual abuse is balancing therapeutic distance. On a continuum, either extreme, overly enmeshed, or coolly distant will have the effect of hindering therapy. Also, varying degrees of emotional availability may be appropriate at different times during treatment. Rita Weingourt (1985) stresses the importance of the therapist not distancing from victims after disclosure. If the therapist's reaction to a disclosure of this type of abuse is to not react and show no shock, then the message the victim receives is rejection. Learned helplessness is entrenched over time as women who have been abused carefully reveal small parts of the abuse to others and frequently if not always get a response that communicates general disregard for the woman's suffering and a blaming of the victim for not stopping the abuse or getting out of the relationship. It is essential that the therapist not send this message to the client who has been victimized.

Although the therapist should not seem distant during the disclosure, it is important during later therapy for the therapist to maintain more emotional distance. If the therapist reacts with anger to the woman's stories of abuse, then the client's anger, if any was present, will be pushed even deeper, allowing the therapist to be angry for her. In many cases, the client may even take a stance protective of the husband/perpetrator. This replicates the abusive relationship, with the therapist as the abuser and the client as the paralyzed victim who blames herself for conflict and feels obligated to soothe tensions (Weingourt, 1985). Maintaining an appropriate emotional distance can be a difficult and delicate endeavor. In these cases the therapist's use of self is extremely important.

These issues are especially salient when the therapist is a male. Clients may be more sensitive to the distancing of a male therapist on disclosure, almost expecting not to be heard and understood. Clients who have experienced spousal sexual abuse also may be hypersensitive to anger reactions from a therapist, even if the anger is directed at the perpetrator (Weingourt, 1985). Victims may be especially sensitive to victim-blaming statements when the helping professional is male.

Whatever happens in therapy, it is important that the woman who has experienced the abuse not be placed in a situation that would be therapeutically isomorphic to the abusive relationship. Clients must never feel they have no control over decisions that are made. They should be empowered with information and decisions so that they can begin to recognize the power they have within themselves to change their lives for the better. Because of this, therapists may decide to be less structured in the therapy room than they might ordinarily be. Clients might be given the freedom to chose the topics to be discussed, or allowed to come late without anything being said. She might also be given more freedom to regulate the emotional temperature of the room. Allowing her to diffuse emotional situations may be very empowering for her, even if it might seem therapeutically counterproductive. Such little efforts as these may make a great deal of difference to a woman who has been dominated and controlled by her most intimate partner.

The areas in which therapists must be careful to avoid recreating the abusive-type relationship are intimacy, power, and control. These are the areas of a sexually abusive relationship that make them so toxic, and these issues must be carefully treated in order to allow clients room to grow. Because these issues are inextricably tied to the intensity and structure of therapy, effective treatment requires a great deal of patience and cooperation with the client, allowing her to unfold at her own pace rather than coercing unwelcome vulnerability.

Structure of the Therapy

Once assessment reveals that sexual abuse has occurred, the issue of the woman's safety must be considered first. At this stage, the treatment would be essentially the same as treatment given to a woman experiencing spousal physical violence. If the woman is still in the relationship, then a physical and/or sexual violence contract may need to be drawn up between the partners. A necessary part of the contract, whether the husband is involved in it or not, is a commitment by the wife to see that changes are made to ensure her safety following the next outbreak of violence. These changes may include one of the partners moving out. Given the frequency of sexually abused wives also being physically abused, this facet of treatment must not be overlooked. Prior to focusing therapy on inter- and intrapersonal healing, an assessment of the client's physical safety and financial security must be made (Shields, Resick, & Hanneke, 1990). A revisiting of Maslow's hierarchy of needs would show that a woman cannot expend much effort in overcoming depression, anxiety, or other presenting problems when she isn't sure about her living arrangements or where meals might come from a few days from now.

Once the client feels relatively safe and stable, then work can begin on the presenting symptoms which may be resulting from the abuse. These symptoms generally can be treated with techniques designed for the specific symptoms. For instance, depression, anxiety, or sexual dysfunction can be treated using standard therapeutic techniques (Shields, Resick, & Hanneke 1990). Depression and anxiety may be treated using traditional cognitive, rational-emotive, or cognitive-behavioral techniques, focusing on breaking the patterns of thought and behavior that tend to maintain these symptoms. Because of the common power, boundary, and sexual violations involved, therapists are encouraged to make use of the literature available on the treatment of adult survivors of incest.

Because of the sexual nature of the abuse, a consistently reported symptomatology is sexual dysfunction (Finkelhor & Yllo, 1985). These dysfunctions may take several forms including sexual aversions or phobias, inhibited sexual desire, and anorgasmia. Treatment plans may include a referral to a sex therapist in cases where the problematic sexual behavior has been in existence for a long time or where the therapist feels ill equipped to treat it due to a lack of training or experience with a particular problem. Another option available to the therapist is the sensate focus technique in which the client is given the opportunity to explore her sensuality in a setting that does not feel threatening and where there are little or no expectations. This form of therapy has helped many individuals overcome difficulties with "inhibited sexual desire" and may be especially helpful for victims of abusive sexual intimacy at the hands of their spouses. Another commonly recommended method for treating sexual disorders is cognitive restructuring, or cognitive-behavioral therapy (Leiblum & Rosen, 1989; LoPiccolo & Friedman, 1988). In cognitive/behavioral therapy, attitudes and feelings about love and sex, intimacy and power are examined and evaluated, and where appropriate modified through "thought stopping", education and experiential exercises.

Judith Becker (1989) even proposes a ten-session treatment plan, including sensate focus techniques and cognitive restructuring, for treating sexual disorders in victims of sexual abuse. Bibliotherapy may be an effective supplement to in-session therapy. There are many excellent books available to help individuals overcome sexual difficulties (Heiman & LoPiccolo, 1976; Kasl, 1989). Selecting the most appropriate book for a particular client depends on the type and severity of the dysfunction being experienced and the desired result.

In addition to treating overt symptoms, relationship issues need to be addressed. Shields et al. (1990) write that after any act of violence has occurred it is difficult to reestablish trust in the relationship. To add a sexual betrayal to the violence may mean that even if the victim can come to feel comfortable with her partner in other ways, they (Shields et al., 1990, p. 176) state that

> Sexual intimacy and fulfillment require a level of relaxation, vulnerability, and trust that would be difficult to attain after such a betrayal. Therefore, it is unlikely that reactions to marital rape can be adequately treated until the woman has successfully extricated herself from the relationship.

Despite the damage that has been done, and the obstacles to trust and intimacy they face, many women will choose to stay in the relationship during treatment. In this situation, part of helping the client to have a balanced view of herself and her relationship includes sharing with her the reality that it is unlikely she will have a satisfying sexual relationship in her marriage any time in the near future. There is also no guarantee, even if the abuse has stopped, that the husband will not abuse the wife again. Whether the client is an individual (married or single) or a couple, working to enhance the abilities of the people involved to be open and vulnerable involves a great deal of relationship modeling and creation of an environment of trust. Because of the damage that is done when abuse occurs within a relationship, it may be the case that for clients to have an intimate, trusting relationship they will have to have a relationship with a new partner.

Regardless of the outcome of the sexually abusive marriage, it is essential that clients find or reestablish close and supportive relationships. These relationships may be with siblings, relatives, or old and trusted friends. Forming and strengthening enduring, intimate relationships is therapeutic for the client's social and emotional adjustment (Burr & Christensen, 1992). Therapists must be cognizant of clients' emotional connectedness, and throughout therapy support efforts to build and strengthen these relationships.

RECOMMENDATIONS/SUGGESTIONS FOR THERAPISTS

Probably the most difficult issues faced by therapists treating victims of spousal sexual abuse are those around separating the victim from the abuser. This issue has been present in the arena of spousal physical violence for some time. There is an ethical paradox for therapists who view marital dissolution as necessary for the best outcomes, while at the same time being constrained by professional guidelines to not advise clients regarding decisions about marital status. One method of dealing with this paradox is to make the issue overt in therapy. If the client is aware that many professionals working with spousal violence find progress difficult until after the couple separates, then it may help her to examine how important the relationship is to her, and it empowers her by putting her in a position of choice about her future. Although decisions will not necessarily be easy to make or to follow through with, she is at least in a more empowered situation than if the therapist is trying to coax or coerce the client into ending the relationship. By informing the client of the broader context of therapy and allowing her to control the decision-making process, a new, less hierarchical relationship is defined. This prohibits the replication of an abusive-style relationship where she is helpless and others make the decisions.

Another way out of the "marriage-buster" ethical dilemma is for the therapist to consider the possibility that all abusive relationships are not created equally. If the therapist can envision that women and marriages are not all affected in identical ways by this type of abuse, then it becomes possible that in any given case, a variety of outcomes might be the best possible outcome for this victim, including staying in the marriage. Holding this view of abuse and victims, in many ways, makes working with these cases more difficult, blurring therapeutic goals and strategies. However, this view also empowers the victim, allowing her the "expert opinion" on her ideal outcome and her needs in the therapeutic process.

CONCLUSIONS

Spousal sexual abuse is a realm clinicians have only recently begun to recognize and study, and relatively little research has been done to explore how it occurs and how its effects can be treated. It often occurs in conjunction with spousal physical abuse, and some attempts have been made to describe it in comparison to spousal physical abuse or extrafamilial rape. These explanations, however, have failed to fully explain or describe the unique aspects of this form of abuse.

Treatment differs depending on the manner in which the client presents for therapy. For most clients, who initially come to therapy seeking help with some other problem, treatment usually involves assessing whether this type of abuse has taken place, and then pursuing disclosure. After the disclosure, treatment generally focuses on removing any symptoms being experienced by the client then shifting toward healing the relationships involved, whether these are an abusive marriage, a new intimate relationship, or a family's relationships surrounding the abuse.

Spousal sexual abuse is a form of abuse that has been largely ignored by both researchers and clinicians. More research must be done to discover the types of social and personality factors that are associated with this type of abuse. Even more important, research needs to be done to identify the types of therapeutic interventions that will be most helpful for women facing lives torn by sexual abuse. Clinicians also have a responsibility to these women. Therapists and other helping professionals need to be aware that this type of abuse occurs in society and that few women who are dragged off to the bedroom against their will fare as well as Scarlet O'Hara.

REFERENCES

Becker, J. V. (1989). Impact of sexual abuse on sexual functioning. In S. R. Lieblum & R. C. Rosen (Eds.), *Principles and practice of sex therapy* (pp. 298–318). New York: Guilford.

Bidwell, L. & White, P. (1986). The family context of marital rape. *Journal of Family Violence, 1*(3), 277–287.

Bowker, L. H. (1983). Marital rape: A distinct syndrome? *The Journal of Contemporary Social Work, 64*, 347–352.

Burr, W. R. & Christensen, C. D. (1992). Undesirable side effects of enhancing self-esteem. *Family Relations, 41*(4), 460–464.

Finkelhor, D. & Yllo, K. (1982). Forced sex in marriage: A preliminary research report. *Crime and Delinquency, 28*, 459–478.

Finkelhor, D. & Yllo, K. (1985). *License to rape: Sexual abuse of wives.* New York: Holt, Rinehart, & Winston.

Frieze, I. H. (1983). Investigating the causes and consequences of marital rape. *Signs: Journal of Women in Culture and Society, 8*, 532–553.

Gelles, R. J. & Cornell, C. P. (1985). *Intimate violence in families.* Beverly Hills: Sage.

George, L. K. & Winfield-Laird, I. (1986). *Sexual assault: Prevalence and mental health consequences.* A final report submitted to the National Institute of Mental Health for supplemental funding of the Duke University Epidemiologic Catchment Area Program, Chapel Hill.

Groth, A. N. & Gary, T. S. (1981). Marital rape. *Medical Aspects of Human Sexuality, 15*, 3.

Hanneke, C. R., Shields, N. M., & McCall, G. J. (1986). Assessing the prevalence of marital rape. *Journal of Interpersonal Violence, 1*, 350–362.

Heiman, J. R. & LoPiccolo, J. (1976). *Becoming orgasmic: A sexual and personal growth program for women.* New York: Prentice-Hall.

Kasl, C. D. (1989). *Women, sex, and addiction: A search for love and power.* New York: Harper & Row.

Kilpatrick, D. G., Veronen, L. J., & Resick, P. A. (1978). Responses to rape: Behavioral responses and treatment approaches. *Journal of Behavior Therapy, 6*, 85.

Koss, M. P., Dinero, T. E., & Seibel, C. A. (1988). Stranger and acquaintance rape: Are there differences in the victims experience? *Psychology of Women Quarterly, 12*, 1–24.

Leiblum, S. R. & Rosen, R. C. (1989). *Principles and practice of sex therapy: Update for the 1990s*. New York: Guilford.

LoPiccolo, J. & Friedman, J. M. (1988). Broad-spectrum treatment of low sexual desire: Integration of cognitive, behavioral, and systemic therapy. In S. R. Leiblum & R. C. Rosen (Eds.), *Sexual desire disorders* (pp. 107–144). New York: Guilford.

Lewis, B. Y. (1984, August). *Wife abuse and marital rape in a clinical population*. Paper presented at the Second Family Violence Research Conference, University of New Hampshire, Durham.

Pesce, C. (1992, April 21). Marital-rape case acquittal fuels protest. *USA Today*, p. 3A.

Prescott, S. & Letko, C. (1977). Battered women: A social psychological perspective. In Roy, M. (Ed.), *Battered women*. New York: Van Norstrand Reinhold.

Russell, D. E. H. (1990). *Rape in marriage*. Bloomington: Indiana University Press.

Shields, N. M. & Hanneke, C. R. (1983). Battered wives' reactions to marital rape. In D. Finkelhor, R. J. Gelles, G. T. Hotaling, & M. A. Strauss (Eds.), *The dark side of families: Current family violence research* (pp. 132–148). Beverly Hills: Sage.

Shields, N. M., Resick, P. A., & Hanneke, C. R. (1990). Victims of marital rape. In R. T. Ammerman & M. Hersen (Eds.), *Treatment of family violence: A sourcebook*. New York: John Wiley.

Walker, L. E. (1979). *The battered woman*. New York: Harper & Row.

Walker, L. E. (1984). *The battered woman syndrome*. New York: Springer.

Weingourt, R. (1985). Wife rape: Barriers to identification and treatment. *American Journal of Psychotherapy, 39*(2), 187–192.

3

PHYSICAL ABUSE OF CHILDREN BY PARENTS

VIRGINIA HULLINGS-CATALANO

> *I distinguish between two kinds of abuse in my experience.*
> *Oftentimes, there were calmly enforced, sadistic rituals,*
> *defined as sadistic...[I have] recollections of being forced to*
> *kneel upright, with piles of books on our outstretched arms*
> *for hours.... The second type of abuse...was that of unpre-*
> *dictable outbursts of rage. I recall incidents such as the time*
> *our father dumped over a fully set table because our mother*
> *had served two starches with dinner. There was also the time*
> *he nailed me to the wall by my braid for laughing too*
> *loudly.... We were slapped and spanked with a stick daily*
> *and every few months received injuries that required*
> *medical attention.* (Cameronchild, 1978, in Williams
> & Money, 1982, pp. 23–24)

Child abuse affects the developmental health of children, from infancy through adolescence. Approximately 5,000 known deaths occur yearly as a result of injuries to the child by the caregiver (Justice & Justice, 1990). Yet the most noticeable signs of child abuse, such as bruises, bite marks, and broken bones, are often overlooked by members of society because of their own naivete or denial that these acts were committed by a family member.

DEFINITIONS OF PHYSICAL CHILD ABUSE

The term "battered child syndrome"" was first used approximately thirty years ago to describe physical injuries inflicted on children by parents (Kempe, Silverman, Steele, Droegmueller, & Silver, 1962). The definition of child abuse has since been expanded to include other forms of abuse and neglect. Public Law 93-247, the Child Abuse Prevention and Treatment Act of 1974, provides a broad definition of child abuse and neglect that states use to provide general legislation governing the welfare and health of the child (Iverson & Segal, 1990). Agencies like Child Protective Services develop an operational or working definition for abusive experiences they encounter under the guidelines of state statutes (Iverson & Segal, 1990).

Nevertheless, regardless of concrete definitions, the difficulty in defining physical child abuse continues. For example, a parent who spanks a child ten times and leaves no physical marks is less likely to be considered abusive than a parent who hits their child three times with a stick, leaving bruises. The presence of physical injury lends more credence to an abusive situation, although the disciplinary action is as painful. Accidental injuries can be abusive and deadly, yet might not be considered abuse; for example, when a parent leaves a child in the tub unsupervised and the child turns on the hot water tap and suffers second degree burns. Questions for clinicians to think about are: Is a child less abused when hit ten times with an adult's hand than with a stick? Are accidental injuries as abusive as the injuries related to harmful intent? Clinicians' personal experiences of discipline within their families also may affect what behavior is labeled abusive or what is not.

The quandary of defining physical child abuse becomes more pronounced because various authors have equated physical child abuse with child maltreatment, child neglect, and/or emotional abuse (Berger, 1980a; Besharov, 1990; Bowdry, 1990; Watkins & Bradbard, 1982; Wolock & Horowitz, 1984). This makes comparison among studies difficult. Within this chapter, *physical child abuse* refers to any physical contact with the intent to harm a child, including disciplinary actions.

Scope of the Problem

Physical child abuse is tabulated with other forms of child abuse and neglect when reports are compiled. The term *child abuse* covers all forms of behaviors having a negative effect on the child's sociopsychological, educational, emotional, and physical well-being, and is reflected in national and state statistics (Tseng & Jacobsen, 1988). The figures given are based on reported child abuse and neglect incidents unless otherwise stated.

From 1980 to 1986, child abuse and neglect reports increased by 66 percent, which indicates that more than 1.5 million children (25.2 children per 1,000) are abused each year (National Center on Child Abuse and Neglect, 1988, in Howling, Wodarski, Gaudin, & Kurtz, 1989). As a result of a national survey conducted in 1985, Straus and Gelles (1986) estimated that a minimum of 1 million children between the ages of 3 and 17 in dual-parent households encountered serious physical abuse that year.

Over representation of black children in the tabulation of official child abuse and neglect reports is noted in surveys. In 1980, 15% of black children were accounted for in the U.S. Census tabulation. However, in 1982, 22% of child abuse and neglect reports were on black children. This percentage rose to 26.8 in 1985 (Hampton, Gelles, & Harrop, 1989). These figures are alarming, yet bias is often present when labels such as"abuse" or "neglect" are applied. Factors such as race, ethnic background, and social class can determine what labels are applied to an injury or situation (Hampton & Newberger, 1985; Katz, Hampton, Newberger, Bowles, & Snyder, 1986).

IMPACT OF PHYSICAL ABUSE ON CHILD DEVELOPMENT

Violence directed toward a child has different effects on a child's development. Research has addressed the following developmental factors: aggressive behavior, self-concept, social cognition, and emotional development. For a clinician, the child's interaction with the family will be dependent on these factors. Individual assessment and treatment for the child will likely revolve around these developmental signposts.

Studies of aggression and its effects on children reveal various findings. Some scholars find that children with severe injuries display less aggression toward others and avoid aggressive interactions (Kinard, 1980; 1982), or engage in aggressive crimes as adolescents (Gutierres & Reich, 1981). Other studies demonstrate more aggressive and noncompliant behaviors (Egeland & Sroufe, 1981b; Egeland, Sroufe, & Erickson, 1983). In addition, Straker and Jacobson (1981) found no significant differences on measures of aggression and fantasies. Maltreated preschool children exhibited more affection than hostility toward adults (Bradley, Caldwell, Fitzgerald, Morgan, & Rock, 1986). Abused boys demonstrated both internalizing (i.e., fearful, inhibited) behaviors and externalizing (i.e., antisocial, aggressive) behaviors and were shown to be more vulnerable to violence occurring in the home (Jaffe, Wolfe, Wilson, & Zak, 1986).

Children whose mothers were referred for psychiatric help after the abuse had negative views of themselves and experienced feelings of unhappiness (Kinard, 1982). With a repetitive style of abusive parent–child interaction, interference with the child's ability to master age-appropriate developmental tasks as noted (Kinard, 1982). It has been shown that the risks involved with abuse are higher with preschoolers than with older children because of cognitive development and the need to supervise them more (Hughes, 1988).

Abused children tend to be more delayed in emotional development and social-cognitive skills than nonabused children (Camras, Grow, & Ribordy, 1983; Dean, Malik, Richards, & Stringer, 1986; Fatout, 1990a, 1990b; Kinard, 1980, 1982; Wolfe & Mosk, 1983). Infants and toddlers who have been abused tended to show insecure attachment patterns to mothers during separation and reunion testing with the Ainsworth Strange Situation Paradigm (Egeland & Sroufe, 1981a). The continuation of disapproval and rejection by mothers led to "overcontrol" or nonexpression of emotions by their children (Cicchetti, 1989). Perry, Doran, and Wells (1983) found that abused children exhibited delayed or low-normal intellectual and communication skills. Differences between abused children and nonabused children exist in social-cognitive abilities, social role comprehension, perspective-taking skills, and social sensitivity (Barahal, Waterman & Martin, 1981; Straker & Jacobson, 1981).

Social cognition refers to "the processing of social cues and the comprehension of interpersonal problems" and is indicative of interpersonal adjustment (Walker & Downey, 1990, p. 253). Social-cognitive styles of children have been perceived as an intergenerational trait due to dysfunctional parenting (Barahal et al., 1981), although Walker and Downey (1990) dispute any correlation between social-cognitive abilities and risk factors, especially associated with parental psychiatric illness. Frodi and Smetana (1984) found that abused and neglected children were unable to identity and discriminate people's emotions compared to the control group, but that all differences disappeared when IQ was co-variated. They concluded that maltreated children's performances were not necessarily inferior, but that in a violent atmosphere, other subskills in social cognition develop which confounds testing. Children may adapt social-cognitive skills that enable them to live within a violent environment (Frodi & Smetana, 1984).

Handicapped Children

Maltreatment of handicapped children has been widely recognized since Gil (1970) documented physical abuse of children (29% of 6,000) who had developed physical disabilities prior to the abuse. Theories suggest that handicapped children are more vulnerable to abuse because of delayed developmental skills and extra demands they place on parents (Frisch & Rhoads, 1982; Morgan, 1987). Physical child abuse has been identified in children who have had low birth weights, prematurity, mental retardation, and developmental disabilities (Benedict & White, 1985; Berger, 1980b; Frisch & Rhoads, 1982; Frodi, 1981; Nesbit & Karagianis, 1982). Physical abuse is also suspected to be one cause of neurological handicapping conditions, such as cerebral palsy and mental retardation, because of head injuries sustained before the children are 1 to 3 years old (Jaudes & Diamond, 1981; Rose & Hardman, 1981; Steele, 1987). Although most parents with developmentally delayed children are able to cope well, lack of environmental and social supports increases the risk of maltreatment (Zirpoli, 1990).

Siblings

If one child is reported as abused, are the siblings also at risk for maltreatment? Studies comparing siblings and maltreated children have found a significant relationship between stressful life events, home environment, and behavior problems (Berger, 1980b; Halperin, 1981; Jean-Gilles & Crittenden, 1990). Siblings who have not been abused in violent families were found to resort to serious, aggressive crimes more often than the maltreated child (Gutierres & Reich, 1981).

Children living in violent homes tend to accept their parents' values and expectations of them, and to judge themselves against those values. Siblings live under the same expectations and readily accept the parents' criticism of themselves (Kempe, 1987). It is thus necessary to assess and possibly treat not only the identified abused child, but the sibling subsystem as well when working with family violence.

PHYSICAL ABUSE AND FAMILY MEMBERS

Parent's Psychopathology

Many studies focus on psychopathological features of the parent as the cause of child abuse (Estroff, Herrera, Gaines, Shaffer, Gould, & Green, 1984; Webster-Stratton, 1985). Child maltreatment and disruptive child behavior are associated with maternal psychopathology (Iverson & Segal, 1990; Watkins & Bradbard, 1982). Clinicians have noted that psychiatric tests of abusive and nonabusive mothers show higher scores on anger-excitability (Green, Power, Steinbook, & Gaines, 1981) and higher incidences of affective and schizophrenic disorders (Kaplan, Pelcovitz, Salzinger, & Ganeles, 1983) for abusive mothers.

Narcissistic or object relations problems are indicated as the parent tries to reenact the repressed phase of an abusive childhood through his or her own child (Criville, 1990), either releasing hostilities generated by experiences of earlier unmet needs (Parens, 1987), or being unable to relate to the child in a personalized manner (Dougherty, 1983; Main & Goldwyn, 1984). Physical abuse occurs when the child is not able to fulfill the parent's fantasies or expectations because the parent attempts to produce a relationship with the child that unrealistically places the child in an adult role.

Poor attachment and bonding issues between mother and child are variables that researchers have studied. Different studies suggest that teenage mothers are more at risk to abuse their children and less capable of forming a nurturing relationship because of immaturity, large numbers of live births, and lack of "experience factors" (Zuravin, 1988). Teenage mothers often have to cope with sociodemographic stressors (e.g., unemployment, loss of high school education, lack of familial support) which add a delayed negative effect to the already stressed parent–child interaction (Creighton, 1985; Zuravin, 1988).

Abusive mothers report high levels of parenting-related stress which they attribute to their children's poor compliance with behavior-directed instructions (Herrenkohl & Herrenkohl, 1981; Mash, Johnston, & Kovitz,

1983) and their own poor tolerance levels toward their children's behavior. Within the parent–child interaction, abusive mothers express more coercive and aggressive verbal and nonverbal behavior toward their children than nonabusive mothers (Bousha & Twentyman, 1984; Lahey, Conger, Atkeson, & Treiber, 1984). Lahey et al. (1984) suggest these parents have greater emotional or somatic distress and are unable to manage their children. Abusive parents perceive such behavior as fighting or arguing, crying or fussing as noncompliance to instructions (Herrenkohl, Herrenkohl, & Egolf, 1983; Theyer, 1987).

Intergenerational Theory

Transgenerational theory posits that child abuse is transmitted from one generation to another by role modeling. Authors have reported different statistics to support the theory that abusive parents have been abused by their parents. In Steele's study of a clinical population, 30 to 60% of the respondents were found to have been abused as children (Steele, 1980). The Toronto Multiagency Child Abuse Research Project reported that 22% of abusive mothers and 9% of fathers were physically abused or neglected as children (Caplan, Waters, White, Parry, & Bates, 1984). Seven out of nine women who have been imprisoned because of fatal child maltreatment had been abused as children (Korbin, 1987).

Reasons suggested for transgenerational violence are reenactment of past abusive situations (Ney, 1988), and inability or resistance to use better (i.e., less coercive and violent, more assertive and affectionate) parenting styles (Ney, 1988). Social learning theory suggests role modeling between the child and parent causes a continuation of abusive behaviors through each generation (Kalmuss, 1984; Straus, Gelles, & Steinmetz, 1980). Conflict becomes part of the family myths, and scripts are continued for the child and parents to follow through family interaction (Ney, 1988).

Sociological Factors

Sociological perspectives focus on sociocultural and environmental factors that together create an abuse-oriented milieu. Sociological factors may include the degree of poverty or low socioeconomic level of the family (Herrenkohl, Herrenkohl, Toedter, & Yanushefski, 1984; Pelton, 1981; Showers & Bandman, 1986), unemployment (Gelles & Hargreaves, 1981), low educational level, marital discord, single parenthood, negative life stressors (Straus, 1983), and social isolation (Berger, 1980a; Gelles & Maynard, 1987).

Although a majority of studies reflect working-class or low-income group characteristics, physical child abuse exists within the middle- and higher-income groups as well. A recent study surveying undergraduate social science students (n = 570) illustrates this point (Stewart, Senger, Kallan, & Scheurer, 1987). The sample was uniformly middle-class, 40% of families had incomes above $50,000, and more than 30% of the remaining families had incomes between $30,000 and $50,000. One percent of the students had been severely physically abused; 6% were witnesses to their fathers beating their mothers. While emotional neglect is four times more frequent within the middle-class group, the evaluation of physical abuse in the middle- and upper-income groups is as important as in the lower-income groups.

The evaluation of mothers and their employment status has not indicated a higher risk of child abuse with mothers who work outside the home. The presence of other sociological factors, such as excess domestic responsibility, unemployment of the husband, and raising preschoolers may contribute to the risk of physical abuse in the family (Gelles & Hargreaves, 1981).

ASSESSMENT OF PHYSICAL CHILD ABUSE

Family Assessment

Family therapy through a systems framework is a relatively new approach in treating child abuse (Pardeck, 1989). The use of systems theory moves assessment and treatment from an intrapersonal level to an interpersonal level. The evaluation of child abuse includes not only that of the individual child, but also of the parents, other family members, and social environmental factors such as family support systems.

The first contact with the family is likely to be by phone, and the presenting symptom may be for an individual in the family such as the mother dealing with stress or a child's disruptive behavior at school. The family therapist must convey the importance of meeting with the whole family, despite the parent's emphasis on an individual's problem. Child abuse may not be recognized by the therapist, even within the assessment sessions, because disclosure of family secrets is threatening to the family unit.

Signs of child abuse are harsh or frequent discipline reported during the interview, unexplained lacerations or bruises noted on a child, or reports by a school referral of possible child abuse. Reluctance to discuss family history, presentation of contradictory information, or information on repetitive crises in the family may indicate extreme chaos and disorganization that is typical of abusive environments. More subtle symptoms are topic changes or distractions by parents and children when talking about responses to a disruptive behavior, the type of punishment used for discipline, lack of social supports and isolation from the community, or extremely rigid and high expectations regarding the children. Table 3.1 summarizes some of the most common signs of abuse.

A history of physical abuse in the parents' nuclear family does not always indicate that they abuse their own children. Yet, it is important to thoroughly interview the parents about their expectations for their children and about how discipline is enforced. The use of circular questioning fac-

TABLE 3.1 • Possible Signs of Physical Abuse*

Children's behavior:

- aggressive behavior
- fearful of adults
- hypervigilance, guarding behavior
- preoccupation with themes of violence or conflict
- provocative behavior
- art work or play that displays violence
- unexplained bruises, lacerations, welts, burns
- sprains, broken bones, other injuries
- bullying other children
- withdrawn or compliant behavior, eager to please
- poor self-image
- checks with parents before replying to questions
- poor eye contact
- negativist, oppositional behavior
- extreme fatigue from sleep disruption

Parent's behavior:

- reluctance to talk about family history
- presentation of contradictory information
- unable to explain child's frequent injuries
- changes topics when discipline is mentioned
- use of harsh punishment for discipline
- history of being abused as a child
- frequent complaints about the children
- yelling at children
- poor eye contact

Family characteristics:

- isolation from their community
- no social or familial supports
- noninvolvement with school affairs
- friends not allowed at home
- poor medical care

*Similar signs may appear in other disorders

ilitates this process without becoming threatening to the parents. Some empathic questions to ask are:

It certainly can be difficult to raise three children under age 4, how do you manage it?

It sounds as if it is extremely frustrating to be at home all day, can you tell me about it?"

Your job appears so stressful; how do you deal with the pressure?

After a stressful day at work, how do you relax at home?

Parents may feel more comfortable responding to questions when the therapist is offering reassurance at the same time.

When the therapist interviews the parents, anxiety and fear may restrict them from being honest about their feelings and the abuse. Parents often are frightened by the authority of the therapist and the possibilities about what may happen to their family. Parents need to be placed at ease. Whether the child is not at risk for physical abuse, or the situation is being monitored by the clinician or professional child protective worker, parental needs still can be addressed. The family's environmental and familial stressors and the parents' ability to negotiate conflict are reviewed. When talking with the family, the parents are considered the "experts" about their children because of their knowledge and experiences with the child.

While discussing the child, the therapist can explore the parents' experiences of childhood. The exploration of the parents' perception of the identified patient (IP) child and their respective history allows the therapist to assess the potential of maltreatment and the underlying structure of the family. The therapist may see similarities between the parents' family upbringing and their present expectations and behaviors with their children.

Questions can be directed to each child individually while the parents are there. This permits the clinician to observe the interactions and responses of both child and parents. Observation may indicate if the parent allows the child to respond to questions about the family or interrupts instead, or what types of contradictions exist between the child's responses and parents'. The therapist may notice body cues of tension or fear during parent–child interactions, or the child may be extremely active or passive within the context of the family transactions. Children may avoid direct eye contact with parents during conversations or the parent may show inappropriate disapproval or displeasure toward the child for behavior during the interview (Seagull, 1987). For example, a child who looks to the parent every time before responding to the therapist's questions may be fearful of making the wrong response. Children often demonstrate unlimited boundaries, push and hit one another, and ignore any directions from parents. How the parents control the behavior of an active child may indicate forms of discipline used at home.

Different tasks, such as play, decision making, or one-to-one conversation, can be given to the family members to see how they interact (McFadden, 1989). Observation of negative interactions—collusion or scapegoating—between family members is possible. Ambivalent feelings of the children toward parents can be observed, as well as the behaviors between different subsystems.

Grandparents or any other significant family members should be invited to these sessions because abusive families generally have dysfunctional features that extend beyond the nuclear family. Dysfunctional behavior, such as the lack of support toward family members, alterations within family boundaries and hierarchies, or the existence of maladapted family myths, may contribute to abusive behavior (Jones & Alexander, 1987). Other family members, or even babysitters who play a large part in the care of children, can participate in the interview. Intergenerational patterns of physical abuse can often emerge when family genealogy is discussed within a therapy session (McGoldrick & Gerson, 1985).

Assessment Scales

Hansen and McMillan (1990) suggest therapists need to be aware of the following items during the assessment of child abuse and neglect: "1) identification of maltreatment; 2) child management; 3) anger and arousal for the abusive parent; 4) parental knowledge and expectations regarding child behavior; 5) problem-solving and coping methods; 6) social supports for the family; and 7) neglectful parenting" (p. 257). Assessment scales can be used to gather information about parenting skills. Parental self-reports that include interviews, self-monitoring, and child behavior reports have not always been accurate and reliable, although they provide information based on the parents' point of view (Hansen & McMillan, 1990).

Several measurement scales (see Table 3.2) that are helpful with assessment of parenting skills are: The Family Crisis-Oriented Personal Scale (F-COPES) which indicates problem-solving tactics when families encounter family or family-related problems; the Family Inventory of Life Events and Changes (FILE) which looks at normative and nonnormative family-related stresses; and the Family Satisfaction Inventory which measures the family's cohesion and adaptability (Knoff, 1986). The MacMillan-Olson-Hansen Anger Control Scale (MOHAC) is effective with identifying anger control issues related to childrearing. The use of these measures appraises issues within the family that interviews may not address, but they should not be used as diagnostic tools. A summary of some of the assessment scales also is presented in Table 3.2.

Dr. Joel Milner (1980) created the Child Abuse Potential Inventory (CAP) to help social service workers assess an individual's potential for child abuse. This inventory reviews predominant characteristics of parents that may indicate the capacity for violence for families whose personal or living situations place them at high risk for child abuse. Items look at unrealistic expectations and attitudes toward childrearing, difficulties with interpersonal relationships, and personal characteristics such as impulsiveness, depression, rigid ideas, vulnerability, feelings of insecurity or loneliness, and if the parent experienced a negative childhood. Overall, the CAP Inventory provides a useful tool to assess parents who are at risk for physically abusing children.

Child Developmental Assessment and Scales

Children adapt to their violent environment with many different behaviors. The behaviors depend on the type and extent of physical abuse that was

TABLE 3.2 • Family Assesment

Test	Description	Assessment	References
The Family Crisis-Oriented Personal Scale (F-COPES)	Consists of 29 items that are measured on a 5-point Likert scale; useful with FILE	Problem-solving approaches and behaviors used by families	McCubbin, Larsen, & Olson (1987)
The Family Inventory of Life Events (FILE); Adolescent File (A-FILE)	Measures of 71 items for each parent to fill out; a shortened version for adolescents for ages 12–18 and has 50 items	Evaluates normative, and nonnormative family stresses; based on systemic theory where one member's stress affects the other	McCubbin, Patterson, & Wilson (1987); McCubbin & Patterson (1987)
The Family Satisfaction Inventory		Evaluates 14 concepts for cohesion (emotional bonding of family members) and adaptability (family adjustment with structure, roles, and rules for crisis situations)	Olson & Wilson (1982)
MacMillan-Olson-Hansen Anger Control Scale (MOHAC)	Consists of 50 child-related situations that are rated by parents	Helps to identify anger control problems related to childrearing; can be used to document effects of treatment	MacMillan, Olson, & Hansen (1988)
The Child Abuse Potential Inventory (CAP)	Self-report instrument of 160 items primarily used to screen for physical abuse; questionnaire is a forced choice, agree–disagree format and has a third grade readability level	Measures of "Abuse," "Random Responding," "Inconsistency," and "Defensiveness" (Lie Scale)	Milner (1980,1986)

inflicted on the child (Ney, 1987). Abused children may have developmental delays in areas of fine- and gross-motor skills, language skills, and/or intellectual skills (Hitchcock, 1987). Disruptions of critical developmental tasks often have cumulative effects for children, leading to emotional and behavioral problems later in their lives (Sroufe & Rutter, 1984).

Siblings also may need assessment. Assessments can be facilitated by having children meet with the therapist in a separate session. Observation of the interactions between siblings will add knowledge of the family relationships for the therapist. If the identified patient (IP) is a child, watching the siblings interact with the IP may provide the therapist with evidence of scapegoating (Pillari, 1991).

Children display different developmental signs of emotional and psychological deficits. Infants may demonstrate failure-to-thrive problems and neurological deficits that are the result of physical abuse. A noticeable lack of coordination and response to any stimuli may indicate withdrawal from the environment. The Bayley Scales of Infant Development (Bayley, 1969) can be used to assess the social and physical development of the infant.

Abused preschoolers tend to have more nonverbal communication during the performance of concrete tasks instead of abstract ones (Martin, 1980) and more deficits in auditory comprehension (Allen & Oliver, 1982) than nonabused children. Preschoolers may demonstrate depression by detachment from the mother–child dyad (Fatout, 1990a). Sleep disturbances, bedwetting, and extreme fears can indicate masked depression (Blumberg, 1981). Toddlers who are physically abused may develop problems with autonomy and control with toilet training (Mayhill & Eastlack-Norgard, 1983).

The effects of physical abuse on a child seem to be mediated by temperament (Salter, Richardson, & Kairys, 1985). Certain children either regress to an earlier stage, withdraw from peers and adults, or display aggressive or destructive behaviors at all ages (Fatout, 1990b).

Clinicians need to screen children for extreme risk-taking behaviors (running into traffic, playing with guns) and suicide attempts (drugs, cutting wrists). Green (1978) found a significantly higher incidence of self-destructive behaviors in a sample of abused children (40%) in comparison to neglected (17.2%) and normal (6.2%) children. Scales, such as the Children's Depression Inventory, the Children's Manifest Anxiety Scale—Revised, and the Fear Survey Schedule for Children—Revised, can promote evaluation of developmental risks. In middle childhood, children begin to resort to delinquent activities that can continue into adolescence. More overt self-destructive behaviors (i.e., substance abuse, runaway behavior, sexual promiscuity) can occur (Kempe, 1987; Mayhill & Eastlack-Norgard, 1983).

Developmental deficits can be assessed through interviews and observation of behavior and with play and standardized tests. The McCarthy Scales of Children's Abilities and the Achenbach Child Behavior Checklist evaluate internalizing and externalizing syndromes. The Kinetic Drawing System for Family and School assesses individual issues on several levels and the Forcer Structured Sentence Completion Test assesses adolescent interpersonal tendencies on different levels such as aggression and emotional attitudes (see Table 3.3).

Contacts with the child's school and teachers are important sources of information for the therapist. Any sudden change in behavior with peers or teachers may indicate problems at home. The school nurse might have administered care to "accidental" injuries at home. The attendance record may reveal a pattern of a child being kept at home because of tell-tale signs of physical abuse (Seagull, 1987). Changes in academic performance are signs of disorganization and chaos in a child's life.

Interviewing

Open-ended questions encourage children to respond with a general picture of their life. Asking about daily routines elicits information about supervision by parents, and can give clues about the neglect of emotional and physical necessities (Seagull, 1987). For example, the clinician may question the child

TABLE 3.3 • Child Assessment

Test	Description	Assessment	References
Bayley Scales of Infant Development	Consists of 163 items on the Mental Scale and 81 items on the Motor Scale; for children 2 1/2 years old	Motor area (gross coordination) and mental area (adaptability, learning, sensory acuity, and fine-motor coordination)	Bayley (1933a, 1933b, 1965, 1969)
Children's Depression Inventory	Consists of 27 items	Evaluates mood disturbances, hedonic capacity, self-feelings, and interpersonal behaviors	Kovacs & Beck (1977); Kovacs (1981)
Children's Manifest Anxiety Scale—Revised (RCMAS)	A 73-item format where children respond yes or no to items applying to them	Measures level of anxiety, and has subscales for Physiological Anxiety, Worry and Oversensitivity, Concentration Anxiety, and a Lie Scale	Reynolds & Richmond (1978)
Fear Survey Schedule for Children— Revised	Self-report inventory for children 7–16 years consisting of 80 items; sensitive to gender	Identifies children sensitive to specific fears or have a high level of fear	Ollendick (1983, 1988)
Achenbach Child Behavioral Checklist	Based on clinical samples; series of child behaviors standardized for children at ages 4–5, 6–11, 12–16	Investigates behaviors of externalizing (aggression, antisocial) and internalizing syndromes (withdrawal, self-destructive)	Achenbach (1978); Achenbach & Edelbrock (1984)
The Kinetic Drawing System for Family and School	Projective drawing techniques relevant to common themes	Assessments of individual issues: perceptions and attitudes toward family, school, and social interactions	Knoff & Prout (1985a, 1985b)
The Forcer Structured Science Completion Test	Projective, sentence completion format; consists of 100 structured sentences	Assesses dominant needs, emotional attitudes, reactions to interpersonal relationships, aggressive tendencies, and affect	Forcer (1950)
Piers-Harris Children's Self-Concept Scale (CSCS)	For children ages 8–18; consists of 80 statements about oneself; self-report statements	Self-concept areas of behavior, intellectual and school status, physical appearance and attitudes, anxiety level, popularity, happiness and satisfaction	Piers (1984)

about how the day starts, the time she gets up, breakfast routines of who is there with her, who feeds her or helps with dressing. The clinician can ask about school—who is her teacher, who does she socialize with, or what are her favorite subjects. The conversation can then lead to after school activities: Does the child go home immediately after school; if not, who does she visit. If the child goes right home, what happens at home in terms of afternoon chores, who does she play with (siblings or friends), and who else is at home.

Inquires like these provide information concerning who is there to supervise the child, if she is physically cared for, or whether she must supervise siblings because parents are absent. These questions give the clinician some understanding of the rules and expectations the child lives by and what position the child has in the family.

During the interview the child should proceed at his or her own pace. Pressuring the child increases ambivalence and feelings of "betraying" the parent. The child has fears of losing the abusive parent's love (McFadden, 1989). Within an individual or family setting, observation of nonverbal cues can elicit information about the family dynamics. Cues to observe may be that the child is sitting away from the family, or she doesn't respond to the therapist before checking with a parent, or maybe she's hitting younger siblings.

Reporting

If the family has been referred for therapy because of child abuse, reporting is not necessary. Child abuse that continues while the family is in therapy must be reported to the proper authorities. Often, a family who came for treatment for another problem will disclose that child abuse is present in their family. This disclosure may be accidental such as a mother speaking about spousal abuse, or a child relating the punishment received for a certain behavior.

Assessment of the child's physical safety within the family is one of the first steps in evaluating child abuse. If the therapist is not part of a team of investigators, she or he must inform the proper authorities. Each state has legislation governing the protection of children. Therapists need to be aware of the designated policies.

If child abuse is revealed to the therapist during therapy, the therapist may attempt to persuade the parent to place the call to the child protective program or be present while the therapist calls. This action motivates the parent to take responsibility for the abuse and continue with therapy, with the child's interest in mind. Seeing a parent report abuse may also decrease feelings of guilt or blame that a child might feel.

Although the therapist is working with the whole family, the primary responsibility is toward the client most at risk (Ammerman & Hersen, 1990; Bentovim, 1987; Hill, 1980; Margolin, 1982). Children, including siblings, have rights to protection. Reporting abuse and its intervention often outweighs the stance of neutrality between the therapist and the individual family members (Bentovim, 1987). This chapter's author has briefly reviewed reporting; the reader will find a more comprehensive discussion of this topic in Chapter 14.

TREATMENT OF PHYSICAL CHILD ABUSE

Family Treatment

A systems perspective examines the underlying structure and organization of the family to understand the family's patterns of interaction. The therapist assists the family to reconstruct new and nonabusive roles in order to break these destructive patterns. As the therapist works with the family unit, the parents are recognized as the respected source of control within the family (Wodarski, 1981).

Goals to achieve may vary depending on the specific family, but one priority Conger (1982) suggests is to help the abusive parents create personal and social controls that will inhibit violence. For the family, the goal would be stabilization of the family unit by establishing appropriate boundaries to allow individuation yet provide support. This might be established by the use of appropriate child management, stress management with anger control techniques, education of child development for parents that would indicate proper adult and child roles or boundaries, and an increased ability to communicate with one another. Initiation of these tasks will depend on the family situations as determined by the therapist.

While it is essential to treat the whole family in conjoint sessions, there may be times when family sessions are not appropriate (Halperin, 1981). One reason is the potential of physical and psychological danger to the child or children. A conjoint session may be too explosive or frightening with all members present. In other instances, the parents cannot legally have contact with the child. An additional reason that family sessions may not be appropriate is when there is violence in the spousal subsystem.

A child may not benefit from conjoint sessions because of fear (Halperin, 1981). Meeting with the child (or children) without the parents facilitates the ability to speak about feelings and abusive incidents. If there are high negative feelings between the identified child and siblings, again, it is more beneficial for the child to meet individually with the clinician until the situation is safe for all of the family members involved (Halperin, 1981; Ney, 1987).

Aderman and Russell (1990) hypothesize that abusive and neglectful parents engage in behavior that distances the family from informal support systems. Any formal attempts by agency workers to help the family are seen as distrustful and intrusive. The workers' attempts to instruct the parents in parenting skills and nonabusive behaviors are seen as "hierarchical" one-upmanship that reinforces the parents' low self-esteem, powerlessness, and anger (Aderman & Russell, 1990). Resistance to treatment is a major course that parents follow to express their discontent and anger at the system.

The clinician's awareness of the clients' perspective promotes a comfortable, therapeutic environment. This constructivist model states that all reality is constructed from a personal perspective of the individual, and systems are autonomous in that they cannot be controlled from the outside (Aderman & Russell, 1990; Hoffman, 1985). The therapist must develop the ability to consider the client's beliefs with respect. As the client interacts with the therapist, the parents may feel less threatened by the therapist's knowledge and authority. The therapist minimizes the use of strategic maneuvers or controls that would create a one-up position with the client (Hoffman, 1985).

Thus, the reason for seeing a therapist must be clarified during the first session. The therapist needs to understand the family's reality in their own words. Clarification of the presenting problem assists the clinician to engage with the family system, and to begin assessment of underlying patterns such as abuse.

If the family was referred because of child abuse, denial of the abuse will stall treatment. Although the parent may have difficulties in speaking about the physical abuse, the clinician can focus on the parent's history of abuse, or what effect the presenting problem has on the family or the child. This presentation of the problem may open up the parent for a dialogue about the abuse, especially if the child or children have been moved to foster care.

Education and Role Transactions

It is often useful for the therapist to elicit a discussion about norms for parenting in the family. Education consists of information about developmental stages and what cognitive, emotional, and psychological tasks a child is prepared to accomplish at different stages. Relating the parent's history of childhood and what she or he wished from their parents may be a first step to initiate compassion toward the abused child (Jones & Alexander. 1987). Exploration of their own memories and feelings of being abused as children can be compared to the children's present situation. The parents may be able to recognize how their abusive behaviors have impacted their children. As the parents gain recognition of their own emotions, the therapist begins structural changes within the family by encouraging them to perceive the children differently but positively (Jones & Alexander, 1987; Talen & Lehr, 1984).

The therapist's empathy for abusive adults can enable the adults to recognize their own needs and provide a role-model for the parent(s) to develop empathy for the children (Hitchcock, 1987; Pardeck, 1989; Steele, 1987). "The most valuable ingredients therapists can provide, beyond the intellectual insights that enable caregivers to grow and develop, are time, attention, tolerance, and recognition of the immeasurable worth of the individual human beings sitting next to them" (Steele, 1987, p. 385).

When educating clients about child development and behavior management, it is important to consider the beliefs of parents. Education is cognitive restructuring designed to alleviate the parent's sense of uniqueness or aloneness and expand their knowledge of parenting and children (Otto & Smith, 1980). Increased knowledge allows the parent to have a different but healthier interaction when dealing with their children, especially when stresses outside the home are intrusive and difficult. Abusive parents often have myths that pertain to parenting. One such myth is that it is easy for other people to parent but not for them. Another common myth is that there is only one specific way to parent.

When the therapist begins to teach appropriate parenting skills, grandparents can be included. Grandparents need support and recognition of their expertise. Roles in the families may need to be restructured to reduce enmeshed grandparents' assistance, and establish authority in the younger family. Resistance will be present, but positive changes may be instituted by presentation of the grandparents' expertise and wisdom and relating it to the grandparent role (Asen, George, Poper, & Stevens, 1989). The establishment of boundaries between subsystems and strengthening hierarchies between grandparents, parents, and children comprises the restructuring of the family unit (Talen & Lehr, 1984).

Behavior Modeling and Role-Play

Role-playing, instructions on child development, child management, and parent training in more appropriate disciplinary techniques have been used to change abusive behaviors (Lutzker, 1983; Lutzker, Frame, & Rice, 1982; Wolfe & Sandler, 1981; Wolfe, Sandler & Kaufman, 1981). In-home parental training with the use of assigned homework, direct instructions, and home aides has been moderately successful in appropriating gains in parental and child interactions (Burgess, Anderson, Schellenbach & Conger, 1981; Conger, Lahey & Smith, 1981; Wolfe, St. Lawrence, Graves, Brehony, Bradlyn, & Kelly, 1982).

The therapist is the educator and the liaison for new beliefs and behaviors for the parents. The therapist models appropriate behavior toward children by speaking quietly to them, listening to the child's responses, and perhaps taking time to play while the parents observe. Role-plays with parents and children using family situations that have occurred is a teaching tool for changing negative behavior.

Role-plays that reinforce positive behaviors between individual members are also instructive for teaching child development. After discussing developmental levels for children, the parents can demonstrate their knowledge by role-playing incidents concerning children of different ages.

Some parents might use their childhood victimization as a reason to excuse their violent behavior. By asking parents what effect their victimization has had on their lives, a therapist may inspire them to recognize and gain insight into the feelings they had as children. How the parents treat their children can then be examined along the same lines. "This double acknowledgment of being abused and of abusing can be a very painful process" (Jones & Alexander, 1987, p. 353). Parents may become more motivated to change their destructive behavior so that their children will not suffer the same harm as they did.

Stress and Anger Control

Abusive families have poor comprehension of stress management and anger control because of inadequate or abusive responses to social, emotional, and economic stressors in their family environment (Egan, 1983; Nomellini & Katz, 1983). Stressors for parents elicit anger and aggression that becomes directed at children. Children may then respond to normal and stressful situations in an angry and aggressive manner.

Suitable responses to different stress components can be introduced through role-playing and modeling. Cognitive-behavior management skills teach parents how to control emotions connected with stress (Egan, 1983; Goldstein, Keller, & Erne, 1985). The use of relaxation techniques will lessen tension building, while time-out periods allow the parents to work on cognitive responses instead of responding with rage (Conger et al., 1981; Goldstein et al., 1985; Lutzker, 1983; Lutzker et al., 1982). Maintaining a diary of anger experiences and expressing anger assertively rather than on a behavioral level are other ways that anger can be decreased (Nomellini & Katz, 1983).

The therapist may find that, with the exception of anger, family members have distorted views about revealing emotions. A family myth may be that strength is connected to anger, but showing hurt or pain is weak or "sissy-like," especially for males. Children also may hold distorted views of responsibility for the physical abuse, especially if a child is scapegoated for the family's problems. Sensitive education about these distortions can help family members explore new ways of interacting.

TREATMENT CONSIDERATIONS
FOR UNIQUE POPULATIONS

Handicapped Clients

Some authors suggest that developmentally challenged children are more vulnerable to abuse because of delays in development of skills and the extra demands they place on parents (Frisch & Rhoads, 1982; Morgan, 1987). Surprisingly, children with more severe functional or developmental impairments have been shown to be at lesser risk for maltreatment, while marginally disabled children are at more risk because of added frustration and unrealistic expectations by the parents (Benedict, White, Wulff, & Hall, 1990). Overall, research has not documented a direct causal link between handicaps and abuse (Starr, Dietrich, Fischhoff, Ceresnie, & Zweier, 1984), although some parents have more difficulties coping with the handicapped condition (Fine, 1986).

Fine (1986) suggests that an alienation factor may contribute to child abuse, and that the connection of the family to community resources and respite care available to parents may offer relief. Sensitivity by the therapist to the parents' issues of feeling "trapped" and overwhelmed by the situation, and parents' involvement with a support network may help alleviate some of the feelings that contribute to physical abuse (Fine, 1986).

Clinicians also may come across cases where the parents are physically, developmentally, or psychologically challenged. In one study, Accardo and Whitman (1990) interviewed 79 families having at least one parent who was mentally disadvantaged and found that 71 out of 107 (66.4%) children were maltreated or neglected. Children who were at risk for abuse were cognitively brighter than their parents and could verbally express themselves. These parents may experience low self-esteem (Justice & Justice, 1990) and negative self-concepts (Robinson & Robinson, 1976) that can contribute to poor parenting and maltreatment of their children.

Increased knowledge of childrearing practices and understanding of child development can encourage these parents to feel competent to handle their children's behaviors. Education can help physically, developmentally, or psychologically challenged parents learn appropriate values for disciplining, problem solving, and communicating with their children (Schilling, Schinke, Blythe, & Barth, 1982). Goals must be tailored to meet the individual abilities of the parents.

Ethnic and Racial Variations

Clinicians encounter clients who have different ethnic and racial experiences that can influence therapy goals and strategies. Populations that have come across different forms of discrimination from a dominant white cultural environment often are reluctant to disclose feelings and opinions because of fears of being judged (Robinson, 1989). Minority clients' various racial experiences have led them to develop different responses to such experiences based on their environments and socioeconomic status (Linville, Salovey, & Fischer, 1986).

It is important for clinicians to recognize their personal biases and values when meeting with families who are of a different ethnic and racial background. Studies have indicated a therapist's differential judgment and treatment of clients can be influenced by the clinician's personal opinions and prejudices (Franklin, 1985; Robinson, 1989). When this occurs, the effectiveness of therapy is lessened as the communication between the clinician and client(s) is distorted by stereotypic attitudes.

Class status is another factor to consider when combined with ethnicity or race. A therapist's perception of the poor lower-class or working-class client can influence the effectiveness of treatment expectations (Franklin, 1985).

Knowledge of racial and ethnic lifestyles of minority populations will help the clinician develop a broad repertoire of responses in therapeutic interactions (Davis & Proctor, 1989; London & Devore, 1992; Ponterotto & Casas, 1990); a heightened sensitivity to different lifestyles is necessary. Robinson (1989) recommends that clinicians become aware of four aspects regarding race and treatment that may negatively affect therapy assessment and outcome. These aspects can be applied to ethnicity as well. She suggests clinicians need to be aware of "1) racial congruence of the client, 2) influence of race on the presenting problem, 3) the clinician's racial awareness, and 4) the clinician's strategies" (1989, p. 324).

ADJUNCTIVE THERAPY

Individual Treatment for Children

Child therapy may be essential to alleviate the developmental effects of maltreatment and to break the cycle of transgenerational abuse (Howling et al., 1989). Therapy has been instrumental in decreasing the incidence of abuse by directly working with the child to eliminate characteristics or behaviors that have become transactional in response to parental abuse. The clinician helps the child to comprehend the confusion of being treated poorly and to handle emotions such as anger and fear. Lack of trust and a primary-attachment figure may exist (Kempe, 1987; Mayhill & Eastlack-Norgard, 1983).

Children do not understand why a parent is abusive. Cognitive confusion is an initial response to the impact of physical violence (van Dalen, 1989). The child attempts to find an explanation of "why is this happening to me" and concludes it is because of "badness." The ability of the child to trust his or her own perception of the world is shifted as the focus becomes centered on the abusive parent's unpredictable behavior. Multiple feelings—anger, hate, and fear toward the parent—as well as personal feelings of guilt, are blocked because the child blames "badness" for the parent's reaction. The child may begin to seek punishment by the parent in order to have that parent's attention, at any cost, or because it reinforces a sense of being bad. Often, by the time the child meets a therapist, resignation about the abuse is a reality (van Dalen, 1989).

The experience of physical abuse needs to become objective in order for children to disengage from the dependency of the parents. Children can learn that the abuse has victimized them, and that they were not at fault (Ney, 1987). Weinbach and Curtiss (1986), though, do not believe that the child's knowledge of being a victim proves any therapeutic purpose. They suggest that just knowing physical abuse is illegal may be sufficient. Working through the pain and distress releases other emotions of anger and fear.

The child may also relate to the clinician on a mature level, which can hide the emotional trauma the child has endured. The child presents a pseudo-adult image and displays very little emotion (Fatout, 1990a; Ney, 1987). One child in a family may be the protector of the other children. It is important to recognize that abused children may present a false, mature, and responsible self, yet have very little self-confidence and security.

There are different techniques to help a child identify emotions. Pictures show different types of feelings can be used to depict what facial gestures go with what emotions. Sometimes the use of a mirror helps the child "see" his or her own facial gestures. Using feeling games like *The Anger Control Game* teaches children how to respond to situations nonviolently. Playing with puppets or role-plays using costumes are important to provide a sense of self-expression for children.

Reading or acting out fairy tales and identifying with different characters who have been abused, deserted, or not loved can help a child work out ambivalent emotions (Thiessen, 1985). Fairy tales can be used as a form of catharsis for children who are unable to speak about or identify their feelings.

When working with children who are not living with their parents, the clinician must build a positive framework to allow future family therapy to occur. The child's attachment to the parent needs to be maintained by asserting that the physical abuse is wrong, yet the parent's feelings for caring are positive. Van Dalen (1989) proposes that the child be told the parent was responding to outside circumstances that resulted in abusiveness toward her or him.

Clinicians who counsel abused children who often exhibit externalizing and internalizing behaviors may find that relaxation techniques can promote a calming effect. Progressive muscle relaxation (PMR) can be especially helpful for older children and adolescents; the technique encourages systematic relaxation of muscle groups (Hansen, Conaway, & Christopher, 1990). Although PMR can be used for younger children in short sessions, deep-breathing techniques also provide a practical approach to relaxation. Counting out loud from one to ten is useful to decrease impulsive behavior for children who become emotionally reactive when aroused with anger.

Children who have been abused generally will be deficient in problem-solving skills and controlling labile emotions. Games for clinicians to use to promote problem solving are available. Such games as *Coping and Decisions*, *The Anger Control Game*, and the *Breakaway* help children recognize their feelings and promote coping and decision-making skills.

Couples Group Treatment

Group treatment with spouses is suggested because of the symbiotic relationship and hierarchy that exists with spouses (Justice & Justice, 1990). Treatment with other spouses fosters a sense of belonging and provides positive feedback for newly learned behavior (Halperin, 1981; Wodarski, 1981). The couples are confronted with issues such as child development, anger control, and the use of appropriate discipline.

Handling anger is a serious problem, especially if their family histories support the use of rage as a solution to problems (Justice & Justice, 1990). Anger and abuse also may be an issue between the partners. The use of no hitting contracts, relaxation techniques, and time-out can be presented within couple groups (Goldstein et al., 1985; Justice & Justice, 1990). Learning to control the escalation of anger responses can be learned through role-plays, and cognitive-behavioral methods (Barth, Blythe, Schinke, & Schilling, 1983; Goldstein et al., 1985).

Doughtery's (1983) program provides a nurturing or holding environment within a group setting to help the parents experience self-awareness and growth. The author believes abusive parents use their children as need-satisfying objects or as "bad" representations of themselves. In this holding environment, parents learn that their children cannot fulfill parents' lost childhood needs, yet they can gain self-gratification in a mature fashion. An important idea portrayed by Dougherty (1983) is that through the mastery of tasks, parenting classes, and constant nurturing, parents can learn to display affection and express empathy.

Group therapy provides emotional support to parents and can be instrumental in teaching child-management techniques. Groups also provide performance comments to the parents as the behaviors displayed become more appropriate. For further information on group therapy through a structured learning process, consult *Changing the Abusive Parent* by Goldstein, Keller, and Erne (1985).

Group Therapy for Children

Group therapy has been successful for treating children and adolescents. The important aspects with group intervention are peer support and socializing (Howling et al., 1989). Communication within groups is essentially productive for adolescents because they are peer-oriented.

There are four general categories of coping skills that are pursued in group therapy: interpersonal, problem solving, cognitive and affective coping, and self-management (Rose & Edleson, 1987). For children from physically abusive environments, social skills can be underdeveloped as abused children are either too aggressive or too withdrawn. Children who become hypervigilant to their environment often are unable to trust even peers enough to let their guard down. Within a group setting, a peer-group approach can help facilitate meeting and interacting with other members.

Problem-solving skills can be generated for alternative thinking, consequential thinking, and means–ends thinking to enable the child to develop a sense of control over the environment. Cognitive-coping skills that facilitate coping with internal and social phenomena are important (Rose & Edleson, 1987). For abused children, problem solving and coping may be limited to dealing with the violence at home; skills for dealing with the outer environment are more likely limited or underdeveloped.

Self-management skills assist children control their behavior as they control their environment. Development of self-control may provide abused children with a sense of self as they learn about controlling aggressive or disruptive behavior.

The use of group therapy in addition to family therapy may be necessary for abused children. Sharing traumatic experiences with other children has had positive influences on changing children's self-images (Steward, Farquar, Dicarry, Glick, & Martin, 1986).

MULTIDIMENSIONAL TREATMENT MODALITIES

Many times, child abuse cases have several professionals involved because of the legal issues surrounding abuse and reporting. Families are often referred to clinicians by family or criminal courts and child protective agencies. With mandated treatment for the parents, therapists meet with clients under adversarial conditions and resistance to treatment may occur (Irueste-Montes & Montes, 1988). Yet research indicates that court-ordered parents are more likely to complete therapy than voluntary parents (Wolfe, Aragona, Kaufman, & Sandler, 1980), although other studies show court-ordered parents and parents who enter treatment voluntarily had no significant differences in completing therapy, and both had significant improvement in parenting (Irueste-Montes & Montes, 1988).

Contact with child protective workers, social services, or court judges may be necessary if legal services are involved with the case. Baglow (1990) presents a model that permits professional input in an organized and competent manner. He suggests that when the initial disclosure and referral originate from either a specialized child agency (e.g., rape crisis center or hospital clinic) or a legal agency (e.g., a child protection agency, police, and/or social services), a planning of a joint case conference can occur where the different agencies and the designated therapist(s) meet to share assessment and clarify legal and treatment responsibilities for the case. Periodic joint reassessments are scheduled for information exchange and to promote legal and therapeutic resolution in the best interest of the child and the family (Baglow, 1990).

This process provides a systemic family model and promotes communication to prevent treatment breakdown. The responsibility of maintaining therapy is distributed between several professional workers. This can be especially helpful with families who are resistant to therapy. Multidimensional treatment promotes cooperation and support with the process of therapy, and containment for the family to maintain treatment goals set by the clinician (Baglow, 1990).

CONCLUSIONS

Child abuse treatment programs are continuously being evaluated and researched, yet the strategies applied to parent–child therapy, individual therapies, and group therapies are many. With child abuse, the involvement of other professionals and agencies contributes to the paradox of what to examine and how to measure results. Multiple variables within the treatment plans limit the evaluation of different treatment strategies and, as Blythe (1983) states, conclusions about what treatment works are replaced by: "What treatment, by whom, is most effective for this individual with that specific problem, and under which set of circumstances?" (p. 332).

Various studies report findings on behavioral or cognitive-behavioral therapy (Azar & Siegel, 1990; Blythe, 1983, Otto & Smith, 1980; Wodarski, 1981), constructive therapy (Aderman & Russell; 1990), demonstration and innovative treatment programs (Cohn & Daro, 1987), and different group therapies for parents and children (Goldstein et al., 1985; Justice & Justice, 1990; Steward et al., 1986).

In studies evaluating the success of different programs, statistical results are varied. One study involving 89 different demonstration treatment programs consisting of 3,253 families dealing with child abuse and neglect, shows that abuse continued in 30 to 47% of the cases investigated (Cohn & Daro, 1987). For these programs, few children experienced direct services for maltreatment. In two studies Jones (1987) reviews, the reabuse rate was 20% (Lynch & Roberts, 1982) to 30% (Rivara, 1985). The effectiveness of family therapy involving nuclear and/or extended families has not been researched thoroughly, except for a single case documentation (Pardeck, 1989).

Strategies used with family systems have been used within other models of treatment. Aderman and Russell (1990) use circular questioning and a systemic meta-level questioning to encourage parents to view their abusive behaviors through their own eyes. These forms of questioning proved to be enlightening to the parents and initiated constructive behavior change. Several treatment programs use structured family therapy while others included parent–child interactions (Asen et al., 1989; Doughtery, 1983).

At this time, it is important to document family therapy with abusive families to determine the effectiveness of the different approaches. The use of a controlled sample may be helpful to determine the potential of family therapy, although there are multiple variables to consider when working with a family. Single case documentation may introduce the treatment protocol used yet will not necessarily be conclusive with a diverse population.

REFERENCES

Accardo, P. J. & Whitman, B. Y. (1990). Children of parents with mental retardation: Problems and diagnoses. In B. Y. Whitman & P. J. Accardo (Eds.), *When a parent is mentally retarded* (pp.123-132), Baltimore: Paul H. Brookes.

Achenbach, T. M. (1978). The child behavior profiles: I. Boys age 6–11. *Journal of Consulting and Clinical Psychology, 46*(3), 476–488.

Achenbach, T. M. & Edelbrock, C. S. (1984). Psychopathology of childhood. *Annuals Review of Psychology, 35*, 227–256.

Aderman, J. & Russell, T. (1990). A constructivist approach to working with abusive and neglectful parents. *Family Systems Medicine, 8*(3), 241–250.

Allen, R. E. & Oliver, J. M. (1982). The effects of child maltreatment on language development. *Child Abuse & Neglect: The Interactional Journal, 6*(3), 299–305.

Ammerman, R. T. & Hersen, M. (1990). Issues in the assessment and treatment of family violence. In R. T. Ammerman & M. Hersen (Eds.), *Treatment of family violence: A source book* (pp. 3–13). New York: John Wiley.

Asen, K., George, E., Poper, R., & Stevens, A. (1989). A systems approach to child abuse: Management and treatment issues. *Child Abuse & Neglect, 13*, 45–57.

Azar, S. T. & Siegel, B. R. (1990). Behavioral treatment of child abuse: A developmental perspective. *Behavior Modification, 14*(3), 279–300.

Baglow, L. J. (1990). A multidimensional model for treatment of child abuse: A framework for cooperation. *Child Abuse & Neglect, 14*, 387–395.

Barahal, R. M., Waterman, J., & Martin, H. P. (1981). The social cognitive development of abused children. *Journal of Consulting and Clinical, 49*(4), 508–516.

Barth, R. P., Blythe, B. J., Schinke, S. P., & Schilling II, R. F. (1983). Self-control training with maltreating parents. *Child Welfare, 4* (July-August), 314–324.

Bayley, N. (1933a). *The California First-Year Mental Scale.* Berkeley: University of California Press.

Bayley, N. (1933b). *The California Infant Scale of Motor Development.* Berkeley: University of California Press.

Bayley, N. (1965). Comparison of mental and motor test scores for ages 1–15 months by sex, birth, order, race, geographical location, and education of parents. *Child Development, 36*, 379–411.

Bayley, N. (1969). *Bayley Scales of Infant Development.* San Antonio: The Psychological Corporation.

Benedict, M. & White, R. (1985). Selected perinatal factors and child abuse. *American Journal of Public Health, 75*, 780–781.

Benedict, M. I., White, R. B., Wulff, L. M., & Hall, B. J. (1990). Reported maltreatment in children with multiple disabilities. *Child Abuse & Neglect, 14*, 207–217.

Bentovim, A. (1987). Physical and sexual abuse of children—the role of the family therapist. *Journal of Family Therapy, 9*, 383–388.

Berger, A. M. (1980a). The child abusing family: I. Methodological issues and parent-related characteristics of abusing families. *The American Journal of Family Therapy, 8*(3), 53–66.

Berger, A. M. (1980b). The child abusing family: II. Child and childrearing variables, environmental factors and typologies of abusing families. *The American Journal of Family Therapy, 9,* 52–58.

Besharov, D. J. (1990). *Family violence: Research and public policy issues.* Washington, DC: The AEI Press.

Blumberg, M. L. (1981). Depression in abused and neglected children. *American Journal of Psychotherapy, 35*(July), 332–335.

Blythe, B. J. (1983). A critique of outcome evaluation in child abuse. *Child Welfare, LXII*(4), 325–335.

Bousha, D. M. & Twentyman, C. T. (1984). Mother–child interactional style in abuse, neglect, and control groups: Natural observations in the home. *American Psychological Association, 93*(1), 106–114.

Bowdry, C. (1990). Toward a treatment-relevant typology of child abuse families. *Child Welfare, LXIX*(4), 333–340.

Bradley, R. H., Caldwell, B. M., Fitzgerald, J. A., Morgan, A. G., & Rock, S. L. (1986). Experiences in day care and social competence among maltreated children. *Child Abuse & Neglect, 10*, 181–189.

Burgess, R. L., Anderson, E. A., Schellenbach, C. J., & Conger, R. D. (1981). A social interactional approach to the study of abusive families. *Advances in Family Interventions, Assessment and Theory, 2*, 1–46.

Cameronchild, J. (1978). An autobiography of violence. In G. J. Williams & J. Money (1982). *Traumatic abuse and neglect of children at home.* Baltimore: The John Hopkins University Press.

Camras, L. A., Grow, J. G., & Ribordy, S. C. (1983). Recognition of emotional expression by abused children. *Journal of Clinical Child Psychology, 12*(3), 325–328.

Caplan, P. J., Waters, J., White, G., Parry, R., & Bates, R. (1984). Toronto Multiagency Child Abuse Research Project: The abused and abuser. *Child Abuse & Neglect, 8,* 343–351.

Cicchetti, D. (1989). Child maltreatment: Theory and research on the causes and consequences of child abuse and neglect. New York: Cambridge University Press.

Cohn, A. H. & Daro, D. (1987). Is treatment too late: What ten years of evaluative research tell us. *Child Abuse & Neglect, 11,* 433–442.

Conger, R. (1982). Behavioral interventions for child abuse. *The Behavior Therapist, 5*(2), 49–53.

Conger, R. D., Lahey, B. B., & Smith, S. S. (1981). *An intervention program for child abuse: Modifying maternal depression and behavior.* Paper presented at the Family Violence Research Conference. University of New Hampshire, Durham.

Creighton, S. (1985). Epidemiological study of abused children and their families in the United Kingdom between 1977 and 1982. *Child Abuse & Neglect, 9,* 441–448.

Criville, A, (1990). Child physical and sexual abuse: The roles of sadism and sexuality. *Child Abuse & Neglect, 14*(1), 121–127.

Davis, L. & Proctor, E. (1989). *Race, gender, and class: Guidelines for practice with individuals, families, and groups.* Englewood Cliffs, NJ: Prentice-Hall.

Dean, A. L., Malik, M. M., Richards, W., & Stringer, S. A. (1986). Effects of parental maltreatment on children's conceptions of interpersonal relationships. *Developmental Psychology, 22,* 753–771.

Dougherty, N. (1983). The holding environment: Breaking the cycle of abuse. *Social Casework, 64* (May), 228–290.

Egan, K. J. (1983). Stress management and child management with abusive parents. *Journal of Clinical Child Psychology, 12*(3), 292–299.

Egeland, B. & Sroufe, L. A. (1981a). Attachment and early maltreatment. *Child Development, 52,* 44–52.

Egeland, B. & Sroufe, L. A. (1981b). Developmental sequelae of maltreatment in infancy. *New Directions for Child Development, 11,* 77–92.

Egeland, B., Stroufe, L. A., & Erickson, M. (1983). The developmental consequences of different patterns of maltreatment. *Child Abuse & Neglect, 7,* 459–469.

Estroff, T. W., Herrera, C., Gaines, R., Shaffer, D., Gould, M., & Green, A. H. (1984). Maternal psychopathology and perception of child behavior in psychiatrically referred and child maltreatment families. *Journal of the American Academy of Child Psychiatry, 23*(6), 642–652.

Fatout, M. F. (1990a). Consequences of abuse on the relationships of children. *Families in Society, 71,* 76–81.

Fatout, M. F. (1990b). Aggression: A characteristic of physically abused latency-age children. *Child and Adolescent Social Work, 7*(5), 365–376.

Fine, M. J. (1986). Intervening with abusing parents of handicapped parents of handicapped children. *Techniques: A Journal for Remedial Education and Counseling, 2,* 353–363.

Forcer, B. R. (1950). A Structured Sentence Completion Test. *Journal of Projective Techniques, 14,* 15–30.

Franklin, D. L. (1985). Differential clinical assessments: The influence of class and race. *Social Service Review, 59,* 44–61.

Frisch, L. & Rhoads, F. (1982). Child abuse and neglect in children referred for learning evaluation. *Journal of Learning Disabilities, 15,* 583–586.

Frodi, A. (1981). The contribution of infant characteristics to child abuse. *American Journal of Mental Defiency, 85,* 341–349.

Frodi, A. & Smetana, J. (1984). Abused, neglected, and nonmaltreated preschoolers' ability to discriminate emotions in others: The effects of IQ. *Child Abuse & Neglect, 8,* 459–465,

Gelles, R. J. & Hargreaves, E. F. (1981). Maternal employment and violence toward *Journal of Family Issues, 2*(4), 509–530.

Gelles, R. J., & Maynard, P. E. (1987). A structural family systems approach to intervention in cases of family violence. *Family Relations, 36,* 270–275.

Gil, D. D. (1970). *Violence against children.* Cambridge, MA: Harvard University Press.

Goldstein, A. P., Keller, H., & Erne, D. (1985). *Changing the abusive parent.* IL: Research Press.

Green, A. H. (1978). Self-destructive behaviors in battered children. *American Journal of Psychiatry, 135,* 579–582.

Green, A. H., Power, E., Steinbook, B., & Gaines, R. (1981). Factors associated with successful and unsuccessful intervention child abusive families. *Child Abuse & Neglect, 5,* 45-52.

Gutierres, S. E. & Reich, J. W. (1981). A developmental perspective on runaway behavior: Its relationship to child abuse. *Child Welfare, LX*(2), 89–94.

Halperin, S. L. (1981). Abused and nonabused children's perceptions of their mothers, fathers, and siblings: Implications for a comprehensive family treatment plan. *Family Relations, 30,* 89–96.

Hampton, R. L., Gelles, R. J., & Harrop, J. W. (1989). Is violence in black families increasing? A comparison of 1975 and 1985 national survey rates. *Journal of Marriage and the Family, 51,* 969–980.

Hampton, R. L. & Newberger, E. H. (1985). Child abuse incidence and reporting by hospitals: The significance of severity, class, and race. *American Journal of Public Health, 75*(1), 56–60.

Hansen, D. J., Conaway, L. P., & Christopher, J. S. (1990). Victims of child abuse. In R. T. Ammerman & M. Hersen (Eds.), *Treatment of family violence: A sourcebook* (pp. 17–49). New York: John Wiley.

Hansen, D. J., & McMillan, V. M. (1990). Behavioral assessment of child-abusive and neglectful families. *Behavior Modification, 14*(3), 255–278.

Herrenkohl, R. C. & Herrenkohl, E. C. (1981). Some antecedents and developmental consequences of child maltreatment. *New Directions for Child Development, 11,* 57–76.

Herrenkohl, R. C., Herrenkohl, E. C., & Egolf, B. P. (1983). Circumstances surrounding the occurrence of child maltreatment. *Journal of Counseling and Clinical Psychology, 51*(3), 424–431.

Herrenkohl, E. C., Herrenkohl, R. C., Toedter, L., & Yanushefski, A. M. (1984). Recent studies in child abuse: Parent–child interactions in abusive and nonabusive families. *Journal of the American Academy of Child Psychiatry, 23*(6), 641–648.

Hill, M. (1980). The manifest and latent lessons of child abuse inquiries. *British Journal of Social Work, 20,* 197–213.

Hitchcock, R. A. (1987). Understanding physical abuse as life-structure. *Individual Psychology, 43*(1), 50–55.

Hoffman, L. (1985). Beyond power and control: Toward a "second order" family systems therapy. *Family Systems Medicine, 3,* 381–396.

Howling, P. T., Wodarski, J. S., Gaudin, J. M. Jr., & Kurtz, P. D. (1989). Effective interventions to ameliorate the incidence of child maltreatment: The empirical base. *Social Work, 34,* 330–338.

Hughes, H. M. (1988). Psychological and behavioral correlates of family violence in child witnesses and victims. *American Journal of Orthopsychiatry, 58*(1), 77–90.

Irueste-Montes, A. M. & Montes, F. (1988). Court-ordered vs. voluntary treatment of abusive and neglectful parents. *Child Abuse & Neglect, 12*, 33–39.

Iverson, T. J. & Segal, M. (1990). *Child abuse and neglect: An information and reference guide*. New York: Garland Publishers.

Jaffe, P., Wolfe, D., Wilson, S. K., & Zak, L. (1986). Family violence and child adjustment: A comparative analysis of girls' and boys' behavioral symptoms. *The American Journal of Psychiatry, 143*(1), 74–77.

Jaudes, P. K., & Diamond, L. J. (1985). The handicapped child and child abuse. *Child Abuse & Neglect, 9*, 341–347.

Jean-Gilles, M. & Crittenden, P. M. (1990). Maltreating families: A look at siblings. *Family Relations, 39*, 323–329.

Jones, D. P. H. & Alexander, H. (1987). Treating the abusive family within the family care system. In R. E. Helfer & R. S. Kempe (Eds.), *The battered child*, 4th ed. (pp. 339–359). Chicago: The University of Chicago Press.

Justice, B. & Justice, R. (1990). *The abusing family*. New York: Insight Books Plenum Press.

Kalmuss, D. (1984). The international transmission of marital aggression. *Journal of Marriage and the Family, 46*, 11–19.

Kaplan, S., Pelcovitz, D., Salzinger, S., & Ganeles, D. (1983). Psychopathology of parents of abused and neglected children and adolescents. *Journal of the American Academy of Child Psychiatry, 22*(3), 328–344.

Katz, M. H., Hampton, R. L., Newberger, E. H., Bowles, R. T., & Snyder, J. C. (1986). Returning children home: Clinical decision making in cases of child abuse and neglect. *American Journal of Orthopsychiatry, 56*(3), 253–262.

Kempe, R. S. (1987). A developmental approach to the treatment of the abused child. In R. E. Helfer & R. S. Kempe (Eds.), *The battered child*, 4th ed. (pp. 360–381). Chicago: The University of Chicago Press.

Kempe, C. H., Silverman, F. H., Steele, B. P., Droegmueller, W., & Silver, H. K. (1962). The battered children syndrome. *Journal of the American Medical Association, 181*, 17–24.

Kinard, E. M. (1980). Emotional development in physically abused children. *American Journal of Orthopsychiatry, 50*(4), 686–695.

Kinard, E. M. (1982). Experiencing child abuse: Effects on emotional adjustment. *American Journal of Orthopsychiatry, 51*(1), 82–91.

Knoff, H. M. (1986). *The assessment of child & adolescent personality*. New York: Guilford Press.

Knoff, H. M. & Prout, H. T. (1985a). The Kinetic Drawing System: A review and integration of the Kinetic Family and School Drawing Techniques. *Psychology in the Schools, 22*, 50–59.

Knoff, H. M. & Prout, H. T. (1985b). *The Kinetic Drawing System: Family and School*. Los Angeles: Western Psychological Services.

Korbin, J. (1987). Child abuse and neglect: The cultural context. In R. E. Helfer & R. S. Kempe (Eds), *The battered child*, 4th ed. (pp. 23–41). Chicago: The University of Chicago Press.

Kovacs, M. (1981). Rating scales to assess depression in school-aged children. *Acta Paedopsychiatrica, 46*, 305–315.

Kovacs, M. & Beck, A. T. (1977). An empirical–clinical approach toward a definition of childhood depression. In J. Schulterbrandt & A. Raskins (Eds.), *Depression in childhood: Diagnosis, treatment, and conceptual models* (pp. 63–87). New York: Raven Press.

Lahey, B. B., Conger, R. D., Atkeson, B. M., & Treiber, F. A. (1984). Parenting behavior and emotional status of physically abusive mothers. *Journal of Consulting and Clinical Psychology, 52*(6), 1062–1071.

Linville, P., Salovey, P., & Fischer, G. (1986). Stereotyping and perceived distributions of social characteristics: An application to ingroup-outgroup perceptions. In J. Dovidio & S. Gaertner (Eds.), *Prejudice, discrimination and racism* (pp. 165–208), Orlando: Academic Press.

London, H. & Devore, W. (1992). Layers of understanding: Counseling ethnic minority families. In K. Arms, J. Davidson, & N. Moore (Eds.), *Cultural diversity and families* (pp. 172–176). Dubuque, IA: W. C. Brown.

Lutzker, J. R., Frame, R. E., & Rice, J. M. (1982). Project 12-ways: An eco-behavioral approach to the treatment and prevention of child abuse and neglect. *Education and Treatment of Children, 5,* 141–155.

Lutzker, J. R. (1983). Project 12-ways: Treating child abuse and neglect from an eco-behavioral perspective. In R. F. Dangel & R. A. Polster (Eds.), *Parent training: Foundation of research and practice.* New York: Guilford.

Lynch, M. A. & Roberts, J. (1982). *Consequences of child abuse.* London: Academic Press.

MacMillan, V. M., Olson, R. L., & Hansen, D. J. (1988). *The development of an anger inventory for use with maltreating parents.* Paper presented at the meeting for the Association for the Advancement of Behavior Therapy, New York.

Main, M. & Goldwyn, R. (1984). Predicting rejection of her infant from a mother's representation of her own experience: Implications for the abused–abusing intergenerational cycle. *Child Abuse & Neglect, 8,* 203–217.

Margolin, G. (1982). Ethical and legal considerations in marital and family therapy. *American Psychologist, 37,* 788–801.

Martin, H. P. (1980). The consequences of being abused and neglected: How the child fares. In C. H. Kempe & R. E. Helfer (Eds.), *The battered child,* 3rd ed. (pp. 347–365). Chicago: The University of Chicago Press.

Mash, E. J., Johnston, C., & Kovitz, K. (1983). A comparison of the mother–child interactions of physically abused and nonabused children during play and task situation. *Journal of Consulting and Clinical Psychology, 12*(3), 337–346.

Mayhill, P. D. & Eastlack-Norgard, K. E. (1983). *Child abuse and neglect: Sharing responsibility.* New York: John Wiley.

McCubbin, H. I., Larsen, A., & Olson, D. (1987). F-COPES Family Crisis-Oriented Personal Scales. In H. I. McCubbin & A. Thompson (Eds.), *Family assessment inventories for research and practice.* Madison: University of Wisconsin.

McCubbin, H. I. & Patterson, J. M. (1983). Stress: The Family inventory of Life Events and Changes. In E. E. Filsinger (Ed.), *Marriage and family assessment: A sourcebook for family therapy* (pp. 275–315). Beverly Hills: Sage Publications.

McCubbin, H. I. & Patterson, J. M. (1987). Adolescent–Family Inventory of Life Events and Changes. In H. I. McCubbin & A. I. Thompson (Eds.), *Family assessment inventories for research and practice.* Madison: University of Wisconsin.

McCubbin, H. I. Patterson, J. M., & Wilson, L. (1987). Family Inventory of Life Events and Changes (FILE), Form A. In H. I. McCubbin & A. Thompson (Eds.), *Family assessment inventories for research and practice.* Madison: University of Wisconsin.

McFadden, E. J. (1989). *Counseling abused children.* Ann Arbor, MI: ERIC Counseling and Personnel Services Clearinghouse.

McGoldrick, M. & Gerson, R. (1985). *Genograms in family assessment.* New York: W. W. Norton.

Milner, J. (1980). *The Child Abuse Potential Inventory: Manual.* Webster, NC: Psytec Corporation.

Milner, J. (1986). *The Child Abuse Potential Inventory: Manual—Revised.* Webster, NC: Psytec Corporation.

Morgan, S. R. (1987). *Abuse and neglect of handicapped children.* Boston: College-Hill/Little, Brown.

Nesbit, W. C. & Karagianis, L. D. (1982). Perspectives: Child abuse—exceptionality as a risk factor. *The Alberta Journal of Educational Research, XXVIII*(1), 69–76.

Ney, P. G. (1987). The treatment of abused children: The natural sequence of events. *American Journal of Psychotherapy, XLI*(3), 391–401.

Nomellini, S. & Katz, R. (1983). Effects of anger control training on abusive parents. *Cognitive Therapy and Research, 7*(1), 57–68.

Ollendick, T. H. (1983). Reliability and validity of the revised Fear Survey Schedule for Children (FSSC–R). *Behaviour Research and Therapy, 21,* 685–692.

Ollendick, T. H. (1988). Fear Survey Schedule for Children—Revised. In M. Hersen & A. S. Bellack (Eds.), *Dictionary of behavioural assessment techniques.* New York: Pergamon.

Olson, D. H. & Wilson, M. A. (1982). Family Satisfaction Scale. In D. H. Olson, H. I. McCubbin, H. L. Barnes, A. S. Larsen, M. J. Muxen, & M. A. Wilson (Eds.), *Family inventories.* St. Paul: Family Social Science, University of Minnesota.

Otto, M. L. & Smith, D. G. (1980). Child abuse: A cognitive behavioral intervention model. *Journal of Marital and Family Therapy, 6,* 425–429.

Pardeck, J. T. (1989). Family therapy as a treatment approach to child maltreatment. *Early Child Development and Care, 42,* 151–157.

Parens, H. (1987). *Aggression in our children.* Northvale, NJ: Aronson.

Pelton, L. (1981). The myth of classlessness. In L. Pelton (Ed.), *The social content of child abuse and neglect.* New York: Human Science Press.

Perry, M. A., Doran, L. D., & Wells, E. A. (1983). Developmental and behavioral characteristics of the physically abused child. *Journal of Consulting and Clinical Psychology, 12*(3), 320–324.

Piers, E. V. (1984). *Manual for the Piers-Harris Children's Self-Concept Scale.* Los Angeles: Western Psychological Services.

Pillari, V. (1991). *Scapegoating in families: Intergenerational patterns of physical and emotional abuse.* New York: Brunner/Mazel.

Ponterotto, J. G. & Casas, J. M. (1990). *Handbook of racial/ethnic counseling research.* Springfield, IL: Charles C Thomas.

Reynolds, C. R. & Richmond, B. O. (1978). "What I think and feel": A revised measure of children's manifest anxiety. *Journal of Abnormal Child Psychology, 6,* 271–280.

Rivara, R. P. (1985). Physical abuse in children under two: A study of therapeutic outcomes. *Child Abuse & Neglect, 9,* 81–87.

Robinson, J. B. (1989). Clinical treatment of black families: Issues and strategies. *Social Work, 34,* 323–329.

Robinson, N. & Robinson, H. B. (1976). *The mentally retarded child.* New York: McGraw-Hill.

Rose, E. & Edleson, J. L. (1987). Working with children and adolescents in groups. *American Journal of Psychotherapy, 42,* 162–163.

Rose, E. & Hardman, M. L. (1981). The abused mentally retarded child. *Education and Training of the Mentally Retarded, 4,* 67–75.

Salter, A., Richardson, C., & Kairys, S. (1985). Caring for abused preschoolers. *Child Welfare, LXIV*(4), 343–356.

Schilling, R. F., Schinke, S. P., Blythe, B. J., & Barth, R. P. (1982). Child maltreatment and mentally retarded parents: Is there a relationship? *Mental Retardation, 20*(5), 201–209.

Seagull, E. A. W. (1987). The child psychologist's role in family assessment. In R. E. Helfer & R. S. Kempe (Eds.), *The battered child,* 4th ed. (pp. 152–177). Chicago: The University of Chicago Press.

Showers, J. & Bandman, R. L. (1986). Scarring for life: Abuse with electric cords. *Child Abuse & Neglect, 10,* 25–31.

Sroufe, I. A. & Rutter, M. (1984). The domain of developmental psychopathology. *Child Development*, 55, 17–29.

Starr, R. H., Dietrich, K. N., Fischhoff, J., Ceresnie, S., & Zweier, D. (1984). The contribution of handicapping conditions to child abuse. *Topics in Early Childhood Special Education*, 4, 55–69.

Steele, B. (1987). Reflections on the therapy of those who maltreat children. In R. E. Helfer & R. S. Kempe (Eds.), *The battered child*, 4th ed. (pp. 382–391). Chicago: The University of Chicago Press.

Steele, B. E. (1980). Psychodynamic factors in child abuse. In C. H. Kempe and R. E. Helfer (Eds.), *The battered child*, 3rd ed. (pp. 382–391). Chicago: The University of Chicago Press.

Steward, M., Farquar, L. C., Dicarry, D. C., Glick, D. R., & Martin, P.W. (1986). Group therapy: A treatment of choice for young victims of child abuse. *International Group of Psychotherapy*, 36, 261–277.

Stewart, M C., Senger, M. M., Kallan, D. & Scheurer, S. (1987). Family violence in stable middle-class homes. *Social Work*, 32, 529–531.

Straker, G. & Jacobson, R. (1981). Aggression, emotional maladjustment, and empathy in the abused child. *Developmental Psychology*, 17, 762–765.

Straus, M. A. (1983). Ordinary violence, child abuse and wife-beating: What do they have in common? In D. Finkelhor, R. Gelles, G. Hotaling, & M. Straus (Eds.), *The dark side of families* (pp. 197–212). Beverly Hills: Sage.

Straus, M. A. & Gelles, R. (1986). Societal change and change in family violence from 1975 to 1985 as revealed by two national surveys. *Journal of Marriage and the Family*, 48, 465–479.

Straus, M. A., Gelles, R. J., & Steinmetz, S. K. (1980). *Behind closed doors: Violence in the American family*. Garden City, NY: Doubleday/Anchor.

Talen, M. R. & Lehr, M. L. (1984). A structural and developmental analysis of symptomatic adopted children and their families. *Journal of Marital & Family Therapy*, 10(4), 381–391.

Theyer, B. A. (1987). Punishment induced aggression: A possible mechanism of child abuse? *Psychological Reports*, 60, 129–130.

Thiessen, I. (1985). A new approach with fairytales as metaphors and anchoring devices in hypnotherapy. *Medical Hypnoanalysis*, 6, 21–26.

Tseng, C. S. & Jacobsen, J. J. (Eds.) (1988). *Sourcebook for child abuse and neglect: Intervention, treatment, and prevention through crisis programs* Springfield, IL: Charles C Thomas.

van Dalen, A. (1989). The emotional consequences of physical child abuse. *Clinical Social Work Journal*, 17(4), 383–394.

Walker, E. F. & Downey, G. (1989). The effects of familial risk factors on social-cognitive abilities. *Child Psychiatry and Human Development*, 20(4), 253–267.

Watkins, H. D. & Bradbard, M. R. (1982). Child maltreatment: An overview with suggestions for intervention and research. *Family Relations*, 31, 323–333.

Webster-Stratton, C. (1985). Comparison of abusive and nonabusive families with conduct-disordered children. *American Journal of Orthopsychiatry*, 55(1), 59–69.

Weinbach, R. W. & Curtiss, C. R. (1986). Making child abuse victims aware of their victimization: A treatment issue. *Child Welfare*, LXV(4), 337–346.

Wodarski, J. S. (1981). Treatment of parents who abuse their children: A literature review and implications for professionals. *Child Abuse & Neglect*, 5, 351–360.

Wolfe, D, A., Aragona, J., Kaufman, K., & Sandler, J. (1980). The importance of adjudication in the treatment of child abusers: Some preliminary findings. *Child Abuse & Neglect*, 4, 127–135.

Wolfe, D. A. & Mosk, M. D. (1983). Behavioral comparisons of children from nonabusive and distressed families. *Journal of Consulting and Clinical Psychology, 51*(5), 702–708.

Wolfe, D. A. & Sandler, J. (1981). Training abusive parents in effective child management. *Behavior Modification, 5,* 320–335,

Wolfe, D. A., Sandler, J., & Kaufman, K. (1981). A competent-based parent training for child abusers. *Journal of Consulting and Clinical Psychology, 49,* 633–640.

Wolfe, D. A., St. Lawrence, J., Graves, K., Brehony, D., Bradlyn, A. S., & Kelly, J. A. (1982). Intensive behavioral parent training for a child abusive parent. *Behavior Therapy, 13,* 438–451.

Wolock, I. & Horowitz, B. (1984). Theory and review: Child maltreatment as a social problem—The neglect of the neglect. *American Journal of Orthopsychiatry, 54*(4), 530–542.

Zirpoli, T. J. (1990). Physical abuse: Are children with disabilities at greater risk? *Intervention in School and Clinic, 26*(1), 6–11.

Zuravin, S. J. (1988). Child maltreatment and teenage first births: A relationship mediated by chronic sociodemographic stress? *American Journal of Orthopsychiatry, 58*(1), 91–103.

4

INCEST

JAN OSBORN

The incidence of incest may always have been as high as it is now, but, with the appearance of the adult survivor's movement and children's rights groups, awareness of its occurrence and information about long-range effects have increased over the past twenty years. Incidence statistics can be difficult to interpret because of a number of factors. Perhaps the most obvious reason is the taboo against incest. Incestuous families often are not identified until a crisis occurs, bringing the secret out into the open. Even if reported to child protective services for abusive behaviors, the sexual abuse may not be discovered.

Cantwell (1983) studied 247 children in a crisis care unit. They were brought to the program because of reports of physical abuse, sexual abuse, being left home alone, or their parent's incarceration. Of these 247 children, sexual abuse was reported for 45. Of the remaining 202 children who were not suspected of having experienced sexual abuse, 45 more were identified as being sexually abused through the use of a routine vaginal examination. For many children, disclosure does not take place until they are adults. Thus, retrospective studies (see Chapter 8 on adult survivors) are likely to reveal higher incidences than studies looking at families presently abusing (Finkelhor & Hotaling, 1984).

DEFINITION OF INCEST

Another difficulty in assessing the incidence of sexual abuse is definition. When looking at reported cases of incest, comparison across states is nearly impossible as each state has the authority to define its own criteria. Some states, for instance do not take a protective role of children unless actual penetration has occurred (Wyatt & Doyle-Peters, 1986). For example, in two large-scale studies of adult women, both Russell (1983) and Wyatt (1985) found the incidence of sexual abuse to rise dramatically when noncontact sexual activities, such as exibitionism were added to the definition. Of the 930 women in Russell's probability sample, 38% reported histories of sexual abuse involving physical contact. When nonphysical sexual activities were added to the definition, the number jumped to 54%. Similarly, Wyatt (1985) reports incidence rates of 45% for physical sexual abuse and 62% when nonphysical abuse was added to the definition.

Currently the legal definitions of incest do not adequately deal with incest that is perpetrated by siblings. In many states, if the perpetrator was a sibling, the family will receive no intervetion from either a treatment or legal perspective, leaving the victim vulnerable to further abuse. The message this sends to the victim is that the victimization was acceptable behavior. This one area of incest reiterates the crucial role of definitions in the lives of victims and other family members.

Perhaps the most important definition should include the child's viewpoint. Elwell and Ephross (1987) studied 20 children reported by child protective services as having experienced sexual abuse. Two factors related to the child's defintion of the sexual experience produced higher levels of trauma on a symptom checklist; the use of force and physical injury to the child produced more traumatic reactions. The researchers also believed that the closer the relationship the child had with the perpetrator, the more trauma experienced by the child. Because of the small sample size, and the variety of perpetrators, significant results were not found. Fathers, however, were associated with higher trauma. Russell (1984) also makes the assertion that the more trust the child had in the relationship with the adult the more trauma the child experienced. The defined relationship had less impact than the feelings the child had for the perpetrator.

Before meaningful incidence statistics can be collected, however, consensus must be reached on criteria for inclusion. The research community and legislative bodies, both holding insider positions and engaged in gathering data, have not yet come to consensus in defining sexual abuse. This lack of consensus is consistent with the societal confusion around defining sexual abuse. No one definition is agreed on nationally. Thus, although reporting of incidence statistics by state began in 1973, it is still extremely fragmented.

Best (1990), in describing how definition and statistics are utilized to further claims, asserts that a broad definition and high statistics serve to make claims of widespread abuse more believable. He further asserts that "official" statistics are more convincing than other research statistics, regardless of the validity of the methods used. Additionally, the way in which statistics are collected has pragmatic relevance such as funding for child abuse agencies. Those states that have less restrictive reporting guidelines will have higher incidence statistics, thus making them more likely to receive governmental aid for prevention and treatment.

A more important question seems to be: What will professionals do with statistics on incest? In the end the exact definition and incidence of incest will continue to be bantered about by interest groups who have a vested interest in either inflating or minimizing the problem. What is more important is the provision of adequate services for families who have suffered through this devastating experience.

SCOPE OF THE PROBLEM

Incidence studies have been implemented by a variety of researchers (Cantwell, 1983; Cupoli & Monaghan-Sewell; 1988; Finkelhor, 1980; Forseth & Brown, 1981; Kendall-Tackett & Simon, 1987; Russell, 1983, 1984; Wyatt, 1985). The research overwhelmingly supports the belief that perpetrators are most often fathers or father surrogates (stepfather, mother's boyfriend) and victims are most often daughters. In a random, retrospective study of 930 women, Russell (1984) reports that 19% of women have been sexually abused by the age of eighteen. This is coroborated by Finkelhor's 1980 study, where he found 20% of female college students were sexually abuse by the age of seventeen. Of the abused women in Russell's study, 60% reported the father as the perpetrator and 33% reported stepfathers as perpetrators. Kendall-Tackett and Simon (1987) report that 89% of the 365 adults seeking treatment at the Child Sexual Abuse Treatment Program of Santa Clara County were female, and 62% reported that the perpetrator was the father or father surrogate. The perpetrator was male in 97% of the cases and known to the victim in 99% of the cases. The high rate of known perpetrators in this sample may be because a clinical sample was used.

Cantwell (1983) in a retrospective chart review of sexual abuse cases reported in Denver in 1979 found 85% of the 226 reported victims to be girls. Fathers and father surrogates accounted for 54% of perpetrators for both boys and girls. There were no reports of abuse by mothers. Cupoli and Managhan-Sewell (1988), in a study of 1,059 children under age 17 attending a metropolitan emergency room over a 44-month period, reported the perpetrator as inter-familial only 28% of the time and known to the child 58.1% of the time. Girls represented 89% of the sample. This may be because parents are leery of seeking medical treatment for their children when they are the perpetrators. Forseth and Brown (1981) surveyed 58 sexual abuse treatment programs and found 58% of perpetrators to be fathers and 20% to be stepfathers.

The main focus of this chapter is the treatment of families in which incest has occurred. Assessment of the family, couple, and individual members is explored as well as treatment goals for each. The rationale for treating the entire family (though not necessarily together in the same room) also is discussed.

CONSEQUENCES

Consequences for the Individual

Children exhibit a wide range of behaviors when experiencing sexual abuse in the home. Any one behavior alone may not be indicative of sexual abuse thus the child's overall adjustment needs to be assessed. Mannarino and Cohen (1986) evaluated 45 children who had been sexually abused, 69% of whom exhibited symptoms. The most pervasive symptoms noted were nightmares, bedwetting, clinging behavior, inappropriate sexual behavior, anxiety, and sadness. In a study of 20 sexually abused children (ages 5–12), Elwell an Ephross (1987) report similar results. Ninety percent of the children experienced some form of physical disturbance such as sleeping difficulties, and 85% experienced difficulties in school. The most common responses of children after a report had been made were excessive dependence (clinging to the parent), fear of specific people, sleeping difficulty, appetite decrease, nervousness, and pain in the area of the sexual abuse.

Studies of children who have recently experienced sexual abuse reveal a consistent set of symptoms (see Table 4.1). Some of these symptoms may continue into adulthood, while others may improve with time. Other behaviors may not be exhibited until adolescence or adulthood. (For information on aftereffects experienced in adulthood see Chapter 8 on adult survivors of incest.)

TABLE 4.1 • Common Behaviors Exhibited by Traumatized Children

Symptoms of Young Children:

Fear	Phobic or avoidant behavior
Inability to trust	Problems in school
Anger and hostility	Somatic symptoms
Inappropriate sexual behavior	Sleep disturbance/nightmares
Depression	Self destructive behavior
Guilt	Daydreaming
Shame	Compulsive masterbation
Explosive anger	Regression
Dissociation	

Additional Symptoms of Adolescents:

Eating disorders	Running away
Self-mutilation	Suicide attempts
Drug and alcohol use	Promiscuity
Seductiveness	Perfectionism

Compiled from Browne and Finkelhor, 1986; Everstine and Everstine, 1986; Green, 1986; Mian et al., 1986; Meiselman, 1978; and Thompson et al., 1988.

In addition, several authors report a flat affect, indicating shock, fear, and depression. Others in the child's life may mistakenly see this as an indication that the child has been unaffected by the abuse, when in fact, these are sometimes the most traumatized children (Burgess & Holstrom, 1974; Sgori, 1978; Terr, 1990).

Consequences for the Family System

The disclosure of incest can momentarily create more of a crisis than the incest itself for the family system (Sgori, 1982; Trepper & Barrett, 1989). This does not imply that the disclosure is more damaging than the incest, only that the disclosure affects the entire family system and creates a crisis of a different sort. The incest affects each member of the family indirectly; the disclosure affects everyone directly (Trepper & Barrett, 1989). Once the disclosure has occurred, family members are forced to see themselves in an entirely different fashion. They are now forced to view themselves as an incestuous family or to hold the belief that the victim is a liar. Either view has a dramatic impact on everyone's experience.

After disclosure, outside agencies such as child protective services become involved, and the victimized child and/or offending parent may be removed from the home, making it impossible to keep the secret. Sgori (1982) suggests families are in need of "total life support" after the disclosure. This includes a mixture of concrete environmental services and intensive day-to-day support. All family members may be at risk for suicide (Everstine & Everstine, 1989).

The Child Sexual Abuse Treatment Program of Santa Clara County (CSATP) utilizes a support group component as a part of treatment, as they have found families who are further along in the treatment process to be extremely helpful at this time. An independent study of the CSATP found that families received an average of twenty hours of support from group members the first week after entering treatment (Giarretto, 1982). The following "composite portrait" of families at intake comes from the data collected on the Child Sexual Abuse Treatment Program of Santa Clara County (Kroth, 1979):

> The intrafamilial sexual abuse case, typically comprised of a father-perpetrator, a nonoffending spouse and one or more victims, provides the following general picture at intake. The victims on the average were 12 to 13 years of age with a range from 6 to 21. Over half of the victims had been molested from at least six months to three or more years duration. Some 29% of the victims had been molested within the two months prior to intake. Nearly half of all the victims at intake display nervous or psychosomatic symptoms. The parents of these children report at intake that they are in some way close to a "nervous breakdown" (67%), and 88% express the feeling that they are "emotionally devastated." Most of the marital partners are unsure they will continue to live together or are actively contemplating separation or divorce.

A substantial number of perpetrators and spouses (38%) describe themselves as arguing "quite a lot" in the two months prior to intake, and 80% report either nonexistent or declining sexual contacts with each other.

This "composite portrait" neglects the common experience of incest that is perpetrated by a sibling. Many of these families would never reach the intake process because they do not fit the definition of incest.

The perpetrator of the abuse may be incarcerated, making therapeutic intervention difficult unless an agreement can be worked out with the court for treatment. Economic difficulty may develop if the perpetrator is incarcerated for a prolonged period of time. Blame for the hardships endured by the family may be placed with the victim for disclosing rather than the perpetrator. In a study of 27 families, Furniss (1983) found that families would often expel a member rather than change the dynamics of the family relationships. The expelled member was often the daughter, not the perpetrator.

Consequences for Larger Social Systems

Clearly, the incidence of incest cannot have a positive effect on the larger social system. Vast amounts of emotional, physical, and financial energy are expended to combat the effects of incest. With each new victim, the message of secrecy and submission is perpetuated. This message of secrecy regarding sexual abuse is clear in the treatment literature as well.

Some still doubt whether abuse actually occurrs very often and many question the veracity of their adult clients' reports. What Rush (1980) terms the "Freudian cover-up" (p. 91) speaks eloquently to this taboo. Early in Freud's work with hysteria, he found that most of his "hysterical female clients" reported being sexually abused by their fathers. In a letter to his friend W. Fliess, Freud reports, "I have come to the opinion that anxiety is to be connected, not with a mental, but a physical consequence of sexual abuse" (Rush, 1980, p. 87). In 1896 Freud presented his findings to the medical community in a series of three papers titled *Aetiology of Hysteria*. He reported that he identified the specific excitement of the genitals resulting from sexual abuse in childhood as the trauma that brought on the hysteria (Rush, 1980 p. 87). Freud went on to cite 18 cases of hysteria, all including sexual abuse; he was met with hostility and ridicule. Ambivalent himself to identify fathers as perpetrators, Freud never again publicly spoke of sexual abuse as a reality, and instead held that it was fantasy on the part of the women he treated. In another letter to Fliess in 1897, Freud writes that "the number of fathers named by his patients as sexual molesters had truly alarmed him; with the father as prime abuser he had inferred from the existence of some hysterical features in his brother and several sisters that even his father had been thus incriminated" (Rush, 1980, p. 87).

The attitudes that continue to be held by the culture influence the continuation of the problem of incest. The attitude toward reporting sexual abuse varies regionally. For instance, in 1978 Georgia reported 28 cases to the National Registry (Finkelhor, 1980), while Minnesota, which is a smaller state, reported 419 cases. It is doubtful that incidence alone accounts for such a dramatic difference.

Cultural attitudes can also be seen in the criminal prosecution of perpetrators. Of the 6,096 cases reported to the National Registry in 1978, perpetrators of sexual abuse were five times more likely to be criminally prosecuted than perpetrators of other types of abuse (Finkelhor, 1980). This, however, also varies from state to state. In Nevada, criminal action was taken in 43% of the cases reported in 1978, 10% in Arkansas, and Massachusetts rarely prosecuted (Finkelhor, 1980). Few cases nationwide end in incarceration. In 1978, 26% of "poor" perpetrators (annual income less than $13,000) were convicted, and 23% of middle-class perpetrators (annual income above $13,000) were convicted. Finkelhor (1980) asserts that this shows no prejudice in relation to class. The author (of this chapter) finds this an astounding assumption because all upper-class families are combined with middle-class families and the two combined do not equal the same rate of conviction for the lower-class group.

The feminist perspective holds that such high rates of sexual abuse and incest occur because of the patriarchal attitudes of our society. This, they hold, is maintained by the way in which both male and female children are socialized. The patriarchal attitudes of individuals and families are isomorphic to the larger society. The lack of consequences for perpetrators, which they feel contributes to the high prevalence, is also influenced by these patriarchal attitudes.

FACTORS ASSOCIATED WITH INCEST

The action of sexual abuse, as the victim-perpetrator model asserts, is linear and the goal of the perpetrator taking responsibility for the abuse should begin immediately. The contributing factors, however, are not linear (see Table 4.2). Several authors have addressed family risk factors (Everstine & Everstine, 1989; Finkelhor, 1980, Larson & Maddock, 1986). Trepper and Barrett's (1986; 1989) Family Vulnerability Model was found by this author to be the most comprehensive and is reviewed briefly here, followed by additional risk factors offered by other authors not already included. Family system factors will then be expanded on. The purpose of assessment is to solve problems, not to pathologize (Trepper & Barrett, 1989). The model asserts that all families have a degree of vulnerability based on four areas: (1) socioenvironmental factors, (2) family of origin of the parents, (3) family systems factors, and (4) individual psychopathology.

Both perpetrators and nonoffending parents often come from abusive families themselves. Goodwin, Cormier, and Owen (1983) submit that 10% of reported cases are perpetrated by grandfathers. In their study of 10 such

TABLE 4.2   •   Risk Factors Associated with Incest

Socioenvironmental Factors Include:

1) Acceptance of male supremacy
2) An imbalance of power (Bograd, 1984; Brickman, 1984; Sgori, 1982)
3) Adherence to the differential manner in which men and women display affection
4) Objects of sexual attraction (children)
5) Differences in relationship with children. Parker and Parker (1986) found the degree of nurturing a parent provided to the child as a primary predictive variable in all forms of child abuse
6) Tolerance to incest in the family's community
7) Social isolation
8) Chronic stress

Family of Origin Factors Include:

1) Traditional roles of men and women
2) Perceived quality of relationship between parent and his or her parents
3) Incidence of abuse in history of parents. Although perpetrators of sexual abuse may not have been sexually abused, nearly all perceive themselves as having been emotionally abused in their childhood (Barrett, 1992).

Family Systems Factors Include:

1) Abusive style
2) Structure
3) Communication

Additional Factors (Trepper & Barrett, 1989) *Include:*

1) Precipitating events
   a) Alcohol and substance abuse
   b) Opportunity
   c) Acute stress
2) Coping
   a) Social network
   b) Religious beliefs
   c) Use of fantasy
   d) Therapy/ Self-help
3) Denial

Additional Risk Factors Include:

1) Stepfather, mother's boyfriend (Finkelhor 1980)
2) Lack of sexual relationship between parents for a considerable length of time (Everstine & Everstine, 1989; Maisch, 1972; Kroth, 1979)
3) Role reversal of mother and daughter (Barrett, 1992; deYoung, 1982; Everstine & Everstine, 1983; Finkelhor, 1980; Furniss, 1984; Maisch, 1972; Meiselman, 1978).
4) Alcoholic father
5) Mother absent or passive (Finkelhor, 1980)

situations, they found that 6 of the 10 mothers of the victims had been abused by the same man (their fathers) in their childhoods. Eight out of ten of these men had abused multiple victims in both the daughter's and granddaughter's generations. The high level of sexual abuse within the family and across three generations calls for a multigenerational family approach to treatment.

TREATMENT

Individual Treatment

Various models of treatment are availible to clinicans. For the purpose of clarification, the distinctions between the models will be delineated, although in practice few therapists hold rigidly to one particular approach. The beliefs the individal clinican has regarding incest impact on the choice of treatment. The perpetrator–victim model is a linear model viewing incest as an aggressive act of an adult against an innocent child (Rosenfeld, 1979). Treatment is focused on individually treating the perpetrator and the child victim; family therapy is not recommended. The goal of treatment is for the perpetrator to take full responsibility for the abuse, and for the child victim to be able to place the blame with the perpetrator, freeing the child from guilt.

Feminist theory asserts that the patriarchal society in which we live places the (predominately male) perpetrator's rights over the rights of children. The power imbalance between men and women in a patriarchal culture calls for the responsibility to be placed solely with the perpetrator. To blame the nonoffending parent, in any way, ignores these power imbalances.

Family Systems Model

The family systems model explains incest as "the product of a problematic family system rather than the cause, and sees all family members as sharing in the cause and maintenance of the incest" (Trepper & Barrett, 1989, p.18). All members are seen as victims and perpetrators (Barrett, 1992; Fredrickson, 1990). The entire family system is seen as the unit of treatment from the perspective of this model. Treatment usually includes a structural component, creating clear and appropriate boundaries between parental and child subsystems (Barrett, 1992; Larson & Maddock, 1986). This does not mean, however, that each member of the system has equal power in maintaining or stopping the abuse.

As awareness of the impact that incest has on all family members has grown, as well as the influence of individual members on the system, the number of family-centered treatment programs has increased. In the early seventies few centers for family treatment of incest existed. Ten years later in a survey of 58 sexual abuse treatment programs, Forseth and Brown (1981) found that 89% of them utilized family treatment. Finkelhor (1986) asserts: "Despite the diversity of the treatment approaches proposed for dealing with sexual abuse, there is almost no approach which does not use family treatment in at least part of its program" (p. 54). Many programs are also incorporating other agencies—police, judges, attorneys, and child protective service—into treatment (Giarretto, 1982; Trepper & Barrett, 1989). In keeping with these recent developments, this chapter focuses on a family systems approach to treatment, incorporating the larger context. Possibilities for incorporating the feminist perspective with family systems also are addressed.

Clarification of "family therapy" is necessary before continuing with assessment and treatment. While all family members are in need of treatment, not all sessions are conjoint (Furniss, 1984). Actually, most treatment programs incorporate a variety of treatment modalities including family, individual therapy for the perpetrator, nonoffending parent (if one exists) and child victim, couple, sibling subsystem, nonoffending parent with the victim, perpetrator with the victim, and group therapy (Everstine & Everstine, 1989; Furniss, 1983; Giarretto, 1982; Trepper & Barrett, 1989). All of these combinations may be necessary in order to reunite the family (Giarretto, 1982). Individual assessment and therapy are considered vital components of family therapy, because valuable information may be shared when not in the presence of other family members (Trepper, 1986).

Feminist Therapy

Feminist theory has raised several concerns regarding the systemic treatment of incest (Bograd, 1984). One of the greatest concerns voiced by feminists is that the family systems model does not take power imbalances into consideration. By considering each family member's part in the system, feminists argue, family therapists miss these power imbalances and do not expect perpetrators to take responsibility for their actions. Mother blaming is inherent in the expanded frame of the family. The feminist perspective further asserts that all blame should be placed with the perpetrator and the focus of treatment should be on the relief of pain and consequences of the incest suffered by the victim. Family sessions, some argue are harmful to the victim's healing process as blame is ascribed to her by the very act of including her in the therapy of her perpetrator (Bogard, 1984). Incest is not seen by feminists as a symptom of a dysfunctional family system as it is in systems theory, but rather as one of the organizing forces behind the family's pattern of interaction. They further argue that family systems theory ignores historical, cultural, community, and political factors. Family systems theory, they argue neglects the context of patriarchy in which families are embedded. The feminist perspective sees incest as a political problem that stems from the patriarchal society's inability to protect its victims.

Feminist-Informed Family Therapy

Feminist theory takes a strong stand against conjoint sessions (Bograd, 1984). Conversely, Barrett, Trepper, and Stone Fish (1990) assert that family therapy is one of the best ways to address some of these concerns. (For a more complete exploration of the use of feminist-informed family therapy and the treatment of interfamilial sexual abuse refer to Barrett et al. 1990. Barrett (1992) holds that "responsible treatment" addressees the social/political/cultural, family and individual levels, and believes that all levels should be woven throughout the course of treatment.

"Incestuous families are so intensely and overtly bound by patriarchal messages from larger social systems that it is impossible to create any kind of lasting change without addressing and challenging these messages" (Barrett et al., 1990, p. 156). These authors contend that the protection of the child and the cessation of the abuse is the goal of therapy and, by changing the family structure, this goal can be met. They also point out that, contrary to common belief, victims and nonoffending mothers often want to have continued contact with the perpetrator, and do, regardless of court mandates. Not permitting the victim to have contact with the perpetrator in the context of therapy when the child is forced to see him outside of therapy, allows for the patterns of abuse to continue without intervention. Further, the victim role of the daughter can be perpetuated by treating her exclusively as an individual. Individual treatment does not afford her the opportunity to confront her abuser and mother. She may be left with the pain of abuse but no opportunity to effect change in her family.

As mentioned previously, family therapy does not imply that all sessions are conjoint, rather, that all members are viewed as in need of support and treatment. Thus, members may be seen individually and in dyads or subsystems before the family is seen together. As is detailed later, when either parent is denying, the victim should not be seen with him or her. Assisting the perpetrator to take full responsibility for the behavior is a primary goal of therapy. Part of this goal includes assisting the perpetrator to examine the ways in which context has influenced behavior. As Barnett et al. (1990) state:

> Feminist-informed family therapy can provide something individual therapy cannot: Access to the family system that maintains the status quo. Synthesis of feminist theory and family systems therapy encourages therapists to discuss important gender-issue changes that are necessary for the abuse to cease forever, while actively altering the dysfunctional sequences of behavior in session. (p. 164)

Family Assessment and Treatment: General Issues

Assessment and treatment are intimately related and ongoing. Assessment of the family and individual members is complicated by the crisis state most families are experiencing at the beginning of treatment. The family's connection with therapy normally follows the disclosure of the incest and is not necessarily voluntary, such as in the case of court-mandated therapy. Important initial information for the therapist is a full account of how the disclosure happened and what has taken place since this time.

As many family members as possible should be seen, though not necessarily together. If the offending parent is incarcerated, the therapist will need to work with the legal system to allow for participation in family treatment, as waiting for release can greatly hinder the treatment process (Furniss, 1984; Giarretto, 1982). Although family treatment is the goal, child safety is the top priority. Parents should be seen individually or as a couple to assess the support of the victim before family sessions are implemented. Even if initially supportive, parents often choose each other over the child, and discount or minimize his or her accounts (Giarretto, 1982; Sgori, 1982; Trepper & Barrett, 1989). As mentioned earlier, in a study of 27 families, Furniss (1983) found that it was often more tolerable to attempt to break up the family by pushing one or more members out than to change family relationships. If this is happening for the child, she or he should not initially be seen conjointly with parents. If the child has been removed from the home, she or he is in great need of the therapist as an ally. At least one ally needs to be found within the family as well. The best person, of course, is the nonoffending parent, though an older sibling or grandparent can be enlisted if this is not possible (Sgori, 1982). If all family members have remained in the home, or the offending parent has not been incarcerated, the safety of the child must be assessed. The question of whether the nonoffending parent is willing to and can protect the child must be answered as accurately as possible.

Assessment of Denial

The level of denial is also an important predictor for the success of treatment, and, in part, determines who will be seen conjointly. Trepper and Barrett (1989) consider four types of denial: (1) denial of facts, (2) denial of awareness, (3) denial of responsibility, and (4) denial of impact. Denial of facts is the most detrimental to the therapy process; this means that the actual events are being denied. It is not uncommon for the perpetrator of abuse to deny all or part of the facts, particularly if criminal charges are pending. An offender's lawyer will often coach the offender to remain vague. This greatly hinders the therapeutic process.

The nonoffending parent (most typically the mother) often denies initially, particularly if the father is denying. The victim also is very likely to deny facts. Sometimes she or he will deny at the time of disclosure, especially if the abuse was discovered by a third party. More common, the victim will recant the story when the pressure of the situation grows too great such as when parents and/or siblings are denying and or blaming. Regardless of the victim's denial, she or he should not be seen conjointly with either parent who is denying facts as this would be further abuse. If only one parent is denying, the child should be seen with the nondenying (usually the nonoffending) parent. If denial of facts, particularly on the part of the perpetrator continues, the prognosis for family therapy is poor. Work can, however, continue with other members of the family.

Denial of awareness is somewhat less serious and more easily worked through. In this case the perpetrator may accept the facts of the abuse, yet claim he was unaware of its occurrence. The most common excuse is alcohol. Perpetrators often claim they were drunk, and therefore don't remember the abuse. Denial of awareness is also common for the mother. Mothers commonly voice shock and amazement at the disclosure. This is true even if there was a previous disclosure by the child. At times this may be, in a sense, denial of facts; mom did know about the abuse and is lying. Much more common, however, even in cases of previous disclosure, is a true lack of awareness. Thus awareness is repressed as the pain of acknowledging the incest would be too great. Daughters deny awareness by claiming they were asleep, or they did not know what was happening was sexual. Because young children are sometimes not developmentally able to distinguish sexual behaviors from other types of affection, they may not recognize the behaviors as abusive, or they may talk about the abuse in terms of it being a dream or fantasy.

Perhaps the most common form of denial is denial of responsibility. This form of denial is particularly dangerous in terms of ensuring that the child will not be abused in the future. Facts are not denied; however, the abuse is justified. For instance, a perpetrator may claim he would not have turned to his daughter if his wife had been sexually active with him. Alternately, a mother may excuse the behavior because the perpetrator was drunk. A common form of denial of responsibility by both the perpetrator and nonoffending parent is to blame the child for being seductive. Children often accept responsibility for the occurrence of the abuse. Assisting the child to place the responsibility with the perpetrator, is a major part of the work with children, and this is discussed in more detail later in the section on the assessment and treatment of children. The child's safety is in jeopardy because other "justifiable" conditions may arise in the future. Thus, the therapist should take particular caution not to collude with the parents in their denial of responsibility, and "let them off the hook."

Accepting the full impact of the abuse can take some time for all family members—minimization and denial of impact are common. Denial and minimization are natural responses to traumatic experiences and help individuals slowly integrate these experiences into their awareness. Rather than pathologize these responses, therapists can acknowledge the roles of denial and minimization while at the same time persistently pushing and confronting family members to move beyond these coping strategies. Assisting all family members to come to terms with the painful realities of the incest, and the dramatic changes that are necessary for the family to improve, can take a considerable amount of time. Barrett (1992) states that the average length of treatment is two years.

Assessment of Family Structure

Assessment of incestuous families is incomplete without an examination of the family structure (Barrett, 1992; Barrett, Sykes & Byrnes, 1986; Everstine & Everstine, 1989; Furniss, 1983; Giarretto, 1982; Larson & Maddock, 1986; Sgori, 1982; 1988; Trepper & Barrett, 1986; 1989). Charles Fishman (1988) speaks to this with his chapter entitled "Incest: A Therapy of Boundaries."

Incestuous families tend to have a rigid boundary between the family and social systems (Larson & Maddock, 1986). This isolation can contribute to the formulation of incest, as well as allow for its continuance. Blurred intergenerational boundaries can push the victim into a spousal role, and the parent into a child role. Also common for incestual families are diffuse personal boundaries, often referred to as enmeshment. Independent thought and feeling is not tolerated. Individuality equates with disloyalty. Parents often have pervasive fears of abandonment, and employ elaborate defense mechanisms to guard against it. Shame and self-doubt are also commonly pervasive in these families according to Larson and Maddock (1986). A variety of double-bind interactions are common too. Disturbances in intrapsychic boundaries can lead to denial and distortion of reality.

On the basis of Minuchin's structural family therapy, Trepper and Barrett (1989) identify five family structures they find to be the most vulnerable to the development of incest. In the functional family structure there is a clear boundary between the parental subsystem and the child subsystem which is neither too rigid nor too permeable. When this boundary breaks down, families are at risk. In the father-executive system, the father clearly has the power in the family and is dominant. Mothers in this arrangement are often passive and dependent and may provide little parenting. Alcoholism, schizophrenia, and other problems in the lives of mothers can contribute to this. One of the daughters may be selected to take over the spousal role, which can initially bring relief to the mother. A child providing spousal functions is particularly prone to becoming a victim of incest.

In the mother-executive structure, the mother is clearly powerful, and the father is dependent. Alcoholic fathers often fit this structure. The father may be referred to as "one of the kids." Sexual abuse may resemble sibling sexual play. In the third-generation structures, the parent who is in a "one down" position still provides some parenting. Sexual abuse has a parental quality.

The chaotic family appears to have no parents, and no one in control. Fathers often state they did not feel like their daughter's father. Sibling and extended family incest also is more likely within this structure. In the estranged father structure, the father is uninvolved, and when he does reenter, he reenters on the daughter's level. Incest may be aggressive in nature.

As stated earlier, the presence of a stepfather in the system greatly increases the likelihood of sexual abuse. The stepfather, at least initially, is not providing the same type of parental function as the mother, including nurturing, which was cited earlier as also putting children at risk. Stepfathers are included in the definition of incest, because the nature of the relationship and the trust the child feels are more important than a biological connection (Sgori, 1982). Mother absence, whether physically or emotionally, also increases the likelihood of sexual abuse (Finkelhor, 1980).

Family Style

The circumplex model (Olson, Russell, & Sprenkle, 1983) is also utilized to assess family structure (Maddock & Lange, 1988; Trepper & Barrett, 1986, 1989). Families are assessed on two dimensions—cohesion and adaptability. *Cohesion* refers to the amount of emotional bonding family members have with each other. This measure ranges from disengaged to enmeshed. *Adaptability* refers to the amount of flexibility family members possess and ranges from rigid to chaotic. While incestuous families can fall anywhere on the continuum, Trepper and Barrett (1989) have found the most common constellation is the rigidly enmeshed family. Family communication style can be seen as an overlay to the two dimensions of the circumplex model. When possible, the entire family should be seen together to assess the family's communication skills. Communication difficulties common to incest families include: (1) secretiveness, (2) inconsistent or unclear messages to one another, (3) infrequent discussion of feelings, (4) little attentive listening or empathy, and (5) lack of conflict-resolution skills (Trepper & Barrett, 1989).

Larson and Maddock (1986) describe four styles of family abuse that play an important role in determining the course of treatment: (1) affection-exchange, (2) erotic-exchange, (3) aggression-exchange, (4) rage–expression. The most common style is the affection-exchange style. These families appear caring and loving of their members. The abuse comes from a need for affection on the part of the offender and the child. The offender inappropriately turns to the child to meet affection needs. The victim often seeks out positive, usually nonviolent, attention from the offender. These families usually want to stay together, and victims often recant their stories to keep the family together. Generally, these families can stay together throughout the course of therapy and have a good prognosis. Individual pathology is minimal for the perpetrator; however, individual pathology of the victim may increase as the child gets older.

In the erotic-exchange, or pansexual family, most activities are sexualized. Family members have a lack of privacy under the guise of trust. Non-family members are often invited into the family "games." Trepper and Barrett (1989) add that these families are more likely to be involved in family "swinging" or group family sex. They also note that mother–son abuse is more common in this type of family than the others. These families also can often stay together, and prognosis is usually good, "provided the therapist can impact their cognitive distortion that family sex is philosophically supportable" (Trepper & Barrett, 1989, p. 87). Individual psychopathology is also minimal for perpetrators in these families. Children in these families commonly are symptomatic, however, including suicidal tendencies, anorexia, self-mutilation, and even psychosis.

Power and control on the part of the perpetrator come into play much more in the aggression-exchange family. The perpetrator uses sexualized anger as a way of dealing with frustration. The sexual abuse is often violent. Boundaries can be diffuse so that the perpetrator abuses a child believing this will hurt his wife, even if she is unaware of its occurrence. Sibling incest is most common within this style (Trepper & Barrett, 1989). Prognosis is only fair, and families are likely to separate during therapy. Family therapy often is not initially possible because of the trauma of the victim. Individual psychopathology is common in this type of family style.

The rage-expression style is the least common and most dramatic form of incest. Sexual abuse is generally very violent. Psychopathology of the offender is often severe. Trepper and Barrett (1989) add that these parents are the most likely to deny facts, leaving children doubting their realities. These families cannot be seen together until the denial of facts ends, the perpetrator is able to be with the victim without double-bind interactions, and the daughter or son feels comfortable. Prognosis for these families is poor. The perpetrator may need extensive treatment, including inpatient therapy. Other individual members also may exhibit severe psychopathology.

Goals of Family Treatment

The primary goal of family therapy is the safety of the child or children. To provide this safety, it is necessary for the perpetrator to take responsibility for the abuse, change the family structure, and improve communication. An important goal in therapy with incestuous families is to create a structure that will not allow for the continuation of the incest. The structure is one in which parents are clearly in charge of the family and share parenting responsibilities.

While this is an ongoing process throughout therapy, and much of the work may be done in couple sessions, Barrett (1992) also uses a formalized session focusing on family structure. This session is both therapeutic and educational. Families are shown diagrams of the various types of family structures along with an explanation of how incest may happen within that structure. Barrett further explains that no family can always maintain an optimal structure, and gives families examples from her own family. This allows families to explore how incest happened in their family in a nonthreatening way. Regardless of the level of denial, Barrett (1992) speaks throughout the entire session as if the incest did occur. The educational component of the session offers the family a language in which to speak about the abuse. Barrett has found that having this new language often allows families who were previously denying to admit to the abuse. Children may or may not be included in this session depending on their ages and the level of denial. Grandparents are included whenever possible, because this gives the therapist and the family insight into the parents' families of origin, abuse that may have occurred there, and the formulation of the present family structure.

Another formalized session utilized by Trepper and Barrett, Madanes, and others to reinforce parental responsibility within the family structure is the apology session (Barrett, 1992; Barrett, et al. 1986; Madanes, 1990; Trepper, 1986; Trepper & Barrett, 1989). This session is more formalized than the structure session and is actually considered a rite of passage for the family into the next stage of treatment. All family members prepare for the ritual of the apology session for weeks or months. For the apology session to take place, the perpetrator must take full responsibility for the abuse and be ready to apologize for the behavior in a real and believable way. The nonoffending parent, although not expected to take responsibility for the abuse, must be able to take responsibility for her role. The perpetrator must also promise that the abuse will never happen again. Similarly, the nonoffending parent is asked to promise the child that she or he will be believed, if further abuse is disclosed.

An important consideration in planning the apology session is the readiness of the victim (Trepper, 1986; Sgori, 1982). If the victim adamantly holds that an apology would let the parents off the hook, or she or he fears further abuse after an apology, the session should not take place. If adequately prepared, however, few children do not want the apology to take place. An equally important component is the inclusion of all family members (Trepper, 1986, Trepper & Barrett, 1989). Secrets are, in part, what allows the continuation of incest. To allow parents to "protect" the other children is a set up for abuse of another child. Parents are coached on how to share the situation with uninformed children, and all are included in the apology session.

The following list contains a summary of the important goals of family treatment in the case of incest:

1. Child safety
2. Perpetrator takes full responsibility
3. Healthy family structure
   a. Clear boundaries between subsystems
   b. Shared parenting and responsibility
   c. Enhanced marital relationship
   d. Strengthened sibling subsystem
   e. Decrease enmeshment or disengagement (depending on family)
   f. Decrease rigidity or increase structure (depending on family)
4. Increase communication skills
   a. Conflict resolution

b. Decrease double-bind communication
c. Decrease secrecy
d. Increased empathy
e. Increased ability to send clear messages

Assessment and Treatment of Perpetrators

Although severe psychopathology of perpetrators is rare, they may be re-gressed, and because of their own psychic trauma, find it difficult to partici-pate in traditional psychotherapy, which demands that they address their thoughts and feelings. Assisting the client to improve ego strength may be the first step for the therapist (Groth & Oliveri, 1989). A complete psychiatric evaluation including MMPI and TAT can be useful for the therapist to iden-tify those with severe pathology (Trepper & Barrett, 1989).

The importance of denial cannot be over-emphasized. As mentioned ear-lier, denial of facts by the perpetrator is a poor diagnostic sign (Everstine & Everstine, 1989; Furniss, 1983; Sgori, 1982). In the early stages of treatment, denial is best worked through in individual therapy, though in the case of denial of facts and adequate evidence, inpatient treatment for the perpetrator may be the treatment of choice (Barrett, 1992). Group treatment is also an important component of work with perpetrators. One of the primary benefits of the group approach for perpetrators is that they are more easily and pow-erfully confronted by fellow perpetrators than by a therapist (Barrett, 1992; Forseth & Brown, 1981; Groth & Oliveri, 1989; Taylor, 1986).

Abuse of power is inherent in incestuous families. "Coercion, manipula-tion, force, and violation are inherent any time an adult sexually abuses a child. . . To minimize what has happened to a child who has been abused by suggesting that there has been no violence done is to tolerate the abuse of power and the use of force" (Conte, 1984, p. 260). In a study of 586 women, Alexander and Lupfer (1987) found that women who experienced sexual abuse perpetrated by their fathers were much more likely to come from "very traditional families in which children are seen as subservient to adults and females are seen as subservient to males" (p. 242). This is the type of abuse of power that comes to mind in the previous quote from Conte. Taylor (1986) suggests that there is also an abuse of power within the families of perpetra-tors who seek strong women to parent them. He suggests that these men seek the control that comes with the "pampered child" role (p. 454). Taylor's com-ments highlight the point that power can be misused in a variety of ways, even from a supposedly "one down" position. The therapist should assist the perpetrator to examine the inadequacies and unmet needs that are being acted out in terms of power and control issues.

The main form of therapy utilized when treating the perpetrator individ-ually has been behavioral therapy (Dixen & Jenkins, 1981; Groth & Oliveri, 1989). Common techniques include, systematic desensitization, covert sensi-tization, assertiveness training, and fantasy training (Dixen & Jenkins, 1981).

Groth and Oliveri (1989) see behavior therapy as a form of symptom relief. Perpetrators are often relieved to find ways to stop their sometimes compulsive behavior. They strongly assert that behavior therapy, however, is not enough; perpetrators must remain hypervigilant to the chance that they may perpetrate again. Psychotherapy including individual, couple, and family is almost always necessary (Groth & Oliveri, 1989).

As many perpetrators have themselves experienced abuse, the perpetrators' victimization must be dealt with for treatment to be successful (Barrett, 1992; Giarretto, 1982; Taylor, 1986). Assisting the perpetrator to heal from the effects of his own abuse does not lessen the chance that he will take responsibility. Conversely, if the perpetrator works through painful experiences, he is more likely to have empathy for the pain the daughter and other family members are experiencing. This may include extensive family-of-origin work. The perpetrator may then be able to become aware of unsatisfied needs and learn to meet them in appropriate ways. He may also be able to take responsibility for the abuse of power in the family and work conjointly with other family members to equalize the power dynamics.

Assessment and Treatment of the Nonoffending Parent

Individual assessment of psychopathology is similar to assessment of the perpetrator. As mentioned earlier, denial is common for nonoffending parents (most typically, mothers). Breaking through denial of the mother is important in order for the victim to have an ally. Anger, guilt, and helplessness are the most common feelings mothers experience. They may feel intense anger toward the perpetrator, victim, or both, and because of the power dynamic operating in the family, feel unable and even fearful of sharing these feelings with the perpetrator. To establish equal parenting and protect the victim and siblings from further abuse, the abuse of power in the relationship needs to change. As with the perpetrators, nonoffending mothers often come from abusive family backgrounds. As will be covered much more thoroughly in the chapter on Adult Survivors of Sexual Abuse, these women often have low self-esteem and entitlement issues. Before the abuse of power can be completely altered, the mother's victimization must be addressed. As with perpetrators, family-of-origin work is an important part of the individual work with mothers.

Mothers usually feel guilty that they did not know about the abuse, or did not stop it if they were aware of its occurrence. This is particularly common if there are serious marital problems, including sexual difficulties. Women often think that if there were no sexual difficulties, the abuse would not have happened. As with victims, nonoffending parents need assistance to place the responsibility with the perpetrator. Individual sessions also prepare the mother for couple and family sessions.

Because the mother is likely to be the primary caregiver and protector in the family after the disclosure, it is important to assess her abilty to handle the additional stress of managing a family on her own. Therapists may need to help her connect with resourses in the community or the extended family to alleviate some of the stress brought on by the incest disclosure. Support groups for spouses of perpetrators can be very valuable too.

Assessment and Treatment of the Marital Dyad

Much of the structural and communication work mentioned in the family session takes place within marital sessions. Communication, intimacy, and sexuality are often problems in a marriage. Before these problems can be addressed, the partner of the perpetrator must have a space to express anger, betrayal, and pain at what the perpetrator has done. If this is not accomplished, communication or other couple work may be sabotaged.

Communication work needs to be implemented early so the couple will be prepared to discuss the many issues facing them. For example, the nonoffending spouse needs to be able to voice feelings to the perpetrator regarding the abuse, the perpetrator needs to take full responsibility for the abuse in the presence of the spouse, and the couple needs to work together to ensure that no further abuse takes place. Therapists often are surprised by the number of couples who choose to remain together. Barrett (1992) reports that over 50% of the couples seen at Midwest Family Resources chose to stay together during the entire two-year treatment program. Whether or not the couple decides to stay together, communication should be improved so that co-parenting arrangements can be discussed. Trepper and Barrett (1989) list the following as goals of treatment:

1. No denial on the part of the perpetrator or the nonoffending parent
2. Awareness of the "abuse of power"
3. Increased communication
4. Conflict resolution
5. Discussion of the future of the marital relationship
6. Establishment of an executive subsystem
7. Address co-dependency issues

Assessment and Treatment of Children

As mentioned earlier, one of the most important indicators for the successful treatment of the children is the parents' response to them. If the parents are in denial, they will very likely attempt to sabotage treatment. Thus, the work done with the parents is as important to treatment for children as the child–therapist sessions are (Sgori, 1982).

Children do not have the same understanding of the abusive situation as adults working through trauma. Everstine and Everstine (1983) point out that for the child the sexual abuse can be less important than the following: (1) feeling that they could have been killed, (2) feeling totally helpless, (3) feeling betrayed, and (4) loss of a loved person who paid attention to them (for some, the perpetrator is the one person who gave them attention). An additional issue for the child can be guilt. It is difficult for some children to see the perpetrator getting punished while they are receiving attention (Jones, 1986). Depending on their developmental level, children feel that the abuse was their fault—they are bad and caused this to happen—thus the perpetrator should not be punished. It is vital that the therapist not make assumptions about what the abuse meant to a child, and rather obtain the child's perception of the abuse, which will often change over time.

As the child may be experiencing feelings of loss and betrayal of a significant relationship, building a trusting relationship with the child is an important intervention in itself for the therapist. Sgori (1982) sees the formulation of a trusting relationship between the child and the therapist as "a critical psychodynamic goal." She adds that this trust is built, in part, by believing the child. Often, a child may need to spend several weeks playing with the therapist before revealing any information or overtly displaying any emotions. Therapists working with these children need to be patient and trust that "work" is being done even if the child is simply becoming more comfortable in the therapist's presence.

Play therapy is crucial when working with young children. Through her study and observation of children having experienced a wide variety of traumas, Terr (1981) has recognized a pattern of play in children she refers to as "posttraumatic play." She describes this as compulsive, repetitive, unimaginative activity that replays the trauma. The child is most often dissociated and oblivious to the presence of the therapist. Abused children spend a significant amount of time involved in posttraumatic play (Terr, 1981, 1990; Gil, 1991; Jones, 1986).

Gil (1991) asserts that therapists should not interfere in this play for several weeks, because reenactment is an important part of the healing process. After that amount of time, the therapist should interrupt the play by gently attempting to gain information and elicit emotion. For instance, the therapist can ask the child what the doll she is playing with is doing. Slowly the therapist can begin asking how the doll feels. If posttraumatic play is not interrupted, the child can become fixated in the trauma, and development will be impaired.

Everstine and Everstine (1989) recommend using Milton Erickson's interpersonal techniques; the therapist periodically interjects a message into the conversation such as, "You have feelings and you don't have to share them now, you can tell me later." This does two things. First, it helps the child recognize feelings, and it plants the seed for telling the therapist feelings at a later time. A child (as well as an adult) often will be able to empathize with a doll or story character before she can with herself. The therapist should intersperse messages to the child that the doll (thus the child) is not in anyway responsible for the abuse. Contradicting the message that the child has no rights is also important (Sgori, 1982). The child's self-concept and view of the world can be greatly affected by abuse (Finkelhor, 1980).

Children will often repeatedly take things apart and put them back together. Everstine and Everstine (1989) view this behavior as an attempt to undo the abuse. They suggest that the therapist give the child the message that broken or hurt things can be fixed and need not stay broken, and people can feel whole again too. Gradually the child can be assisted to express anger at the perpetrator and at those who did not protect her, as well as grieve for herself. As the child is able to place the blame with the perpetrator, her self-concept and view of the world can be restored.

All the toys in the therapist's office should facilitate therapeutic play. Toys below the child's developmental level should be available because children often exhibit regression. These include toys such as baby bottles, clay, fingerpaints, and soft stuffed animals. Drawing materials should also be present for children may well draw what they cannot speak. Many interpretations can be made of a child's drawings, the most important one, of course, being what the child herself says about the drawings. Dolls and puppets are invaluable in allowing children an outlet for reenactment. Children often will invite the therapist to take a puppet. If the office is equipped with anatomically correct dolls, children may explicitly reenact the trauma using the dolls.

Therapists working with sexually abused children should possess a working knowledge of the aftereffects outlined previously in the consequences section and an understanding of play therapy. Children of trauma, however, can be incredibly resilient, and therapists should be aware of the signs of resilience, not just pathology. Mrazek and Mrazek (1987) offer the following guidelines:

Signs of Resilience in Children

- Rapid responsivity to anger
- Dissociation of affect
- Positive visualization of future
- Conviction of being loved
- Optimism
- Precocious maturity
- Information seeking
- Decisive risk taking
- Altruism
- Hope
- Formulation and utilization of relationships for survival
- Idealization of aggressor's competence
- Cognitive restructuring of painful experiences

Sibling Subsystem Sessions

The incest also obviously affects the siblings of the victim, and they are in tremendous need of support. Siblings need to be informed honestly about the situation for a number of reasons. Children from abusive homes have learned to be hypervigilant and know on some level that something is wrong in the family. Without honest explanation, children make up their own stories and catastrophize the situation (Trepper & Barrett, 1989). Often, the victim or perpetrator may be removed from the home. If the children are not given adequate explanations for the removal, they may exhibit great anxiety, expecting to be sent away themselves. Finally, other children may also have been victimized. This victimization may take the form of having witnessed a sibling being abused. Children who have witnessed traumatic events can exhibit symptoms similar to those exhibited by "victims" and often engage in posttraumatic play in the same way (Terr, 1990).

The overriding feelings for siblings tend to be anger and guilt (Sgori, 1982; Trepper & Barrett, 1989). Siblings may be angry at the perpetrator, nonoffending parent, and/or another sibling. Family members are placed in a position of taking sides. Often siblings will feel angry with the abused sibling for breaking up the family. Other children in the family may show little empathy for her, because they feel she has had a favored position with the perpetrating parent. They may also take the side of the victim, or refuse to see the perpetrating parent because they fear him. "Survivor guilt" is common among siblings; they may have known about the abuse and felt helpless to stop it.

Play therapy is very useful for working with the sibling subsystem. They can quite accurately reenact family situations with the use of puppets and can even find it fun. This can also prepare them for sessions with their parents. Depending on the family dynamics, siblings may need as intensive treatment as the victim.

CONCLUSIONS

Therapy with families who have experienced incest must be comprehensive. Treating only the victim and/or perpetrator is not enough. Comprehensive treatment programs for incestuous families use a variety of treatment modalities including family therapy, individual treatment for the victim, perpetrator and nonoffending parent (most commonly the mother), couples therapy, and sessions for the sibling subsystem and the mother–victim dyad. Assessment and treatment recommendations for these modalities, as well as guidelines for deciding which family members to see together, have been discussed. Significant emphasis was placed on structure because balancing the family structure is a significant therapeutic goal. Because the presence of denial in one or both parents greatly impedes treatment, denial was also covered in depth. In addition, child safety, which is the highest priority, is difficult to ensure when parents are denying.

As is evident by the content of this chapter, there are a multitude of issues therapists need to address when working with incest victims, perpetrators, and families. Tremendous resources are necessary to take these families from a traumatized place to one where healing can occur. Unfortunately, the vital resources of time and money are rarely available. This reality demands that therapists prioritize their treatment goals and collaborate as much as possible with agencies that are already involved with the family.

REFERENCES

Alexander, P. C. & Lupfer, S. L. (1987). Family characteristics and long-term consequences associated with sexual abuse. *Archives of Sexual Behavior, 16*(3), 235–245.

Barrett, M. J. (1992, March). *Treating perpetrators of sexual abuse.* Paper presented at the 15th Annual Family Therapy Networker Symposium, Washington, D.C.

Barrett, M. J., Sykes, C., & Byrnes, W. (1986). A systemic model for the treatment of intrafamily child sexual abuse. In T. S. Trepper & M. J. Barrett (Eds.) *Treating incest: A multiple systems perspective* (pp. 67–82). New York: Haworth Press.

Barrett, M. J., Trepper, T., & Stone Fish, L. (1990). Feminist-informed family therapy for the treatment of intra-familial child sexual abuse. *Journal of Family Psychology, 4* 151–166.

Best, J. (1990) *Threatened children: Rhetoric and concern about child-victims.* Chicago: The University of Chicago Press.

Bograd, M. (1984). Family systems approaches to wife battering: A feminist critique. *American Journal of Orthopsychiatry, 54*(4), 558–568.

Brickman, J. (1984). Femisnist, nonsexist, and traditional models of therapy: Implications for working with incest. *Women and Therapy, 3,* 49-67.

Browne, A. & Finkelhor, D. (1986). The impact of child sexual abuse: A review of the research. *Psychological Bulletin, 99,* 66–77.

Burgess, A. W. & Holstrom, L. L. (1974). Rape trauma syndrome. *American Journal of Psychiatry, 13*(9), 981–986.

Cantwell, H. B. (1983). Vaginal inspection as it relates to child sexual abuse in girls under thirteen. *Child Abuse & Neglect, 7,* 171–176.

Conte, J. R. (1984). Progress in treating the sexual abuse of children. *Social Work, 29,* 258–263.

Cupoli, J. M. & Monaghan-Sewell, P. (1988). One thousand fifty-nine children with a chief complaint of sexual abuse. *Child Abuse & Neglect, 12,* 151–162.

deYoung, M. (1982). Innocent seducer or innocently seduced? The role of the child incest victim. *Journal of Clinical Child Psychology, 11*(1), 56–60.

Dixen, J. & Jenkins, J. O. (1981). Incestuous child sexual abuse: A review of treatment strategies. *Clinical Psychology Review, 1,* 211–222.

Elwell, M. E. & Ephross, P. H. (1987, February). Initial reactions of sexually abused children. *Social Casework, 68,* 109–116.

Everstine, D. S. & Everstine, L. (1989). *Sexual trauma in children and adolescents: Dynamics and treatment.* New York: Brunner/Mazel.

Everstine, L. & Everstine, D. S. (1983). *People in crisis.* New York: Brunner/Mazel.

Finkelhor, D. (1980). Risk factors in the sexual victimization of children. *Child Abuse & Neglect, 4,* 265–273.

Finkelhor, D. (1986). Sexual abuse: Beyond the family systems approach. In T. S. Trepper & M. J. Barrett (Eds.), *Treating incest: A multiple systems perspective* (pp. 53–65). New York: Haworth Press.

Finkelhor, D. & Hotaling, G. T. (1984). Sexual abuse in the national incidence study of child abuse and neglect: An appraisal. *Child Abuse & Neglect, 8,* 23–33.

Fishman, H. C. (1988). *Treating troubled adolescents: A family therapy approach.* New York: Basic Books.

Forseth, L. B. & Brown A. (1981). A survey of intrafamilial sexual abuse treatment centers: Implications for intervention. *Child Abuse & Neglect, 5,* 177–186.

Fredrickson, R. (1990, November). *Advanced clinical skills in treatment of sexual abuse.* Paper presented at the Psychological Association Conference, Syracuse.

Furniss, T. (1983). Family process in the treatment of intrafamilial child sexual abuse. *Journal of Family Therapy, 5,* 263–278.

Furniss, T. (1984). Organizing a therapeutic approach to intra-familial child sexual abuse. *Journal of Adolescence, 7,* 309–317.

Giarretto, H. (1982). A comprehensive child sexual abuse treatment program. *Child Abuse & Neglect, 6,* 263–278.

Gil, E. (1991). *The healing power of play: Working with abused children.* NY: Guilford.

Goodwin, J., Cormier, L., & Owen, J. (1983). Grandfather–granddaughter incest: A trigenerational view. *Child Abuse & Neglect, 7,* 163–170.

Green, A. H. (1986). True and false allegations of sexual abuse in child custody disputes. *Journal of the American Academy of Child Psychiatry, 25,* 449–456.

Groth, A. N. & Oliveri, F. (1989). Understanding sexual offense behavior and differentiating among sexual abusers: Basic conceptual issues. In S. M. Sgori (Ed.), *Vulnerable populations, Vol.2.* Lexington, MA: Lexington Books.

Kendall-Tackett, K. A. & Simon, A. F. (1987). Perpetrators and their acts: Data from 365 adults molested as children. *Child Abuse & Neglect, 11,* 237–245.

Kroth, J. A. (1979). Family therapy impact on intrafamilial child sexual abuse. *Child Abuse & Neglect, 3,* 297–302.

Jones, D. P. H. (1986). Individual psychotherapy for the sexually abused child. *Child Abuse & Neglect, 10,* 377–385.

Larson, N. R. & Maddock, J. W. (1986). Structural and functional variables in incest family sytems: Implications for assessment and treatment. In T. S. Trepper & M. J. Barrett (Eds.), *Treating incest: A multiple systems perspective* (pp. 27–44). New York: Haworth Press.

Madanes, C. (1990). *Sex, love, and violence: Strategies for transformation.* New York: W. W. Norton.

Maisch, H. (1972). *Incest.* New York: Stein & Day.

Mannarino, A. P. & Cohen, J. A. (1986). A clinical-demographic study of sexually abused children. *Child Abuse & Neglect, 10,* 17–23.

Meiselman, K. (1978). *Incest: A psychological study of causes and effects with treatment recommendations.* San Francisco: Jossey-Bass.

Mrazek, P. J. & Mrazek, D. A. (1987). Resilience in child maltreatment victims: A conceptual exploration. *Child Abuse & Neglect, 11,* 357–366.

Olson, D. H., Russell, C. S., & Sprenkle, D. H. (1983). Circumplex model of marital and family systems: VI. Theoretical update. *Family Process, 22,* 69–83.

Parker, H. & Parker, S. (1986). Father–daughter sexual abuse: An emerging perspective. *American Journal of Orthopsychiatry, 54,* 531–547.

Rosenfeld, A. (1979). Endogamic incest and the victim–perpetrator model. *American Journal of Diseases of Children, 133,* 406–410.

Rush. F. (1980). *The best kept secret: Sexual abuse of children.* Englewood Cliffs, NJ: Prentice-Hall.

Russell, D. E. H. (1983). The incidence and prevalence of intrafamilial and extrafamilial sexual abuse of the female child. *Child Abuse & Neglect, 7,* 133–146.

Russell, D. E. H. (1984). The prevalence and seriousness of incestuous abuse: Stepfathers vs. biological fathers. *Child Abuse & Neglect, 8,* 15–22.

Sgori, S. M. (1978). Child sexual assault: Some guidelines for intervention and assessment. In A. Burgess, N. Groth, & L. Holstrom (Eds.), *Sexual assault of children and adolescents.* Lexington, MA: Lexington Books.

Sgori, S. M. (1982). *Handbook of clinical intervention in child sexual abuse.* Lexington, MA: Lexington Books.

Taylor, J. W. (1986). Social casework and the multimodal treatment of incest. *Social Casework, 67* (Oct.), 451–459.

Terr, L. (1981). Forbidden games: Post-traumatic child's play. *Journal of the American Academy of Child Psychiatry, 20,* 740–759.

Terr, L. (1990). *Too scared to cry: Psychic trauma in childhood.* New York: Harper & Row.

Trepper, T. S. (1986). The apology session. In T. S. Trepper & M. J. Barrett (Eds.), *Treating incest: A multiple systems perspective* (pp. 93–101). New York: Haworth Press.

Trepper, T. S. & Barrett, M. J. (1989). *Systemic treatment of incest: A therapeutic handbook.* New York: Brunner/ Mazel.

Wyatt, G. E. (1985). The sexual abuse of Afro-American and white American women in childhood. *Child Abuse & Neglect, 9,* 507–519.

Wyatt, G. E. & Doyle-Peters, S. (1986). Methodological considerations in research on the prevalence of child sexual abuse. *Child Abuse & Neglect, 10,* 241–251.

5

PHYSICAL ABUSE OF PARENTS BY ADOLESCENT CHILDREN

JOHANNA WILSON

Family violence is a relatively new field of study. It was not until the 1960s that child abuse was "discovered" and concern for these children became an issue of national proportions. During the seventies professionals began to write about battered women (Gelles, 1987). The remaining areas of family violence, such as sibling, parental, and elderly abuse, consistently have been overlooked by researchers and lay people.

Although children of any age can abuse their parents, the focus of this chapter is on physical abuse of parents by children between the ages of 10 to 24 (Harbin & Madden, 1979; Cornell & Gelles, 1982). They often live in the home with their parents and are economically dependent on them (Harbin & Madden, 1979). The age range of the children is slightly older than what would usually be considered "adolescence" in order to reflect the age range typically used by researchers of this problem. This is distinguished from abuse that involves adult children who abuse their elderly parents. The adult children do not necessarily live with them and are not usually economically dependent on their elderly parents.

Parental abuse by children also needs to be distinguished from adolescent parricide. *Adolescent parricide*, the murder of significant others, is the most extreme form of parental assault. The literature suggests that this is a distinct phenomenon and is usually studied separately from parental abuse (Heide, 1992; Post, 1982). Parricide is found when there is extreme child abuse in families, often involving a threat or the witnessing of a threat against a family member with a weapon. The combinations of the severity of the abuse from the parent to a child, the onset of adolescence, and the imbalance brought about by emotional and behavioral changes build pressure to the breaking point, which may result in the murder of a parent (Heide, 1992).

Post (1982) states that parricide is the culmination of child abuse that can no longer be tolerated. These children are unlikely to attempt murder again, but it is important to distinguish these cases from those who have other motives, or those who enjoyed the murder and would be in danger of killing again (Heide, 1992). Parental abuse does not usually result in murder. It is more often the pattern that the behavior results from a reaction to family stress and a reversal of hierarchy (Harbin & Madden, 1979) rather than a one-time reaction to extreme abuse like the common pattern in parricide.

The question of how to address issues of parental abuse is difficult. Because it is a newly identified problem in our society, most of the research seems to focus on what causes children to become violent toward their parents and in discovering the extent of the problem rather than looking for potential treatment methods (Cornell & Gelles, 1982; Kratcoski, 1982; Evans & Warren-Sohlberg, 1988; Straus & Gelles, 1988; Paulson, Coombs, & Landsverk, 1990).

SCOPE OF THE PROBLEM

Most of the research addressing child-to-parent abuse evolved from studying the general issue of family violence. Richard Gelles and his associates (Cornell, 1982; Straus, 1988, 1990; Steinmetz, 1985) have been studying issues of family violence since the early 1970s, but parental abuse was not a specific topic of study until the early 1980s. Harbin and Madden (1979) identify parent battering as a distinct subtype of family violence; this study is the earliest identification of the problem as a syndrome.

Harbin and Madden (1979) report that almost 10% of children between the ages of three and eighteen have attacked their parents. The preliminary empirical research correlated with this estimate (Cornell & Gelles, 1982; Kratcoski, 1982). These estimates are startlingly similar to spousal abuse rates (Straus & Gelles, 1988). More recently, the estimates range from 5% (Evans & Warren-Solberg, 1988) to 21% (Kratcoski, 1985), with the more consistent average ranging between 7 to 13% (Paulson et al., 1990; Peek, Fischer, & Kidwell, 1985). These ranges varied in accordance with the extent of violence being exhibited by the child. The rate of severe violence toward parents was typically on the lower extreme of the scale, while the overall incidence rate was higher.

The rates also vary because of the means of collecting data. Because this is a new area of research, there is not yet an identified or recommended instrument to measure the extent or severity of violence. Data-collection methods included reports from parents, reports from adolescents, past case reports, and secondary analyses of surveys (Agnew & Huguley, 1989; Cornell & Gelles, 1982; Evans & Warren-Solberg, 1988; Kratcoski, 1982; Kratcoski, 1985; Paulson et al., 1990; Peek et al., 1985). The lack of consistency creates difficulty in making an accurate assessment of the prevalence of parent battering.

FACTORS ASSOCIATED WITH
ADOLESCENT-TO-PARENT VIOLENCE

Characteristics of Violent Adolescents

It seems that adolescent males and females are equally likely to assault a parent. Gender was not found to be a significant factor in identifying violent youth in most of the research (Agnew & Huguley, 1989; Cornell & Gelles, 1982; Paulson et al., 1990), but Evans and Warren-Sohlberg (1988) did find that sons were significantly more likely to be abusive toward their parents than were daughters.

Although often regarded as more violent, minority groups display less violence against their parents than Caucasians do. Agnew and Huguley (1989) found this difference to be significant when they compared Hispanic to Anglo adolescents' assaults toward their parents. Paulson et al. (1990) only found statistical significance among females when comparing black and white teens, but did notice a trend that more white children assault their parents than do black children. This is attributed to two factors. One is that minority parents do not tolerate disrespect and administer immediate consequences (Agnew & Huguley, 1989; Charles, 1986). The other factor includes the element of a unifying religion in the home. Paulson et al. (1990) note that the Hispanic parenting style has an emphasis on "religiously sanctioned paternal authority," which decreases assault on parents (p. 130).

Younger children were significantly less aggressive than older children (Paulson et al., 1990). Several researchers found that the peak age for aggressive adolescents was between 15 and 17 years old (Evans & Warren-Sohlberg, 1988; Straus & Gelles, 1988). Agnew and Huguley (1989) found the peak age for females to be 17 to 18 years old, but they were unable to identify a peak age for males. They did find that as male children age, they become less likely to hit their mothers and more likely to hit their fathers.

Agnew and Huguley (1989) measured the size of the adolescent, based on the height and weight of the individuals, but found no correlation between size of children and their aggressive behavior toward parents. They also found no relationship between social class and battered parents although this syndrome is typically considered a lower-class phenomenon (Agnew & Huguley, 1989; Paulson et al., 1990; Peek et al., 1985).

Characteristics of the Family

Often families characterized by violence and parent abuse are chaotic and disorganized (Heide, 1992; Madden, 1982; Wells, 1987). This chaos can lead to a shift in the roles of the family members so that the parents release their authority and the child steps in to take control. This reversal of roles happens not because the child wants the control, but because the child feels that someone needs to be in charge and knows that the parents are unable or unwilling to take charge (Harbin & Madden, 1979; Wells, 1987).

In a related vein, Kratcoski (1985) found that the highest proportion of violence against parents occurred among disengaged families. Conversely, Harbin and Madden (1979) claim that families with violent adolescents tend to be overly enmeshed and are seeking a disconnection by becoming violent. Kratcoski (1985) also states that violent youths were more likely to have witnessed or been victims of considerable violence in the home. This finding is consistent with the most commonly cited correlate to parent battering—the presence of other forms of family violence in the home (Harbin & Madden, 1979; Kratcoski, 1982; Madden, 1982; Power, 1988; Straus & Gelles, 1990; Wells, 1987).

Families who have adolescent children that abuse parents tend to deny the abuse. This tendency toward denial reinforces the concept of keeping secrets and teaches children what they learned from their parents: that they do not have much hope; that they are helpless to change their situation; and that the means of coping is to become violent (Kratcoski, 1985).

Peek et al. (1985) and Paulson et al. (1990) found that in two-parent households, the parents who were abused by their children did not have a strong spousal relationship. Cornell and Gelles (1982) found that in households where there was wife abuse there was a high pattern of abuse toward the mother (and no abuse of the father).

Social Factors

Paulson et al. (1990) found that children who assault their parents were less likely to be interested in school. They also found that these children felt school was unimportant. Cornell and Gelles (1982) found that when a child in the home is kicked out of school, it is more likely that she or he will use violence toward a parent. Truancy, suspension, and harassment of teachers are some behaviors that Kratcoski (1985) found indicative of parental assault.

Kratcoski (1985) and Agnew and Huguley (1989) found that when families do not meet the emotional needs of their children, the children often relate to peers who are deviant and reinforce delinquent and deviant values. Youths who assault their parents tend to feel better understood by their peers than their parents and do not have high self-esteem (Paulson et al., 1990). Evans and Warren-Sohlberg (1988) found that 66% of their adolescent sample had some history of involvement with law enforcement and/or social services, and 52% of the families surveyed had histories of domestic violence.

Substance abuse is found to be highly correlated with family violence (Livingston, 1986; Potter-Efron & Potter-Efron, 1985). "A majority of families with chemically dependent adolescents have also experienced or are currently experiencing one or more types of family violence" (Potter-Efron & Potter-Efron, 1985, p. 3). Evans and Warren-Sohlberg (1988) found that substance use was a factor in disagreements leading to abuse incidents in almost

20% of parental assaults. Straus and Gelles (1988) also found a strong association between alcohol use and family violence.

CONSEQUENCES OF ADOLESCENT-TO-PARENT ABUSE

For the Adolescent

One of the tasks that adolescents face is individuation from the family system. Because of the dysfunctional nature of a violent family system, this becomes a difficult, if not impossible, task for the adolescent (Harbin & Madden, 1979; Madden, 1982; Wells, 1987). The reversal of the parent–child hierarchy leads to a pseudo-independence. Harbin and Madden (1979) describe how the process happens. They state that the lack of parental authority forces the adolescent to take on an independent role before it is developmentally appropriate. The result is that "while the child appears to be a parent to his own parents, he remains emotionally dependent" (p. 1290).

It is likely that because of the chaotic nature of the home environment, the children are not taught a variety of methods for problem resolution; therefore violence is the method of choice (Harbin & Madden, 1979; Wells, 1987) Adolescents who use violence against parents learn that violence is an acceptable form of problem solving. This often leads a child into delinquency and involvement with the legal system (Agnew & Huguley, 1989).

The most significant consequence for the adolescent is the perpetuation of the cycle of violence. Cornell and Gelles (1982) claim that this form of violence is the "missing link" in the study of the intergenerational transmission of violence. The question that remains is whether the transmission is a continuous learning process, where children who witness violence begin to express themselves violently within their family of origin and then continue to be violent with their family of procreation. Alternately, violence may be a discontinuous process, where they repress feelings of violence until they have their own family on whom they can express their anger (Peek et al., 1985).

For the Family

The most significant consequence for the family is the teaching and reinforcing of the cycle of violence. Straus, Gelles, and Steinmetz (1980) state that when children are witnesses to and/or victims of family violence, there are several unintended messages. The first of these messages is that hitting is equated with loving. Those who love you hit, and conversely, you hit those you love. Observing violence in the home also justifies the moral use of hitting other family members or people outside the family. The final indirect message family violence gives is that being violent is an acceptable alternative when other methods of negotiation do not work.

There are several reasons for the parents/family to deny or avoid the violence issue. Parents may be trying to protect their child or they may be ashamed to admit that they are the victims of abuse by their child (Harbin & Madden, 1979; Madden, 1982; Potter-Efron & Potter-Efron, 1985). Harbin and Madden (1979) explain the long-term consequences of denial as being "the sanctioning of the child's violent behavior, entrenching the feelings of helplessness in both the parents and child, and sabotaging therapeutic intervention" (p. 1290).

Because violence from adolescents to parents is relatively common, is related to several other problems in the family and peer group, and is shrouded in denial, it can be difficult in therapy. The following section introduces several issues that may help therapists address this problem.

ASSESSMENT OF ADOLESCENT-TO-PARENT ABUSE

Between 1979 and 1993, there were seven empirical studies and five reviews done on the topic of adolescent violence against parents (Agnew & Huguley, 1989; Cornell & Gelles, 1982; Evans & Warren-Sohlberg, 1988; Kratcoski, 1982; Kratcoski, 1985; Paulson et al.,1990; Peek et al., 1985). None of these articles directly addressed treatment. All of the studies concentrated on finding theories of causality and identifying traits and circumstances of parental abuse.

Most often treatment issues refer to the general area of treating violent families. Yet, Harbin and Madden (1979) feel that the "battered parent" family represents a different form of family violence and needs to be treated accordingly. The reversed hierarchy, separation, and family secrets have features which distinguish this form of family violence from adult-initiated violence. Peek et al. (1985) agree with this assessment, but neither suggest possible treatment approaches.

Agnew and Huguley (1989) integrate a framework to explain the specific pattern of parental assault. They combine theories of family violence (as discussed before) with theories of delinquency. However, the focus of their study is again on theories of causality and characteristics rather than treatment approaches.

Paulson et al. (1990) and Stouthamer-Loeber and Loeber (1988) state that parent training would probably be the best form of treatment intervention. The goals of this type of intervention would be "to help permissive and uninvolved parents learn to be firm yet supportive with their offspring, and to become more involved in helping them with their problems, activities, and interests" (Paulson et al., 1990, p. 131). This approach would be most helpful in a preventive program setting.

What System Should Be Addressed?

It is important to consider the connection between parental assault and familial behavior patterns, thus comprising the need to assess the violent individual and the family system. Shapiro (1984) states that "violence between family members is an expression of interactional behavior" (p. 116). The issues that are present in adolescent-to-parent violence center on family structure, family processes and dynamics, establishment of and respect for authority, rule expectations, and role fulfillment (Wells, 1987).

The family context is the crucial system in need of assessment. It is typical that other forms of family violence have been used or observed in families where adolescents strike out at their parents (Cornell & Gelles, 1982; Peek et al., 1985; Wells, 1987). It is also important to assess any form of substance abuse by either a parent or the abusive child (Potter-Efron & Potter-Efron, 1985).

Although assessing the family is important, it is also necessary to look beyond the family context to identify other possible areas of delinquency or misconduct for the individual. This enables the therapist to identify how much the adolescent has externalized his or her feelings of hopelessness, rage, disappointment, and powerlessness to the general society and how much remains within the household. The adolescent may also be embedded in a violent peer group such as a gang that reinforces the use of violence on others.

General Assessment

When a family comes in for treatment, they may or may not readily acknowledge that family violence is a problem. Often they will present with an acting-out adolescent whom the parents cannot manage, a "stubborn child," and/or problems with truancy and other difficulties at school. The family needs to be asked directly if there is any violence in the home and if anyone is currently abusing drugs.

When a family is being treated for substance abuse, it is crucial that therapists look for signs of violence and are prepared to address the issue as part of treatment. The reverse is also true; when one is working within the context of family violence, substance abuse by any family member should be explored. Potter-Efron and Potter-Efron (1985) identify an indicator of violence as any history of family violence in a current or former relationship. They also offer general characteristics of individuals or families with violent and chemical difficulties and encourage clinicians to further investigate the potential of violence when these are noted within a family. The characteristics are:

1. A family that cannot agree on a common reality;
2. A family in which one or more members cannot and do not handle fear or anger appropriately or where several members show this inability in relation to another specific family member;

3. A family that expresses all feelings through anger—when family members give extra space to one particular member and appear to respond immediately to that person's verbal or nonverbal cues;
4. A family that keeps secrets and interacts with a revenge-type of communication.

The instruments used are not specific to adolescent-to-parent violence, but remain in the realm of measuring violence and conflict. Cornell and Gelles (1982) constructed a Violence Severity Index. This questionnaire evaluates both the severity and the frequency of violent acts by assigning a weight to a violent act and multiplying it by the frequency it was enacted.

The other instrument identified by Straus and Gelles (1988) is the Conflict Tactics Scales (CTS). This measures three separate variables: reasoning, verbal aggression, and violence of physical aggression. Again, these measures are not specific to adolescent-to-parent assaults. They measure family violence, but do not address the issues of hierarchy and separation.

A violent family system may be responding to external pressures, interpersonal difficulties, or a crisis situation. They may be a multiproblem unit in a state of constant conflict and chaos. Often parents do not or cannot distinguish themselves from their children, and their own needs overcome those of their children (Power, 1988).

It is also important to consider the developmental stages and needs of each of the individuals in the family. For instance, as previously noted, the adolescent is trying to individuate and establish himself or herself as an autonomous person. At the same time, parents are usually at or entering their mid-life or retirement years, and assessing their own parents' mortality. This could be the first child to leave home or the last (Power, 1988). These stages have a powerful impact on each member of the system. A case example illustrates some of the assessment and treatment processes.

> A mother (Carol) applied for services because her 16-year-old son, Mike, was acting out in school and becoming increasingly difficult at home, and she did not know what to do with him. Carol suspected that he was using drugs, but she had no proof. She had tried to confront Mike about it, but he consistently denied any usage.
>
> The family was a blended system: Carol had been married for close to ten years to a man who was not Mike's natural father. Carol and Joe had two children together, ages eight and six. Before the other children were born, the stepfather (Joe) adopted Mike, and they had a good relationship. Mike's natural father (Kevin) lived locally, but had only erratic contact with Mike. While gathering historical information, it was discovered that Kevin had been (and still was) abusing drugs and had been violent toward Carol early in their relationship. They were young when they met and had Mike (Carol was 16, and Kevin was 18) and never got married although they lived together for a few years before Carol took Mike and moved in with her parents. Carol never finished high school and was working as a receptionist.

The developmental stages of the family members were that Mike was the oldest, the first child to leave home. Carol was still young (32), had two small children, and was not ready to let this child leave. Joe was frustrated and upset that Mike was causing so much trouble and wanted him out. They had just bought an unfinished house and were struggling to make ends meet. Joe was a motorcycle repairman and often bartered with his customers to have work done on the house. The other children stated that they were often scared someone would get hurt, but they remained relatively uninvolved with the disputes. Another factor impacting this system was that Mike's maternal grandmother (with whom he had lived for a few years in between his mother's relationships) was declining in health; Carol and Mike were constantly worrying about her.

Parental Subsystem

Stouthamer-Loeber and Loeber (1988) discuss the assessment process as needing to include an assessment of both the children's behavior and the parents' behavior and attitudes. It is important to identify the parents' strengths and weaknesses in order to know what interventions can and should be used in treatment. Certain attitudes toward parenting may be indicative of abusive situations. When parents have low empathy, have a strong belief in corporal punishment, hold inappropriate age expectations, and/or promote a role reversal within the family, there is a greater chance that abuse has or will occur in the household (Potter-Efron & Potter-Efron, 1985).

The parental subsystem may be characterized by permissiveness, uninvolvement, and sparse affectionate interaction with their adolescent offspring. This may be the result of the parents being preoccupied with their own mid-life assessment or because they do not know how to attend to the needs of their adolescents. These behaviors contribute to assaultive reactions from the children (Paulson et al., 1990). Wells (1987) also notes that older parents (aged 50 to 60), where the mother is overprotective and the father is unsupportive, were more likely to experience assaultive behavior by the adolescent.

Another theme to look for is parents who may have been unable or unwilling to provide nurturance and continuous care for the child. If the child has not had protection and structure in their early years, the transition to adulthood is made even more difficult. As adolescents, they respond by exhibiting behaviors of violence modeled earlier by their parents. They may also try to challenge their parents through brute force (Wells, 1987).

Charles (1986) and Paulson et al. (1990) found a trend of parental abuse in middle- and upper-class families. These parents would overintellectualize and examine their child's behavior rather than respond with appropriate interventions (Charles, 1986). This has been attributed to the fact that these educated adults were trying to be more understanding and therefore allowed more "challenges" and "verbal expressions" from their children (Charles, 1986, p. 354).

In the case example, the parental subsystem consisted of a triangle, involving Carol, Joe, and Kevin. Although Kevin was not in contact with either of the other two, he was involved to some degree with Mike. Because Mike could manipulate Kevin to be in the middle, he could and did stress the other ends of the triangle. Kevin was still abusing drugs, according to Carol and Joe. Carol and Joe had marital stressors, many of which stemmed from their financial situation. This stressful situation was exacerbated by Mike's defiance and disrespect toward the other family members (especially Carol and Joe). Joe's focus tended to stay on the finances, the house, and the other children. Carol was trying to be the mediator between Joe and Mike, trying to care for her other children, and trying to help with the finances and the house. They did not express much affection toward one another and were not often physically or emotionally intimate.

Child Subsystem

Adolescence is a time of transition. The goal of this adolescent period is to move into adulthood. It is a time of becoming independent, while at the same time, still wanting and needing to hold onto a sense of dependence. Adolescents often receive conflicting messages. One may be that they are not capable of being responsible, while another may be that they need to be responsible. They are told they need to be independent, yet they have restrictions imposed on them by their parents and by society. Their bodies are developing and they are experiencing sexual desires and fantasies, yet they are told they should not follow through on their desires.

If adolescents have a strong sense of identity and self-esteem, they will be better equipped to negotiate these conflicts. When children do not have these qualities, the conflicts may become overwhelming and they sometimes engage in a variety of activities, which may include violence toward their parents.

Generally, children are seeking resolution of a conflict regarding what is expected of them in the community versus what the expectations and rules are in the home. The messages may be so different that they are hard to reconcile. This conflict creates further distance between themselves and their home and/or their community. They receive conflicting information on what is important and how to communicate. While they may learn that, in the home, violence is the means to satisfying one's needs, they also learn that, in the outside community, violence leads them to punishment and rejection from authority figures (school teachers and officials, law enforcement officers, and so on) and sometimes peer groups.

In families where the adolescent has reversed roles and has become the parental authority, there may be a "grandiose sense of self and an enormous sense of entitlement" on the part of the child (Harbin & Madden, 1979, p. 1290). This child does not fear any retaliation and has an exaggerated need to control. More often, there is an unstable sense of self and identity underneath the mask of control and violence. The violence displays the lack of internal control that adolescents carry within them (Charles, 1986). Many adolescents have not developed the emotional maturity or appropriate social skills to respond to these conflicts or other personal issues involving relationships, sibling rivalry, stress, and peer pressure (Wells, 1987).

If adolescents have learned to resolve conflict through violence, then they will attempt to end the conflict by becoming violent toward the source of the conflict, their parents. Parents receive the brunt of the conflict because there is a message from peers and society that parents should be encouraging and supporting their children through this process of individuation. When physical violence is the only type of communication they see that has any impact, adolescents will follow suit.

Patterson, DeBaryshe, and Ramsey (1989) describe two interpretations for antisocial behavior in adolescents. They describe control theory, which says that harsh discipline and lack of supervision from the parents is a result of a disrupted parent–child bond, as one interpretation. This "poor bonding implies a failure to identify with parental and societal values regarding conformity and work. These omissions leave the child lacking in internal control" (p. 329). An alternative interpretation is the social-interactional perspective which states that children are trained to become antisocial and this behavior is necessary for the child's survival in a "highly aversive social system" (Patterson et al., p. 330). An important factor is that while the child is being trained to perform deviant behaviors, she or he is also *not* being taught many prosocial skills.

This author proposes that adolescents from both types of households sometimes become violent toward others, but the crucial difference between these groups is that one group has bonded with their family and the other has not. Children fitting into the Patterson et al. (1989) control theory, which claims a disrupted parent–child bond, would likely have a lack of desire to connect with either the family or society. It is these adolescents who may quickly become identified as antisocial delinquents.

The social-interactionist perspective states that children are taught antisocial behaviors within the family. It is these children who learn hitting is an expression of love, a means of survival. This does not mean the family has not been able to bond; in fact, they may be overly bonded. The problem of violence in these children is a result of not being taught other, more healthy, means of expressing their emotions. It is probably these adolescents who learn the difference between their household and their community and are able to adapt to societal norms when involved outside their household.

> Mike was alone. He did not feel connected to his family, yet he had a strong attachment to his mother. He once stated, "I'm not a bad kid, just misunderstood." He had witnessed some of the abuse of his mother and was concerned with her safety and well-being. He was also trying to leave the system but still have a connection. Even within the house, he had no bedroom of his own—he slept on the couch. He felt he had been replaced by this new family and that he

no longer belonged. He also was being given double messages. His mother "wanted to trust him" but couldn't because of his "bad" behavior.

The peers he chose were also troubled. They might have been considered a "gang." Thus, he had a place where violent behavior was reinforced and rewarded in terms of belonging. Mike would fit into the group of peers that had bonded with his family (especially his mother and grandmother), but had not had enough attention or focus to learn prosocial behaviors and techniques to respond to his feelings of frustration and emptiness.

Parent–Child Interaction

Families in which violent adolescents emerge interact on the extreme ends of the spectrum in terms of connection with family. Most researchers agree that families are either closely connected or distant in their relationships with one another (Charles, 1986; Paulson et al., 1990; Peek et al., 1985). There is also a focus on parental involvement. If the parents are able to establish their authority, maintain respect for authority, be consistent with their expectations and discipline, and promote positive support and encouragement for the growth and development of their children, then the children are less likely to be assaultive (Agnew & Huguley, 1989; Paulson et al., 1990; Peek et al., 1985).

Parental discipline is another factor to regard as an indication of family interaction. If parents are rigid and strict, adolescents often feel restricted and unable to grow and develop. On the other extreme, children feel abandoned and lost if their parents are too lenient. Both cases generally lead to some form of rebellion from the adolescent. Families that do not promote healthy forms of communication and affection are the most likely to be impacted by violent adolescents. Children who cannot challenge the rules in their family because they fear reproachment and punishment are not able to establish their own values and create an identity for themselves.

It is important to remember that the path to violence is a slow progression. Children who are violent as adolescents have probably been testing their parents' limits for some time. It is during adolescence that the power struggle becomes overt (Wells, 1987). When a child is younger, he or she might respond to frustration by having a temper tantrum or mumbling comments under his or her breath. If this less intensive behavior has little or no negative consequences, the behavior slowly becomes more aggressive. For example, it moves to assaulting the parents verbally, then throwing items at walls or other objects, then throwing objects at other people, and so on. From here, the behavior becomes even more physically aggressive. When parents do not set limits or respond to these more subtle behaviors in the early stages, they are inadvertently reinforcing and strengthening the likelihood of the behaviors increasing in both frequency and intensity. It is this reinforcement of passive–aggressive behaviors that promotes the cycle of violence for the adolescent (Harbin & Madden, 1979). The adolescent is given the message that aggressive behavior will gain the desired outcome which includes an increase in power and control within the family.

Harbin and Madden (1979) note that "usually one or both parents have abdicated the executive position, or there is so much covert competition between them that neither rules effectively" (p. 1289). This is the time when the child begins to take charge. While the parents are busy being distracted by their chaotic and stressful environment, they do not notice they have given up their authority to their adolescent, thus creating the reversed hierarchy. The children do not respond to or respect their parents' authority in the home. This comes from a lack of clearly defined rules and roles consistently enforced by their parents (Wells, 1987). Adolescents receive mixed messages from their parents about what is expected of them. When they try to clarify the expectations, they still do not get a direct answer. They then begin to make their own rules and decisions and begin to view their parents as equals rather than as authority figures (Charles, 1986).

Wells (1987) believes both the child and the parent feel victimized by one another. She states that the child "is straining at the parents' seemingly inappropriate limits to his or her activities and behaviors, while the parents see the child's provocativeness and out-of-control actions as direct assaults upon them" (p. 127).

Adolescents who assault their parents do not know how to appropriately connect with their parents, although this would seem to be the underlying desire of abusive children. They may have learned that the only way in which to express or obtain their connection is through hitting. Or, as Harbin and Madden (1979) suggest, they may be so connected to their family that the violence acts as a "primitive distancing mechanism from the parent/victim" (p. 1290).

Adolescents who become violent are struggling with two critical and conflicting issues. They are walking the line of becoming independent, yet they are not allowed to cross over the line. They begin to challenge authority and establish an identity for themselves. When the dimension of a reversed hierarchy is added to the equation, there are some complications. First of all, there is the issue of a false sense of independence because the adolescent assumes an independent role before she or he is developmentally ready, as previously stated (Harbin & Madden, 1979). The adolescent who has bonded with parents will begin to question the process by asking these types of questions: "If I break away from my family and become independent, who will take care of them?" or "Who will be in charge if I leave?" and "Do I take care of myself or my family first?"

Thus, the struggle for independence is further complicated by the adolescent feeling responsible for the family's well-being. If the adolescent carries this burden, a resentment grows within him or her toward parents for not doing their job as parents—taking care of the family. Because these children do not know how to resolve this conflict, they begin to challenge the parents to take over. At the same time, they do not trust that their parents are capable of being in charge and they resist giving up the power they have. The adolescents like having the power because it allows them to make their own decisions, yet they also want their parents to put some restrictions on them so that they know their parents are concerned about them.

If the adolescent has not bonded, then there is less concern with other members of the family; the primary concern is with herself or himself. This adolescent seeks self-satisfaction and self-fulfillment regardless of other people's feelings.

The parents may respond by trying to take back the power, but it is difficult for the child to give it up; sometimes resistance results in violence. Thus the cycle continues with the parents feeling responsible and not enforcing consequences on the child. They excuse the behavior and blame themselves instead of giving consequences and forcing the child to take responsibility for his or her own actions.

> The interaction between Mike and his parents was limited in scope and in duration. His mother, in trying to give him the benefit of the doubt, was very permissive and then would try to be very restrictive. His adoptive father would always vote for the restrictive route, constantly imposing punishments and negative reinforcements. His natural father was unavailable to Mike, and his grandmother was permissive because she no longer had the strength to set boundaries and because she felt sorry for Mike.
>
> Mike threatened violence toward his mother often, seemingly in an attempt to reach out to her. He wanted to know if she would just let him go, or if she wanted him to stay as a part of the family. His struggle was "If I leave, do I disappear from their lives like my natural father or do they want to continue to have me in their lives?" His response to those questions would have been they did not want him in their lives; they would be just fine without him; they would not miss him at all. Their response would have been quite different, but they had no means of expressing their feelings in a way that he could hear them.

TREATMENT OF ADOLESCENT-TO-PARENT ABUSE

Family therapy is the treatment of choice when working with cases of adolescent-to-parent abuse, especially in situations where members are willing to "unlearn" the patterns of violence they grew up with and replace them with positive, healthy patterns of interaction and negotiation (Kratcoski, 1985; Wells, 1987). Although there is almost no literature directly written for the treatment of adolescent-to-parent abuse, there are several resources in the general area of family violence and delinquency that can be effectively applied to this problem. The approaches to the treatment of family violence are reviewed in the next section before addressing treatment issues for delinquents and their families.

Treatment of Family Violence

Youngerman and Canino (1983) include a multidimensional approach to working with violent adolescents and their families. They feel it is important to use psychiatric treatment in conjunction with family therapy. They identify the familial patterns of violence and lithium-responsiveness and encourage an intersystemic approach to working with violent youth, specifically with violent manic-depressives. The benefit of this approach is the comprehensive treatment. Future research should explore when hospitalization and drug treatment are necessary and when they are not. Because this is an extremely expensive form of treatment, hospitalization should probably be used as a last resort.

When chemical dependency is an issue with family violence, Potter-Efron and Potter-Efron (1985 pp. 6–7) have established common messages that need to be repeated to the family as a means of helping them learn and practice their new family interactions. These messages are:

1. Violence is never an acceptable solution for family problems and only leads to more violence.
2. The use of alcohol or drugs promotes family violence and cannot be accepted.
3. Secrets keep a family sick; denial of family problems to others, to the family, and to yourself perpetrates the problems.
4. Each member of the family has the right to a decent life, a life free from daily fear, pain, dishonesty, or shame.
5. The entire family has been affected by the use of chemicals or violence by some members. Everyone gets hurt together and all need to work together to get well.
6. Change is possible, both individually and for the family.

These messages reinforce the family's work in therapy and can inspire members when one is feeling helpless. They need to be repeated often in order for the family to accept them.

Shapiro (1986) offers another approach to working with violent families. He asks whether the status of violence is an issue of crisis needing immediate attention or one where time can be taken to make a complete evaluation with all members present. He also attends to issues of resistance in the therapy session and discusses the dilemmas faced by family members, both the perpetrators and the victims. In the joining phase, the therapist needs to make a positive connection with the perpetrator, in this case, the adolescent. The parents, or victims, may also be resistant to disclose that they are being abused by their child because of shame or the need to protect. It is the job of the therapist to create an atmosphere of openness and honesty and to establish rules to address the issues of violence in therapy. Shapiro (1986) recommends that all family members stay involved with therapy, and that it may be necessary to see certain subsystems of the family. The marital couple may need separate sessions to address marital or parental issues, while the siblings may need to be seen either individually or as a subsystem. Work continues with the family to address interactional patterns, communication issues, and conflict resolution.

The following steps are taken from Haley (1992) who worked with violent families. The first step for the therapist is to work together with other agencies and colleagues involved with the family to promote a sense of direction and common goals.

Next, one needs to bring out the family secrets as soon as possible; this does not always happen in the history-taking session, but it should take place in the initial therapy sessions. Haley (1992) states that usually families are more apt to disclose unpleasant information before they have developed a relationship with the therapist.

The third step is to make an agreement for change. If the family is not ready to do so, one needs to find motivation for them to do so. Sometimes this includes involving extended family members to gain support for changing behaviors that have been ingrained throughout the generations.

Once the family has contracted for change, one must take action. The therapist needs to organize the family by issuing directives that begin to challenge established family patterns. Power shifts need to be balanced and successful treatment needs to be reinforced. Families need to take the responsibility for change, but often they attribute success to the therapist.

The case presented was not one in which there was an immediate concern for safety. It seemed that although Mike threatened to be violent with his mother, he had not followed through recently because of fear that Joe would retaliate. Mike was never violent toward his siblings—he was actually protective of them in his own way. Although family therapy was the treatment of choice, Joe was refusing to attend and he did not see the necessity of the other children attending. He felt so strongly about this that, if the therapists had refused treatment, he would have let it be and kicked Mike out of the house.

The work proceeded with Mike and his mother, sometimes alone and sometimes together. Joe did agree to attend some of the sessions with just his wife and one family session at the end. The treatment was time limited and not all of the stages were completed, but the family made some progress in learning about their roles and how to modify some behaviors to lessen the need for threats and to communicate in a more prosocial manner.

Carol learned how to shift away from her "victim" stance and talk to Mike and Joe more openly and honestly. Mike was able to express some of his fears and anger. At first this was in a passive–aggressive manner (not showing up for his scheduled appointments), but then he gradually moved to more appropriate behaviors (stating his anger or discomfort, crying). The parent–child bond improved as did the husband–wife bond, reducing the likelihood of violence.

Treatment of Delinquency

Alexander's Functional Family Therapy approach (Alexander, Waldron, Newberry, & Liddle, 1988) has been proven more effective than other approaches in treating delinquents, and it has been empirically generalized to work effectively with different delinquent populations (Barton, Alexander, Waldron, Turner, & Warburton, 1985). Functional Family Therapy (FFT) focuses on the family's realities and perceptions of the problems. The therapist focuses on how families regulate distance, improving communication and helping the family see how their behavior is interrelated. The change techniques used "must produce the changes identified by the therapist, but at the same time the changes must make sense to the family" (Alexander et al., 1988, p. 145).

Atkinson and McKenzie (1987) provide one of the few reviews of treatment failures in working with delinquents served by FFT. They categorize these failures into two basic types. The first group is one in which the therapist has failed to facilitate change in the family patterns. The second group involves the youth continuing to engage in delinquent behaviors despite changes in the family's interactional patterns. It is this group on which they focus their intervention and research. They emphasize that their methods of treatment should only be used in conjunction with family therapy, and only after the family therapy procedures have failed to stop the offending behaviors. This procedure also involves collaborating with the juvenile justice system.

The "Hard Line" method might be appropriate when working with violent adolescents. It involves working independently with the parents for a few sessions to help them prepare their plan of consequences for the child's unacceptable behaviors. Once a plan is made and the parents feel capable of following through with it, they discuss what these consequences are with the child prior to the enactment of the delinquent behavior so that the child is prepared for what is coming. This usually involves reporting the behavior, regardless of the seriousness of the offense, to the authorities. This gives the parents power, while allowing the child the choice to make a decision, knowing what the potential consequences will be. The power of this intervention lies in the change in the interaction between parent and adolescent.

Integration of Family Violence and Delinquency

When working with family violence or delinquency, the structure of therapy varies depending on the treatment approach taken, although some of the concepts are similar. Most of the approaches identify a series of stages through which the process runs. Generally, approaches utilize a joining period, followed by an assessment phase, then an intervention or therapy period and finally a termination period.

The key to structuring the interventions and treatment approaches is to incorporate the issue of safety for the family members and to allow for the healthy individuation of the adolescent. Treatment approaches need to reverse the hierarchy—(put the parent back in charge)—while allowing the adolescent to continue the natural struggle for independence.

The therapist should take charge of the family sessions from the beginning of treatment. It needs to be demonstrated to the family that the therapist holds the power to structure and direct the sessions. This will increase safety for the family and reduce the risk that the therapist will be inducted into the family (Shapiro, 1986). As the therapy continues, the therapist should become less involved. As the family makes progress and is able to resolve their own issues, the therapist can be less directive.

> It was crucial for Carol to see the importance of following through on setting limits with Mike, as the Hard Line approach suggests. She was able to incorporate this thinking into her actions and also to convince Mike that they were on the same side and it was an issue of safety, not of her "siding" with Joe. This therapist spent some time focusing on Carol and the reasons she was unable or unwilling to follow through in order to make this work, not just stressing the importance of her being able to do it.
>
> It was also critical to give Mike some other resources and to pay attention to his perspective so that he felt understood. Once he felt this effort, especially on the part of his mother, but beginning with the therapist, he was much more receptive to change.
>
> Another important piece was to slowly bring Joe into the therapy. He was so angry and resistant to giving Mike "yet another" chance that it was extremely difficult to make any significant changes in the system without his support. Once all these pieces were in place, the issues of connectedness/individuation were able to be resolved because the family understood some of the underlying issues.

Goals of Therapy

The most immediate, most important goals for therapy, in all cases, are the involvement of all family members and the discontinuance of the violence. It is important to include everyone in treatment so that the most accurate assessment and interventions can be made by the therapist.

The issue of safety is primary in all cases of family violence. This might mean that one of the members is removed from the home for a short period of time to ensure the safety of the other members. Alternately, an agreement may be made that in case of a violent episode, someone, usually the adolescent, will spend a designated period of time outside the home at a friend's or relative's (Shapiro, 1986).

Shapiro (1986) suggests that once the issue of violence has been addressed and is under control, the main task is to provide guidelines to ensure families learn how to talk and listen to one another so that they are able to negotiate without violence. Long-term goals for cases involving adolescent-to-parent abuse include going beyond the improvement of interaction and into the realm of individual factors and extended family systems. Individual issues include building the self-esteem of both the adolescent and the parent, deepening confidence in one's abilities, increasing the ability to trust oneself and one another, and promoting an overall increase in one's happiness.

Family issues include addressing the issues of individuation, helping the adolescent to separate from the family while finding a healthy way to stay connected. Family-of-origin issues may interfere with this process for the parents, and these issues need to be resolved for the benefit of the family. Other family issues include strengthening the marital dyad or building the strength and confidence of a single parent to support generational boundaries that put and keep parents in charge.

Prevention

Prevention and early intervention are the Paulson et al. (1990) solutions to violent adolescents. They state that if parents are trained to be more involved in their children's lives, then the children will feel more valuable and be less likely to strike out at their parents. They claim that adolescents need an atmosphere of firm support and affectionate interaction. Stouthamer-Loeber and Loeber (1988) discuss the connection between parent behaviors and circumstances and children's problem behaviors and agree that parent training would be the ideal form of prevention.

LEGAL AND ETHICAL CONSIDERATIONS

The primary issue in a case of family violence rests with the issue of safety. All family members must be safe. If the family cannot contract to discontinue violence in the home, then separation needs to occur. This issue creates difficult legal and ethical issues.

The legal responsibility for the health and welfare of a child is with the parents until the child reaches the age of 18 years, unless they chose to sign over these rights to the state (Steinmetz, 1985). If it is the adolescent that is to be removed from the household because of safety issues, he or she needs to be placed in a safe place, not "thrown out" of the house. Ideally, provisions would be made to stay with friends or relatives, unless the state has become involved and provides an alternate home placement for the child.

Safety may also create an ethical issue for the therapist. If the therapist feels a family member is unsafe, even though all members are agreeing not to use violence, there is a dilemma of whether to trust what the family is saying, or to act on one's instinct and provide immediate protection through insistence on separation. There are a number of issues involved in this assessment/decision.

The unique structure of the family creates many difficult issues with which to contend. Power (1988) identifies some distinct group characteristics of the family such as a diverse age range; intense, long-term relationships; and involuntary membership. It is a group with a high level of both conflict and commitment (Straus & Gelles, 1988). These characteristics create loyalties and complications for the members involved. They may claim to feel safe even though they are fearful for their safety; they are either torn by a need to protect the individual, especially in the case of the violent adolescent, or fear retribution from the abuser following the meeting. "Family members are usually torn between discomfort with the violence in their midst and the need to preserve unity" (Shapiro, 1986, p. 129). Siblings of the violent adolescent are in a double bind and usually follow the lead of their parents to protect loyalties. They do not want to expose their parents as being weak and also fear the reaction of their violent sibling. It is vital that the therapist be aware of these dilemmas for the family members when making their assessment of the family's safety.

There is not much literature that discusses the range of legal options for parents to control their adolescent. Arrigo (1982) offers one of the few perspectives on the legal responses to parent battering. In cases of parent battering, she states that parents need to file formal assault-and-battery charges against their child. This is a rare occurrence because of the shame and guilt parents have in these circumstances.

Police hesitate to make an arrest in these disputes because the parent usually refuses to testify against the child. The Dixon Bill states that a child who is brought into the system as a status offender cannot be detained in a juvenile detention center. Thus, families with children labeled as "incorrigible" and "uncontrollable" are not able to receive any type of respite or temporary separation from a violent situation unless they run away, are hospitalized, or seek emancipation.

Emancipation laws vary from state to state. In California, a child can become emancipated if he or she is 14 years old and can meet the following criteria: There is agreement between the parents and minor for emancipation, the child is able to manage financially, and the court finds that emancipation is not contrary to the child's best interest. Arrigo (1982) does not feel this option is good for children before therapeutic interventions have established a sense of stability for the adolescent being emancipated.

In 1982, Cornell and Gelles stated that there was a need for the social service and criminal justice systems to take notice of this type of family violence. It is more than ten years later and there is still very little discussion about encouraging parent victims to seek amelioration and stop blaming themselves.

CONCLUSIONS

The issue of adolescent-to-parent abuse is a relatively new area of family violence. Although it is as prevalent as spousal abuse (Straus & Gelles, 1988), it is still a neglected area of developing research and treatment approaches. The approaches this chapter identifies are a merging of the available resources addressing family violence and juvenile delinquency.

There are many additional factors that need to be considered when working with violent individuals. Substance abuse has a high correlation with violence, and these issues should be addressed simultaneously when appropriate.

Working with violent adolescents also adds the dimension of legal responsibilities for the parents. A child under the age of 18 is the parents' responsibility. While in the case of spousal abuse, a partner can hold the expectation that the other partner not be allowed in the home, a child is legally protected against this type of ultimatum. This can create an ethical dilemma for the therapist and the family.

Parents have few resources to fight against their victimization. Until society recognizes the true impact of adolescent violence against parents, parents will continue to be victimized and will continue to hide the circumstances under which they are living.

REFERENCES

Agnew, R. & Huguley, S. (1989). Adolescent violence towards parents. *Journal of Marriage and the Family, 51,* 699–711.

Alexander, J. F., Waldron, H. B., Newberry, A. M., & Liddle, N. (1988). Family approaches to treating delinquents. In E. W. Nunnally, C. S. Chilman, & F. M. Cox (Eds.), *Mental illness, delinquency, addictions, and neglect* (pp. 128–146). Newbury Park, CA: Sage.

Arrigo, M. J. (1982). Battered parents in California: Ignored victims of domestic violence. *San Diego Law Review, 19,* 781–800.

Atkinson, B. J. & McKenzie, P. N. (1987). Family therapy with adolescent offenders: A collaborative treatment strategy. *American Journal of Family Therapy, 15*(4), 316–325.

Barton, C., Alexander, J. F., Waldron, H., Turner, C. W., & Warburton, J. (1985). Generalizing treatment effects of functional family therapy: Three replications. *American Journal of Family Therapy, 13,* 16–26.

Charles, A. V. (1986). Physically abused parents. *Journal of Family Violence, 1,* 343–355.

Cornell, C. P. & Gelles, R. J. (1982). Adolescent to parent violence. *The Urban and Social Change Review, 15*(1), 8–14.

Evans, E. D. & Warren-Sohlberg, L. (1988). A pattern analysis of adolescent abusive behavior toward parents. *Journal of Adolescent Research, 3*(2), 201–216.

Gelles, R. J. (1987). *Family violence.* Newbury Park, CA: Sage.

Haley, J. & Madanes, C. (1992, November). *Working with violent and abusive families.* Paper presented for Family Therapy Workshops, a Consortium of Family Service of Rochester, Hillside Children's Center and the University of Rochester Family Therapy Training Program, Rochester, NY.

Harbin, H. T. & Madden, D. J. (1979). Battered parents: A new syndrome. *American Journal of Psychiatry, 136*(10), 1288–1291.

Heide, K. M. (1992). *Why kids kill parents: Child abuse and adolescent homicide.* Columbus: Ohio State University Press.

Kratcoski, P. C. (1982). Child abuse and violence against the family. *Child Welfare, 61*(7), 435–445.

Kratcoski, P. C. (1985). Youth violence directed toward significant others. *Journal of Adolescence, 8,* 145–157.

Madden, D. J. (1982). Adolescent violence in the family. In J. Hansen (Ed.), *Clinical approaches to family violence* (pp. 92–104). Rockville, MD: Aspen Systems.

Patterson, G. R., DeBaryshe, B. D., and Ramsey, E. (1989). A developmental perspective on antisocial behavior. *American Psychologist, 44*(2), 329–335.

Paulson, M. J., Coombs, R. H., & Landsverk, J. (1990). Youth who physically assault their parents. *Journal of Family Violence, 5*(2), 121–133.

Peek, C. W., Fischer, J. L., & Kidwell, J. S. (1985). Teenage violence toward parents: A neglected dimension of family violence. *Journal of Marriage and the Family, 47*(4), 1051–1058.

Post, S. (1982). Adolescent parricide in abusive families. *Child Welfare, 61*(7), 445–455.

Potter-Efron, R. T. & Potter-Efron, P. S. (1985). Family violence as a treatment issue with chemically dependent adolescents. *Alcoholism Treatment Quarterly, 2*(2), 1–15.

Power, R. (1988). Differential models of social work groups with family violence. *Social Work with Groups, 11*(3), 9–31.

Shapiro, R. J. (1984). Therapy with violent families. In S. Saunders, A. Anderson, C. A. Hart, & G. Rubenstien (Eds.), *Violent individuals and families* (pp. 112–136). Springfield, IL: Charles C. Thomas.

Shapiro, R. J. (1986). Passing the buck: Too often therapists steer clear of violent cases. *Family Therapy Networker, 10*(May-June), 48–66.

Stouthamer-Loeber, M. & Loeber, R. (1988). Parents as intervention agents for children with conduct problems and juvenile offenders. *Child and Youth Services, 63,* 127–148.

Straus, M. A. & Gelles, R. J. (1988). Violence in American families: How much is there and why does it occur? In E. Nunnally, C. Chilman, & F. Cox (Eds.), *Family in trouble series: Vol. 3. Troubled relationships* (pp. 141–162). Newbury Park, CA: Sage.

Straus, M. A. & Gelles, R. J. (1990). *Physical violence in American families.* New Brunswick, NJ: Transaction Publishers.

Straus, M. A., Gelles, R. J., & Steinmetz, S. K. (1980). *Behind closed doors: Violence in the American family.* New York: Anchor Books.

Steinmetz, S. K. (1985). Parent to child—child to parent: Obligation and abuse in America. *Delaware Lawyer Summary, 4,* 20–25.

Wells, M. G. (1987). Adolescent violence against parents: An assessment. *Family Therapy, 14*(2), 125–133.

Youngerman, J. K. & Canino, I. A. (1983). Violent kids, violent parents: Family pharmacotherapy. *American Journal of Orthopsychiatry, 53*(1), 152–156.

6

ABUSE OF THE ELDERLY BY ADULT CHILDREN

SABINE KRUMMEL

In the past three years things have gotten steadily worse. My daughter locked me in the garage and left me there.... Whenever I tried to cook a meal, she would appear and turn off the gas and remove the grills so that the only way I could cook was to hold the pan over the fire.... My daughter's treatment of me kept getting worse. Always hurting me physically and mentally, kicking me, pushing me, grappling with me.... She is a well-educated person. (Schlesinger & Schlesinger, 1988, p. 4)
—*VOICE OF AN ELDERLY WOMAN*

The thing that bothered me most about my mother-in-law was constant demands—unreasonable demands—towards the end she really got bad. She wouldn't let me sleep. Ten to fifteen minutes, then she would call me again. All day and night she would do this, all day and night.... (Steinmetz, 1988, p. 262)
—*VOICE OF A CAREGIVER*

Victimization of the elderly by their adult children has only recently been acknowledged as a significant social problem (Hudson, 1986; Pillemer & Finkelhor, 1988; Steinmetz, 1988). Within the last two decades the consensus on the prevalence of elder abuse has been estimated to range from 3 to 5% of all elders (Bookin & Dunkle, 1985; Pillemer & Finkelhor, 1988; Rathbone-McCuan & Goodstein, 1985). This suggests that elder abuse is almost, if not equally, as pervasive as child abuse in our society (Bookin & Dunkle, 1985; Hudson, 1986). In addition, it is all too readily assumed that elder abuse occurs primarily in nursing homes rather than at the hands of loved ones.

This belief is unfounded; at any given time, fewer than 5% of individuals over the age of 60 live in institutions (Hudson, 1986). What is currently a significant social problem may escalate into an unmanageable quandary if ignored. Currently industrialized countries are experiencing an elder "boom" because of rapid advances in medical interventions (Hardin & Schlater, 1987; Quinn & Tomita, 1986). The fastest growing age group is 85 years and over (Steinmetz, 1988). Approximately 33% of the U.S. population in 2020 will be 55 years old or older. It is estimated that within 10 to 20 years, close to 50% of all deaths will occur after the age of 80 (Steinmetz, 1988). Obviously, the future implications for the family are immense in terms of time, emotional support, and financial assistance required from the younger generation for the elderly.

In addition, the "younger generation" may no longer be so young, because parents in their eighties tend to have children in their sixties (Steinmetz, 1988). Caretakers in their retirement years often express frustration, anger, and guilt regarding responsibility for their elderly parent. This frustration is verbalized by a 66-year-old daughter caring for her 86-year-old father.

> He has lived his life. I should have a chance to live mine. I worked forty-five years of my life and I would like to have a little time to live before I die. There are times when it crops up…when I feel so guilty about feeling like I do that I just think I must be no good to anybody …. There are times when I think, if I could die and get out of the whole stinking mess… without having to live with it day in and day out (Steinmetz, 1988, pp. 263–264).

Besides the increased percentage of the elderly in our society, it becomes essential to incorporate the broader context of sex differences in both the caregivers and the elderly. Although the title "caregiver" portrays a sexless image, research indicates that a disproportionate number of elders are cared for by the women in our society (Brody, 1981; Cantor, 1983; Couper, 1989; Johnson, 1983; Stoller, 1983). In general, single, divorced, or widowed daughters provide more care than do married daughters (Horowitz, 1985). Daughters tend not only to live closer to their parents, but also to feel more responsibility for their parents' well-being (Kending & Rowland, 1983; Marshall & Rosenthal, 1982). Whereas sons provide financial support, daughters are more closely involved with daily caregiving for the elderly such as chores, meals, and emotional support (Brody, 1981; Cantor, 1983; Johnson, 1983). Paradoxically, married sons have a higher tendency to take in an elderly parent than single sons, which suggests that they rely on their wives to provide the major caregiving (Horowitz, 1985).

Similar to "caregiver," the word *elderly* does not identify any gender differences. Nevertheless, research has consistently indicated that women have a longer life expectancy than men. In 1979 for every 100 women over the age of 65, 68.4 men existed. This disproportion tends to increase with age (Breckman & Adelman, 1988). In addition, older women struggle not only with ageism, but also with sexism. Older women are often portrayed as "hags" or "old bags" long before men receive equally slanderous remarks (Quinn & Tomita, 1986). Besides outer appearance, a large discrepancy exists between older men and women regarding the financial resources available to each. Whereas men tend to be able to rely on at least a limited pension, most women have no financial security in old age. As few as 2% of older women benefit from widows' survivor benefits following their husband's deaths (Block, 1983). Many women perceive their economic crisis as a personal failure rather than as a social and economic injustice within the social system (Quinn & Tomita, 1986).

DEFINITION OF ELDER ABUSE

When dealing with the abused elderly, the practitioner's first hurdle is to decide what exactly constitutes abuse (Quinn & Tomita, 1986). A workable definition describes *elder abuse* as physical injury or neglect, financial exploitation, mental torment, unreasonable confinement, or denial of services necessary for the maintenance of mental and physical health (Breckman & Adelman, 1988; Pillemer & Finkelhor, 1989; Powell & Berg, 1987; Rathbone-McCuan & Goodstein, 1985; Quinn, 1990). Five categories provide a multifaceted criterion by which to identify elder abuse:

Physical abuse refers to being beaten, slapped, bruised, cut, burned, physically restrained, or drugged by a caretaker (Breckman & Adelman, 1988; Gray Panthers of Austin, 1983). Multiple bruises at different stages of healing are a common indication of elder abuse (Quinn, 1990).

Psychological abuse refers to the instance of an elderly person being ridiculed, manipulated, treated as a child, frightened, humiliated, shamed, or called names (Gray Panthers of Austin, 1983; Powell & Berg, 1987). Although psychological abuse tends to be difficult to measure, it is consistently reported that it tends to cause even more distress and anguish than does physical abuse.

Financial abuse refers to inappropriate and illegal exploitation of the elderly's resources (Breckman & Adelman, 1988; Gray Panthers of Austin, 1983). Indications of financial abuse include excessive and expensive "gifts," multiple withdrawals from a bank account over a short period of time, disappearance of valuable possessions, or illegally signed checks and documents (Quinn, 1990).

Active neglect involves the violation of rights of all citizens. These rights include freedom of speech, religion, and the rights to vote and assemble (Quinn, 1990). Active neglect, therefore, includes withholding food, medicine, or bathroom assistance, as well as denying the elderly the right to open their own mail, attend the church of their choice, maintain contact with friends, or use the telephone (Gray Panthers of Austin, 1983; Quinn, 1990).

Passive neglect is defined as harm inflicted on the elderly because of inadequate knowledge of the changing needs of aging adults. Appropriate food intake and medical supervision are ignored and result in starvation, dehydration, and medical emergencies. The elderly person is often left alone for unreasonable time spans, isolated from stimulation, or altogether forgotten (Gray Panthers of Austin, 1983).

VICTIM AND ABUSER PROFILE

The majority of research on elder abuse identifies the victims as primarily white women who are widowed or single and over the age of 75 (Powell & Berg, 1987; Wolf & Pillemer, 1989). Many victims are physically or mentally impaired and are dependent on their caregivers. Abusers of the elderly are described as primarily being adult sons, who suffer from some form of psychopathology and are dependent on their elderly parents (Douglass & Hickey, 1983; Wolf & Pillemer, 1989). A more recent study has challenged these findings, suggesting that perpetrators of elder abuse are spouses in up to 60% of cases (Pillemer & Finkelhor, 1988). This study also suggests that men are as likely to be abused by caregivers as women. Nevertheless, most studies agree that women suffer more severely from both physical and psychological abuse than men do (Pillemer & Finkelhor, 1988). Elders who live with their perpetrators are at higher risk for abuse by their adult children than those living alone because of the greater opportunities for interaction (Pillemer & Finkelhor, 1988).

Studies repeatedly suggest that abuse is present in all age groups, economic levels, and various ethnic groups among the elderly (Breckman & Adelman, 1988). Nevertheless, the limited research on African American families suggests that black elderly individuals experience far less abuse by their adult children than do white elders (Williams & Griffin, 1991). It is speculated that the extended family network and strong cohesiveness within black families serve as a buffer to abuse. In addition, African American families often encourage their adult children to return to the home of their elderly mothers because of a strong matriarchal family structure. By contrast, elderly white persons tend to move into their children's home (Williams & Griffin, 1991). Similar patterns are found in Latin American and native American families. Nevertheless, research on these three ethnic groups continues to be limited and more attention is needed in the future (Quinn & Tomita, 1986).

FACTORS RELATING TO ELDER ABUSE

Extensive review of empirical and theoretical research indicates seven factors particularly relevant in the understanding and treatment of elder abuse (Anetzberger, 1987; Bookin & Dunkle, 1985; Breckman & Adelman, 1988; Pillemer, 1986; Quinn & Tomita, 1986). The remainder of this chapter is dedicated to a treatment model incorporating the following seven characteristics.

1. Caregiver stress
2. Caregiver psychopathology
3. Caregiver dependence
4. Intergenerational transmission of abuse

5. Role changes and identity adjustment
6. Negative attitudes and values about the elderly
7. Social isolation

Caregiver Stress

Caregiver stress is the most widely cited risk factor of elder abuse (Kosberg, 1988; Steinmetz, 1988; Steinmetz & Amsden 1983). Nevertheless, numerous authors have challenged the idea that caregiver stress is directly responsible for the abuse of the elderly (Breckman & Adelman, 1988; Pillemer & Finkelhor, 1989). According to these findings, stress alone does not foster elder abuse. Regardless of the controversial research results, it is necessary for practitioners to take caregiver stress seriously, because it can indirectly fuel other risk factors. The most common sources of caregiver stress are feeling "caught in the middle," sleep deprivation and physical exhaustion, constant criticism, and growing resentment of the elder's needs (Steinmetz, 1988). These sources of stress are powerfully portrayed by a 57-year-old daughter-in-law caring for her 81-year-old mother-in-law:

> When you have small children who also need your time and attention and a home to manage and you are working five days a week and you have an older person whose needs are even in excess of those of the children, it is almost next to impossible to handle it all and do it to any degree of satisfaction. You always feel like you are not cutting the mustard. What you do is just handle the priorities and emergency situations (Steinmetz, 1988, p. 261).

Caregiver Psychopathology

Several studies suggest that characteristics of the perpetrator, rather than those of the victim, are most often correlated with elder abuse (Anetzberger, 1987; Pillemer & Finkelhor, 1989; Pillemer, 1985; Suitor & Pillemer, 1988; Wolf, Godkin & Pillemer, 1984). High rates of alcoholism, arrests for various violations of the law, and other deviant behaviors of caregivers are especially prevalent. It has also been suggested that disabled, cognitively impaired, or mentally ill caretakers tend to demonstrate abusive behavior at a much higher rate than those who are mentally and socially stable (Anetzberger, 1987; Breckman & Adelman, 1988; Pillemer, 1986). A brief excerpt of a case study from official court records provides a tangible description of a caregiver suffering with severe psychopathology:

> The daughter had apparently cut electrical and telephone wiring and had let the home deteriorate; the house was filthy, and the floors were covered with a large collection of garbage. The daughter, a former Las Vegas showgirl, had a long psychiatric history of paranoid schizophrenia. She had become delusional and had barricaded herself in the house and was keeping her mother locked in the garage... (Quinn, 1990, p. 278).

Caregiver Dependency

Caregivers who are dependent on the elderly, either financially or for housing reasons, are more likely to abuse their parents than are caregivers who are financially independent (Pillemer & Finkelhor, 1989; Pillemer, 1985; Wolf, et al., 1984). Generally, dependent abusers tend to be unmarried, socially isolated, and poorly educated. They present themselves as poorly groomed, quite immature in a "childlike dependence" way, and with no desire to alter their circumstances (Anetzberger, 1987). An example illustrates these various characteristics of caregiver dependency:

> This 87-year-old woman lives with her 50-year-old son, Henry, whom she refers to as her baby.... Henry is an unemployed veteran. He has a worried, unsmiling look, sagging shoulders, and stooped posture. He moves slowly, dragging his feet.... Henry was also in poor health because of his gouty arthritis, alcohol abuse, and perception of himself as a failure....[Concerning the abuse inflicted on this elderly woman]: She seemed passive and withdrawn, saying "I always give in to Henry, especially when he's drinking. If you be meek and humble, they will like you" (Ferguson & Beck, 1983, pp. 303–304).

Intergenerational Transmission

The theory of intergenerational transmission of abuse suggests that violence in many families tends to be a learned behavior transmitted through several age groups and numerous generations (Bookin & Dunkle, 1985; Holmes, 1981; Pillemer 1986; Straus, 1988). Although this theory is highly popular, several researchers encourage caution because of the lack of concrete empirical research (Breckman & Adelman, 1988; Wolf & Pillemer, 1989). Nevertheless, bitter memories of the past often resurface in adult children caring for their elderly parents. A 66-year-old daughter caring for her 86-year-old father shares her struggle with having been a victim herself, and the temptation to use violence herself to control her elderly parent.

> I would say that if a parent has been a very loving parent and caring parent, then a child could handle that, but when you know they haven't been, it is very difficult to handle, very difficult. It's said that you have to forget what is in the past. Honey, you don't forget these things. Even an old dog, if you have beaten him, will cringe when he sees you. Even he doesn't forget (Steinmetz, 1988, p. 268).

Role Changes

As the mental and physical functioning of the elderly person decreases with age, the realignment of family responsibilities becomes a necessity. Rarely do family members take time to assess role changes, clarify expectations, and identify new functions for the whole family. The natural process of structural change is hindered as the family moves into new life cycle change (Ferguson & Beck, 1983; Walsh, 1988). When a family is unable to accommodate to the changing needs of the elderly person, family members experience high anxiety, resentment, and confusion. One adult child describes her struggle with these new role adjustments as her elderly parent loses various functions:

> You never think that this will happen to you. Mom and I always helped each other. We'd shop together, do gardens together. Now it's like I'm her mother and she's a little baby. I never thought it would be like this, with me doing everything for her (George, 1986, p. 84).

Attitudes Toward Aging

Perhaps the most global social problem confronting the elderly today is the pervasive negative attitude directed toward them from the general public (Achenbaum, 1983; Anetzberger, 1987; Breckman & Adelman, 1988). *Ageism*, like sexism or racism, is a rigid, biased, and destructive belief system that impedes positive interactions between generations. Aging has become synonymous with illness, lack of control, loss of memory, and depression. Perhaps the most destructive belief is that the elderly inevitably become senile. "I must be getting old" or "Alzheimer's must be setting in" have become flip remarks in our daily language (Quinn & Tomita, 1986). Froma Walsh (1988, p. 311) writes:

> Old age. We dread becoming old almost as much as we dread living long enough to reach old age. The elderly in our society have been stereotyped and discussed as old-fashioned, rigid, senile, boring, useless and burdensome.

Social Isolation

Like other forms of domestic violence, social isolation is highly correlated with abuse of the elderly (Breckman & Adelman, 1988). Social isolation tends to feed into caregiver stress because fewer resources are available for a temporary rest. Research has consistently demonstrated that abuse tends to occur primarily in instances of isolation, and decreases as nonviolent observers are available to witness violent acts (Pillemer, 1986).

TREATMENT

Practitioners will be confronted with the reality of elder abuse through a number of different circumstances. Current studies suggest that slightly over 80% of cases are reported by individuals outside the abusive family system, such as hospital staff or employees at mental health agencies (Bookin & Dunkle, 1985; Powell & Berg, 1987). By contrast, elderly individuals rarely report abuse themselves. The most astonishing finding is the reporting rate of relatives or friends. Although relatives are aware of abuse inflicted on the elderly, in almost half of these cases, less than 20% of the relatives actually report the abuse (Powell & Berg, 1987). Many fear anger and retaliation from the perpetrator, the responsibility of having to take in the elderly individual themselves, and/or a bewilderment as to what to do to rectify the situation (Powell & Berg, 1987).

These statistics indicate that unless it is detected by social agencies, abuse of the elderly will continue to fester unnoticed. It is, therefore, the role of practitioners to attune themselves to the possibility of elder abuse in families already engaged in therapy. Families may have initially come to therapy to deal with teenage delinquency or marital problems and may either be ignorant that elder abuse is occurring or downplay these facts during therapy.

ASSESSMENT

Prior to any intervention strategies, a comprehensive assessment should provide as clear a picture as possible of the abuse inflicted and the role played by the perpetrator in the older person's daily life (Breckman & Adelman, 1988). Strong controversy exists around whether to interview the victim and perpetrator separately or together. Generally, separate interviews have been recommended, with the assumption that it encourages honest sharing and highlights inconsistencies (Quinn & Tomita, 1986). Although there are several benefits to a separate interview, numerous drawbacks accompany this strategy as well. The practitioner not only becomes a vessel for highly significant and possibly explosive information, but is restricted in using this pertinent information out of fear of shattering the fragile trust level of the clients. In addition, meaningful intervention strategies are generally possible only once painful experiences are discussed openly among family members. Finally, the information gained through individual interviews may be no more extensive or honest than if done conjointly.

In case the practitioner does decide that the interviews should be conducted separately, it is highly recommended that one immediately follow the other (Marin & Morycz, 1990). This will eliminate collusion or threats by the perpetrator. Although the abusers may initially resist an interview, they may be more forthcoming if the interviewer requests "help" and is sympathetic rather than judgmental and skeptical (Quinn & Tomita, 1986). For example, one may approach the suspected perpetrator by saying:

> "Your mother and I have been talking about ways in which I might be of help to her. Because you are so closely involved in her day-to-day care, I wouldn't want to make any plans without getting your description of what her needs are and what you think should be done to help her" (Marin & Morycz, 1990, p. 153).

Assessment Tools

Often, through a narrow field of vision, we ignore pertinent areas within the victim's and perpetrator's life and zoom in much too early on one isolatedroblem or relationship dynamic. The therapist needs to evaluate three major criteria: the individual characteristics of the victim and abuser, characteristics of the relationship between the victim and abuser, and social–cultural characteristics. The evaluation guideline suggested in Table 6.1 covers all of these areas in detail and provides examples of questions appropriate for each category. Although all example questions are directed toward the perpetrator, they can easily be adjusted to apply to the victim.

Besides a broad understanding of the individual, relational, and societal characteristics, it is essential to clearly outline the type and the severity of

TABLE 6.1 • Guidelines for Evaluation of Abuse

I. Individual Characteristics

   A. Caregiver Stress

      Example: "Obviously, taking care of an elderly parent is a tremendous responsibility. Where do you feel the strain the most?" or "Have you ever gotten so overwhelmed that you have felt like hitting your mother?"

      1. Caught in the middle
      2. Sleep deprivation and physical exhaustion
      3. Constant demands and criticism
      4. Growing resentment and guilt

   B. Caregiver Psychopathology

      Example: "In order to be of help to your Mom you and I need to get a sense of what has been tough for you in the past and how you have coped with stress. Do you consider yourself a normal drinker? Have you ever used alcohol to get over tough times?"

      1. Alcoholism/drug abuse
      2. Mental disability of caregiver
      3. Cognitive disability of caregiver
      4. A history of arrests
      5. Previous violence

   C. Caregiver Dependency

      Example: "It looks like all of your siblings have flown the nest. Can you give me an idea what still keeps you at home?" or"Money can be a touchy topic in many relationships. Can you explain to me how you and your Dad pay all the bills?"

      1. Financial dependence
      2. Length of time living with parent
      3. Length of time held current job
      4. Education level
      5. Maturity level
      6. Motivation level— actively engaged or passively withdrawn
      7. Appearance—self-care, self-image, and grooming

Continued

TABLE 6.1 • *Continued*

II. Relational Characteristics

  A. Intergenerational Abuse

    Example: "Most of us walk around with unfinished business with our parents. Even when they try to do their best, they have sure screwed things up for us at times. I wonder whether you remember those moments too?"

    1. Caregiver experienced abuse as a child
    2. Caregiver observed abusive behavior as child
    3. Attitudes toward abuse as means of control
    4. "Unfinished business" or resentment from past

  B. Role Adjustments

    Example: "It sure gets confusing. First parents are there to help us and then all of a sudden it all gets switched around. I wonder who in your family is most confused by that?"

    1. Unrealistic expectations of elderly
    2. Unrealistic expectation of caregiver
    3. Hierarchical layout (using Minuchin's diagram)
    4. Power balance
    5. Intimacy and love
    6. Self-esteem of elderly in current role
    7. Self-esteem of caregiver in current role

III. Social–Cultural Characteristics

  A. Ageism

    Example: "You are obviously much more of an expert on what its like living with an elderly parent than most people. What do you think, are all these things we hear about older people true or not?"

    1. Myths

      a. Old age starts with 65
      b. Old age is synonymous with senility
      c. Old age and illness are interchangeable
      d. Old people are all the same
      e. Old people are infantile
      f. Old people are depressing
      g. Old people are unproductive

  B. Social Isolation

    Example: "It is only logical that we can't meet all the needs of another person–especially when they are so needy. I wonder who you can turn to when you've just had it up to here?"

    1. Social network (letters, phone calls, visits, outings)
    2. Options for temporary time-out

      a. Other relatives—in house
      b. Other relatives—out of house
      c. Friends/neighbors
      d. Community resources

abuse inflicted on the elderly by the caregiver. Discussion of the abuse in concrete detail emphasizes that abuse toward an elderly parent cannot and should not be hushed up and desensitized through global, nonspecific language.

The practitioner needs to assess both the *severity* and the *frequency* of the abuse inflicted on the elderly person. For example, "I am a bit confused. I wonder if you can help me understand how your Dad got those bruises," or "I wonder what you do when your Dad just won't do what he is supposed to do?"

The following is a list of the types of abuse inflicted on the elderly:

- *Physical abuse*—beat, starve, slap, bruise, sexually molest, cut, burn, restrain physically, drug
- *Psychological abuse*—ridicule, manipulate, infantalize, frighten, humiliate, shame, call names
- *Financial abuse*—illegal exploitation of funds, excessive "gifts," multiple withdrawals, illegally signed checks
- *Active neglect*—violate basic rights such as freedom to speak, vote, practice religion, open own mail, use telephone, meet with friends
- *Passive neglect*—neglect because of incompetence or lack of knowledge by caregiver of how to care for the elderly

In addition to assessing abuse inflicted on the elderly victim, it is equally essential to evaluate the numerous strengths available in each individual, relationship, and surrounding family system. Questions that emphasize the intimacy and love between the generations, as well as the joys one can experience with an elderly parent, are equally important. For example, one may suggest, "Many grandchildren miss out on really knowing their grandparents. I guess your family is one of the lucky few who still keeps up this rich tradition." Another statement may be, "You know, with all the struggles this family is experiencing, I am just really aware of the tremendous love you seem to have for each other. I wonder if we can get through the rough stuff together so you can enjoy all the goodness you already have in your family?"

TREATMENT STRATEGIES

Intervention strategies vary drastically depending on the severity of the abuse, the risk factors involved, and the number of family members willing to participate in therapy. Much too often, a fourth factor outweighs the previously mentioned factors—namely, the willingness of the therapist to work in a family context rather than with an isolated victim or perpetrator. The current literature available on the treatment of elder abuse predominantly emphasizes an individual framework, with a few suggestions on group therapy. A therapist who is willing to work with the entire family or various subsystems is left stranded. Because of the dearth of intervention strategies available to therapists for conjoint therapy, the suggestions that follow have a strong emphasis on involving numerous family members.

Social Buffers Against Abuse

The top priority in the treatment of elder abuse is to prevent further abuse (Quinn & Tomita, 1986). Prior to working on abusive relationship dynamics, social buffers against further abuse through other family members, friends, neighbors, and community resources need to be explored.

Studies have repeatedly indicated that abused elders are more socially isolated than nonabused control groups (Breckman & Adelman, 1988; Wolf & Pillemer, 1989). Family members and concerned outsiders are able to moderate life stresses and reduce tension before they erupt into violence. Perpetrators of crime usually commit their offenses in private to reduce the likelihood of being caught. Finally, elderly persons inside a caring social network can find allies and thereby develop the strength to voice their plight themselves. This does not imply that social isolation is necessarily the cause of abuse (Wolf & Pillemer, 1989). On the contrary, causality may work in the opposite direction, in that perpetrators actually purposefully reduce social contact for the elderly. One victim explained, "He makes it hard for me to talk on the telephone. He mimics me while I'm talking. Sometimes I just throw the phone down" (Wolf & Pillemer, 1989, p. 79). The primary responsibility of a clinician, therefore, is to increase the social network as a buffer against further abuse prior to dealing with abusive dynamics between the perpetrator and the victim. The flow chart in Figure 6.1 provides a succinct graphic representation of various alternatives.

Practitioners should not be included in the social network because they function as temporary social network coordinators rather than as permanent resources acting as buffers to abuse. Nevertheless, a social case worker may need to be included in the system on a permanent basis to provide the necessary link between the family and community resources.

As a temporary social network coordinator, the therapist needs to deliberately include other family members in sessions. This may mean inviting family members currently living at the same residence, or coordinating an extended family session by including family members from other states. Often traveling costs or difficulties in scheduling restricts participation from essential family members. Creative means need to be employed to alleviate this gap in communication. For example, sessions can be videotaped and mailed to missing family members who are then able to provide additional information. A family session can make extensive use of the telephone by either making individual telephone contacts with missing family members or using a party line. Broadcasting telephone conversations through loudspeakers within a session allows all members to participate simultaneously. To

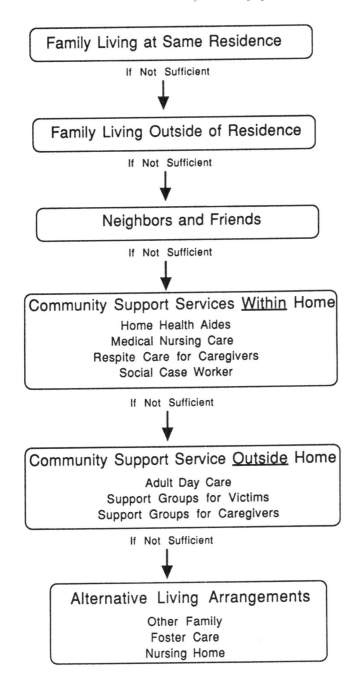

FIGURE 6.1   •   Expansion of Social Network

open up communication, the practitioner can encourage "family letters" by addressing everyone simultaneously through copies or personalized letters.

Finally, a social network can be increased through direct contact with concerned neighbors and friends, social agencies, home aides, or an elderly companion. Therapists should provide clients with pamphlets on available resources—senior companions, adult day care, home aides, or support groups (Marin & Morycz, 1990). Victims and perpetrators often experience shame and fear of public exposure to reach out and make necessary inquiries on their own. Practitioners often shy away from such mundane tasks like providing families with networking information; they would rather get "to the meat of things." Nevertheless, it is often these ordinary things that prove to be most helpful (Pierce & Trotta, 1986).

Family Therapy

The remainder of this chapter reviews three levels of intervention, beginning with the least severe abusive situations, and ending with the most violent and destructive circumstances. This three-stage framework has been summarized from Ferguson and Beck (1983) and includes primary prevention, secondary intervention, and finally, tertiary intervention. At the first level of abuse, or the primary intervention, the goal is to decrease the risk of abuse before it has even reached any significant proportion. In the secondary intervention the aim is to diagnose and interrupt abusive dynamics at an early stage to ensure prompt treatment. Finally, in the third stage of intervention, the primary goal is to reduce the level of abusive behavior, often through temporary or permanent removal of the victim from the dangerous living situation with the perpetrator. The focus here is mainly on the primary and secondary intervention strategies. Especially in these first two levels family therapists have the strongest leverage. The tertiary level, in which abuse has an outstanding history and separation between victim and perpetrator becomes necessary, social case workers may be of greater help.

Primary Intervention

Families who benefit most from primary intervention have experienced excessive stress, resentment, or confusion for a significant period of time. Family members find themselves struggling with an ever-mounting tension, which is dealt with either by denial or by short, vicious outbursts. Physical abuse is relatively rare, although emotional and psychological abuse may be escalating as family members attempt to deal with the tension. Therapy therefore focuses on decreasing caregiver stress, assisting in healthy role adjustments, providing education on the aging process, and creating a reward system (Ferguson & Beck, 1983).

Decreasing Caregiver Stress.   Although only a relatively small proportion of caregivers deliberately abuse their elderly parents exclusively due to excessive demands (Breckman & Adelman, 1988), expression of caregiver stress must serve as a warning signal, because it may indirectly affect other risk factors. Studies suggest that caregiver stress is not merely one global experience but can be divided into stress experienced because of instrumental tasks and expressive tasks (Steinmetz, 1988). *Instrumental tasks* include daily activities such as food preparation, transportation, grooming, and financial tasks. By contrast, tending to the emotional needs of the elderly, and experiencing incessant demands, and a lack of privacy are considered *expressive tasks*. Studies repeatedly demonstrate that expressive tasks are associated with much higher stress levels than are instrumental tasks (Steinmetz, 1988). In other words, the emotional work tends to be more stressful than the physical work.

In helping family members reduce the global stress level, individual stressors need to be clearly outlined. A therapist may choose to write down the various stressors on a blackboard during a session. This not only openly validates the client's experience, but may also reduce the global sense of helplessness. Stressors related to instrumental tasks are often based on excessive physical demands and can be reduced through coordination of family and community resources. An open discussion of male–female tasks within the family can be used to challenge the typical roles to allow for a more balanced distribution of the various responsibilities. In addition, periodic respite activities, such as dates or vacations, allow caregivers to build up their tolerance level. "Emergency breaks" can be implemented so a caregiver can spontaneously catch fresh air or relax under a shower while others temporarily take over responsibilities for short periods of time.

Stress related to expressive tasks is often based on an emotional overload. The clinician can assist family members to create greater personal space and privacy through rearranging their living area. Caregivers can be encouraged to attend support groups or even begin their own small group within their neighborhood. The practitioner can help the family set crisis guidelines (Steinmetz, 1988). A list of emergency numbers, names, and activities tacked up on the fridge can help reduce excessive anxiety. Often, families find themselves in the role of caretakers without even having concretely decided to take on this tremendous responsibility. A specific trial period for caregiving can be agreed on rather than the ominous "until death." A suggestion box in the family room may be helpful in allowing everyone to be assured that gripes and ideas will be remembered during family sessions.

Role Adjustment.   Rarely do family members take time to assess role changes, clarify expectations, and identify new functions (Ferguson & Beck, 1983). Whereas "role adjustment" becomes a necessity, "role reversal" often sabotages smooth family functioning (Walsh, 1988). Rather than frame the readjustment of care given and care received as "role reversal" or "generational inversion," the therapist may normalize the situation as a natural process in a life span. It is a rounding of a cycle rather than an unnatural, isolated freak event. Regardless of the degree of physical and emotional support given to an elderly parent, the adult child does not become the "parent" to the elderly "child" (Couper, 1989; Walsh, 1988) The caregiver's tendency to infantilize elderly parents is not only highly demeaning for the older person and frustrating for the caregiver, it also fosters even greater dependency than may actually be necessary (Quinn & Tomita, 1986; Walsh, 1988).

It is also highly myopic, in our technological society, to measure individual worth primarily through the single characteristic of physical and mental performance. Elders in numerous cultural and historical contexts have been treasured and respected simply for their old age, regardless of their current productivity. Children's books can become a helpful tool in providing positive impressions of the elderly. *Sachika Means Happiness* by Kimiko Sakai is a wonderful children's book, which shows a girl's frustration with her aging grandmother, that gradually changes to understanding of her grandmother's confusion (ages 4–8). *Nana Upstairs and Nana Downstairs* by Tomie DePaola is a charming picture book about a boy's relationship with his grandmother and great-grandmother, and death (ages 4–9).

After a reevaluation of structure, the family can begin to explicitly discuss expectations and responsibilities. Role conflicts often become apparent as one asks circular questions. A therapist could ask a child, "Daniel, I wonder what happens when Grandma needs to go to the bathroom and Mom is in the middle of washing dishes?" An exploration of who does what, when, and for whom provides a glimpse of the relationship dynamics between the various generations. Throughout the discussion of roles, responsibilities, and expectations, it is essential to make explicit the tendency for women to be the primary caregivers for the elderly (Brody, 1981; Cantor, 1983; Johnson, 1983; Stoller, 1983). A genogram is especially helpful in tracing the underlying expectations of men and women in the caregiver role of the elderly. Often, women consider their resentment as a unique problem experienced exclusively in their family (Luepnitz, 1988). Through a greater context of past generations, and education on the sexist arrangements of society, the entire family may begin to challenge their assumption "that this is just the way it is supposed to be."

Finally, the therapist helps the family strengthen its ability to perform the newly assigned roles (Ferguson & Beck, 1983). For example, an adolescent child may need some training in grooming the elderly person on a regular basis, or younger children may serve as messengers and fetchers for an elderly for fifteen-minute periods dispersed throughout the week. It is also essential for elderly persons to enhance their self-esteem and sense of worth (Ferguson & Beck, 1983) by having responsibilities in the family which they are capable of meeting. Storytelling or reading can become a routine bedtime ritual shared by young children and the elderly.

Education on the Aging Process. Old age brings with it major life transitions and tasks. Retirement, widowhood, grandparenthood, illness, and many losses require adaptational changes (Walsh, 1988). These late-life transitions directly interact with the changes taking place in the two younger generations. Regardless of the particular tasks required of each generation, families tend to shift together in either a movement of connecting and intimacy, or in one of autonomy and distancing (Combrick-Graham, 1985). Whereas nodal points—childbirth, weddings, and deaths—pull the three generations toward greater intimacy and connectiveness, adolescence, the forties reevaluation, and retirement tend to shift the three generations toward greater autonomy and distance. Lee Combrick-Graham (1985) captures these movements succinctly in her Family Life Spiral and her System Oscillation diagram, which may prove helpful as a teaching tool for families.

In the case of disabilities of an elderly person, the need for autonomy and distance in one generation may collide with the need for greater intimacy and nurturance in another. A family can experience tremendous frustration and resentment when the elderly person is in need of greater assistance when simultaneously, the adolescents and the middle generation are in the process of seeking greater autonomy and distance. Often a family can find great relief when their different needs are no longer perceived as wrong, uncaring, or overdemanding, but seen in the context of life-cycle stages. Gernerally, adjustments can be made with much less reactivity as each family member becomes more cognizant of their differences.

In addition to education on life-cycle transitions, the practitioner may encourage family members to acquire new skills in managing difficult behaviors in elders suffering with chronic illness. Although nurses and physicians are a tremendous resource in explaining diagnoses and potential medical interventions, many clients shy away from deliberately seeking out these professionals in our impersonal health-care system (Ansello, King, & Taler, 1986). Often, gently empowering a client gives them permission to make demands on their physician's time. Similarly, additional information about prescription drugs and over-the-counter medications can reveal previously ignored side effects. Knowledge of nutrition, special diets, and drug–food interactions can lead to greater independence for the elderly person.

Finally, education needs to incorporate an open discussion on death and dying. The five stages of dying suggested by Küebler-Ross (1969) provide a wonderful framework, which lends words to an array of highly charged emotions. The stages are denial, anger, bargaining, depression, and finally acceptance. This process of letting go is intuitively familiar to even small children. A two-year-old may experience denial at the disappearance of a favorite toy, similar to that of an elderly individual on losing excellent eyesight. Temper tantrums in children are not very far removed from expressions of anger by adults. Bargaining with Mom or a higher power both place hope on an outside omnipotent force. Depression or sadness sets in with the realization of the inevitable. Gradually, acceptance of one's loss of either a favorite toy or one's eyesight allows for peace. Numerous excellent books have been written on this topic and can easily be found at public libraries. *Fall of Freddie the Leaf* by Leo Buscaglia is a story for all ages about life and death through the changing seasons. *Annie and the Old One* by Miska Miles is a beautifully illustrated book about a Navajo girl and her dying grandmother (ages 6–12).

Create a Reward System.   Several authors suggest that a balancing of rewards and costs is essential to maintaining satisfactory relationships (Gelles, 1984). Exchange theory basically suggests that most, if not all, interactions are guided in pursuit of rewards and an avoidance of costs or punishments (Anetzberger, 1987). Reward comes in numerous forms—praise, love, helping behavior, or even monetary gain. As the cost of the relationship grows and the rewards diminish, the caregiver may turn to abusive behavior to balance the perceived unfairness.

Elders may actually shy away from verbally acknowledging the tremendous sacrifices a caregiver makes in their daily life because of shame. Some elderly parents may be unable to express appreciation due to lack of full mental functioning, thereby perpetuating the great imbalance of cost and reward. Other family members tend to ignore the feats of caregivers. Whereas adult children, generally adult sons, who are exempt from the daily stress of caregiving, are praised for the slightest contribution, actual caregivers, generally women, receive the least credit and are often blamed the most (Quinn & Tomita, 1986). Our society at large does not reward caregivers for their enormous sacrifices. Families caring for an elderly parent do not receive any special allowances or direct reimbursements even though they are actually saving the government money. In fact, these families are penalized by the government by a reduction in Social Security insurance benefits (Pierce & Trotta, 1986). Paradoxically, although society recognizes mothers, fathers, secretaries, and bosses on special holidays, caregivers of the elderly are ignored.

For the therapist to balance this discrepancy in the reward system, numerous avenues can be explored. An open discussion of rewards and costs within the family system can be introduced. Initially, the family may shy away from an explicit expression of costs and resentments because of deeply ingrained taboos. Nevertheless, brainstorming of rewards, costs, and unexpressed wishes can become a lively and fun discussion with the whole family through the use of play-tokens or a blackboard. To give homage to the various caregivers of the family, the therapist can help the family create rituals such as special dinners, cards, or small presents. Finally, the therapist needs to help the elderly parent explore feelings of guilt associated with being dependent, which ultimately inhibit them from expressing appreciation. A word of thanks can often carry more weight than any deed or boxed present.

Secondary Intervention

Secondary intervention becomes a necessity when physical, psychological, emotional, and financial abuse and neglect have already occurred for an extended period of time. Violence by the caregiver is less a product of a temporary overload or stress level, and is instead more ingrained in the family system as a legitimate method of control. The goal at this stage of therapy is to decrease caregiver dependency, teach nonviolent coping behaviors, and work through intergenerational abuse issues.

Decrease Caregiver Dependency. Numerous studies indicate that caregivers dependent on their elderly parents, either financially or emotionally, have a higher tendency to abuse them than do independent caregivers (Pillemer & Finkelhor, 1989; Suitor & Pillemer, 1988; Wolf et al., 1984). Finkelhor (1983) suggests that adult children who are dependent on their elderly parents may abuse them in an attempt to compensate for their perceived lack of power. This feeling of inadequacy is fueled by society's strong expectation that dictates grown children are supposed to be independent from their parents (Pillemer & Suitor, 1990). The dependent caregivers may therefore abuse their elderly parent to regulate their sense of powerlessness.

Simultaneously, elderly victims may be equally invested in perpetuating strong dependence of their adult child for a number of reasons. An elderly person may fear abandonment and rejection and consider the inflicted abuse as a lesser of two evils. After all, a dependent caregiver can not walk away. A second alternative is that the elderly victim gains a sense of purpose in life by continuing to be the support source for their dependent adult child. Finally, greater dependence may be perceived as love and devotion, whereas independence may threaten a highly enmeshed relationship.

Because of the numerous functions this dependency serves both the victim and the perpetrator, the practitioner must invest significant energy to understand these dynamics. In the event the elderly person fears abandonment, the practitioner needs to balance greater independence in the caregiver with more functional joint activities between the adult child and the parent. When dependency is a function of the parent's purpose in life, the practitioner can help the elderly victim increase their social network in order to reduce the limited focus on a dependent child. Finally, when dependency is due to low functioning of the adult child, the practitioner can search for talents and special skills and attempt to empower the dependent adult child to seek additional skill training.

Working through Intergenerational Abuse Issues. Experiencing abuse by loved ones, either directly or through observation, leaves significant imprints. Regardless of whether abuse patterns are perpetuated or discontinued in any particular family, past abuse lingers, and may periodically surface like a wave of unexpected stench, although it may never be directly acknowledged. Similar to the experience of many Germans following the Holocaust, or of Americans following Vietnam, shame rests deep within a population regardless of direct participation in an atrocious act. Similarly, the impact of violence between loved ones rarely stops with direct participation. Often, the use of a genogram can trace abuse patterns along the extended family tree. The taboo of open discussion of the stench is gently challenged. Therefore, uncovering past abuse cycles serves all families, regardless of whether abuse is still a current practice in a family or not. Current abusers are able to see themselves in a larger context and to possibly find a mission in ending the family legacy. In addition, both populations may connect with their shame and openly grieve the wrongs committed in their family.

Teaching Nonviolent Coping Behaviors.   Abuse is often based on a hierarchical imbalance, in which the hierarchically superior individual forces punitive control on the person in the inferior position. To break this abuse cycle, it is essential that the therapist does not fall into the same behavior patterns under the guise of treatment. For example, a therapist may misuse her or his power to force an abusive individual to sign a "nonviolence pledge," and threaten termination for noncompliance. Indirectly, the therapist is modeling that coercive control is acceptable "in certain instances." A change from punitive control to self-care and personal integrity is necessary. Rather than demanding a signature on a completed nonviolent document, the client needs to own their agreements, including personalized goals and consequences. It becomes the abuser's project to define and personalize their agreement. The therapist becomes the coach, educator, and sounding board.

If abusive behavior persists and the client demonstrates no motivation to change, the therapist needs to encourage police involvement, legal actions, and temporary or permanent removal of the abuser or victim. Even though these actions appear to mirror the abusive cycle of punitive control within a hierarchically imbalanced relationship, a reframe of self-care and personal integrity of the abuse victim and therapist can drastically change the meaning of the intervention. A call to the police, in other words, does not "punish" another, but protects one's personal space.

Other behavior changes need to follow the same reframe of personalized project and self-care. Alternatives to violence—time-out, relaxation procedures, and physical exertion—can be suggested by the therapist but never forced on the client. Excessive talking or lecturing by the therapist is often a sure sign of a hierarchical imbalance and power control.

Tertiary Intervention
Within tertiary intervention, the primary goal is to reduce and finally eliminate the abusive behavior through drastic measures such as periodic visits by agency employees, legal devices, and possible police intervention. At this

stage, temporary or permanent removal of the victim from the offender may prove to be the only viable alternative.

Psychopathology of the Caregiver.   Caregivers suffering from psychopathology tend to be the most difficult clients to work with (Anetzberger, 1987). Alcohol and drug abusers often have a long history of violent and unpredictable outbursts. They may deny or minimize their abusive behaviors or justify their actions by explaining that the elders got "what they deserved" (Bookin & Dunkle, 1985; Quinn & Tomita, 1986). The remainder of this chapter discusses the status of mandatory reporting laws, legal devices, and police interventions available to abused elders.

Mandatory Reporting Laws.   Although most states have passed mandatory reporting laws for elder abuse within the last five years, the definition of abuse, obligated reporters, and the department responsible for investigation vary widely from state to state. Thobaben (1989) provides extensive information on the different reporting laws within the various states in the United States. In addition, mandatory reporting laws continue to be highly controversial for numerous reasons (Crystal, 1986; Faulkner, 1982; Thobaben, 1989).

Nevertheless, states with and without mandatory reporting laws tend to have one thing in common: assistance to elderly victims continues to be scarce. Simply reporting and verifying abuse does not imply automatic aid to elderly victims (Wolf & Pillemer, 1989). Because of the lack of a comprehensive national policy regarding elder abuse, states and communities have had to rely on their own resources. Various models have been implemented and tested, such as the Syracuse, New York, "Service Coordination" model and the Massachusetts "Service Brokerage" model.

The two major characteristics of the Syracuse Service Coordination Model are an attempt to coordinate already existing services and the use of specially trained aides (Wolf & Pillemer, 1989). Follow-up studies have verified that the trained aides, who periodically visit abused elders and their families, significantly reduce elder abuse (Wolf & Pillemer, 1989). The friendly visits include socialization, advocacy for both the victim and the perpetrator, and assistance with household tasks. One aide noted, "We don't think of ourselves as counselors, but friends who have information about services and some knowledge to share" (Wolf & Pillemer, 1989, p. 118). Another aide reported, "At the start, we went in primarily as an advocate for the victim. Now, we kind of ride the fence on a lot of cases. You're an advocate for the relatives, as well as the elderly" (Wolf & Pillemer, 1989, p. 118).

The Massachusetts Service Brokerage Model relies primarily on "a large multiservice agency that provides nonmedical home care services to persons over 60" (Wolf & Pillemer, 1989, p. 105). Homemaker services, home-delivered meals, legal services, and counseling are immediately available to eligible victims. Homemaker services monitor abuse, relieve stress, and provide cleaning help. They are often authorized to work up to four hours a day, five days a week. Generally, victimized elders become clients of the agency receiving continuous abuse monitoring, crisis intervention, and long-term support services.

In sum, mandatory laws will hopefully increase awareness of this social problem on a national level, allow investigation in cases of suspicion, and assist weak and frightened victims. Nevertheless, resources continue to be scarce and insufficient. Buffers against abuse toward the elderly must therefore come from more intrusive intervention strategies such as the legal devices available to the elderly.

Legal Devices.   Especially in cases of severe physical abuse and financial exploitation, legal protection becomes necessary. The practitioner needs to have sufficient knowledge of various legal devices and support when legal or police assistance is necessary. A guiding rule for the practitioner when introducing legal or police force is to use the least restrictive option to allow the greatest personal freedom and independence in the life of the victim (Quinn & Tomita, 1986). A sense of control over personal decisions directly influences life-satisfaction, self-worth, and purpose in life. The following paragraphs review numerous legal devices available to an elderly victim, beginning with the least restrictive measures and progressing to more involved interventions.

Direct deposit allows the elderly person to have all their checks deposited directly to a bank, credit union, or savings and loan account (Quinn & Tomita, 1986). The advantage of this arrangement is that checks cannot be stolen, forged, misplaced, or destroyed by perpetrators. A *representative payee* is a relative, friend, or agency appointed by the Social Security Administration to collect checks for an elderly person in order to pay their bills (Quinn & Tomita, 1986). Annual reports are usually required in order to inhibit fraud. *Trusts* provide financial management to the elderly by a trust department at a bank. Because trust officers do not make house visits, personal and medical needs are not supervised under this option.

Joint tenancy allows two people to share equal rights to property, accounts or assets (Quinn & Tomita, 1986). A will is therefore not required in the event of the death of either one of the individuals. Abuse of joint tenancy can occur if an elderly person is threatened or bribed into this legal agreement. A *power of attorney* can be either a temporary or a permanent authorization of one or more persons to make legal and/or medical decisions for the elderly individual (Quinn & Tomita, 1986). Regardless of the name, no lawyer is required, and the necessary legal forms are available in most stationary stores. There is no supervision over powers of attorney, and unless criminal charges are filed, investigations do not occur. Very specific terms of agreement limit the scope of possible abuse.

Conservatorship and guardianships are too often the first choice due either to a lack of knowledge of alternatives or to convenience (Quinn & Tomita, 1986). Courts tend to grant conservatorship simply because of old age, or medical or psychiatric diagnoses, regardless of the elderly person's level of functioning. Nevertheless, revisions are in the process in many states due to the abuse of this legal document.

Protection orders are granted by a judge and mandate that the abuser make no contact with the victim (Quinn & Tomita, 1986). An elderly person can immediately request a order of protection regardless of actual physical harm (i.e., threats and fear for one's safety provide grounds for a protection order). Finally, *criminal charges* can be brought against a perpetrator by an elderly victim (Quinn & Tomita, 1986). Once the charges have been pressed, the elderly person loses "control" of the case by placing it in the hands of the prosecutor. This can be a highly stressful route, because "the victim must withstand multiple delays in the criminal proceedings, be willing to be interviewed by both the prosecutor and the attorney for the defense, be consistent in telling her story, and not be afraid that the abuser, who sometimes may be out of jail on bail, will torment her" (Quinn & Tomita, 1986, p. 221).

Often when considering involvement of the police or the court, the elderly victim fears public exposure and feels tremendous shame for having raised a child who abuses (Quinn & Tomita, 1986). Victims fear that by testifying in court against their abusers, they are ultimately responsible for the imprisonment of their own children (Quinn & Tomita, 1986). Although victims show a genuine interest in exploring interventions, many feel "caught between a rock and a hard place." They may find their present situation increasingly unacceptable, yet available alternatives seem equally unpleasant (Breckman & Adelman, 1988). Ultimately, elders may turn inward through self-blame, low self-esteem, and bewilderment in order to justify a life-threatening situation.

CONCLUSIONS

Abuse of the elderly continues to be ignored in all levels of society, whether within the family, the community, or the nation. Research continues to be limited, funds are scarce, and social awareness is barely significant. Therefore, marriage and family therapists need to make a continuous effort to battle the ignorance and apathy connected to this reality. Within the initial phone contact and especially throughout assessment, the therapist needs to inquire about the presence of an elderly person. Regardless of possible abuse, an elderly person deserves the respect and consideration to be acknowledged and discussed. After all, when all pictures in our offices portray youth and beginnings, we are modeling ignorance. When even house pets overshadow the presence of the elderly within a session, we are encouraging disrespect.

When we continuously channel the discussion away from the last life-cycle stage, we are supporting blindness.

The therapist, needs to answer the same questions previously posed to clients: "Since you are an expert, what do you think? Does old age start at 65? Are old people infantile, depressing, unproductive and all the same?" Or, is it possible that old age has a rich message that has been lost in our society of production, technology, and high speed? Maybe it is not old age that needs to be pitied, but us, who have forgotten to listen to its messages.

REFERENCES

Achenbaum, W. A. (1983). *Shades of gray: Old age, American values and federal policies since 1920.* Boston: Little, Brown.

Anetzberger, G. J. (1987). *The etiology of elder abuse by adult offspring.* Springfield, IL: Charles C Thomas.

Ansello, E., King, N. R., & Taler, G. (1986). The environmental press model: A theoretical framework for intervention in elder abuse. In K. A. Pillemer & R. S. Wolf (Eds), *Elder abuse: Conflict in the family.* Dover, MA: Auburn House.

Block, M. R. (1983). Special problems and vulnerability of elderly women. In J. Kosberg (Ed.), *Abuse and maltreatment of the elderly: Causes and interventions.* Littleton, MA: John Wright.

Bookin, D. & Dunkle, R. (1985). Elder abuse: Issues for the practitioner. *Social Casework, 66* (January), 3–12.

Breckman, R. S. & Adelman, R. D. (1988). *Strategies for helping victims of elder mistreatment.* Beverly Hills: Sage.

Brody, E. M. (1981). Women in the middle and family help to older people. *The Gerontologist, 21,* 471–480.

Cantor, M. H. (1983). Strain among caregivers: A study of experience in the United States. *The Gerontologist, 23,* 597–604.

Combrick-Graham, L. (1985). The developmental model for family systems. *Family Process, 24*(2), 139–150.

Couper, D. P. (1989). *Aging and our families.* New York: Human Science Press.

Crystal, S. (1986). Social policy and elder abuse: In K. A. Pillemer & R. S. Wolf (Eds.), *Elder abuse: Conflict in the family.* Dover, MA: Auburn House.

Douglass, R. L. & Hickey, T. (1983). Domestic neglect and abuse of the elderly: Research findings and systems perspective for service delivery planning. In J. I. Kosberg (Ed.), *Abuse and maltreatment of the elderly: Cause and interventions.* Littleton, MA: John Wright.

Faulkner, L. R. (1982). Mandating the reporting of suspected cases of elder abuse: An inappropriate ineffective, and ageist response to the abuse of older adults. *Family Law Quarterly, 16,* 69–91.

Ferguson, D. & Beck, C. (1983). H.A.L.F. A tool to assess elder abuse within the family. *Geriatric Nursing, 4*(5), 301–304.

Finkelhor, D. (1983). Common features of family abuse. In D. Finkelhor, R. J. Gelles, G. T. Hotaling & M. A. Straus (Eds.). *The dark side of families: Current family violence research.* Beverly Hills: Sage.

Gelles, R. J. (1984). An exchange/social control theory. In D. Finkelhor, et al. (Eds.), *The dark side of families: Current family violence research.* Beverly Hills: Sage.

George, L. K. (1986). Caregiver burden: Conflict between norms of reciprocity and solidarity. In K. A. Pillemer & R. S. Wolf (Eds.), *Elder abuse: Conflict in the family.* Dover, MA: Auburn House.

Gray Panthers of Austin (1983). *A survey of abuse of the elderly in Texas.* Austin: Gray Panthers of Austin.

Hardin, E. & Schlater, T. (1987). Dynamics of parental abuse. *Journal of the National Medical Association, 76*(6), 674–676.

Holmes, S. A. (1981). A holistic approach to the treatment of violent families. *Social Casework, 62,* 594–600.

Horowitz, A. (1985). Sons and daughters as caregivers to older parents: Differences in role performance and consequences. *The Gerontologist, 25,* 612–617.

Hudson, M. R. (1986). Elder mistreatment: Current research. In K.A. Pillemer & R. S. Wolf (Eds.), *Elder abuse: Conflict in the family.* Dover, MA: Auburn House.

Johnson, C. L. (1983). Dyadic family relations and social support. *The Gerontologist, 23,* 377–383.

Kending, H. L. & Rowland, D. T. (1983). Family support of the Australian aged: A comparison with the United States. *The Gerontologist, 23,* 643–649.

Kosberg, J. I. (1988). Preventing elder abuse: Identification of high risk factors prior to placement decisions. *The Gerontologist, 28,* 43–50.

Küebler-Ross, E. (1969). *On death and dying.* New York: Macmillan.

Luepnitz, D. A. (1988). *The family interpreted: Feminist theory in clinical practice.* New York: Basic Books.

Marin, R. S. & Morycz, R. K. (1990). Victims and elder abuse. In R. T. Ammerman & M. Hersen (Eds.), *Treatment of family violence.* New York: John Wiley.

Marshall, V. W. & Rosenthal, C. J. (1982). Parental death: A life course maker. *Generations, 61,* 30–31, 39.

Pierce, R. L. & Trotta, R. (1986). Abused parents: A hidden family problem. *Journal of Family Violence, 1*(1), 99–110.

Pillemer, K. A. (1985). The dangers of dependence: New findings on domestic violence against the elderly. *Social Problems, 33,* 146–158.

Pillemer, K. A. (1986). Risk factors in elder abuse: Results from a case-control study. In K. A. Pillemer & R. S. Wolf. *Elder abuse: Conflict in the family.* Dover, MA: Auburn House.

Pillemer, K. & Finkelhor, D. (1988). The prevalence of elder abuse: random sample survey. *The Gerontologist, 28*(1), 51–57.

Pillemer, K. & Finkelhor, D. (1989). Causes of elder abuse: Caregiver stress versus problem relatives. *American Journal of Orthopsychiatry, 59*(2), 179–187.

Pillemer, K. A. & Suitor, J. J. (1990). Prevention of elder abuse. In R. T. Ammerman & M. Hersen (Eds.), *Treatment of family violence.* New York: John Wiley.

Powell, S. & Berg, R. (1987). When the elderly are abused: Characteristics and intervention. *Educational Gerontology, 13,* 71-83.

Quinn, M. J. (1990). Elder abuse and neglect: Treatment issues. In S. M. Smith, M. B. Williams, & K. Rosen (Eds.), *Violence hits home: Comparative treatment approaches to domestic violence.* New York: Springer.

Quinn, M. J. & Tomita, S. K. (1986). *Elder abuse and neglect: Causes, diagnosis and intervention strategies.* New York: Springer.

Rathbone-McCuan, E. & Goodstein, R. (1985). Elder abuse: Clinical considerations. *Psychiatric Annals, 15*(5), 331–339.

Schlesinger, B. & Schlesinger, R. (1988). *Abuse of the elderly.* Toronto: University of Toronto Press.

Steinmetz, S. (1988). Elder abuse by family caregivers: Process and intervention strategies. Special issue: Coping and victimization. *Contemporary Family Therapy: An International Journal, 10*(4), 256–271.

Steinmetz, S. & Amsden, D. (1983). Dependency, family stress and abuse. In T. Brubaker (Ed.), *Family relationships in later life.* Beverly Hills: Sage.

Stoller, E. P. (1983). Parental caregiving by adult children. *Journal of Marriage and the Family, 45,* 851–858.

Straus, M. A. (1988). *Abuse and victimization across the lifespan.* Baltimore: The John Hopkins University Press.

Suitor, J. J. & Pillemer, K. (1988). Explaining conflict when adult children and elderly parents live together. *Journal of Marriage and the Family, 50,* 1037–1047.

Thobaben, M. (1989). State elder/adult abuse and protection laws. In R. Filinson & S. Ingman (Eds.), *Elder abuse: Practice and policy.* New York: Human Science Press.

Walsh, F. (1988). The family in later life. In B. Carter & M. McGoldrick (Eds.), *The changing family life cycle.* New York: Gardner Press.

Williams, O. J. & Griffin, L (1991). Elder abuse in the black family. In R. L. Hampton (Ed.), *Black family violence.* Lexington, MA: Lexington Books.

Wolf, R. S., Godkin, M. A., & Pillemer, K. A. (1984). *Elder abuse and neglect: Final report from three model projects.* Worcester, MA: University of Massachusetts Medical Center, University Center on Aging.

Wolf, R. S. & Pillemer, K. A. (1989). *Helping elderly victims.* New York: Columbia University Press.

7

ADULT SURVIVORS OF CHILDHOOD PHYSICAL ABUSE

KIM L. SUMNER

I hate it when I get angry and spank my children too hard. I feel awful when I see the bruises made by my own hand. I feel like some kind of monster. But what would you expect? I have scars all over my legs that my father made with an extension cord. At least I don't do that to my children! (Elliot & Tanner, 1988, p. 3)

—MARY, MOTHER OF THREE

...I lived in some kind of a crazy house. I remember I used to do this thing, I used to pinch myself because I would think, well, maybe this is a nightmare or maybe I am really dead. So if I feel something that must mean I am alive... I remember feeling really angry and really alone. I always felt very alone, very helpless. (Miller, Downs, & Testa, 1990)

—VOICE OF AN ALCOHOLIC WOMAN ABUSED IN CHILD AND TEEN YEARS

These children resemble cases of "shell-shock" in adult[hood]. They display a profound blunting of all the external manifestations of inner life.... It appears not so much that their inner life is distorted or idiosyncratic, but rather that it has been completely suspended. (Inglis, 1978, p. 83)

—VOICE OF A CLINICIAN

These passages lend the reader a vantage point to the deeply ingrained memories and effects of childhood violence. Mary (the mother quoted), who was embroiled in a well-learned pattern of abuse in her family of origin, finds it very difficult to break the cycle of abuse even with her own children. The intergenerational transmission of violence is but one of many possible long-term outcomes of childhood physical abuse. Other effects of childhood physical abuse have been appearing in the literature in the last decade, and therapists are realizing a need for therapeutic guidelines for dealing with the varied effects of growing up in a violent home. What other effects of childhood physical abuse might a clinician observe, and how can the clinician help someone experiencing problems as a result of childhood physical abuse?

DEFINING ABUSE

Before accurately assessing the scope of the problem of adults abused as children or devising assessment and treatment strategies, it is necessary to have some consensus on what consititutes abuse. Many forms of physical punishment (i.e., spanking, slapping) are accepted culturally and considered to be appropriate means of disciplining children (Gelles & Straus, 1988). Should these tactics be considered abusive? Murray Straus and Richard Gelles have studied physical abuse in families extensively and have developed definitions of abuse that will be used throughout this chapter. In the 1975 and 1985 National Family Violence Survey and Resurvey (Straus & Gelles, 1987; Straus, Gelles, & Steinmetz, 1980), they differentiate the type of abuse by its severity, as follows: *violence* refers to"an act carried out with the intention, or perceived intention, of causing physical pain or injury to another person" (Straus & Gelles, 1988, p. 15). Within this definition, slapping and spanking constitute acts of violence, even though these practices are culturally accepted means of disciplining children. *Severe violence* includes hitting the child with an object such as a belt or stick. *Very severe violence* includes throwing something at the child; pushing, grabbing, or shoving the child; beating up the child; burning or scalding the child; threatening the child with a knife or gun; and using a knife or gun on the child (Straus & Gelles, 1988).

SCOPE OF THE PROBLEM

An estimated number of adults currently living who experienced physical abuse as children can be ascertained by examining data from the 1975 and 1985 National Family Violence Survey and Resurvey (Straus & Gelles, 1987; Straus et al., 1980). Based on the 1985 Resurvey data, approximately 2.3% of children under the age of seventeen, or 1.5 million children, currently experience very severe violence, and 11%, or 6.9 million children, currently experience severe violence at the hands of their parents or caregivers (Straus & Gelles, 1988). Abuse at the hands of siblings is even more prevalent. Approximately 80%, or 50.4 million children under the age of seventeen, currently experience some form of violence at the hands of their child siblings. Of these, approximately 53%, or 33.3 million children, suffer severe abuse at their siblings' hands (Straus & Gelles, 1988).

One can extrapolate from the Straus and Gelles data from the 1975 survey and 1990 U.S. Census information to obtain a conservative estimate of 25.86 million adults, or 14 out of 100, at least seriously physically abused by parents or caregivers as children.* Of course, this number does not include those who were abused by siblings. For the clinician, then, it routinely becomes necessary during assessment to inquire into each client's history of physical abuse in his or her family of origin (Carmen, Rieker, & Mills, 1984).

CONSEQUENCES OF THE PROBLEM

Clients often do not identify themselves as having been abused, and they may not recognize various symptoms associated with past abuse. Therefore, it becomes necessary for the clinician to know what to look for in clients struggling with the lasting effects of abuse.

Factors Influencing Consequences

The degree to which an individual is negatively affected by childhood abuse varies from person to person depending on a number of factors such as the severity of the abuse (Egeland, Jacobvitz, & Papatola, 1987; Herrenkohl, Herrenkohl, & Toedler, 1983), the resiliency of the individual (Mrazek & Mrazek, 1987), and the existence of other mitigating or protective factors (Werner & Smith, 1982; Widom, 1988).

Severity of Abuse
Herrenkohl and colleagues (1983) provide empirical evidence that the more severe the abuse in the family of origin, the more likely a child is to grow up to be an abuser and to use more severe forms of abuse. They hypothesize that this cycle of abuse is perpetuated by parents having an inner deficit in their ability to nurture their children. As a result, the child feels rejected and receives little nurturance. Without the experience of receiving nurturance, the child turned adult will sustain an impoverished ability to provide nurturance, thus making them more likely to physically abuse their children.

Resilience
Resilience factors can aid in coping with abuse (Mrazek & Mrazek, 1987). Resilience may be described as "influences that modify, ameliorate, or alter a

---

*These figures were derived by multiplying the Straus and Gelles 1975 severe violence rates by 1990 U.S. Census figures on the number of adults (persons over the age of eighteen) currently living in the United States (U.S. Department of Commerce, 1990). Data from 1975 rather than 1985 data were used since those children studied in 1975 are currently adults (or are becoming adults). Thus, a figure of 184.71 million adults was obtained by subtracting the number of children (64 million) from the total number of people living in the United States—248.71). This figure was then multiplied by .14 and .80, for parent-to-child and sibling-to-sibling violence, respectively, yielding the prevalence rates cited above.

person's response to some environmental hazard" (Rutter, 1985, as cited in Mrazek & Mrazek, 1987, p. 359), through various personal characteristics and skills. Nevertheless, strategies and defenses that are functional for a child at one time may not be functional at a later time. Thus, for some survivors, these resiliency factors, while helpful in childhood, become troublesome symptoms if continued into adulthood (Rosenthal, 1988). Of course, many survivors' coping strategies do not become problematic in adulthood; nonetheless, the clinician can be maximally useful if she or he understands the possible dysfunctional patterns arising from once-functional coping strategies. Specific examples of such coping strategies are reviewed in the assessment section of this chapter.

Protective Factors

Like resilience factors, protective factors serve to lessen the blow (*pun intended*) of physical abuse; however, these factors are external to the child. They are environmental circumstances that buffer the child from some of the effects of violence. These protective factors include being in an upper socioeconomic strata (SES); having well-educated parents; having little or no family pathology in one's background; having a supportive family milieu (unfortunately, this is unlikely to exist in an abusive household); having access to good health, education, and social welfare services; having additional caregivers besides the primary caregiver; and having relatives or neighbors available to provide social support (Werner & Smith, 1982). It should be noted that this does not mean that abuse does not occur in upper SES families, or that education per se is a vaccine against violence. Rather, many of these factors are related to being socially well-connected and having various stress-reduction outlets available, versus experiencing social isolation and a high level of stress.

Consequences for the Individual System

Long-Term Emotional Effects of Abuse

In later life, adults who were abused as children may struggle with poor self-esteem, identity problems, a reduction in coping skills, and depression (Steele, 1986; Trimpey, 1989). Poor self-esteem arises perhaps from learning that inner feelings and desires are unimportant compared with those of the abusers. Identity problems are incurred by learning not to pay attention to one's own feelings and to suppress self-initiative, thus inhibiting self-direction and self-definition. The clinician may observe a reduction in coping skills that leaves the client vulnerable and likely to function poorly under stress. Adults abused as children also experience depression at a higher rate than do those who were not abused (Bryer, Miller, Nelson, & Krol, 1986; Steele, 1986).

Distrust of others and hypervigilance are additional long-term psychological effects of childhood physical abuse (Steele, 1986). Because the child's caregiver most likely responded to the child inconsistently, the child has no sense of an internal world reality. She or he must always look for external cues as to what will occur in the environment. As a result, the child grows to distrust inner wisdom, constantly looking to the outside for such guidance. Such a moment-to-moment existence precludes the development of a strong ego and the ability to look to the future, fostering hypervigilance and distrust. As one might expect, intimacy and bonding suffer in adulthood.

Authors have also noticed that some abuse survivors' use of dissociation accompanied occasionally by panic attacks and intrusive thoughts comprises the experience of Post-Traumatic Stress Disorder (PTSD) subsequent to victimization in childhood (Cornell & Olio, 1991; McCormack, Burgess, & Hartman, 1988). Anger, guilt, and shame are also commonly experienced by adults abused as children (McCann, Sakheim, & Abrahamson, 1988).

Long-Term Behavioral Effects of Abuse and Sex Differences

These effects include increased social withdrawal (Gelles & Straus, 1988) and increases in aggressive and antisocial behavior (Gelles & Straus, 1988; Kroll, Stock, & James, 1985; McCord, 1983, 1988; Singer, 1986; Widom, 1989a). There is much evidence to warrant the conclusion that physical abuse in childhood affects men and women differently. Conflict resolution skills may be deficient (Burnett & Daniels, 1985), with men tending to use physical aggression more readily than verbal skills to solve a problem (Brown, 1982; Pollock, Briere, Schneider, Knop, Mednick, & Goodwin, 1990). Carmen, Rieker, and Mills (1984) observe that men who have been abused tend to turn their anger outward, as evidenced by the increased criminality, physical aggression, and poor conflict resolution skills discussed previously. They may do so as a defense against feelings of helplessness and vulnerability.

Women, on the other hand, are more likely to turn anger inward toward themselves in the form of substance abuse and self-destructive behavior (Carmen et al., 1984; Cohen & Densen-Gerber, 1982; Covington, 1983; McCord, 1983; Miller et al., 1990). Covington (1983) found that alcoholic women are more likely than nonalcoholic women to report having been physically abused during childhood. Downs, Miller, and Gondoli (1987) confirm this correlation with their findings that alcoholic women are more likely to have experienced moderate and severe parental violence, compared with a random sample of women. There appears to be a connection between violence and negative emotions toward the self that may set the stage for substance use as a coping or escape mechanism (Miller et al., 1990; Oates, Forrest, & Peacock, 1985).

There is also some evidence to suggest that, for women, having been abused in childhood is correlated with revictimization by a partner in adulthood (Downs, Miller, Testa, & Panek, 1990; Lewis, 1987; Marshall & Rose,

1988; McCann et al., 1988). Although this is not by any means a definite outcome for those who have been abused, the possibility exists that an adult abused as a child develops expectations that she will not be able to protect herself from others, and that others will exploit or abuse her, thus paving the way for revictimization in adulthood.

Carmen et al. (1984) hypothesize that both abused men and abused women experience anger and damage to their self-image. The authors conclude: "Patterns of sex role socialization obviously shape the differential responses to abuse of males and females" (Carmen et al., 1984, p. 582).

Consequences for the Family/Interpersonal Relationship Systems

Attachment Disorders

People who were physically abused as children experience attachment disorders at a higher rate than do those who were not abused (Steele, 1986). Attachment disorders arise because of an inhibited ability to respond empathically. Therefore, establishing and maintaining an intimate relationship is often difficult for adults who were physically abused as children; they have great difficulty trusting others and allowing themselves to experience affect without dissociation (Cornell & Olio, 1991; McCann et al., 1988). The clinician may recognize a total lack of affect as the client recounts a story of an incident of severe abuse, or she or he may observe an inhibited ability to express emotions appropriately. As one might expect, trust is difficult for these people to develop and maintain (Carmen et al., 1984).

Intergenerational Cycle of Abuse and Victimization

In recent years family violence clinicians and researchers have noticed that a disproportionate number of abusive adults were physically abused as children (Bernard & Bernard, 1983; Gelles & Straus, 1988; Herrenkohl et al., 1983; Herzberger, 1983; Widom, 1989a, 1989b). Because the topic of intergenerational cycles of abuse has been extensively debated among both researchers and clinicians, it deserves special attention and scrutiny here.

Various researchers have estimated the rate of intergenerational transmission (the percent likelihood that a person who was abused as a child will become a child abuser), ranging from 7% (Gil, 1973) to 17 and 18% (Hunter & Kilstrom, 1979; Straus, 1983), up to 70% (Egeland & Jacobvitz, 1984), depending on study design and sample. As Kaufman and Zigler (1987) point out, it is difficult to determine the accuracy of most researchers' estimates because methodological limitations restrict the generalizability of studies. They carefully examined the data from the studies cited here to derive a rate of 30%, plus or minus 5%. In other words, approximately one in three persons who were abused as children grow up to abuse their children. It is also important, however, to observe that, according to Kaufman and Zigler's (1987) estimate, two out of every three persons who were abused as children do not grow up to become abusers. Moreover, although there is a correlation between having been abused and abusing, the majority of abusing parents were not themselves abused as children.

To date, the emphasis in the literature has been on establishing whether or not violence leads to violence. "...The time has come for the intergenerational myth to be put aside and...to cease asking, 'Do abused children become abusive parents?' and ask, instead, 'Under what conditions is the transmission of abuse most likely to occur?'" (Kaufman & Zigler, 1987, pp. 190–191). They point out that the unqualified acceptance of the intergenerational hypothesis has been extremely detrimental to some. Maltreated young persons are told repeatedly that they are destined to become abusers, contributing to a self-fulfilling prophecy. Alternatively, many who have broken the cycle of violence in their adult lives feel like "walking time bombs" (p. 191), destined to explode and fulfill the intergenerational hypothesis' prediction at any time.

Thus, as a clinician it becomes important to understand both under what conditions an adult abused as a child is likely to resort to violence, and to understand what factors are operating for those who have not themselves resorted to violence. In short, those who do repeat the cycle of violence in their families of procreation commonly experience an inadequate social support network; more ambivalent feelings about their pregnancies; less healthy babies; less awareness of and ability to be openly angry about their early abuse experiences; more than one childhood abuser; onset of abuse before age 13; an absence of a supportive relationship while growing up; a higher level of stress/ poorer coping abilities; and more severe forms of discipline in their families of origin (Egeland & Jacobvitz, 1984; Gelles & Straus, 1988; Herrenkohl et al., 1983; Hunter & Kilstrom, 1979; Kaufman & Zigler, 1987; Milner, Robertson, & Rogers, 1990).

Consequences for the Societal System

Some authors argue that violence is a model for love relationships in society (Bernard & Bernard, 1983; Gelles & Straus, 1988). This inculcates in people's minds the acceptability and normalcy of violence within intimate and family relationships. As violence is an acceptable practice in problem solving at the family level, it will remain an acceptable means of problem solving at national and global levels (Carmody & Williams, 1987; Williams, 1990); thus, family violence presents a danger not only to the individuals in the family, but also to world safety and peaceful problem resolution.

ASSESSMENT AND TREATMENT

Very little literature exists on systemic treatment approaches to working with adults physically abused as children. Because of this, much of the material presented in the following sections on assessment and treatment strategies has been drawn from literature of adult survivors of incest and on the treatment of currently physically abusing families. Clinicians may find themselves assessing individuals, couples, or families; aspects of each system in assessment will be discussed.

Assessment

Individual Assessment

Constructivist Self-Development Theory (McCann & Pearlman, 1989) is a cognitive (and systems-adaptable) model which posits that life experiences affect the formation of schema, or beliefs about self and others. These beliefs then influence the development of psychological response patterns (thoughts and feelings), which inform a person's behavior and affect that person's subsequent life experiences. Schemas develop through early experience; they are frameworks for understanding oneself and the world. McCann and colleagues (1988, 1989) envision a cycle in which life experiences continually inform, enhance, or deconstruct schema. These schemas, in turn, determine thoughts and feelings, which then affect life experiences and behavior.

Traumatic events are especially powerful in shaping schemas (McCann & Pearlman, 1989). For example, a traumatic event may affect a client's schema about her safety. She may believe that she is powerless to protect herself from a basically unsafe world. Consistent with this belief, the client pays extra attention to the newspaper police blotter and to television crime shows, confirming her belief in a savage world. Her safety schema may justify agoraphobia and avoidant behavior.

Individual assessment touches on three psychological dimensions of the individual: the self capacities—abilities "that allow [people] to regulate self-esteem and maintain an enduring sense of [their] value and worth" (McCann & Pearlman, 1989, p. 308), the traumatic memories themselves, and psychological needs and related beliefs (schemas). In addition, the thoughts, feelings, and behaviors (psychological response patterns) the clinician observes are important in assessment.

Assessing the Client's Self.   The self comprises various capacities and resources that are important in maintaining self-esteem and in dealing with painful memories. Self capacities include the ability to tolerate strong affect, the ability to be alone without being lonely, the ability to calm and sooth oneself, and the ability to regulate self-esteem and to moderate self-loathing (adapted from McCann & Pearlman, 1989, 1990a). Capacities can be assessed both indirectly (by observing the client's interactions with the therapist and with others) and directly, by asking the client how they achieve (or don't achieve) the tasks involved in each capacity.

It is important to assess these areas first because the client's ability to integrate and work through the traumatic memories depends on these capacities and resources. For example, a client who has a limited capacity to self-soothe and to tolerate strong affect will not benefit from a premature unearthing of traumatic, affectively loaded memories. Clinicians should also assess the partner of the "identified patient" client, if there is one and the couple is presenting for conjoint therapy. If the clinician finds that his or her client's capacities are all somewhat limited, or that one or two areas are extremely deficient, then the initial treatment focus will be on self-building (to be discussed in the treatment section).

Assessing Traumatic Memories.   Many adult survivors of childhood physical abuse will be able to remember what happened during their childhood. For others, however, the traumatic memories are too powerful and difficult; parts of memories, or all of some memories, are repressed and/or denied. Memories of abusive incidents are often fragmented and experienced in pieces as mysterious triggers to intense feelings (McCann & Pearlman, 1989; McCormack et al., 1988). Unable to put the whole memory together, the adult suffers from intrusive and disruptive memory flashes, never quite understanding why they suddenly feel panicked or rageful. The clinician needs to assess the traumatic memories along with the self and cognitive schemas to make a determination of readiness to begin *memory work*—pulling together fragmented pieces of memories into whole memories and exploring the meanings of these memories in other life experiences.

It is helpful to ascertain what the perpetrator may have said to the client as well as the client's cognitive processes before, during, and after the victimization. Clinicians should explore the statements made by perpetrators that have become internalized into the survivor's memories and schemas (McCann & Pearlman, 1989). They can also ask clients questions like, "Tell me everything that was going through your mind at that moment," or "What exactly did he say to you?" Clinicians should also listen for indications of psychic numbing alternating with intrusive symptoms, including images and sudden onset of strong emotions. Ask about the occurrence of nightmares, flashbacks, and intrusive thoughts. Because intrusive visual images are often loaded with strong feelings, in-depth exploration of these images should be delayed until a determination of adequate self-capacities (especially ability to tolerate strong affect) has been made.

Assessing Needs and Schemas.   Next, the clinician should assess the psychological needs and beliefs (cognitive schemas) of the client. Schemas develop in the areas of safety, trust, esteem, power, intimacy, independence, and frame of reference. Individuals will differ in terms of the centrality to their life and experience of certain needs and beliefs (McCann & Pearlman, 1989).

Assessing Psychological Adaptation and Interpersonal Relationships. It must be emphasized that, because symptoms differ depending on which cognitive schemas are most central to an individual, presenting problems vary widely and clinicians will not be able to guess what they will see in a client based simply on knowledge of a history of physical abuse in the family of origin.

A special set of short-term responses to child abuse deserves discussion here. Several resilience factors, or personal characteristics and skills, can help a child cope with abuse at the time it is occurring (Mrazek & Mrazek, 1987). To summarize, these coping strategies include dissociation of affect, developing a rapid response to danger, decisive risk-taking, forming relationships for survival, idealizing the aggressor's competence, cognitively restructuring painful experiences, behaving altruistically, maintaining positive future expectations and fantasies, and maintaining optimism and hope.

Clinicians need to be watchful for behaviors that may represent vestiges of old coping patterns. Many adults abused as children use appropriate coping strategies to deal with adult stressors. Some, however, may find that the strategies they developed as children have followed them into adulthood and become dysfunctional in the context of dealing with adult stressors. It must be noted that the present behavior a clinician observes may not be attributed definitively to earlier coping strategies. The value in exploring possible links to childhood coping lies in identifying the positive, healthy needs and intentions behind the problematic behaviors and in assisting clients in setting treatment goals to get these needs met in ways that are not destructive to adult relationships.

One frequently observed result of having been physically abused as a child is a lack of trust in one's perceptions. Many child victims are told that they are bad, or that they are being hit for their own good, or because their parents (siblings, etc.) love them, or that they aren't actually being abused. All of these messages serve to contradict the child's lived experience and, in so doing, undermine their belief in the validity of their own perceptions. The child learns not to trust feelings. They may as an adult continually second-guess themselves and look to others for validation and proof that their feelings and perceptions are right. This self-doubt will manifest itself in adult relationships and in the therapy room (to be discussed later).

Couple and Family Assessment

In assessing couples and families in which one or both spouses was physically abused as a child, the clinician should be mindful of the functioning of boundaries, role expectations, communication, conflict resolution skills, and adaptability of the family, in addition to all the routine components of couple evaluation a clinician would normally perform. The components of individual assessment also are important when working with couples and families; after all, the family is made up of the system and the individuals in the system.

Boundaries. Because there is great variability in couples and families in which one or both spouses were physically abused as children, boundary functioning will differ across families. In general, though, establishing flexible but firm boundaries is difficult. The boundary between the executive or parental subsystem and the sibling subsystem may be extremely rigid, with authoritarian disciplining styles and a definite distinction between the adults and the children in the family. Probably more often, however, generational boundaries are extremely diffuse. Normal developmental expectations are ignored or unacknowledged, and parents expect adultlike behavior of their children. In couples, especially when there is an overfunctioning/underfunctioning dynamic (to be discussed later), the overfunctioning partner may engage in "mindreading" of the partner, while the underfunctioner indeed expects the partner to be able to know his or her needs, thoughts, and wishes; this, too, is indicative of diffuse personal boundaries.

As opposed to the boundaries commonly observed within the family, the boundary between the family and the community is usually a rigid one that allows little flow of information into or out of the family system (Justice & Justice, 1982; Nichols, 1986; Schilling, 1990). These families tend to be socially isolated.

Role Expectations. Within abusing couples and families (and in some families where active abuse is not occurring, but one or both spouses were abused as children) there is often a constant struggle to be cared for (Justice & Justice, 1982; Dougherty, 1983). In Transactional Analysis (Berne, 1961) terms, parents who pursue nurturing and caring in this passive manner are vying for the "child" position; the clinician should be watchful of comments or behaviors that represent beliefs about who is responsible for meeting the parent's needs. For example, one parent called her 18-month-old child "Mama" and expected her five-year-old son to organize her belongings (Dougherty, 1983). In working with couples when there are no children involved, clinicians may notice that each partner expects emotional and physical caregiving by the other.

Another variation on this theme is observed when one partner in the relationship perceives the other person (and is perceived by the other) as fragile, "damaged goods," and in need of protection and comfort beyond what one would normally expect. The other partner, then, becomes the hero, the comforter, the protector, the worker in the relationship. Either of these roles may be occupied by an adult abused as a child. This can pave the way for an overfunctioner/underfunctioner dynamic to develop, which prevents each partner from seeing the other accurately. The "hero" partner probably does not feel free to be vulnerable or to ask for help, whereas the underfunctioning partner does not realize the ways in which they are strong and functional. In this scenario each person perceives himself or herself and the partner in a limiting way which precludes the development of true intimacy and personal growth.

Yet another incantation of this self-limiting theme occurs when, as a result of childhood abuse, the adult has an overblown sense of ownership and responsibility for events and interactions. Many abuse victims are told that they are being punished because they are bad, and the association between something happening and "I must have caused it" can become automatic. In relationships this can set up a dynamic where partners collude in blaming one person rather than sharing responsibility. It can also result in the overresponsible party believing that she or he has the power (no less, the duty) to change the partner if they deem change desirous. The overresponsible partner may be solely responsible for keeping track of therapy appointments or homework assignments, for example, because it is her or his "job" to make change occur.

Clinicians may utilize a genogram to trace parenting patterns and the impact of childhood abuse on marital role expectations (of self and partner) and attitudes toward children and childrearing (Nichols, 1986). An exploration of the unconscious marital contract will also reveal couple and parental role expectations (Sager, 1976).

Related to caregiving expectations is parents' knowledge of normal child development. Parents who were abused as children often had unrealistic expectations placed on them at an early age. Many of these parents do not have an adequate working knowledge of child development (Dougherty, 1983, 1990; Pardeck, 1989; Schilling, 1990). Combined with their sometimes intense neediness, this can make for a situation that perpetuates abuse. Parents may have expectations of their own children that are totally unrealistic given the children's developmental stage. Clinicians can utilize both observations of parent–child interactions and direct questioning to assess parents' knowledge of normal child development.

Clinicians should also ask the children about their household responsibilities. The therapist might ask these questions: "Can you tell me what you do when you come home from school? Oh, so you check on your baby sister, maybe change her diaper. Then what do you do?...Oh, I see, and then what happens?"

Communication/Conflict Resolution Style.   The clinician should also assess the special connections and loyalties family members have with each other. Conflict and confrontation often take on a supercharged quality in couples/families where one partner or parent has been physically abused during childhood. Frequently, the abused partner/parent maintains on some level the fear of being hit or abused by their partner, even if the partner has never given them a reason to expect this. If the nonabused partner in this situation knows of the partner's fears, then they may use that fear to dominate the partner. Alternatively, they may feel stifled and unable to behave congruently when they feel angry, disappointed, betrayed, and so forth, because they do not want their partner to be frightened or distressed. Open conflict is often perceived as dangerous and to be avoided at all costs. Many "normal" angry feelings may be sent "underground," thus squelching the couple's ability to deal overtly with conflict. When this happens, negative feelings and conflict will be expressed covertly. Unfortunately, this serves to perpetuate the abused partner's doubt in the validity of his or her own perceptions because there is an overt denial of conflict and a covert expression of it.

For families with children, triangling in a child as one parent's covert ally may be observed (Minuchin, 1974). This child may then bear the physical and/or emotional brunt of a parent's displeasure with his or her spouse. One treatment goal will be to make communication more direct among all family members and to lessen the need for a third party and for covert conflict. The clinician can assess conflict resolution styles in couples and families both by observing in-session interactions and enactments and by asking open-ended and circular questions to gain a sense of the family's typical style of working through their differences.

Adaptability. Clinicians should assess the family's flexibility in responding to changes, both sudden or situational and developmental. Because role expectations can be rigid in these couples and families, the family may have trouble dealing with change. In couples, roles, such as "overfunctioner" and "underfunctioner" as described before, can become entrenched, reinforcing the limited images of each partner in the relationship. In families with children, if a girl has been expected to attend to her parents' and younger siblings' needs, it will be helpful to know how the family reacts as she grows older and becomes interested in pursuing interests outside of the family. Therapists can ask family members about times of change and their style of solving problems. Because change creates stress, and stress is positively correlated with violence (Werner & Smith, 1982), the therapist should inquire as to the family's usage of stress-reducing factors such as social relationships and community resources. To summarize and provide a rudimentary checklist, the clinician can refer to Table 7.1.

Assessment Instruments

Although currently there are no assessment instruments available that focus exclusively on adults physically abused as children, there are some instruments available to assess aspects of family functioning which may have been affected by physical abuse in childhood. Further research on the specific

TABLE 7.1 • Couple and Family Assessment Checklist

A. Boundaries
 1. Internal (within family)—rigid or diffuse?
 2. External (between family and community)—isolated?
B. Role Expectations
 1. Spousal/family caretaking expectations
  • Mutual caregiving
  • Overfunctioner/underfunctioner dynamics
  • Overresponsible partner
 2. Knowledge of normal child development
C. Communication/Conflict Resolution
 1. Identify patterns around conflict
 2. Conflict detoured through children? television? food? sex? drugs? work?
 3. Function of detouring—what's difficult about being direct?
  • Enact discussions in session
D. Adaptability
 1. Developmental changes
 2. Problem-solving style

effects of childhood physical abuse on adult relationships is required to produce an assessment instrument geared specifically for this purpose.

The Family Environment Scales (FES) (Moos & Moos, 1981) is a 90-item,
true/false self-report instrument that measures family members' perceptions
of the following family dimensions: cohesion, expressiveness, and conflict
(relationship dimensions); independence, achievement orientation, intellectual orientation, activity–recreational orientation, and moral–religious emphasis (personal growth dimensions); and organization and control (system
maintenance dimensions). Although, because of questionable reliability and
validity (Roosa & Beals, 1990), this instrument should not be used for diagnostic purposes, it does offer the clinician a comparison between family member's perceptions of their family as it currently functions and their ideal
concept of family functioning. This information can be useful in determining
role expectations and the family's view of optimal functioning, both important factors in assessment and treatment planning.

In working with couples, clinicians may choose to use the Personal
Assessment of Intimacy in Relationships (PAIR) self-report instrument
(Schaefer & Olson, 1981), which elicits from each partner an assessment of the
intimacy they perceive presently in their relationship and the intimacy they
each deem desirable. Intimacy is broken into five subscales: emotional, social,
sexual, intellectual, and recreational. Clinicians can use this instrument in
conjunction with a genogram to improve couples' understanding of the
meaning of intimacy for each, and as a guide to discussing differences
between perceived and ideal levels of intimacy between partners. The PAIR
boasts high reliability and validity and is a valid predictor of marital satisfaction.

Establishment of Therapeutic Goals

General treatment goals for survivors of childhood physical abuse include establishing healthy self-esteem, particularly the belief that each person has some amount of control over his or her own circumstances (empowerment) without feeling overresponsible. Another major goal in systemically treating adults abused as children is for them to work through the traumatic memories of childhood abuse so that they may learn to live with affect rather than suppressing it. Ideally, clients will develop the capacity to experience cognitive understanding and emotional and bodily awareness without triggering coping mechanisms such as denial, dissociation, or counterproductive family interactions (Cornell & Olio, 1991; Williams, 1990; McCann & Pearlman, 1990a; Lundberg-Love, 1990; Rieker & Carmen, 1986).

In addition, many adults abused as children need to learn how to express their needs and feelings to others who can help them meet these needs (Dougherty, 1983; Smith (1985), as cited in Cornell & Olio, 1991). If the clinician is observing a family in which violence has been transmitted intergenerationally, the primary goal is for the violence to stop.

Finally, another general treatment goal in working with individuals, couples, or families is to develop greater flexibility in interpersonal functioning. The specific form this goal takes will depend on the client's presenting problem(s). In a couple, for example, this may mean an overresponsible client refusing sole blame for the couple's disappointments, or an underfunctioning client expanding her or his self-definition beyond that of victim and discovering and putting to use some relational strengths. In a family, this may take the form of developing less restrictive and more age-appropriate role expectations for family members.

Treatment Strategies

Structure and Process of the Therapy

In this section group, individual, and couple and family therapy modalities are discussed based on literature available from the areas of incest survivorship and the treatment of currently abusing families. Before entering into a discussion of the different treatment modalities, however, it is necessary to review a concept that is important in every modality: dealing with denial and dissociation in the face of traumatic memories and feelings.

Some clients may deny that they have been abused, dissociate, or blank out to distance themselves from powerful feelings (Cornell & Olio, 1991; Williams, 1990; McCann & Pearlman, 1989, 1990a; Gudim, Kelsay, & Nickles, 1986; Blake-White & Kline, 1985). Alternatively, they may talk at length and in detail about specific abuse memories or personal and interpersonal events with blunted affect, appearing as if they are meaningfully processing their abuse history by virtue of talking about it, while actually avoiding the powerful feelings.

When this is happening it is very important that the therapist not prematurely challenge the client to delve into painful feelings and memories. Therapists must incorporate respect for a client's defenses/coping skills with patience in order to maintain an "affective edge" (Cornell & Olio, 1991) and provide a balance between approaching painful things and providing safety for the client.

Individual Therapy

In individual therapy, the therapist plays a unique role with the client in that they play out the client's interpersonal relations with people outside the therapy room. The role of the therapist is to facilitate the drawing out of the client's true self, with all its coping strategies, strengths, and fears. During individual therapy for adult survivor issues, many clients experience one or more time periods when they are in need of more-frequent-than-usual sessions; this usually happens when traumatic memory work is becoming intense and clients feel they need help maintaining control.

Self-building.   Therapy progresses through the general stages of assessment, self-building (if necessary), challenging negative schemas, restoring positive schemas, and memory and affect integration work. Self-building involves the client developing his or her capacities sufficiently to tolerate moving on to the work of challenging and rebuilding schemas and recounting traumatic memories. Self-building around the areas of self-esteem, self-soothing, tolerating strong affect, and tolerating solitude may take many forms, as briefly reviewed in Table 7.2.

Challenging Negative Schemas.   Once self-capacities are adequately built to tolerate the demands of therapy, the next step is to challenge negative beliefs (schemas). In individual therapy, the client's beliefs about self and others will play out in the therapeutic relationship. The therapist–client relationship becomes the canvas on which the painting of new schemas is accomplished.

The therapist can gently challenge clients to question the validity of negative schemas by asking them to envision a time when they would be able to behave in concordance with a positive schema. One may ask clients to envision and describe in detail what will be different when they are able to do whatever it is that they most struggle with at present (McCann & Pearlman, 1989, 1990a; Hudson-O'Hanlon & Weiner-Davis, 1989).

Another way clinicians can challenge clients' negative schemas is by refusing to comply with the client's requests and demands that perpetuate these schemas, such as asking the therapist to help with everyday decisions. As clients begin to question the validity of their negative schemas, their fears about changing and their anger and frustration will be expressed within the therapeutic relationship. The therapist must tolerate being the target of these feelings in order to serve as the vehicle through which clients can learn different ways of believing and relating. This is the essence of rebuilding positive schemas. As clients begins to experience the world differently through their interactions with the therapist, they are better able to initiate change in other relationships in their lives. The clients' level of trust in the therapist should be high enough, and their self-capacities strong enough, to tolerate exploring traumatic memories, which should be approached respectfully. Clinicians can encourage clients to share how much access they have to memories, even if they don't yet feel ready to explore them in detail.

Exploring Traumatic Memories. When the client is ready, the clinician can start asking questions aimed at exploring the memories themselves (McCann & Pearlman, 1990a). For example: "What's the first thing you remember?... next?... last?" "Are there missing pieces? Do you need to find them out? What aspect(s) are most important to you?" "When you remember, do you see any pictures or images?" "Do you remember the smells, sounds, sensations, colors, etc.?"

If the client is able to share the memories but does so in an overly cognitive or emotionally devoid manner, she or he is not prepared to explore the affect-laden aspects of the memories. The therapist can comment on this and

TABLE 7.2 • Self-Capacity Techniques for Self-Building

Self-soothing
- Guided imagery and relaxation; self-talk
- Imagine another person in the same situation and how they would comfort that person; then, do the same for self

Tolerating Solitude
- Journaling/tuning in to inner dialogues and feelings
- Work up to spending reflective time alone by first listening to music, painting, etc., while alone

Moderating Self-loathing
- Model empathy and compassion toward parts of client's self that he or she dislikes
- Imagine another person in same situation
- Cognitive therapy techniques for reducing distortions, overgeneralizations, and so on.

Tolerating Strong Affect
- Establish holding environment to allow client to risk experiencing strong feelings; indicate willingness to work with affect as a reassurance that the client is capable of doing so
- Therapeutic metaphors; guided imagery; transitional objects

Compiled from Atwood and Levine, 1990; McCann and Pearlman, 1989, 1990a; Dougherty, 1983; and Beck, 1979.

observe that maybe it is too painful to share just yet. The client's fears and fantasies about experiencing the memories can then be addressed overtly. If a client is experiencing recurrent or intrusive memories, the therapist can frame this as the mind's way of letting the client know there is some unfinished business to deal with. As clients begin to reexperience memories, any of the techniques discussed in the chapter on working with incest survivors to help them stay with and process feelings will also be useful here.

Integrating Memories and Affect.   Affect integration is accomplished as the client is increasingly able to reexperience the trauma (i.e., replay the memories at will) without pushing the feelings away. This is incredibly empowering for those clients who have been afraid to allow themselves to feel too deeply, or who feel out of control when they do. During this stage, it may be possible to decrease session frequency and discuss ending therapy. Clinicians should make it clear that the reason for suggesting a decrease in session frequency and/or talking about ending therapy in the near future is because they have confidence in the client's competence.

Nonetheless, some clients will experience this suggestion as yet another abandonment by a person whom they thought they could trust. This is an excellent opportunity to talk openly with clients about their feelings about the loss of the therapeutic relationship, their doubts about their coping ability, and their feelings of abandonment. It is helpful for the clinician to be able to express his or her feelings of loss around the issue of terminating with the client as well.

Couple Therapy

This section discusses issues that couples with childhood histories of abuse (one or both partners) are likely to encounter and systemic treatment strategies are proposed. The present author emphasizes that because adults physically abused as children deal with various presenting problems, it is impossible (and clinically irresponsible) to lump them all into a few manufactured categories for treatment purposes. Because the present author works on the assumption that the spousal dyad is the single most influential relationship in the family (Kirschner & Kirschner, 1986), when there is a dyad present, everything in this section also applies to family therapy work. The family therapy section focuses more exclusively on interactions with children and other family members.

The structure of couple therapy is similar to that of individual therapy: The therapist should assess the couple's capacities and how the schemas play out between them (in the form of relationship rules and role functions), and then focus on skill building, challenging the negative schemas, and building positive schemas (negotiating for change). Along the way, traumatic memories can be processed. The problem areas discussed in the couple and family assessment section will be dealt with in this framework. The therapist facilitates interaction between family members to highlight the operation of schemas, expressed through relationship rules, role expectations, and repetitive interactional patterns. The therapist will also serve as a reparental agent for many clients, modeling self-nurturing, validation, and confidence in their strivings for change.

Building the Holding Environment. As mentioned in the assessment section on communication and the holding environment, the experience of feeling appreciated and having faith and trust in one's partner can be very elusive. The first step in couple or family work, then, is to help the partners develop their abilities to serve as an adequate holding environment for each other. To do this, the therapist must walk a delicate line between responding empathically and providing comfort and support, and occupying the caregiver position (Chu, 1988). A therapist could not possibly provide either partner with all the nurturing they need, and partners must learn to provide nurturing for themselves and for each other. To occupy the caregiver role would be to collude with the partners in their hope that "someone else" should be capable of and responsible for providing that nurturing. Once an enriched couple holding environment is established, the couple relationship can become more of a healing place in which to overcome dysfunctional behaviors and beliefs.

The therapist can help the couple build up the shared holding environment, couple capacities, by providing the couple with an environment conducive to testing out fears around expressing feelings and trusting another person. The couple can then be encouraged to take small risks in these directions; behavioral couples therapy techniques (Jacobson & Holtzworth-Munroe, 1986) may be utilized by creating an awareness of the rewards that are the spoils of risking in a relationship. Likewise, some of the activities prescribed in Imago Relationship Therapy (Hendrix, 1988), such as Mirroring exercises, Caring Behaviors Lists, and Surprise Lists (Reromanticizing exercises), can serve to improve the couple's holding environment and encourage risk-taking. This stage of therapy can be seen as parallel to the self-building work of individual therapy in that it builds a backdrop of greater trust and risking so that relationship change can become the focus of the work. The self-building work discussed in the section on individual treatment is also helpful in improving the shared couple holding environment. As the partners improve their capacities, they are better able to provide for some of their own nurturance and acceptance needs. Simultaneously, they are better able to take responsibility for helping to meet their partner's nurturance needs. For those clients who behave in an overresponsible way, these exercises can help them challenge and reality-test the beliefs that contribute to their partners' reluctance to share responsibility for the relationship. This improves the couple's level of trust and positive feelings.

When the holding environment between the therapist and the couple and between the partners themselves has been strengthened, it is possible to begin the work of figuring out how the history of childhood physical abuse affects the couple's relationship. This is accomplished by identifying troublesome interactional patterns in the couple's and then tracing them back to the family of origin.

Using Genograms to Elucidate Family-of-Origin Patterns.   Because the family of origin has been so influential in the development of these patterns, family-of-origin-related techniques are helpful in this regard. The clinician can begin with a multigenerational genogram tracing each partner's families of origin with regard to the quality and structure of marital relationships, family myths and secrets, patterns of enmeshment or emotional cutoffs, major emotional events in the client's life and what they meant to the client, beliefs about the proper places of men and women in relationships, and beliefs about child development and discipline (Nichols, 1986; McGoldrick & Gerson, 1985). Clients can begin to understand where some of their beliefs about life and about relationships come from. If, for example, a client's parent was also physically abused as a child, the client may begin to understand why the parent was unresponsive to his or her need for affection and nurturance. This type of understanding can also go a long way toward fostering forgiveness toward one's abusers.

Moreover, a genogram can help abused clients put into perspective their part in the abuse. It can be especially helpful for those who have blamed themselves for their abuse, or have felt overly responsible for their couple relationship, to examine the "anatomy" of their family via genogram and to challenge their belief that if only they were different, could do more, and so on, then they would know no harm. The genogram adds an element of context to couples work that can also improve the holding environment because many dysfunctional relationship behaviors become understandable to both partners in light of family-of-origin history and patterns.

Using the Negative Velcro Loop to Elucidate Current Negative Patterns. Eleanor Macklin's (1991) adaptation of Bunny Duhl's negative velcro loop concept can also enlighten couples to role expectations and rules derived from their families of origin. Basically, the *negative velcro loop* describes a process that occurs in couples wherein one partner's vulnerabilities spark her or his defenses, which in turn triggers the other partner's vulnerabilities and defenses, and so on. Once each partner understands her or his own and the partners' vulnerabilities, each of them can devise ways to avoid resorting to the typical defenses. Some common vulnerabilities include the fear that one will not be able to help or heal the other and that this equates to failure; the fear that one will not be taken care of adequately by the other; the fear of being hit or hurt in any way; and the fear of strong feelings and/or dependence associated with being vulnerable in a relationship or trusting another person.

The negative velcro loop is an excellent tool for graphically mapping out potential change in the couple relationship. Moreover, it can serve as a balancing mechanism in cases where the partners have a consensus that one of them is the "sick" one who really needs treatment, since the loop cannot function without reciprocal and circular input from both partners.

Through genograms and the negative velcro loop (as well as routine couple therapy techniques comfortable to the practitioner), couples will gain a greater intellectual and affective understanding of how their schemas play out in the couple/family arena. The discovery process reviewed above should enlighten clinicians to the complicated patterns of interwoven negative schemas they may encounter.

Challenging Negative Patterns.   Once it is clearer how schemas and generational patterns are playing out in the couple relationship, it becomes possible to challenge them and to negotiate for change. As in individual therapy, it is important at this stage to respect clients' (couples') defenses against change.

One way of challenging negative schemas or patterns in the couple relationship is to ask the couple about times when one or both of them have not felt or behaved in the usual or prescribed manner (Hudson-O'Hanlon & Weiner-Davis, 1989; White & Epston, 1990). For example, when working with an overfunctioning/underfunctioning couple in which the underfunctioner perceives herself as a victim, a good probe would be "Tell me about a time when you stood up for yourself" or "Tell me about a time when you accomplished something important on your own." Every person has experiences like this in his or her life. Once they remind themselves of one such time it becomes possible to remember other times when they have also behaved differently from their prevailing view of themselves, thus paving the way for a new self-definition and eventually a new definition of the couple relationship.

If the individual cannot come up with an example or memory of this nature, the partner may be helpful in this regard. In some cases, though, the partner may be heavily invested in believing in this limited image of the other partner, because these beliefs justify his or her own behavior. In these instances it is useful to ask the couple what they think would happen if either or both of them changed. In this example, the therapist could ask what would the overfunctioner do if the victim awoke tomorrow and suddenly was assertive, self-confident, and able to function independently. It may also be useful to ask the underfunctioner how she or he feels about the partner believing her or him to be so fragile and in need of care. Interventions aimed at interrupting common patterns in the relationship are useful here (Hudson-O'Hanlon & Weiner-Davis, 1989). Role reversals may be utilized to help couples become more conscious of their everyday scripts' influence on behavior. Basically, the therapist is challenging couples to expand their definition of themselves and their relationships by pointing out aspects of their self-definitions that are limiting and aspects of their lived experience that do not fit these self (and couple)-definitions.

If conflict is usually dealt with covertly by the couple, the clinician can address this by claiming the therapy room as a "safe haven" for conflict to bloom. In this way the couple can "try on" direct confrontation and negotiation with the knowledge that someone else is there to help keep it safe. The couple can make overt their fears about conflict. The therapist, in turn, can send a supportive message of confidence in the couple's ability to get through this by overtly offering to work on conflict in the therapy room. This also provides the therapist with an opportunity to introduce lessons on "fair fighting" if necessary (Mantooth, Geffner, Franks, & Patrick, 1987). Once the couple has demonstrated an improved ability to work through conflict in the therapy room, the therapist can suggest that they try it on their own at home when it arises.

Dealing with Traumatic Memories.   It should be mentioned that when traumatic memories arise they can provide opportunities to enrich the holding environment, improve understanding for both partners, and lead to greater risk-taking. The therapist can direct the partner not having the memory to support and encourage the one who is, and then the couple can process how those experiences have affected their relationship. They may try tracing the meaning and influence of that memory into their negative velcro loops. The therapist can encourage them to recognize that they can overcome many of the behaviors and feelings learned in the family of origin if they agree to help each other. Through these processes the couple can negotiate changes and promote deeper awareness and understanding of each other. This contributes to improved adaptability and greater possibilities for managing change and conflict effectively and overtly.

Comparison of Couple Work Versus Individual Work.   The major difference between individual and couple work, then, is the act of bringing family-of-origin issues into the here and now via the couple relationship. In both individual and couple/family work, the therapist begins by tracing the impact of childhood abuse on each person's schemas. From here, individual therapy progresses by capitalizing on the relationship between the client and the therapist. Couple and family work, on the other hand, progresses by capitalizing on the richness of current and past interactions between partners/ family members, with the therapist playing a more facilitative (versus a transference) role. This is not to say that the therapist is not perceived by the couple to be an important part of the therapy; rather, the couple is the *most* important unit of action in couple/family work.

The differences between the individual and couple approaches can be detected by the differences in dialogue of individual versus couple sessions. The hypothetical vignettes of the same (fictional) case that follow give the reader a sense of the differences. Some background information:

> Dan is a 30-year-old married man who suffered physical abuse from his mother as a child and adolescent. In the first vignette, he has entered individual therapy because of what he describes as an inability to offer comforting and to trust his wife, Connie. In the second vignette, he and Connie have entered marital therapy together and Connie is bringing up a time in their relationship when Dan has had difficulty offering comfort. Connie has had a recurring nightmare, during which she becomes very agitated and feels a need to be held by Dan.

Individual Therapy

DAN: …so, lately I've been noticing more when I don't feel comfortable with someone.

THERAPIST: Can you say more about that?

D: Yeah. Like, a few days ago Connie was really mad at me because she had her nightmare again and I didn't hold her when she was upset. I talked to her, but I didn't touch her. She was mad at me the next day. She said she couldn't understand why I wouldn't hold her, since that's what she needed.

T: Were you aware that that was what she wanted from you at the time?

D: Oh, sure. She says that's what she wants me to do, but I'm not always sure. I just didn't want to do it.

T: What got in the way of wanting to do it?

D: Well, it's not as easy as you think. These nightmares have happened before, and I used to try to touch her, but she would move around a lot, you know, like squirm. I thought she didn't want me to touch her when she would do that.

T: That's understandable. Yet she has told you that she does want to be held. What prevents you?

D: Well, for one, she's hit me in the past when I've tried. I mean, she didn't mean to; she was asleep and she was thrashing around. But I don't enjoy getting hit. It reminds me too much of when I was a kid.

T: Have you told her that?

D: Hell, no, she'd think I'm a wimp! Besides, she's my wife; shouldn't she know?

T: You know, I'm just thinking that, of course, it makes a lot of sense that you wouldn't want to put yourself in a position of being hit again. No wonder it's hard for you to trust her when she's like that. But I wonder if that happens sometimes here, too, with us.

D: What do you mean?

T: Well, I'm thinking of a few weeks ago, when we were doing relaxation training exercises and you seemed to be having a lot of trouble settling down. I remember that you had a particularly hard time keeping your eyes closed. You kept opening them and looking around. But when I asked if everything was alright, you said yes.

D: Well, now that you mention it, I did feel a bit uncomfortable. I mean, there I am on the floor, on a bunch of pillows laid out, my eyes are shut, and you're sitting there like normal.

T: What was uncomfortable about that, Dan?

D: Well, I couldn't see what you were doing. You could have been doodling, making faces at me, anything.

T: So you found it difficult to trust me at that moment.

D: Yes.

T: And you also found it difficult to tell me that while it was happening?

D: Yes.

T: I see. Well, I wonder what we could have done about that if I had known you were uncomfortable.

D: You should have known anyway; you're the therapist!

T: That's partially true, Dan. I had some awareness that you weren't feeling really comfortable. However, I don't see it as my job to read your mind and accommodate without knowing from you what is going on.

D: I guess you're right.

T: Do you think Connie understands how you feel about her hitting you?

D: Well, she should; I mean, she knows that my Mom was rotten to me when I was little.

T: Do you think she would have any way of knowing that, just from what you describe happening between you? I mean, she's asleep, right? So she probably doesn't understand anything except she's scared and she wants you to comfort her. She may not even know she does it.

D: I guess so.

T: Let's go back for a minute to us. I'm wondering if there's some way that we can agree on to help you feel comfortable in sessions telling me when you're having a hard time.

The therapist brought a familiar pattern from the client's life into the realm of the therapeutic relationship. Then she challenged his beliefs around this interaction. From here, Dan and the therapist can negotiate a new way of relating in the therapy room. Then, Dan can bring this new skill back into his relationship with Connie. This is the essence of individual therapy work. Let us look at how the same situation would be handled in couple therapy:

Couple Therapy

CONNIE: He won't comfort me, help me out.

DAN: I always ask if you want to talk about it.

C: I don't want to talk. If you'd just hold me, I'd be okay. See, he never will help me out the way I need helping.

Therapist: Connie, I hear how much you need him to comfort you. Dan, what's happening for you when Connie has nightmares?

D: Well, it's tough. I want to help her, but I'm afraid.

T: What do you feel afraid of?

D: You (Connie) get a little crazy when you have these dreams. I used to touch you but you would flail around a lot. I thought that meant you didn't want me to touch you.

C: But I'm telling you now that I want you to.

T: Connie, do you have any idea what is tough for Dan about holding you when you have nightmares?

C: Well, he says I thrash around, but I don't see why that should bother him. I'm telling him I want him to hold me.

T: Dan, can you explain to Connie what is difficult about that for you?

D: I guess part of it is that I was confused. I thought you didn't want me to. Now I know you do. But, still,…

C: Then why don't you? What's the big deal?

D: I get afraid…of being hit.

T: Has Connie ever hit you, Dan?

D: Not on purpose. But sometimes when she is thrashing around like that she has hit me. It's hard for me because it reminds me of when my mother used to do that.

C: I hit you?

D: Yes.

C: I never knew. Why didn't you ever say anything about it?

D: I thought you'd think I was a wimp to be afraid of you. Besides, I thought you didn't want me to touch you, anyway.

T: It makes sense that you would be afraid of being hit again. What about that is bad for you, Dan? How do you feel when Connie hits you in her sleep?

From here the therapist can explore Dan's memories of his abuse and engage Connie in a process of empathizing with him. Then it becomes possible for behavioral change, as introduced in the following vignette, taken from later in the same hypothetical session:

C: Well, I understand now why you have a hard time reaching out to touch me when I'm that upset. But I still need you to.

D: I can't really do it without being afraid. I want to, Connie. I really do, but I just can't.

T: I wonder if there is something the two of you could agree on that would help you, Connie, feel comforted and wouldn't put you, Dan, in a scary spot. What types of things do you think you could do for Connie when she has nightmares?

D: I could talk to you, like I have been. I could turn on the lights so you'd wake up.

C: I really need you to hold me when I'm that scared.

D: I can do it when you're awake, because I know you're not gonna hit me.

C: You're great about holding me when I'm awake.

T: How about if Dan were to wake you up first in a way that doesn't put him at risk, and then he could hold you, Connie?

D: I could do that.

C: I think that could work.

T: Why don't you talk about some different ways you could do that and decide on one to try for the next time this happens.

In this vignette, the therapist is directing the flow between Dan and Connie. Solutions are to be worked out between them, using the therapist as a guide and model, but the affective material is processed by the couple.

Throughout these steps (which are by no means discrete and orderly), the therapist has hopefully positioned herself so as to be slightly in and slightly out of the couple relationship. The therapist prods, encourages discussion and conflict, acknowledges fears, helps control the flow of information and communication, and supports each partner without undermining the other. At the same time, however, the therapist establishes rules and limits in the therapy room.

Family Therapy

In this section, approaches to working with families, two-parent or single-parent, are discussed. In families with two adult partners present, all relevant couple issues from the couple therapy section apply here as well. After addressing the immediate crises and presenting problems, couple issues can be dealt with either by alternating sessions from couple to family sessions, or by working with the spousal dyad separately for periods of time during family sessions. Likewise, it will be helpful to work only with the children at times. All family members who live with the nuclear family should be regularly included, and those close friends or relatives who interact with the family regularly and intimately (ex-spouse, a close family friend who babysits the children a few times per week) can be invited as needed. Single parents should be encouraged to consider joining a therapy group if one is available; if not, they may contract with the therapist to meet alternately alone and with their children so as to give them an opportunity to work through things like traumatic memories without placing an undue burden of witnessing this on the children.

As in couple therapy, a genogram can be an excellent way of gathering information which takes into account everyone's perceptions and opinions. With older (junior-high and teenaged) children, the genogram will help them better understand their family.

Dealing with Role Expectations.   One area of concern for these families is the role expectations placed on the children. As previously discussed, it is not uncommon for parents in these families to expect caregiving, instrumental, and emotional capacities beyond their children's developmental levels. Thus, in these families the children may appear as extremely capable and mature beyond their years. In some cases the children may have earned "junior adult" status and the privileges that accompany this status will be difficult for them to relinquish. In other cases and depending on the ages of the children, they may be experiencing regressive symptoms (bedwetting) or acting out behaviors (vandalism), perhaps as an attempt to get some nurturance and care.

Whatever the case may be, the therapist should work with the children through verbal or play therapy to help them express their feelings of what it's like to live in their family. Sometimes airing sadness or disappointment may seem disloyal to the child. Therefore, the therapist should try to talk with the parent beforehand about the needs of children and the importance of letting them have their feelings without being punished in any way. Especially if the children are young, parents should have opportunities to work through some of the self issues discussed in previous sections so that they are able to provide empathy and reassurance to their children.

Establishing a Boundary Between Discipline and Abuse.   If the parent is having difficulty establishing the boundary between disciplining children and abusing them, the therapist should be clear with her or him what the limits are and should work with the parent (with the children present) to identify what warning signs are for feeling overwhelmed; the parent should contract with the therapist and the children to handle these feelings. If there is an executive dyad, the other partner can take responsibility for the children for a period of time. If the client is a single parent, he or she should either have a designated friend or relative to do the same, have a time-out plan, or call the therapist if absolutely necessary.

Negotiating Change in the Parent–Child Relationship.   Once everyone's feelings about the family have been made overt, the therapist can help negotiate change in the parent–child relationship. For children who need to be reassured of their parent's ability to nurture them, the therapist can prescribe a special time just for them to play, talk, and so on. For those who have occupied a junior adult role in the family, recognition must be given for the work they have done to keep the family going, and parents need to negotiate with these children to give up some of their burdens/privileges. The therapist should support parents in their efforts to remain at the heads of their families, and this includes challenging them to stretch themselves to meet their children's needs and seek help from appropriate sources. Other treatment recommendations for families can be found in Chapter 3 on child physical abuse.

Group Therapy

Group therapy with individuals helps to diminish isolation and shame among physical abuse survivors and to encourage disclosure of painful memories and feelings associated with the childhood abuse (Goodwin & Talwar, 1989; Gudim et al., 1986). In general, group therapy work progresses through three stages. The stages, as adapted from Paula Lundberg-Love's (1990) ideas on therapeutic work with incest survivors, comprise recounting the abuse, repairing the "damage" done by the abuse, and resolving residual behavioral and interpersonal issues associated with the abuse. Because group therapy for adults physically abused as children closely parallels group therapy for incest survivors, the reader is directed to consult Chapter 8 on working with incest survivors for this information.

Group Family Therapy focuses mainly on giving parents accurate information about normal child development, learning to observe their own and their children's behavior more objectively and systematically, and learning and practicing behavioral child management techniques (Dougherty, 1983; Schilling, 1990; MacMillan, Olson, & Hansen, 1991). The reader can refer to Chapter 3 on child physical abuse for more information on this type of group format.

RECOMMENDATIONS/SUGGESTIONS
FOR THERAPISTS

Special Problems

Lisa McCann and Laurie Pearlman (1990b) have studied the impact on therapists of working with victims of childhood trauma. Within the framework of their Constructivist Self-Development Theory (1989, 1990a; McCann et al., 1988), they identify a process they call *vicarious traumatization*. Vicarious traumatization occurs when therapists working with trauma victims "find their cognitive schemas and imagery systems of memory...altered or disrupted by long-term exposure to the traumatic experiences of their victim-clients" (p. 132). They offer the example of a therapist who had worked extensively with survivors of childhood sexual abuse strongly suspecting her daughter's teachers and friends' parents of being perpetrators and feeling hesitant to let her daughter come into contact with these people at all. Another therapist, having worked with childhood physical abuse survivors, would wake during the night with recurrent intrusive thoughts and images of a burglar breaking into his house and terrorizing his family. In many cases, therapists develop symptoms strikingly similar to those of PTSD sufferers. Vicarious traumatization is akin to what noted trauma specialist Charles Figley calls *compassion fatigue* (Figley, 1993).

According to McCann and Pearlman (1990b), all therapists who work with trauma survivors experience alterations in their schemas that impact their feelings and relationships. Whether these alterations interfere with therapeutic work, however, depends on the therapist's ability to integrate and transform these affective experiences. The therapist must be able to process the traumatic images and experiences. This processing involves becoming aware of the therapist's own most salient need areas and schemas, because the central areas are the ones most likely to be negatively impacted by vicarious traumatization.

It is very important that therapists acknowledge, express, and work through vicarious traumatization and understand how it affects their schemas (McCann & Pearlman, 1990b). To accomplish this, therapists must have a supportive professional environment. Therapists who work with trauma survivors can avoid professional isolation by organizing a group of professionals to meet regularly for three purposes: (1) to normalize therapists' reactions to their work and to view vicarious traumatization as an opportunity for growth (rather than as a pathological embodiment of the therapist's underlying personal and family of origin issues); (2) to explore therapists' central schemas; and (3) to provide a safe environment in which to work through negative reactions. McCann and Pearlman (1990b) emphasize that in these groups the participants must strike a balance between the need to work through traumatic material and the need to protect colleagues from having to assimilate more traumatic material in this process. They recommend dealing with this by talking about it and being honest when they cannot listen at the moment. Hopefully, if there are enough group members, someone else who can listen will be available.

McCann and Pearlman (1990b) and Figley (1993) also offer some excellent suggestions for coping professionally and personally with working with trauma survivors. These include, but are not limited to, striving for a balance between personal and professional life (maintaining personal boundaries); balancing clinical work with other professional endeavors (research or education, for example), if possible; balancing victim and nonvictim cases; giving themselves permission to experience emotional reactions; doing political work for social change to offset feelings of helplessness about the problem of violence; seeking out nonvictim-oriented activities providing hope and optimism; being aware of one's own conflict areas and unresolved traumas; and developing realistic expectations of themselves.

Ethical/Legal Issues When Dealing with Adults Abused as Children

By nature, working with adults abused as children means that most clients will be of legal age; thus, therapists are not mandated by law to report child abuse to the appropriate social and legal agencies. There are, however, some circumstances under which therapists have an ethical obligation to report past child abuse (Urquiza, 1991). Some of these circumstances are when a client continues to be in danger of being abused and when the client informs the therapist that there are other children (usually siblings or stepsiblings) still under legal age (18) who are being abused or are at risk of being abused. In either case, the clinician has a moral and ethical obligation to report abuse. In the latter circumstance many practitioners will also have a legal obligation to report suspected abuse under mandated reporting laws, which include provisions for reporting when the practitioner has reasonable cause to suspect that abuse may be occurring, depending on professional licensing and state laws. Practitioners should become educated as to the extent of their legal obligations.

Systemic Issues

This chapter reflects the current struggle in the field to integrate the individual and the system so as to capture the true complexity of family life and individual history. In closing, it is important to consider the larger systems to which we and our clients belong.

Just as individuals are parts of the family system, so family systems are smaller parts of larger systems: cultural systems. Throughout this chapter, the author urges clinicians to consider the special meanings and associations physical violence in the family of origin has had for each individual client and family. Each client's ethnicity, race, and experience with the dominant culture in society will influence those special meanings and associations. To be truly systemic, every clinician must become better informed about the race, ethnicity, and cultural experiences of each of their clients. Erwin R. Parson, in his eloquent commentary on the need to integrate the client's cultural identity in assessment and treatment, highlights the importance of transethnic competence: "Ethnicity shapes how the [client] perceives, understands, accepts, and adapts to his or her traumatic stress…. Transethnic competency is thus essential, and there is the need for therapist awareness of the [client's] 'cultural–behavioral norms,' as well as for overcoming ethnocentric views in their transcultural or transethnic interventions…." (Parson, 1985, pp. 314–315). Any intervention that fails to consider the client's cultural identity, says Parson, is doomed to fail.

The task of clinicians working in a culturally competent manner with adults physically abused as children, then, is to understand the abuse as experienced by the client. This will be reflected in goalsetting as the client defines what it is that is important to change, as well as in assessment and treatment.

In assessing a client's schemas, clinicians should consider the role ethnicity, race, and racism play in contributing to a client's primary need areas. For example, if safety needs are salient for an inner-city client, the clinician should consider that person's social reality as contributing to that need. This is important, because, if a treatment goal of reducing fears about people's and the world's safety is not met to the therapist's satisfaction, treatment may be labeled a failure when it may not necessarily be adaptive or healthy within the client's day-to-day environment to meet this goal. More likely than this, however, if clients in this example feel pressured by the therapist to buy into the treatment goal, they are likely to drop out of therapy.

CONCLUSIONS

Throughout this chapter, the emphasis has been on the importance of understanding each client through his or her unique way of organizing experiences in his or her life. This is especially true when working with adults who have been physically abused as children because family violence is so common in society that the effects can be diffuse and difficult to spot. Only when we are willing to examine what family violence has meant to each victim are we able to work with its effects.

REFERENCES

Atwood, J. & Levine, L. (1990). The therapeutic metaphor. *Australian Journal of Clinical Hypnotherapy & Hypnosis, 11*, 17–40.

Bernard, M. L. & Bernard, J. L. (1983). Violent intimacy: The family as a model for love relationships. *Family Relations, 32*, 283–286.

Berne, E. (1961). *Transactional analysis in psychotherapy: A systematic individual and social psychiatry.* New York: Grove Press.

Blake-White, J. & Kline, C. (1985). Treating the dissociative process in adult victims of childhood incest. *Social Casework, 66*(7), 394–402.

Brown, S. E. (1982). An analysis of the relationship between child abuse and delinquency. *Crime and Justice, 5*, 47–51.

Bryer, J. B., Miller, J. B., Nelson, B. A., & Krol, P. A. (1986). Adult psychiatric symptoms, diagnoses, and medications as indicators of childhood abuse. Paper presented at the 94th Annual Convention of the American Psychological Association, Washington, DC.

Burnett, E. C. & Daniels, J. (1985). The impact of family of origin and stress on interpersonal conflict resolution skills in young adult men. *American Mental Health Counselors Association Journal, 7*(4), 163–171.

Carmen, E., Rieker, P. P., & Mills, T. (1984). Victims of violence and psychiatric illness. *American Journal of Psychiatry, 141*, 378–383.

Carmody, D. C. & Williams, K. R. (1987). Wife assault and perceptions of sanctions. *Violence and Victims, 2*(1), 25–38.

Chu, J. A. (1988). Ten traps for therapists in the treatment of trauma survivors. *Dissociation, 1*(4), 24–32.

Cohen, F. S. & Densen-Gerber, J. (1982). A study of the relationship between child abuse and drug addiction in 178 patients. Preliminary results. *Child Abuse & Neglect, 6*, 383–387.

Cornell, W. F. & Olio, K. A. (1991). Integrating affect in treatment with adult survivors of physical and sexual abuse. *American Journal of Orthopsychiatry, 61*(1), 59–69.

Covington, S. S. (1983). Sexual experience, dysfunction and abuse: A descriptive study of alcoholic and nonalcoholic women. Ph.D. dissertation, The Union of Experimenting Colleges and Universities. Cincinnati, OH.

Dougherty, N. (1983). The holding environment: Breaking the cycle of abuse. *Social Casework, 64* (5), 283–290.

Downs, W. R., Miller, B. A., & Gondoli, D. M. (1987). Childhood experiences of parental physical violence for alcoholic women as compared with a randomly selected household sample of women. *Violence and Victims, 4*, 121–138.

Downs, W. R., Miller, B. A., Testa, M., & Panek, D. (1990, November). Long-term effects of parent-to-child violence for women. Paper presented at the Annual Convention of the National Council on Family Relations, Seattle.

Egeland, B. & Jacobvitz, D. (1984). Intergenerational continuity of parental abuse: Causes and consequences. Paper presented at the Conference on Biosocial Perspectives in Abuse and Neglect, York, ME.

Egeland, B. Jacobvitz, D., & Papatola, K. (1987). Intergenerational continuity of abuse. In R. J. Gelles & J. Lancaster (Eds.), *Child abuse and neglect: Biosocial dimensions* (pp. 255–276). Hawthorne, NY: Aldine De Gruyter.

Elliot, L. D. & Tanner, V. L. (1988). *My father's child: Help and healing for the victims of emotional, sexual, and physical abuse.* Brentwood, TN: Wolgemutt & Hyatt.

Figley, C. R. (1993). Compassion stress: Toward its measurement and management. *Family Therapy News, 24*(1), 3, 16.

Gelles, R. J. & Straus, M. A. (1988). *Intimate violence.* New York: Simon & Schuster.

Gil, D. (1973). *Violence against children: Physical child abuse in the United States.* Cambridge: Harvard University Press.

Goodwin, J. M. & Talwar, N. (1989). Group psychotherapy for victims of incest. *Psychiatric Clinics of North America, 12*(2), 279–293.

Gudim, L., Kelsay, D. A., & Nickles, L. F. (1986, June). "Battered women" and previous victimization: Is the question relevant? (Report No. C6 020570). Cheyenne, WY: Research project for Division of Community Programs, Department of Health and Social Services. (ERIC Document Reproduction Service No. ED 291 038)

Hendrix, H. (1988). *Getting the love you want: A guide for couples.* New York: Harper-Perennial.

Herrenkohl, E. C., Herrenkohl, R. C., & Toedler, L. J. (1983). The intergenerational transmission of violence. In D. Finkelhor, R. J. Gelles, G. T. Hotaling, & M. A. Straus (Eds.), *The dark side of families: Current family violence research* (pp. 305–316). Beverly Hills: Sage.

Herzberger, S. D. (1983). Social cognition and the transmission of abuse. In D. Finkelhor, R. J. Gelles, G. T. Hotaling, & M. A. Straus (Eds.), *The dark side of families: Current family violence research* (pp. 317–329). Beverly Hills: Sage.

Hudson-O'Hanlon, W. & Weiner-Davis, M. (1989). *In search of solutions: A new direction in psychotherapy.* New York: W. W. Norton.

Hunter, R. & Kilstrom, N. (1979). Breaking the cycle in abusive families. *American Journal of Psychiatry, 136*, 1320–1322.

Inglis, R. (1978). *Sins of the fathers.* New York: St. Martin's Press.

Jacobson, N. S. & Holtzworth-Munroe, A. H. (1986). Marital therapy: A social learning-cognitive perspective. In N. S. Jacobson & A. S. Gurman (Eds.), *Clinical handbook of marital therapy* (pp. 29–70). New York: Guilford Press.

Justice, B. & Justice, R. (1982). Etiology of physical abuse of children and dynamics of coercive treatment. In J. C. Hansen & L. R. Barnhill (Eds.), Clinical approaches to family violence (pp. 1–20). Rockville, MD: Aspen.

Kaufman, J. & Zigler, E. (1987). Do abused children become abusive parents? *American Journal of Orthopsychiatry, 57*, 186–192.

Kirschner, D. A. & Kirschner, S. (1986). *Comprehensive family therapy: An integration of systemic and psychodynamic treatment models.* New York: Brunner/Mazel.

Kroll, P. D., Stock, D. F., & James, M. E. (1985). The behavior of adult alcoholic men abused as children. *The Journal of Nervous and Mental Disease, 173*, 689–693.

Lewis, B. Y. (1987). Psychosocial factors related to wife abuse. *Journal of Family Violence, 2*, 1–10.

Lundberg-Love, P. K. (1990). Adults survivors of incest. In R. T. Ammerman & M. Hersen (Eds.), *Treatment of family violence* (pp. 211–242). New York: John Wiley.

MacMillan, V. M., Olson, R. L., & Hansen, D. J. (1991). Low- and high-deviance analogue assessment of parent-training with physically abusive parents. *Journal of Family Violence, 6*(3), 279–301.

Macklin, E. (1991, November). The use of the negative velcro loop in couple therapy: An adaptation of a concept developed by Bunny Duhl (manuscript). Workshop given at the Annual Conference of the American Association of Marriage and Family Therapists, Dallas, TX.

Mantooth, C. M., Geffner, R., Franks, D., & Patrick, J. (1987). *Family preservation: A treatment manual for reducing couple violence.* Tyler: The University of Texas Print Shop.

Marshall, L. L. & Rose, P. (1988). Family-of-origin violence and courtship abuse. *Journal of Counseling and Development, 66*, 414–419.

McCann, I. L. & Pearlman, L. A. (1989). Constructivist self-development theory as a framework for assessing and treating victims of family violence. In S. M. Stith, M. B. Williams, & K. Rosen (Eds.), *Violence hits home: Comprehensive treatment approaches to domestic violence* (pp. 305–329). New York: Springer.

McCann, I. L. & Pearlman, L. A. (1990a). *Psychological trauma and the adult survivor.* New York: Brunner/Mazel.

McCann, I. L. & Pearlman, L. A. (1990b). Vicarious traumatization: A framework for understanding the psychological effects of working with victims. *Journal of Traumatic Stress, 3* (1), 131–149.

McCann, I. L., Sakheim, D. K., & Abrahamson, D. J. (1988). Trauma and victimization: A model of psychological adaptation. *The Counseling Psychologist, 16*(4), 531–594.

McCord, J. (1983). A forty-year perspective on the effects of child abuse and neglect. *Child Abuse & Neglect, 7*, 265–270.

McCord, J. (1988). Parental aggressiveness and physical punishment in long-term perspective. In G. T. Hotaling, D. Finkelhor, J. T. Kirkpatrick, & M. A. Straus (Eds.), *Family abuse and its consequences: New directions in research* (pp. 14–37). Newbury Park, CA: Sage.

McCormack, A., Burgess, A. W., & Hartman, C. (1988). Familial abuse and post-traumatic stress disorder. *Journal of Traumatic Stress, 1*(2), 231–242.

McGoldrick, M. & Gerson, R. (1985). *Genograms in family assessment.* New York: W. W. Norton.

Miller, B., Downs, W., & Testa, M. (1990, August). Relationship between women's alcohol problems and experiences of childhood violence. Paper presented at the Annual Convention of the American Psychological Association, Boston.

Milner, J. S., Robertson, K. R., & Rogers, D. L. (1990). Childhood history of abuse and adult child abuse potential. *Journal of Family Violence, 5*(1), 15–34.

Minuchin, S. (1974). *Families & family therapy.* Cambridge: Harvard University Press.

Moos, R. H. & Moos, B. S. (1981). *Family Evaluation Scale Manual.* Palo Alto: Consulting Psychologists Press.

Mrazek, P. J. & Mrazek, D. A. (1987). Resilience in child maltreatment victims: A conceptual exploration. *Child Abuse & Neglect, 11,* 357–366.

Nichols, W. C. (1986). Understanding family violence: An orientation for family therapists. *Contemporary Family Therapy, 8*(3), 188–207.

Oates, R. K., Forrest, D., & Peacock, A. (1985). Self-esteem of abused children. *Child Abuse & Neglect, 9,* 159–163.

Pardeck, J. (1989). Family therapy as a treatment approach to child abuse. *Family Therapy, 16*(2), 113–120.

Parson, E. R. (1985). Ethnicity and traumatic stress: The intersecting point in psychotherapy. In C. Figley (Ed.), *Trauma and its wake* (pp. 314–337). New York: Brunner/Mazel.

Pollock, V. E., Briere, J., Schneider, L., Knop, J., Mednick, S. A., & Goodwin, D. W. (1990). Childhood antecedents of antisocial behavior: Parental alcoholism and physical abusiveness. *American Journal of Psychiatry, 147*(10), 1290–1293.

Rieker, P. P. & Carmen, E. (1986). The victim-to-patient process: The disconfirmation and transformation of abuse. *American Journal of Orthopsychiatry, 56*(3), 360–369.

Roosa, M. W. & Beals, J. (1990). Measurement issues in family assessment: The case of the Family Environment Scale. *Family Process, 29*(2), 191–198.

Rosenthal, K. (1988). The inanimate self in adult victims of child abuse and neglect. *Social Casework: The Journal of Contemporary Social Work, 69*(8), 505–510.

Sager, C. J. (1976). *Couples therapy and marriage contracts.* New York: Brunner/Mazel.

Schaefer, M. T. & Olson, D. H. (1981). Assessing intimacy: The PAIR Inventory. *Journal of Marital and Family Therapy, 7,* 47–60.

Schilling, R. F. (1990). Perpetrators of child physical abuse. In R. T. Ammerman & M. Hersen (Eds.), *Treatment of family violence: A sourcebook* (pp. 243–265). New York: John Wiley.

Singer, S. I. (1986). Victims of serious violence and their criminal behavior: Subcultural theory and beyond. *Violence and Victims, 1,* 61–70.

Steele, B. (1986). Notes on the lasting effects of early child abuse throughout the life cycle. *Child Abuse & Neglect, 10,* 283–291.

Straus, M. A. (1983). Ordinary violence, child abuse, and wife beating: What do they have in common? In D. Finkelhor, R. J. Gelles, G. T. Hotaling, & M. A. Straus (Eds.), *The dark side of families: Current family violence research* (pp. 213–234). Beverly Hills: Sage.

Straus, M. A. & Gelles, R. J. (1987). Is child abuse increasing? Evidence from the National Family Violence Resurvey (Report No. 296 190). Durham, NH: University of New Hampshire, Family Research Laboratory. (ERIC Document Reproduction Service No. ED 296 190)

Straus, M. A. & Gelles, R. J. (1988). How violent are American families? Estimates from the National Family Violence Resurvey and other studies. In G. T. Hotaling, D. Finkelhor, J. T. Kirkpatrick, & M. A. Straus (Eds.), *Family abuse and its consequences: New directions in research* (pp. 14–37). Newbury Park, CA: Sage.

Straus, M. A., Gelles, R., & Steinmetz, S. (1980). *Behind closed doors: Violence in the American family.* Garden City, NY: Anchor.

Trimpey, M. L. (1989). Self-esteem and anxiety: Key issues in an abused women's support group. *Issues in Mental Health Nursing, 10,* 297–308.

Urquiza, A. (1991). Retrospective methodology in family violence research: Our duty to report past abuse. *Journal of Interpersonal Violence, 6* (1), 119–126.

U. S. Department of Commerce (1990). 1990 Census of population and housing: Summary population and housing characteristics—United States. Washington, DC: U.S. Government Printing Office.

Werner, E. E. & Smith, R. S. (1982). *Vulnerable but invincible: A study of resilient children.* New York: McGraw-Hill.

White, M. & Epston, D. (1990). *Narrative means to therapeutic ends.* New York: W. W. Norton.

Widom, C. S. (1989a). Child abuse, neglect, and adult behavior: Research design and findings on criminality, violence, and child abuse. *American Journal of Orthopsychiatry, 59*(3), 355–367.

Widom, C. S. (1989b). The cycle of violence. *Science, 244*(4901), 160–166.

Williams, M. B. (1990). The treatment of the traumatic impact of family violence: An integration of theoretical perspectives. In S. M. Stith, M. B. Williams, & K. Rosen (Eds.), *Violence hits home: Comprehensive treatment approaches to domestic violence* (pp. 330–351). New York: Springer.

8

ADULT SURVIVORS OF INCEST

LAURIE B. LEVINE

Incest, a type of childhood abuse, is unique in that the perpetrator is a trusted person in the person's life and enlists cooperation through the use of threats and secrecy. Incest is often inflicted under the guise of love. The use of love and the secrecy of incest serve to confuse the victim and reinforce feelings of shame and responsibility. Mothers' denial is a very common reaction as many women have difficulty accepting this type of abuse, especially when the mother is an incest survivor herself (Briere & Runtz, 1987; Browne & Finkelhor, 1986; Covington, 1989; Finkelhor, 1979; Follette, Alexander & Follette, 1991; Gil, 1988; Jackson, Calhoun, Amick, Maddever, & Habif, 1990; Levang, 1989; Russell, 1986; Wyatt, 1985). Sue's story is not unlike the ones told by other incest survivors.

> Sue, 27, and Don, 29, sought marital therapy for a sexual dysfunction. During their two-year marriage, Sue has had an extramarital affair with one of Don's co-workers, the couple has had difficulties with communication, and are generally unhappy with their relationship. In the first session, Sue revealed that she was an incest survivor and the perpetrator was her stepfather. Charges were filed and the stepfather was mandated to therapy. Sue's mother and stepfather are still married.
>
> Sue and Don live about a thousand miles from her family and she still has tremendous fears that her stepfather will "get her." She is afraid to emotionally separate herself from her family of origin for fear that the stepfather will move on to her younger sister. In order to protect this child, Sue endures sexual comments and inuendos from her stepfather and the denial of what happened from her mother. Sue feels rejected by her extended family who also does not believe her. She worries that Don's family will see her as dirty and responsible for what happened.
>
> Sue's primary definition of herself is that of an incest victim. She feels a tremendous sense of guilt and shame about the experience. Sue has vivid memories of the abuse, including nightmares and conscious flashbacks particularly during

sex with her husband. She has shared many of her memories and experiences with Don who is uncomfortable with some of the information. He has a great deal of anger toward Sue's stepfather and is very confused about how to help his wife.

The number of reported cases of incest has increased dramatically in the last several decades as awareness of this problem has expanded. Growing awareness has led to changes in attitudes regarding incest and has fostered many studies on the subject (Blume, 1990; Briere & Runtz, 1987; Browne & Finkelhor, 1986; Dinsmore, 1991; Finkelhor, 1979; Gelinas, 1983; Gil, 1988; Maltz & Holman, 1987; Russell, 1986; Wyatt, 1985). The main focus of this chapter is on the treatment of adult survivors of incest. Assessment, therapeutic approaches, common therapeutic goals, and the role of the therapist are explored. In addition, it examines common reactions incest survivors encounter as individuals and in their subsequent intimate and family relationships.

DEFINITION OF INCEST

The findings of current incest research depend in great part on how incest is defined in a given study. Researchers can only find what is within the parameters of what they are examining. This ambiguity in defining incest significantly affects the reported prevalence and incidence of incest in our society.

The definition of incest that will be used in this chapter is the most inclusive one found by the author. "Incest can be seen as the imposition of sexually inappropriate acts, or acts with sexual overtones, or any use of a minor child to meet the sexual or sexual/emotional needs of one or more persons who derive authority through ongoing emotional bonding with that child" (Russell, 1986, p. 4).

Bronson (1989) suggests that any definition of incest requires some attention to the "imputed trust and power imbalance" that are integral parts of incest (p. 21). Definitions of sexual contact should include all forms of sexual behavior. Incestuous acts include the showing of pornographic materials to a child. Fondling, forcing a child to undress, forced touch, and sexual comments all constitute incestuous acts (Blume, 1990; Bronson, 1989).

Blume (1990) offers a more inclusive definition of incest that includes an examination of the emotional bond that exists between the victim and perpetrator. "Incest—unlike abuse by a stranger or an acquaintance—violates an ongoing bond of trust between a child and a caretaker" (p. 2). This definition considers the fact that the perpetrator has authority over the victim based on dependency in their relationship. The victims' trust and love are violated as well as their bodies. Blume (1990) further suggests that the real damage results from the fact that the child is taken advantage of by the person she or he relies on most. The child really has no choice as the adult is larger, older, and socially dominant. Subsequently, the child's "emotional and physical survival depends upon her acquiescence" to the perpetrator (Blume, 1990, p. 3).

The only arenas where the definition of incest is extremely important seem to be research and the legal system. In these arenas it is necessary to decide when incest has occured as well as the severity of the abuse. To the survivors of incest, however, the exact definition is unimportant because damage is done regardless of the form of the abuse. The distinction between forced intercourse and fondling is irrelevant in relation to the child (Courtois, 1989). Damage occurred at the time when touch became unsafe and inappropriate. It is this aspect of the definition of incest that is significant for the therapist. Blume (1990) and Courtios (1988) further stress the necessity for understanding and the acknowledgment that there are categories of abuse but not degrees.

SCOPE OF THE PROBLEM

Weinberg (1955) reports that there were 1.1 million reported cases of incest in the United States in 1930. Russell (1986) examined the prevalence of incest as it refers to the percentage of victims who experienced incest at some point in their lives. The data reveals that 80 to 90% of reported victims are female and that 90% of the perpetrators are male. (The pronouns used in this chapter reflect this.) Russell's (1986) study indicates that 16% of the 930 sampled reported at least one experience with incest before the age of 18. When Russell (1986) expanded the definition of incest to include exhibitionism and other unwanted sexual contact, 54% of the 930 women reported at least one incestuous experience before the age of 18 (p. 62).

Finkelhor (1979) based his study on a nonclinical population and found that of the 530 women who participated, 10% had experienced some form of sexual abuse from a relative. A later study conducted by Finkelhor (1984) revealed that 15% of the 521 women who participated were sexually abused before 16 years of age; 5% of those women were sexually abused by a relative. Kilpatrick and Amick (1984) reported that 1% of their sample experienced incest. Wyatt (1985) found that of the 248 women interviewed for her study, 62% reported some incidence of sexual abuse before the age of 18. Wyatt's (1985) definition of incest included "contact of a sexual nature, ranging from those involving non-body contact such as solicitation to engage in sexual behavior and exhibitionism, to those involving body contact such as fondling, intercourse and/or sex" (p. 510). When examining the studies on incest and their findings, the importance of how incest is defined by the researchers becomes evident.

CONSEQUENCES

Initial attention given to incest often took the form of negating its existence outside the realm of the victim's imagination. Rush (1977, 1980), Herman (1981), and Masson (1984) provide examples of Freud's work where he attributed his patients' descriptions of incest to fantasies or figments of their imaginations. While Freud's comments on incest apparently served to discount its very existence, the 1953 Kinsey Report served to minimize its effects on the child. Kinsey and his associates did acknowledge cases in which child sexual abuse was damaging to the child but they deemphasized the point by saying: "These cases are in the minority…we only have one clear cut case of serious injury done to the child, and very few instances of vaginal bleeding which, however, did not appear to do any appreciable damage" (Kinsey, Pomeroy, Martin, & Gebhord, 1953, p. 122).

In 1990, Blume stated that "incest ravages childhood. For the child victim and the woman she will become, incest is more than rape of her body…incest is a rape of her trust as well" (p. 12). The disparity between the earlier comments of Freud and the Kinsey Report and the more recent comments of Blume (1990) is an indication of the progress research has made in heightening awareness of the problem of incest and moving away from blaming the victim.

Consequences for the Individual

There has been a great deal of research on incest that suggests that survivors of incest often encounter a number of psychological problems in adulthood. Common symptoms associated with incest or childhood sexual abuse may be expressed cognitively, emotionally, psychologically, or behaviorally. Cognitive reactions or symptoms may take the form of nightmares, hallucinations, and obsessive ideas (Blume, 1990; Briere & Runtz, 1987; Browne & Finkelhor, 1986; Dinsmore, 1991).

Common emotional/psychological symptoms include uncontrollable weeping, fear, feelings of panic, depression, anxiety, suicide attempts, and low self-esteem (Blume, 1990; Briere & Runtz, 1987; Browne & Finkelhor, 1986; Dinsmore, 1991; Gil, 1988; Maltz & Holman, 1987; Russell, 1986).

Behavioral symptoms may take the form of compulsive talking about the experience, bodily reenactment, artistic renderings of the trauma, self-destructive behaviors, and substance abuse. Incest survivors also experience difficulties in intimate relationships. Such difficulties might take the form of transient relationships or sexual dysfunctions (Blume, 1990; Browne & Finkelhor, 1986; Dinsmore, 1991; Gil, 1988; Maltz & Holman, 1987; Russell, 1986).

Dissociation is a common defense used by the victim at the time of the abuse and continues later in life in times of stress. Dissociation allows the child to block cognitive, sensory, motoric, or affective memory and subsequently, to have no recollection of certain periods of time or events in adulthood (Briere, 1989; Courtois, 1988; Dinsmore, 1991; Gil, 1988; Maltz & Holman, 1987; Russell, 1986; Wyatt, 1985). The dissociated symptoms include confusion and disorientation (Bronson, 1989).

Gelinas (1983) suggests that symptoms related to developmental maturity are what eventually brings an incest survivor to seek therapy, and describes three effects of incest and the "secondary elaborations" associated with such effects. These include chronic traumatic neurosis, relational imbalances, and intergenerational risk of incest. Chronic traumatic neurosis are discussed here while relational imbalances and intergenerational risks are described in the next section on consequences for the family system.

There has been research that indicates that Multiple Personality Disorder (MPD) is a possible symptom of incest survivors (Blume, 1990; Briere, 1989; Courtois, 1988; Dinsmore, 1991; Gil, 1988; Maltz & Holman, 1987; Putman, 1985; Russell, 1986; Stern, 1984; Wilbur, 1985; Wyatt, 1985). Putman (1985) found that 97 out of 100 patients with MPD had experienced some form of child abuse including some form of sexual abuse. Schultz, Braun, and Kluft (1987) reported similar findings in that 97.4% of 309 MPD patients experienced abuse as children.

In addition to MPD, Post-Traumatic Stress Disorder (PTSD) is a common response to childhood sexual abuse. According to the *Diagnostic and Statistical Manual of Mental Disorders IIIR* of the American Psychiatric Association, PTSD is the

> development of characteristic symptoms following a psychologically distressing event that is outside the range of usual human experience (i.e., outside the range of such common experiences as simple bereavement, chronic illness, business losses, and marital conflict). The stressor producing this syndrome would be markedly distressing to almost anyone, and is usually experienced with intense fear, terror, and helplessness. The characteristic symptoms involve re-experiencing the traumatic event, avoidance of stimuli associated with the event or numbing of general responsiveness, and increased arousal (p. 247).

There are some studies that have found a correlation between PTSD and child sexual abuse (Donaldson & Gardner, 1985). Other studies on childhood trauma provide information that may be applied to incest survivors (Ayalon, 1983; Black, 1982; Newman, 1976; Covington, 1989; Levang, 1989; Blume, 1990; Jackson et al., 1990; Follette et al., 1991). The findings of these studies are similar to the symptoms reported by adult survivors of incest. These PTSD symptoms include a "sense of overwhelm and threat as they remember early trauma, intrusive flashbacks, physical sensations [throbbing, stinging, internal pain]" (Gil, 1988, p. 160).

Consequences for the Family System

Incest is viewed as one aspect in a dysfunctional family. It is not an isolated incident in the family and does not stop with one act with one child. Some research suggests that incest is passed through generations where the victim may become the victimizer or the mother of a victim (Russell, 1986). Relational imbalances often lead to intergenerational risks for the incest survivor. Mothers who are survivors may be less likely to notice incest occurring in their present families. The tendency here is to subconsciously block any reminder of their own experiences of incest. The secondary elaborations associated with these effects of incest include marital problems, sexual dysfunction, problems with parenting, or depression. It is these symptoms that often bring the incest survivor to therapy (Gelinas, 1983). Goodwin and DiVasto (1979) found similar results in their study. Incest may curtail the mother's ability to parent. The neediness of these mothers contributes to role reversal with their children early on in the their childhood (Courtois, 1988). The result of the relational imbalances for children is "destructive triangulation—they meet the needs of their parents while their needs go unheeded and their development unattended" (Courtois, 1988, p. 41).

Consequences for Current Relationships

Relationships can be difficult for incest survivors as their basic trust has been violated as part of the abuse. Abusive relationships are common for incest survivors. These women often enter relationships where they take the role of the pursuer. She pursues the partner and focuses a great deal of attention on the partner's attitudes and behaviors in an attempt to allay the fear that he will leave. The incest victim may also occupy the role of the withdrawer in an intimate relationship. The withdrawer fears engulfment and attempts to control this fear by creating distance between herself and her partner. Regardless of the position the survivor takes in the relationship, both pursuer and withdrawer are based on feelings of powerlessness or lack of control (Gil, 1988).

Adult survivors often feel needy and fragile in response to the childhood incest and these feelings can surface in intimate relationships. Separation is difficult for survivors to experience without having a great sense of loss. Survivors learn to be caretakers from an early age, putting other people's needs ahead of their own. This experience puts them at risk of being involved in a co-dependent or caretaking roles in a relationship (Courtois, 1988).

Intimacy may be difficult for incest survivors because it requires self-awareness and responsibility for ones' feelings and vulnerabilities. These aspects of intimate relationships may not be easy for incest survivors to achieve (Russell, 1986). "Self-awareness means being aware of her feelings instead of 'acting out,' acknowledging that she is angry, needy, afraid rather than abusing, demanding, or running" (Courtois, 1988). Responsibility for ones' feelings refers to the "individual's willingness to understand that her reactions come from inside her and that an interpersonal conflict is an opportunity not to describe what is wrong with the other person, but to explore more thoroughly her weaknesses, strengths, associations, history and problem areas" (Blume, 1990, p. 254). Frequently, being vulnerable is difficult and frightening for incest survivors. Vulnerability is often associated with being weak and open. It is the openness of intimacy that enables the partners to fully experience one another. This ability to be open in a relationship may be blocked for incest survivors as a protective mechanism.

Numerous problems with sexuality in adult relationships can be a result of childhood incest. For the survivor, affection can mean sex, therefore when sexual advances are not accepted it is seen as a rejection of intimacy. Other survivors feel that true intimacy does not include sex, as sex can "dirty up the intimacy" (Trepper & Barrett, 1989). Additional sexual problems are addressed in the Treament section.

TREATMENT

There has been an abundance of material written on the treatment of incest. Most of this literature is in the form of clinical reports or case histories on father/daughter incest. Incest treatment approaches have only recently become the focus of empirical research (see Cahill, Llewelyn, & Pearson, 1991). It is common for incest survivors to seek therapy for a variety of psychological problems, which they do not relate to any sexual abuse. It is important for the therapist to be able to recognize indications of possible childhood sexual abuse (Briere,1989; Jehu, 1991; Dolan, 1991).

Treatment of survivors and their families may take a variety of forms: individual, couple, family, and group therapy. The same therapist may find it necessary to make interventions in a variety of the systems through a variety of treatmenet modalities in order to best help the survivor and the family. The following section outlines underlying principles for treatment of the population and provides an overview of various treatment modalities.

Underlying Principles

Courtois (1988) outlines philosophical principles to be considered when doing therapy with incest survivors. It is necessary to include both the original and compounded effect of incest in treatment. Courtois (1988) advocates a variety of therapeutic approaches in the treatment of incest survivors, including techniques for the treatment of traumatic stress. Feminist and family systems models are helpful in gaining an understanding of incest and its effects and symptoms, and they facilitate the creation of an appropriate treatment plan. Like other treatment plans, those devised for incest survivors should be individualized within the broader framework to meet the specific needs of the client. Finally, the therapeutic relationship is paramount in creating a safe environment for the client to explore issues (Courtois, 1988, p. 165).

Assessment

Adult survivors come to therapy with either a vast amount of information about their abuse or almost no information at all. Some clients do not associate present psychological problems with the experience of abuse (Jehu, 1991; Gelinas, 1983). The main focus of therapy is on the abuse and how the abuse affects the client's functioning in the present situation. It is important to give the abuse credence so that the client feels validated. The client is encouraged to recall the details of the abuse and the associated emotions in order to work through the trauma and the nonproductive symptoms and defenses (Courtois, 1988). It is essential that the symptoms and defenses not be viewed through a medical-model lens where they may be pathologized. These elements of the client's experience should be understood in the context in which they occur. The difficulties that often bring the incest survivor to seek therapy are the very things that may have served her or him well as a child in getting through the abuse. Viewing incest in terms of the larger sociohistorical context is advocated by the feminist approach to therapy with survivors.

The first task of the therapist is to identify clients who may be experiencing problems as a result of childhood sexual abuse (Cahill, Llewelyn, & Pearson, 1991). The therapist may be required to initiate a conversation about the abuse by questioning clients with regard to sexual abuse. Some indications that incest has occurred are a history of repeated victimization, such as battering or rape or adolescent turmoil, including running away; alcohol or drug dependency; women whose mothers were ill or absent from the home, or women who took adult caretaking responsibilities in their families from an early age (Cahill et al., 1991, p. 2). The necessity for an individualized treatment plan refers to the need to address idiosyncratic experiences of the individual client. Such a treatment plan should include emphasis on the abuse experience in addition to other traumatic experiences, the client's unique personality structure and defenses and methods of adapting, and the idiosyncratic meaning of the incest experience (Courtois, 1988, p. 169). After assessing factors associated with adult survivors of incest, the therapist may deem it necessary to help the client disclose experiences of sexual abuse. The disclosure of the abuse is considered to be part of the therapeutic process and is discussed in greater detail in the section on individual treatment strategies.

Role of the Therapist

The therapeutic relationship is a crucial factor in therapy with survivors of incest as it is in any type of a therapeutic situation. Therapists should communicate feelings of mutual like, respect, and trust (Jehu, 1991). Therapists should offer a nonjudgemental accepting attitude and should not appear shocked or embarrassed by what the client reports. Josephson and Fong-Beyette (1987) conducted a study that examined factors that facilitated disclosure of incest. They found that adult survivors require reassurance, encouragement, and validation from therapists. Additionally, therapists must emphasize that the client is not responsible for the abuse and that they can, in fact, overcome the psychological effects of the incest. Therapists should be sure to acknowledge and validate clients' ambivalent feelings. It also is crucial for the therapist to accept the clients' reality about the abuse (Faria & Belohlavek, 1984; Herman & Hirschman, 1981; Josephson & Fong-Beyette, 1987; Meiselman, 1978).

Additionally, the therapist should be careful not to be parental or authoritarian with incest survivor clients or create an atmosphere where the clients are without power. Clients also need to feel they are the experts on their own experience. Therapists should avoid interventions that are controlling so as not to reperpetrate clients. The role of the therapist may be seen as one of a facilitator who assists in the process of confronting the memories of the abuse and working through the associated emotions (Courtois, 1988; Rosenfeld, 1986).

It is also important for the therapist to be aware of the fact that clients often feel guilt and shame after having disclosed the nature of the incest. The therapeutic relationship is critical at this time. Many therapists believe that telling the story of incest is in and of itself a therapeutic experience because it desensitizes the client to her own memories (Briere & Runtz, 1987; Gelinas, 1983; Joy, 1987; Jehu, 1991). Jehu (1991) emphasizes the importance of pacing clients as they tell their stories. Time should be spent working with the client to improve coping mechanisms and reduce anxiety, stress, anger, and fear before beginning to work on the repression, denial, and emotional avoidance associated with the original trauma (Cahill et al., 1991).

Establishment of Therapeutic Goals

There are many specific approaches to therapy with survivors. However, Courtios (1988) defines several conceptualizations of the therapy process that should be part of any therapy with incest survivors. This type of therapy may be viewed as "a healing or recovery process or an abreaction of the trauma, which generally involves breaking the secret, catharsis, and reevaluation of the incest, its circumstances, and its effects" (p. 170). Therapy with survivors may also be described as a remembering process where the primary focus of therapy is family rules, self-destructive behaviors as survival mechanisms, and internalized guilt and shame (Wise, 1985).

Therapy should pay special attention to the "victim/survivor paradox" where the client has prevailed through the abuse by resourcefulness and continues to see herself as a victim. The goal is to resolve that paradox and move the client past the victim stance to the survivor stance and onto a new definition of herself (Courtois, 1988). There are developmental aspects to therapy with survivors, including "reparenting" as the clients reexperience and rework the tasks of maturation that were either missed or experienced prematurely (p. 171). The client has the opportunity to reexperience painful events of the past with a supportive ally, to mourn what was lost in childhood, and to find meaning in the experience (Courtois, 1988; Silver, Boon, & Stones, 1983).

Because incest takes place in childhood, the abuse has an impact on the development of incest survivors. Traumatic events are associated with developmental milestones. It may be necessary to specifically address such traumatic events. This may be accomplished through a trusting therapeutic relationship, education about the recovery process, stress management, and reexperiencing the trauma in a safe environment. The therapist may also aid the survivor in working toward disclosure and confrontation about the abuse with the family of origin.

Briere (1989) outlines a useful approach to therapy with adult survivors of incest with specific techniques for working with these clients. As stated before, Briere (1989) emphasizes that the quality of the therapeutic relationship is an essential factor in successful therapy. An initial goal of therapy is to normalize the client's feelings and reactions to the incest. It is important that the therapist help the client understand she is not "crazy" or "weird" and her current reactions and behaviors are common responses to childhood sexual abuse. This may be accomplished by imparting information regarding the frequency of the occurrence of abuse, giving the client the message that she is not alone in her struggles (Jehu, 1991; Josephson & Fong-Beyette, 1987; Meiselman, 1978). The therapist should also explain common psychological effects of sexual abuse so that the client is able to see that her reactions are not pathological and unique to her but are common and predictable. Contact with other survivors also facilitates the client's ability to feel that she is not alone. This may be accomplished by group therapy as an adjunct to other types of therapy or abuse-oriented organizations.

Individual Therapy

Dolan (1991) has applied a solution-focused therapeutic approach to therapy with survivors of incest (Berg, 1990; de Shazer, 1982, 1984, 1985; Lipchik & de Shazer, 1986; O'Hanlon & Weiner-Davis, 1989). The basis for the solution-focused approach to therapy is the notion that solutions are the co-creation of the therapist and the client(s). It is assumed the clients have the inner resources to construct highly individualized and uniquely effective solutions to the problems that bring them to therapy. The therapist empowers clients to create and experience their own particular meaningful and effective therapeutic changes (Dolan, 1991). The interventions included in this approach for incest survivors are "symbol for the present" (Dolan, 1989), "pre-treatment changes" (Weiner-Davis, de Shazer, & Ginderich, 1987), the "miracle question" (de Shazer, 1988), and various forms of solution-focused questions appropriate for use in therapy with incest survivors (Dolan, 1991).

Facilitating Disclosure of Incest

Josephson and Fong-Beyette (1987) outline guidelines for facilitating disclosure, including direct questioning about the occurrence of sexual abuse in childhood. This may be accomplished by the use of a structured questionnaire that provides the therapist with a complete sexual history. It is helpful for the therapist to point out similarities in the clients' experiences with common histories of those who have experienced incest in childhood. Often, it is useful to define incest for clients and explore their best and worst memories of childhood.

The therapist needs to be aware of his or her own reactions to the disclosure of incest; reactions of the therapist may inhibit clients from expressing themselves. Josephson and Fong-Beyette (1987) found that clients who experienced their therapist as calm, empathic, and encouraging felt relief and trust after having disclosed the incest. Others who experienced the therapist as "minimizing of the effect of the incest, ignoring or rushing disclosure, excessive interest in sexual details, or anger directed at either the client or the offender reported a subsequent lack of trust in the therapist, and either stopped attending counseling or dropped the subject" (Cahill et al., 1991, p. 3). Reactions that could impede clients' process of disclosing incest include the therapist giving even subtle indications that clients were to blame in some way for the incest or that they are not believed. A therapist's discomfort with violence or threats of violence can inhibit the client from revealing the experiences of incest.

The solution-focused approach emphasizes the need for the client to disclose the details of victimization in an atmosphere of support, respect, and compassion to avoid any further secrecy or stigmatization. Although recounting the details of the abuse is essential, therapy should not be completely focused on this process. "In order to respectfully and effectively address the client's treatment needs, therapy needs to include and strongly emphasize an active utilization of the client's present life resources and images of future goals and possibilities" (Dolan, 1991, p. 25).

Symbol for the Present

A solution-focused approach can be particularly useful in helping the client tell the details of victimization in a constructive nonvoyeristic atmosphere. The therapist may begin by saying, "Please tell me everything that you feel I need to know in order for you to know that I understand" (Dolan, 1991, p. 26). This question allows the client to feel in control of what is shared about the experience of incest at her own pace. As part of this process, it is important to help the client choose something in the room that is a "symbol for the present" so she can be easily reminded of the here and now in the face of frightening flashbacks. The therapist may ask the client to look around the room and describe what she sees in the here and now. "This external focus on visual and the descriptive task provides a conscious break from the memory of the trauma and reduces the emotional impact of talking about the abuse" (Dolan, 1991, p. 28). This process of reconnecting with the present provides the client with a sense of control over her symptoms from the beginning of treatment.

Challenging the Victim Frame

Asking the client about changes she has noticed between the initial phone contact and the first session draws attention to and lays the ground work for a solution-focused approach highlighting exceptions that exist prior to treatment (Weiner-Davis et al., 1987; O'Hanlon & Weiner-Davis, 1989). The discussion of pretreatment changes paves the way for using the Solution-Focused Recovery Scale for Survivors of Sexual Abuse. The purpose of this scale is to aid the client in identifying and talking about ways in which she has already begun to heal herself as well as the resources she possesses to continue the process in the future. This procedure lays a foundation for hope and shifts the focus of therapy toward healing.

After having identified ways in which the client is already healing herself, the therapist may ask her to speculate about subsequent signs of healing. This forces the client to begin to identify herself as a person who is healing and not just as a person who has been victimized. It is important for the therapist to emphasize the smallest signs of healing initially and build from there: "At what times do you feel less depressed?" "What is different for you at those times?" The client may feel overwhelmed by having to identify more distant exceptions: "When do you feel hopeful?" With clients who are more depressed and therefore less able to identify the signs of healing, it may be helpful to ask, "What do you think your (significant other) would say your first small healing sign would be…and your next small sign of healing?" This technique allows the client to borrow hope from her partner when she cannot readily draw on her own resources.

The miracle question (de Shazer, 1988) enables clients to envision solutions to the problems that seem "hopeless" to them. Dolan (1991) modified de Shazer's miracle question for incest survivors. "If a miracle happened in the middle of the night and you had overcome the effects of your childhood abuse to the extent that you no longer needed therapy and felt quite satisfied with your daily life, what would be different?" (p. 34). This question helps clients project themselves to a time where they have dealt effectively with the problem and simultaneously gives them the message that there is in fact a time when they will be without the problem in their lives. Areas in which clients already have control over their lives are also identified. Clients may then be asked to notice times when these healthy behaviors and perceptions are already present and asked to pay closer attention to these differences in the future (de Shazer, 1988). It is essential for the therapist to be careful not to trivialize the clients' experiences and that they feel as though the therapist has an accurate understanding of the victimizations.

de Shazer's (1985) first-session formula task, where clients are asked to think about things that are occurring in their lives that they would like to have continue, has been modified by Dolan (1991) for work with incest survivors. Dolan (1991) suggests that clients make a list of such things. The list is important especially at the beginning of therapy when focusing on past trauma may tend to eclipse clients' awareness of the safety, comfort, and support available in their everyday lives in the here and now (p. 35).

Moving Toward Healing

Asking the client to write a letter to her "older, wiser self" about the struggle she is experiencing is helpful in drawing on the healing resources already present within herself. The client then takes the role of the "older, wiser self" and responds, offering comfort, advice, and ways in which to deal with the problem based on the wisdom and experience of the older, wiser self. Note, this technique should be used with caution with clients who are experiencing MPD (Dolan, 1991).

Constructive questions (Lipchik & de Shazer, 1986) are an integral part of the solution-focused approach that also "help clients focus on what they are already doing that is working (even to some degree), on imagined solutions, and ideas about how to make the solutions occur. The client's responses to these questions provide a useful and highly personalized map for therapy" (Dolan, 1991, p. 37). Individually oriented constructive questions help clients identify specific solutions for their lives.

Systemically oriented constructive questions "evoke and utilize the resources of supportive family, friends, and meaningful others" (Dolan, 1991, p. 37). Examples of individual constructive questions from Dolan (1991) include:

> What will be the first (smallest) sign that things are getting better, that the sexual abuse is having less of an impact on your current life?
> What will you be doing differently when sexual abuse trauma is less of a current problem in your life?
> Are there times when the above is already happening to some (even small) extent?
> What is different about those times?
> What is helpful about those differences?

Dolan (1991, p. 38) also lists these examples of systemic constructive questions:

> What do you think your significant other would say that would be the first sign that things are getting better?
> What do you think your significant other will notice first?

What positive differences will these healing changes you've identified make over time in your relationship with (significant other)?

What differences will these healing changes you've identified make in future generations of your family?

Dolan (1991) describes the tendency of clients to be unaware of psychological resources and healthy coping mechanisms when they experience a regressed state that symbolizes or reminds clients of their trauma. In keeping with a solution-focused approach, Dolan (1991) suggests several techniques that are useful in healing this dissociative split. These include imaging and answering the solution-focused questions, self-induced pattern interruption, notes to the self, and nondominant handwriting. *Pattern interruption* refers to teaching clients that repetitive posttraumatic responses, such as drug and alcohol abuse, over eating, and so on, can be broken by "doing something different" (Berg, 1990; de Shazer, 1985). Having the clients stop and do something different may enable them to break the self-destructive cycle and access more appropriate resources. The "something different" may in fact be the same thing every time. It needs only to be a behavior that "elicits an inner state different from current trauma-focused one" (Dolan, 1991, p. 98).

Treatment of Flashbacks

Dolan (1991) presents a four-step solution-focused approach to addressing flashbacks in therapy with incest survivors. *Flashbacks* are often triggered by some "traumatic associational cue" that takes the form of a sight, sound, smell, taste or touch, or an event that symbolizes or reminds the client of the abuse. The following four-step approach enables the client to have more control over flashbacks. First, ask the client about times she has felt this way before: "What situation were you in the last time you felt this way?" Second, "In what ways are your current situation and your past situation similar?" The goal is to identify a particular time of year, setting, sight, or sound that has triggered the flashback. Third, "How is your current situation different from the situation in the past in which you felt similar feelings? What is different about you, your sensory experience and your current life circumstances and personal resources?" Fourth, "What action, if any, do you want to take to feel better in the present?" If the client is experiencing feelings of being unsafe, it is useful to identify self-protective actions that could be taken to change the current situation (Dolan, 1991, p. 107).

The Inner Child

Traumatic events and experiences are often split off through dissociation—the adult survivor removes herself from the pain and discomfort connected with remembering abuse experiences. The result of this splitting off through dissociation is that large sections of the survivor's memory is repressed and not readily available. The therapist must be aware that these memories are often not the concrete integrated memories of adults. These are memories of small children and remain that way regardless of the chronological age of the survivors. These childlike memories may simply be feeling memories or "knowings" (Osborn, 1992); the memories may surface in the face of stress where the adult survivor will employ impulsive solutions to the difficulties she experiences as an adult. The adult survivor exhibits very adult, functional behavior in addition to the childlike impulsivity of the inner child. This vacillation between excessively childlike, less than competent behaviors, and highly functional, greater than competent behaviors, is similar to Breunlin's theory of oscillation. Breunlin (1988) describes the oscillation between less than competent and greater than competent behaviors as a door swinging open and closed on its hinges.

Parts work is particularly helpful in therapy addressing the inner child. The therapist asks the client to identify and describe different parts of herself with the inner child or little girl being just one part. Other parts may include the competent women, the best friend, and the perpetrator. The survivors may be encouraged to look toward the competent women to take care of the inner child. Questions about how this might happen will be helpful in revealing the already present resources within the adult survivor: "What behaviors will be obvious when the competent woman is taking care of the inner child? What will the competent women do to take care of the inner child? How will the inner child know that the competent woman is taking care of her? How will the competent woman know that the inner child needs her?" (Dolan, 1991; Satir, 1983) The perpetrator may be the part of the survivor that keeps her from talking about her abuse or makes her feel shameful or guilty. Care should be exercised when using this technique with clients that present symptoms of MPD. However, for others this technique is extremely helpful in locating healthy and helping aspects of the client and challenging her self-definition, which may be that of a helpless victim.

Family-of-Origin Therapy

In therapy with the family of origin several questions must be answered to determine if such therapy is an appropriate modality: "Should the family be involved in treatment? Should the perpetrator participate in therapy?" The therapist must consider the survivor's relationship with the nonabusing parent and siblings to determine if they should participate in therapy (Briere, 1989; Gil, 1988). A traditional family systems therapist would include all family members in therapy for the purpose of assessing and planning interventions with the entire family system. According to Courtois (1988), family therapy is useful in identifying interaction patterns, boundaries, role reversal, enmeshment, triangulation, and intergenerational processes as they relate to the abuse, but it is not sufficient in and of itself. Family therapy should be a part of the overall treatment of the incest survivor and is extremely useful in addressing the intergenerational aspect of sexual abuse.

Courtois (1988) suggests that family-of-origin therapy is contraindicated in the treatment of incest survivors. The perpetrator has relinquished his right to participate in therapy based on his offending actions, and the survivor makes more significant progress without the presence of the perpetrator in therapy. This philosophy may not address the client's ambivalent feelings about the perpetrator. The assumption is that there are no ambivalent feelings on the part of the client and that she is relieved to be rid of the perpetrator. This may certainly be true in some cases; however, there are still others where the survivor's feelings about the perpetrator are not as clear. Many incest survivors attempt disclosure at some point during the abuse and are met with unfavorable responses (Courtois, 1988; Gil, 1988). Confrontation of the perpetrator may be an important aspect of family-of-origin therapy. These sessions must be highly structured and controlled by the therapist to protect the survivor from being revictimized. The decision to confront the perpetrator must be made by the survivor not the therapist. When such a decision is made, the therapist should prepare the client for the confrontation through role-plays. The incest survivor should be made aware that the perpetrator may not admit to or apologize for the abuse and that other family members may be in denial about the abuse (Dolan, 1991). The client should also be made aware of alternative strategies to direct confrontation such as letter writing and empty-chair techniques.

Defensiveness is a common response to a disclosure of incest to the family of origin. The therapist should review other attempts at disclosure and the results of such attempts. Prediction of possible reactions to the abuse is an important part of preparing the client for disclosure or confrontation. Past reactions of family members will provide the therapist with a sense of present reactions. The family's interaction and communication patterns will determine how they will incorporate and handle the disclosure information (Watzlawick, Beavin, & Jackson, 1967). If families are emotionally expressive, they will react in emotional ways to the disclosure or confrontation. The same is true if family members tend to intellectualize their feelings (Dolan, 1991).

The purpose of the confrontation is to give the survivor the opportunity to tell the perpetrator directly how he hurt her as a child, how the incest has affected her, and how she feels about him in the present. This confrontation allows the survivor to make the secret of the abuse overt and enables her to express feelings of anger and guilt. This process facilitates the externalization of such feelings and moves the survivor toward closure around the incest (Briere, 1989; Courtois, 1988; Jehu, 1991; Josephson & Fong-Beyette, 1987). The family may react in a manner that places blame for the abuse on the survivor. The client must be prepared for this possibility.

Dolan (1991) suggests that clients write down "their healthy inner truth about their victimization, specifically the fact that is in no way their fault and that they are in not in any way to blame" (p. 62). Examples include: "I am doing this for the little girl I used to be. I need to do this to finally protect that little girl. I must do this so that he can't hurt anyone else" (Dolan, 1991, p. 62). This list can be carried by clients at the time of the disclosure or confrontation as a physical reminder of healthy parts inherent inside and the facts of the experience. The therapist must also be careful not to pressure clients or allow other family members to pressure them into forgiving the perpetrators.

Family-of-origin therapy that does not include the perpetrator may include the survivor's other parent and siblings. This type of therapy may provide the survivor with the opportunity to confront the other parent for not protecting her in childhood and deal with the issues associated with such a confrontation. The survivor may have significant anger toward the other parent and her siblings for not protecting her. The other family members might blame her for the break up of the family. This is particularly true if the other siblings have not experienced sexual abuse. Feelings of abandonment and betrayal also are common: "Why didn't she do anything? He hurt me a lot, and Mom never did a thing" (Briere, 1989). It is often easier for the survivor to have feelings of hatred for the other parent because she is less threatening.

One of the primary goals of family-of-origin therapy is for the other parent to become aware of the abuse and its impact on the adult child. It is common for the other parent to have a sense that something was wrong but not be consciously aware of the abuse. Even in cases where the other parent was aware of the abuse, she may have been psychologically unable to protect her daughter from her husband. Protection of the daughter would require the mother to acknowledge and accept the incest as being real; this is difficult for many spouses of perpetrators. Reconnection with the other parent and siblings is an important facet of family-of-origin therapy. Such reconnection minimizes the isolation that incest survivors experience. Communication patterns are clarified between mother and daughter and the other siblings to eliminate the need for blaming and scapegoating (Watzlawick et al., 1967; Haley, 1976; Satir, 1983).

Boundaries within the family should be redefined so that subsystems and individuals are more delineated and distinct from one another. Diffuse internal family boundaries are characteristic of families where incest has occurred and structural family therapy is appropriate for the realignment of these boundaries, reducing the enmeshment, and realigning the family hierarchy (Fishman, 1991; Minuchin, 1974; Minuchin & Fishman, 1981; Trepper & Barrett, 1989).

When other family members are included in therapy, it may become necessary for the therapist to address issues of survivor guilt (Trepper & Barrett, 1989). Siblings may have also been sexually abused by the same family member and may or may not be aware of such abuse. Siblings often feel guilt and self-blame for not protecting the other sibling. Mothers may feel similar feelings of blame and self-guilt about not protecting their daughters from the abuse. These feelings need to be validated in therapy and siblings also should have opportunities to explore them in greater depth. It is common for both siblings and the other parent to shift loyalties from the survivor to the perpetrator. Issues of loyalty must be addressed in therapy. This may be accomplished by covert loyalty and power issues being discussed openly in the therapy session (Boszormenyi-Nagy & Spark, 1973; Boszormenyi-Nagy & Ulrich, 1981; Framo, 1981; Paul, 1976; Williamson, 1981, 1982a, 1982b).

Solution-focused questions are useful in shifting family members' perceptions away from the trauma and toward a frame of healing. Questions for the survivor include: "How will your sister or brother know that you are continuing to heal? What signs can be looked for to know that your healing is progressing? What will your sibling be noticing? What is your sibling doing now that is helpful? What would you like more of, less of?" Solution-focused questions for the siblings include: "How will you know that you sister has continued to heal? What will you be noticing in her behavior, in what she says? How will she know that you, too, are healing from this trauma?" Questions useful for the other parent include: "What would you have done differently if you had been aware of the abuse as soon as it happened? How would you have protected your child? What differences, if any, would this make in your current relationship with your daughter?" (Dolan, 1991, pp. 48–49).

Couple Therapy

The literature on couple therapy with incest survivors is sparse and certainly an area for research that would be a significant contribution to both survivor treatment and couple therapy. Although there are specific issues for incest survivors that might be better addressed in individual therapy, aspects of the abuse will certainly have an impact on the survivor's intimate relationships. Adult survivors can feel needy and fragile in response to the childhood incest and these feelings are often exhibited in intimate relationships. Separation is difficult for survivors to experience without having a great sense of loss. Survivors learn to be caretakers from an early age, putting other people's needs ahead of their own. This experience puts them at risk of being involved in a co-dependent or caretaking role in a relationship (Courtois, 1988).

Frequently, being vulnerable is difficult and frightening for incest survivors. Vulnerability is often associated with being weak and open. It is the openness of intimacy that enables the partners to fully experience one another. This ability to be open in a relationship may be blocked for incest survivors as a protective mechanism. Incest survivors may feel unsafe being open and vulnerable with their partners. Couple therapy would be indicated to address the areas in which the couple is affected by the abuse. Such areas would encompass a range of couple issues—communication, intimacy, and sexual difficulties.

Barrett and Stone Fish (1992) present a model for doing couple therapy with incest survivors and their partners based on the development of a therapeutic relationship between the partners. This therapeutic relationship creates the environment where both partners can explore areas in their lives in which they were victimized. Individual sessions for both partners and couple sessions are suggested to accomplish this goal. Individual sessions allow each partner to address his or her own experiences of victimization. Simultaneously, the couple sessions create a forum for the partners to share their experiences with one another. Couples often seek therapy at a time when they are totally reactive and fighting, distant and colluding not to impact one another, or when one partner has the problem and the other is the helper.

Developmental markers, such as adulthood, permanent relationships, parenthood, and children leaving home, will trigger issues around incest and victimization for the couple. The therapist must work with the individual partners and the couple on three levels. The first is resilience, which is the area of competency for both partners. The therapist should help the couple identify such areas. The second level is the defenses which protect survivors and partners from the incest experience; Barrett and Stone Fish (1992) refer to this as the "terrible knowledge." The resiliency model is the model of challenge or growth whereas the model of defense is the damage model.

Maltz (1988) developed a model for treating sexual difficulties that incest survivors and their partners experience. Maltz's approach is based on the Masters and Johnson model for sex therapy where the relationship is the focus of intervention rather than the individual. Most frequently reported sexual problems are lack of arousal, lack of orgasm during sex, and fear of sex (Maltz, 1988). One of the most important aspects of sex therapy with couples where one partner is an incest survivor is helping survivors remember that their present partner is not the perpetrator. This may be accomplished by asking the survivor to choose a stuffed animal or some other symbolic representation of their partner that they can hold or keep near them during sex. The purpose of this is that, when a flashback occurs or when the survivor confuses her partner and the perpetrator, she can use the stuffed animal as the physical reminder of the here and now and what is occurring in the present.

Maltz (1988) outlines a four-stage model for therapy which addresses sexual problems with survivors and their partners. This model integrates sex therapy, couple therapy, and incest-resolution therapy. Initial sessions are devoted to the assessment of the sexual problem. The main focus of the assessment process is to determine whether the sexual problem is a result of the incest. Standard sexual histories and inventories are useful in this process (Hof & Berman, 1986).

Partners of incest survivors often experience anxiety, depression, emotional distress, erectile difficulty, loss of sexual desire, or hypersexual interest (Maltz, 1988). Partners are often confused and feel insecure about the nature of the intimacy problem. "Sexual rejection may be reframed as a sign that the survivor now trusts the partner enough to let her true feelings be apparent to him" (p. 154). For partners who are aware of the incest, sadness, anger, and disgust may be common reactions. Partners may also blame themselves in some way for not being able to protect their partner from the abuse. Other partners may blame the survivor for allowing the abuse to interfere in their present life (Maltz, 1988).

The therapist should make education about incest part of the therapeutic process. Dissociation and flashbacks should be explained to the couple so that they gain an understanding of the impact the incest has on their relationship. Time should be spent distinguishing the partners' feelings and attitudes about sex from those of the perpetrator (Maltz, 1988).

Disclosure of the incest to the partner can be a difficult challenge for the survivor, but according to Maltz (1988), it is a necessary part of healing. Disclosure also gives the partner information about what sexual behaviors are likely to trigger flashbacks for the survivor.

To alter the couples' interactions and communication around sex, sex should be removed as an obligation and placed in the control of the survivor. This enables her to have control over her sexuality and her life. Further, the therapist should help the couple directly and clearly define how sexual activity can be initiated and declined.

Both family and couple therapy are useful in the treatment of incest survivors because both therapeutic approaches consider the overall context of the woman's life. As stated earlier, the consequences of the incest often surface in adult intimate relationships. More traditional approaches to therapy with incest survivors emphasize individual and group therapy as the treatment modalities of choice. However, many researchers and clinicians suggest that incest survivors participate in individual and group therapy as an adjunct to family and couple therapy.

Family Therapy

Family therapy with the survivor's current family is helpful in preventing the transmission of relational patterns that often occur across generations. Research suggests that incest may be passed through generations where the victim may become the mother of a victim (Russell, 1986). Relational imbalances and faulty hierarchies often lead to intergenerational risks for incest survivors. Adult survivors of incest may be less likely to notice the sexual abuse of their children in their present families. These mothers often subconsciously block any reminder of their incest experiences even though they may perceive them currently. Survivors tend to experience problems in parenting and depression (Russell, 1986). Previous incest may curtail mothers' ability to parent (Goodwin & DiVasto, 1979). It is these symptoms that often bring incest survivors and their families to therapy. The neediness that is characteristic of these mothers contributes to role reversal with their children (Courtois, 1988). The result of the relational imbalances for children is "destructive triangulation—they meet the needs of their parents while their needs go unheeded and their development unattended" (Courtois,

1988, p. 41). The emotional and sexual needs of the parent supersede the emotional, psychological, and developmental needs of the child. Structural family therapy may be used to address structural issues such as realignment of family boundaries to relieve the need for the triangulation of the survivor's children. Problems occur when there is confusion or a blurring of the boundaries that separate the subsystems. The parentified child is a common example (Minuchin, 1974; Minuchin & Fishman, 1981).

In this situation a child is elevated from the sibling subsystem into the parental subsystem. This child may have more responsibilities in terms of caring for younger siblings or running the household. Despite the blurring of generational subsystems, the family will continue to function as long as family members' needs are being met. Problems occur if and when the child becomes a significant source of emotional support for one parent and the child does not or is not able to participate in age-appropriate activities. Parentified children often feel excluded from the sibling subsystem and not completely part of the parental subsystem. The structure of the system must be challenged or unbalanced in order to move it toward change (Minuchin, 1974; Minuchin & Fishman, 1981).

This may be accomplished by the use of techniques that realign boundaries. These techniques are useful in reorganizing the parental subsystem, eliminating the need for the parentified child. The therapist may achieve this by having separate sessions with each of the subsystems. This physically depicts separation between the parental and sibling subsystems. A therapist may also draw physical boundaries around subsystems in sessions by asking family members to change seats, removing the parentified child from between his or her parents and replacing him or her with another sibling. The therapist also can physically demonstrate appropriate boundaries by sitting between the parent and sibling subsystems or by placing a chair between the two subsystems (Minuchin & Fishman, 1981).

Metaphors and reframes may be helpful in making the family's process or structure overt in a way that is less threatening and easier for the family to hear. Making the structure overt challenges perceptions of their situations. The family can no longer behave in the same ways or maintain the same meaning for their behaviors after perceptions have been successfully challenged. Metaphors, like reframes, give the family situation new meaning which is isomorphic to the family's structure and language. The metaphor creates dissonance for the family where the old definition no longer fits. The family experiences discomfort as a result and begins to search for a new definition. The metaphorical expression changes the family's frame, helps redefine reality, and subsequently, leads to a second order change (Atwood & Levine, 1990,1991).

Parents who have had sexual abuse in their backgrounds sometimes have an inaccurate or insufficient understanding of normal sexual development in children. Adding a sex education component to family therapy that provides information, modeling, and sexual abuse prevention can be extremely important in stopping sexual abuse from continuing into the next generation.

Group Therapy

The most common treatment for incest survivors appears to be group therapy (Herman & Schatzow, 1984; Goodman & Nowack-Scibelli, 1985; Alexander et al., 1989; Roberts & Lie, 1989; Follette et al., 1991). Group therapy is viewed as a useful addition to individual therapy and often as a powerful therapeutic modality in its own right (Cahill et al., 1991; Joy, 1987; Forward & Buck, 1978). Group therapy provides clients with the opportunity to meet other victims and realize that they are not alone in their experience. The group experience also affords clients the chance to resolve some of the issues of secrecy and shame because they can see that other people have had similar experiences and have similar feelings.

Tsai and Wagner (1978) authored a ground breaking study in the area of group therapy for the treatment of incest survivors. On the basis of this initial study, others have done subsequent research on the short-term time-limited format for this kind of therapy. The short-term time-limited approach includes one and half hour sessions weekly for a period of 8 to 12 weeks. The groups consist of five to eight participants and are led by a co-therapy team of two therapists. Alexander and Follett (1988) suggest particular advantages of this model. Bonding among members of the group is facilitated and the group provides a clear structure for dealing with painful and intense emotions. The focus is kept on incest and clear boundaries are established. These factors serve to counteract the denial and confusing expectations that are characteristic of incestuous families. This creates an atmosphere that is both safe and supportive for the survivors to share their experiences and work through the effects of such experiences (Goodman & Nowack-Scibelli, 1985). This group model highlights the strengths of the group members and enables them to take control. These aspects are particularly important as these women often feel helpless and powerless especially around the abuse.

Goodman and Nowack-Scibelli (1985) outline several phases of the group therapeutic approach. The introductory phase is where the group members meet and basic ground rules are set for conducting the group. This phase establishes a foundation for the subsequent phases. In the second phase, group members "tell their stories." This is seen as the initial introduction to the therapeutic process. Group members can see the difficulty members have in sharing the stories and the intense, painful emotions associated with recounting the abuse. The group also serves as a support system for the depression that often follows recounting the details of abuse (Herman & Schatzow, 1984; Goodman & Nowack-Scibelli, 1985). The final phase prepares participants for termination and deals with issues of abandonment, personal achievements, and plans for the future (Herman & Schatzow, 1984; Goodman & Nowack-Scibelli, 1985).

Special Concerns for the Therapist

Working in a therapeutic setting with adult survivors of incest often evokes strong reactions about safety, danger, love, and betrayal. As a result of general feelings about incest, isolation is a significant concern for the therapist. It is the therapist's role to hear and absorb clients' recounting of the abuse and the pain associated with the abuse without reaction. In many cases, the stories of victimization, exploitation, and rage may be physically and emotionally moving to therapists, yet they must maintain a stance of acceptance and show no shock as they listen to the clients. It is not uncommon for therapists who frequently work with incest survivors to experience PTSD in a secondary fashion (Figley, 1985). A therapist may experience nightmares or be concerned with personal danger in situations where she or he previously was not. The ability to be empathic to adult survivor clients may leave the therapist open to allowing some of the client's trauma into his or her own life. Indications that this is happening include increased irritability, free-floating anxiety, difficulties in dealing with stress and personal relationships, questioning therapist's belief in a just world, and cynicism (Briere, 1989).

Repeated exposure to adult survivors of incest in a therapeutic setting can produce a skewed perspective for the therapist (Briere, 1989; Dolan, 1991). Therapists may become either overinvested or underinvested in their clients. Therapists who become overinvested may cross the therapeutic boundary and become personally involved with them in terms of needing to rescue clients by lending money or taking clients home with them. Conversely, those therapists who underinvest in survivors dissociate from client's trauma; they appear to be cool and professional and experience numbness in the face of situations that might otherwise elicit anger or depression. The clients simply become cases that are viewed in a very clinical manner.

In both situations, supervision would be warranted because the reactions of the therapist are specific to his or her own state of mind and are not about the adult survivor client. However, the client will certainly be affected by the emotional and psychological state of the therapist. As a result of his or her internal processes, the therapist may be unable to create a productive therapeutic atmosphere for the client (Briere, 1989; Dolan, 1991).

Effectiveness of Various Approaches

Incest treatment approaches have only recently become the focus of empirical research, and what has been done is limited (Cahill et al., 1991). The literature on treatment of incest is replete with discussions of various approaches to therapy with survivors; however, the majority of the treatment approaches have not been empirically tested. Much of the treatment literature consists of models for therapy illustrated and supported by examples from case studies.

What empirical research that has been done on incest is based on data collected by quantitative measures. These data and related research findings are certainly contributions to the study of incest and its impact on women. The data have provided the field with increased awareness of incest; indications of the prevalence of incest in society; and the common psychological, emotional, and behavioral reactions to incest. However, the present body of research could be augmented by qualitative research studies that examine the common reactions to incest within a broader context. It may be useful to explore why some survivors exhibit certain symptoms while others experience very different symptoms. An examination of the idiosyncratic nature of incest survivors' symptoms may serve an important function in determining treatment (Osborn, 1992).

In addition, exploration and research in the areas of family and couple therapeutic approaches with survivors are needed. While the empirical research is limited in the area of treatment in general, the exploration and discussion of ways in which family and couple therapy may be useful in working with survivors is sorely lacking. Literature on individual and group therapy with survivors is vast; however, these therapeutic approaches do not directly consider or address the impact of the abuse on the survivor's current family and intimate relationships. Addressing symptoms as they relate to the individual is certainly an essential part of the therapeutic process, but it does not address the systemic nature of such symptoms. Drug abuse, depression, and PTSD are individual symptoms that surely have an impact on the survivor's current relationships. If an individual is having a primary relationship with drugs or alcohol, for example, this would have a significant impact on the other relationships in that individual's life.

The lack of research and writing on couple therapy with survivors and their partners is a major gap in the childhood sexual abuse survivor literature. More work needs to be done in this area that includes the partner in the therapeutic process beyond the realm of sexual dysfunction. An area of inquiry may be what impact does sexual abuse have on the relationship between the survivor and the spouse? What are the idiosyncratic facets of the relationship and how do they differ from those where neither partner is a survivor? It may also be helpful to explore the meanings that couples give the abuse and subsequent symptoms and why some couples have more difficulty dealing with abuse than others.

CONCLUSIONS

Incest is an emotionally charged issue for all concerned because it impinges on the basic trust of childhood. In the last several decades, research on incest has changed dramatically. General attitudes have changed—the victim or survivor is no longer blamed for the incest. The focus has shifted to one where the concern lies in how to help incest survivors deal with the effects of incest on their lives. The impact incest has on survivors can be extraordinary and research reflects this.

The consequences of incest are varied and farreaching. Survivors experience a variety of psychological, emotional, and behavioral reactions, which have an impact on the individual survivor herself, her relationships, and her family. It is not uncommon for incest survivors to experience PTSD symptoms in response to the abuse. When one considers that survivors experience the same symptoms as earthquake or plane crash victims, one begins to get a sense of the profound effects incest may have on children.

The treatment of incest has been an expanding area of research and study. The major treatment approaches include group and individual therapy. Family-of-origin therapy, family therapy with the survivor's current family, and couple therapy are considered adjuncts to individual, intrapsychic therapy. There is a growing trend to incorporate such intrapsychic work into systemic family therapy and couple therapy. The assumption here is that we all bring elements of our past relationships and experiences into present relationships and experiences. These elements of the past certainly impact on experiences in the present. The same is true for incest.

Although there are certainly merits in individual-oriented therapies for incest survivors, they seem to only address part of the work that needs to be done. If we assume that the members of family systems are interrelated and interdependent, then it follows that the experience of incest has an impact on all family members both in families of origin and current families. Therefore it follows that it would be useful to integrate the processes of individual, family, and couple therapy for survivors and their families.

REFERENCES

Alexander, P. & Follette, V. (1988). Personal constructs in the group treatment of incest. In R. Neimeyer & G. Neimeyer (Eds.), *Personal construct therapy casebook*. New York: Springer.

Alexander, P., Neimeyer, R., Follette, V., Moore, M., & Harter, S. (1989). A comparisaon of group treatments of women sexually abused as children. *Journal of Consulting and Clinical Psychology, 57*, 479–483.

American Psychiatric Association (1987). *Diagnostic and Statistical Manual*, Third Edition—Revised. Washington, DC: APA.

Atwood, J. & Levine, L. (1990). The therapeutic metaphor. *Australian Journal of Clinical Hypnotherapy and Hypnosis, 11*, 17–40.

Atwood, J. & Levine, L. (1991). Ax murders, dragons, spiders, and webs: Therapeutic metaphors for couple therapy. *Compemporary Family Therapy, 13*, 1–31.

Ayalon, O. (1983). Coping with terrorism. In D. Meichenbaum & M. Jaremko (Eds.), *Stress reduction and prevention*. New York: Plenum.

Barrett, M. & Stone Fish, L. (1992). Couples therapy with adult survivors of incest. Presented at the Fifteenth Annual Family Therapy Network Symposium, Washington, DC.

Berg, I. (1990). *Solution-focused approach to family based services*. Milwaukee: Brief Family Therapy Center.

Black, D. (1982). Children and disaster. *British Medical Journal, 285*, 989–990.

Blume, S. (1990). *Secret survivors*. New York: John Wiley.

Boszormenyi-Nagy, I. & Spark, G. (1973). *Invisible loyalties*. New York: Harper & Row.

Boszormenyi-Nagy, I. & Ulrich, D. (1981). Contextual family therapy. In A Gurman & N. Kniskern (Eds.), *Handbook of family therapy*. New York: Brunner/Mazel.

Breunlin, D. (1988). Oscillation theory and family development. In C. Falcov (Ed.), *Family transitions: Continuity and change over the life cycle*. New York: Guilford Press.

Briere, J. (1989). *Therapy for adults molested as children*. New York: Springer.

Briere, J. & Runtz, M. (1987). Post-sexual abuse trauma: Data and implications for practice. *Journal of Interpersonal Violence, 3*, 367–379.

Bronson, C. (1989). *Growing through the pain*. Englewood Cliffs, NJ: Prentice-Hall.

Browne, A. & Finkelhor, D. (1986). Impact of child sexual abuse: A review of the research. *Psychological Bulletin, 99*, 66–77.

Cahill, C., Llewelyn, S., & Pearson, C. (1991). Treatment of sexual abuse which occurred in childhood: A review. *British Journal of Clinical Psychology, 30*, 1–12.

Courtois, C. (1988). *Healing the incest wound*. New York: W. W. Norton.

Covington, C. (1989). Incest: The psychological problem and the biological contradiction. *Issues in Health Nursing, 10*, 69–87.

de Shazer, S. (1982). *Patterns of brief family therapy*. New York: Guilford Press.

de Shazer, S. (1984). The death of resistance. *Family Process, 23*, 11–27.

de Shazer, S. (1985). *Keys to solutions in brief therapy*. New York: Guilford Press.

de Shazer, S. (1988). *Clues: Investigating solutions in brief therapy*. New York: W. W. Norton.

Dinsmore, C. (1991) *From surviving to thriving*. Albany: State University of New York Press.

Dolan, Y. (1989). Only once if I really mean it: Brief treatment of previously dissociated incest. *Journal of Systemic and Strategic Therapies*, (Winter).

Dolan, Y. (1991). *Resolving seuxal abuse*. New York: W. W. Norton.

Donaldson, M. & Gardner, R. (1985). Diagnosis and treatment of traumatic stress among women after childhood sexual abuse. In C. Figley (Ed.), *Trauma and its wake: The study of treatment of post-traumatic stress disorder*. New York: Brunner/Mazel.

Faria, G. & Belohlavek, N. (1984). Treating female adult survivors of childhood incest. *Social Casework, 65*, 465–471.

Figley, C. (1985). *Trauma and its wake: The study of treatment of post-traumatic stress disorder*. New York: Brunner/Mazel.

Fishman, C. (1991). *Treating the troubled adolescent*. New York: Basic Books.

Finkelhor, D. (1979). *Sexually victimized children*. New York: Free Press.

Finkelhor, D. (1984). *Child sexual abuse: New theory and research*. Beverly Hills: Sage.

Follette,V., Alexander, P., & Follette, W. (1991). Individual predictors of outcome in group treatment of incest survivors. *Journal of Consulting and Clinical Psychology, 59*, 150–155.

Foward, S. & Buck, C. (1978). *Betrayal of innocence: Incest and its devastation*. Los Angeles: Tarcher.

Framo, J. (1981). The integration of marital therapy with sessions of family origin. In A. Gurman & N. Kniskern (Eds.), *Handbook of family therapy*. New York: Brunner/Mazel.

Gelinas, D. (1983). The persiting negative effects of incest. *Psychiatry, 46*, 312–332.

Gil, E. (1988). *Treatment of adult survivors of childhood sexual abuse*. Walnut Creek, CA: Launch Press.

Goodman, B. & Nowack-Scibelli, D. (1985). Group treatment for women incestuously abused as children. *International Journal of Group Psychotherapy, 35*, 531–544.

Goodwin, J. & DiVasto, P. (1979). Mother-daughter incest. *Child Abuse & Neglect, 3,* 953–957.

Haley, J. (1976). *Problem-solving therapy.* San Francisco: Jossey-Bass.

Herman, J. (1981). *Father–daughter incest.* Cambridge: Harvard University Press.

Herman, J. & Hirschman, L. (1981). Father–daughter incest. Signs. *Journal of Women in Culture and Society, 2,* 735–756.

Herman, J. & Schatzow, E. (1984). Time-limited group therapy for women with a history of incest. *International Journal of Group Psychotherapy, 34,* 605–616.

Hof, L. & Berman, E. (1986). The sexual genogram. *Journal of Marital and Family Therapy, 12,* 39-47.

Jackson, J., Calhoun, K., Amick, A., Maddever, H., & Habif, V. (1990). Young adult women who report childhood intrafamilial sexual abuse. *Archives of Sexual Behavior, 19,* 211–221.

Jehu, D. (1991). *Beyond sexual abuse.* New York: John Wiley.

Josephson G. & Fong-Beyette, M. (1987). Factors assisting female clients' disclosure of incest during counseling. *Journal of Counseling and Development, 65,* 475–478.

Joy, S. (1987). Retrospective presentation of incest. *Journal of Counseling and Development, 65,* 317–319.

Kilpatrick, D. & Amick, A. (1984). Intrafamilial and extrafamilial sexual assault. Paper presented at the Second National Family Violence Research Conference, Durham, NH.

Kinsey, A., Pomeroy, W., Martin, C., & Gebhard, P. (1953). *Seuxal behavior in the human female.* Philadelphia: Saunders.

Levang, C. (1989). Father–daughter incest families. *Contemporary Family Therapy, 11,* 28–41.

Lipchik, E. & de Shazer, S. (1986). The purposeful interview. *Journal of Strategic and Systemic Therapies, 5,* 88–89.

Maltz, W. (1988). Identifying and treating the sexual repercussions of incest: A couples therapy approach. *Journal of Sex and Marital Therapy, 14,* 145–163.

Maltz, W. & Holman, B. (1987). *Incest and sexuality.* Lexington, MA: Lexington Books.

Masson, J. (1984). *The assault on truth: Freud's suppression of seduction theory.* New York: Farrar, Straus & Giroux.

Meiselman, K. (1978). *Incest: A psychological study of causes and effects with treatment recommendations.* San Francisco: Jossey-Bass.

Minuchin, S. (1974). *Families and family therapy.* Cambridge: Harvard University Press.

Minuchin, S. & Fishman, J. (1981). *Family therapy techniques.* Cambridge: Harvard University Press.

Newman, C. (1976). Child of disaster: Clinical observations at Buffalo Creek. *American Journal of Psychiatry, 133,* 306–310.

O'Hanlon, W. & Weiner-Davis, M. (1989). *In search of solutions.* New York: W. W. Norton.

Osborn, J. (1992). Unpublished manuscript.

Paul, N. (1976). Cross confrontation. In P. Guerin (Ed.), *Family therapy: Theory and practice.* New York: Gardner Press.

Putman, F. (1985). Dissociation as a response to extreme trauma. In R. Kluft (Ed.), *Childhood antecedents of multiple personality.* Washington, DC: American Psychiatric Press.

Roberts, L. & Lie, G. (1989). A group therapy approach to the treatment of incest. *Social Work with Groups, 12,* 77–90.

Rosenfeld, A. (1986). Treatment for serious mental health sequelae. Panel presented at the Fourth National Conference on the Sexual Victimization of Children, Children's Hospital National Medical Center, New Orleans.

Rush, F. (1977). *The Freudian cover-up*. Chrysalis, 31–45.

Rush, F. (1980). *The best kept secret*. Englewood Cliffs, NJ: Prentice-Hall.

Russell, D. (1986). *The secret trauma*. New York: Basic Books.

Satir, V. (1983). *Conjoint family therapy*, 3rd ed. Palo Alto: Science and Behavior Press.

Schultz, R., Braun, B., & Kluft, R. (1987). The most significant findings of the interface between multiple personality disorder (MPD) and Borderline Personality Disorder (BPD). Unpublished raw data.

Silver, R., Boon, C., & Stones, M. (1983). Searching for meaning in misfortune: Making sense of incest. *Journal of Social Issues, 39*, 81–102.

Stern, C. (1984). The eitiology of multiple personalities. *Psychiatric Clinics of North America, 7*, 177–193.

Trepper, T. & Barrett, M. (1989). *Systemic treatment of incest*. New York: Brunner/ Mazel.

Tsai, M. & Wagner, N. (1978). Therapy groups for women sexually molested as children. *Archives of Sexual Behavior, 7*, 417–427.

Watzlawick, P., Beavin, J., & Jackson, D. (1967). *Pragmatics of human communication*. New York: W. W. Norton.

Weinberg, K. (1955). *Incest behavior*. New York: Citadel.

Weiner-Davis, M., de Shazer, S., & Ginderich, W. (1987). Building on pretreatment change to construct the therapeutic solution. *Journal of Martial and Family Therapy, 13*, 359–363.

Wilbur, C. (1985). Multilpe personality and child abuse. *Psychiatric Clinics of North America, 7*, 3–8.

Williamson, D. (1981). Personal authority via termination of the intergenerational hierarchical boundary: A new stage in the family life cycle. *Journal of Marital and Family Therapy, 7*, 441–452.

Williamson, D. (1982a). Personal authority in the family experience via termination of the intergenerational hierarchical boundary: Part III. *Journal of Marital and Family Therapy, 8*, 309–323.

Williamson, D. (1982b). Personal authority in the family experience via termination of the intergenerational hierarchical boundary: Part II. *Journal of Marital and Family Therapy, 8*, 25–37.

Wise, M. (1985). Incest victim survivor paradox. Presented at the Annual Convention of the American Association of Counseling and Development, New York.

Wyatt, G. (1985). *The aftermath of child sexual abuse: The victim's experience*. Newbury Park, CA: Sage.

9

SYMPTOMS OF SURVIVORS OF PHYSICAL AND SEXUAL ABUSE

DEAN M. BUSBY

Articles dealing with the consequences and treatment of abuse have become common in almost every major professional journal in the family field (Malone, Tyree, & O'Leary, 1989; Morrow & Sorell, 1989; Willbach, 1989; Egley, 1991). As a result, the clinician who is trained today has a wide variety of information and resources available to address the effects of abuse. Nevertheless, there are still considerable gaps in the existing research that hamper applied professionals in their work with abused family members.

Recent literature on sexual and physical abuse indicates that these extreme forms of mistreatment can place an individual at risk for developing the symptoms that are described in the DSM–IIIR as Post-Traumatic Stress Disorder (PTSD) (American Psychiatric Association, 1987; Figley, 1985; Finkelhor, 1987; Frederick, 1985; Goodwin, Cheeves, & Connell, 1990; Lindberg, & Distad, 1985; Meek, 1990; van der Kolk, 1987). Some of the common characteristics or symptoms of PTSD are: (1) reexperiencing the traumatic event in an emotional, psychological, or physical sense that can include nightmares, dissociation, flashbacks, or distressing recollections; (2) avoidance of situations or people that remind the survivor of the trauma; and (3) various symptoms of increased arousal such as sleep problems, outbursts of anger, depression, or difficulty concentrating (APA, 1987).

Although research shows that individuals appear to have different levels of vulnerability to extreme stressors, the stressors appear to be more important than predisposing personality factors in determining the development

Note: This article is an adapted version of the following published material: Busby, D. M., Glenn, E., Steggell, G. L., Adamson, D. W. Treatment issues for survivors of physical and sexual abuse. Reprinted with permission from Volume 19, Number 4, of the *Journal of Marital and Family Therapy.* Copyright 1993, American Association for Marriage and Family Therapy.

of psychological symptoms (Horowitz, 1986; Meek, 1990; Silver, 1985; Singer, 1981). The authors of the DSM–IIIR place additional emphasis on this principle when it states that the distressing event producing PTSD would be "markedly distressing to almost anyone, and is usually experienced with intense fear, terror, and helplessness" (APA, 1987, p. 247). The words "fear," "terror," and "helplessness" are remarkably similar to terms clients use to describe their feelings associated with child abuse. Other comments in the DSM–IIIR, such as "the disorder is apparently more severe and longer lasting when the stressor is of human design" and "sometimes there is a concomitant physical component of the trauma…" are particularly relevant to physical and sexual abuse (p. 248).

Traumatic stress theory, the theory underlying PTSD, is especially appropriate for marriage and family therapists working with survivors of physical and sexual abuse because some of the principles are similar to systems concepts (Figley, 1985; Finkelhor & Brown, 1985; Gelinas, 1983; Goodwin, 1985; Krugman, 1987). For example, Figley (1985) remarks that the experiencing of "post-traumatic stress reactions" is an attempt to "deal with the memories" that are related to the catastrophe (p. xix). An appealing aspect of this description of stress reactions is that the development of symptoms is an ordinary, if not healthy, response to an extraordinary catastrophe. This facet of trauma theory is closely related to systems principles in that symptoms in the individual are not pathological per se, rather they are seen to be a manifestation of how the individual is attempting to fit into the larger system (Hoffman, 1981, p. 348).

An additional systemic principle, which has been related to child abuse, is the "double bind." Speigel (1986) comments on how child abuse creates the classic double-bind experience for the victim:

> Severe trauma inflicted by parents…has elements of a macabre double bind…. Rape by a father or physical abuse imposed by a mother has the bizarre quality of combining intense and longed-for attention from the parent with pain and humiliation. Furthermore frequently the parents rationalize the behavior by telling children that it is "for your own good," will "whip you into shape," will "teach you what you need to know about life," and so on. Thus, these patients are left with intense and irreconcilable feelings, pain, fear, and humiliation on one hand and on the other the desire for something positive from their parents and the half-belief that the mistreatment is indeed for their own good (pp. 69–70).

Is it possible that some of the double-bind communication that was discovered by the Palo Alto group is a symptom of parental abuse (Bateson, Jackson, Haley, & Weakland, 1956)? Regardless of the answer, it is striking how many double-bind messages surround physical and sexual abuse. Survivors are often confused by a perpetrators extreme hostility at one moment and expressions of love immediately following the abuse. Even spouses, neighbors, and friends of perpetrators demonstrate their confusion from the double messages when they express surprise or refuse to believe that anyone "so nice" could have done the unspeakable acts reported by the victims.

Traumatic stress theory, as used by several authors, proposes that there are numerous ways symptoms can emerge (Brown & Finkelhor, 1986; Figley, 1985; Horowitz, 1976, 1986; Krugman, 1987; Laufer, Brett, & Gallops, 1985; Miller-Perrin & Wurtele, 1990; Williams, 1987). There can be an acute reaction that is short in duration, a delayed response that can occur several years or decades after the event, a chronic reaction, or a combination of several of these responses. The initial symptoms often are of a denial (depression, avoidance) type or a reexperiencing (anxiety, somatic) type. Researchers report that many victims of trauma exhibit "sub-clinical" symptoms in that they do not meet all of the requirements for PTSD but are nevertheless experiencing significant distress. They suggest there is a problem with the PTSD diagnosis because it requires that both the denial and reexperiencing symptoms must occur simultaneously whereas in many cases they occur sequentially (Laufer et al., 1985; Williams, 1987).

Many authors have proposed that over time the initial reactions to trauma can develop into secondary problems which often include characteristics of borderline, antisocial, passive-aggressive and other personality patterns that are related to numerous interpersonal problems (Goodwin et al., 1990; Hunter, 1990; Krugman, 1987; Laufer et al., 1985; Miller-Perrin & Wurtele, 1990; O'Connor, 1986; Wheeler & Walton, 1987). Consequently clients who have experienced physical and sexual abuse in their backgrounds and later seek therapeutic assistance can present with primary, secondary, or associated interpersonal problems. Therapists, then, will often diagnosis problems that fit their orientations (i.e., a clinical psychologist might determine there is a personality disorder, while a marriage and family therapist might determine there is relationship problem), all the while overlooking the trauma from the abuse.

According to traumatic stress theory, it is likely that many clients who are survivors of abuse and who are presenting for a wide variety of relationship issues at a marriage and family therapy center exhibit primary and secondary reactions to trauma. The purpose of this chapter is to examine the question of whether survivors of physical and sexual abuse exhibit symptoms associated with traumatic stress theory and PTSD. These symptoms could be of the denial type such as avoidance or depression, and or the reexperiencing type such as anxiety and somatic problems (Horowitz, 1986; Laufer et al., 1985; Williams, 1987). Additionally, the symptoms could be secondary symptoms like borderline, antisocial, and passive-aggresive behavioral patterns that interfere with relationship development (Courtois, 1988; Hunter, 1990; Krugman, 1987; Meek, 1990; Wheeler & Walton, 1987).

This is a summary of a previous work by Busby, Glenn, Steggell, and Adamson (1993). In the 1993 study the trauma symptomology of 226 adults was explored using samples of clients who reported no abuse and clients who reported physical abuse, sexual abuse, or both forms of maltreatment in their families of origin. The trauma symptomology was measured by the Millon Clinical Multiaxial Inventory (MCMI) (Millon, 1984). The MCMI provides a solid estimation of primary and secondary reactions to trauma (Millon, 1981; Butcher, 1984). In addition, the MCMI is closely tied to the DSM–IIIR which is the primary reference for diagnosing personality disorders, clinical syndromes, and PTSD (APA, 1987).

RESULTS

The results of the Busby et al. (1993) study demonstrate that all of the abused groups had significantly higher scores than the nonabused group (on the MCMI a higher score indicates more distress or symptomology). In addition, the physically abused group was significantly less avoidant than the clients who suffered sexual abuse or both physical and sexual abuse (see Table 9.1).

The consistent pattern evident in this table is that scores progressively increased as group membership moved from the nonabuse group to those who experienced both physical and sexual abuse. It appears that as abuse moves from physical to sexual and then to both combined, clients exhibit higher levels of dysfunction with respect to the avoidance, passive-aggressive, borderline, anxiety, somatoform, and dysthymic areas.

Table 9.2 presents the percentage of clients who fell within the clinical range (above 75) on the six scales of the MCMI. It is apparent from this table that as the type of abuse becomes more severe, clients are more likely to fall within a clinical range of functioning on avoidant, passive-aggressive, borderline, anxiety, and dysthymic scales. It is particularly noteworthy that over 70% of the clients who experienced sexual abuse with or without physical violence scored in the clinical range on the borderline, dysthymic, and anxiety scales. The nonabused group, on the other hand, had less than 44% of its members in the clinical range on these three scales.

DISCUSSION

These results provide a preliminary validation of some of the tenets of traumatic stress theory. It did appear that clients who experienced physical and/ or sexual abuse presented with the primary and secondary symptoms associated with trauma. Even though the abused clients were seeking help for relationship difficulties, they were experiencing higher levels of primary symptoms (depression, avoidance, and anxiety) and secondary symptoms (borderline and passive-aggressive behavior patterns) commonly found in clients diagnosed with PTSD (Brown & Finkelhor, 1986; Horowitz, 1976, 1986; Krugman, 1987; Laufer et al., 1985; Miller-Perrin & Wurtele, 1990; Williams, 1987). The symptomology that was exhibited by victims of abuse

TABLE 9.1 • **Means and Standard Deviations of the Four Groups on the MCMI Scales**

Scale Sample	Mean	Standard Deviation
Avoidant		
No abuse (n=148)	50.45*	25.46
Physical abuse (n=36)	61.31*	19.98
Sexual abuse (n=32)	72.77	21.03
Physical and sexual abuse (n=15)	74.20	21.27
Passive-aggressive		
No abuse	51.52*	27.54
Physical abuse	70.56	24.04
Sexual abuse	73.37	22.16
Physical and sexual abuse	77.67	24.99
Borderline		
No abuse	65.22*	19.53
Physical abuse	76.31	13.01
Sexual abuse	79.17	13.36
Physical and sexual abuse	84.67	16.72
Anxiety		
No abuse (n=148)	71.68*	23.61
Physical abuse (n=36	86.28	18.90
Sexual abuse (n=32)	91.33	16.24
Physical and sexual abuse (n=15)	88.87	20.76
Somatoform		
No abuse	63.36*	14.19
Physical abuse	70.19	16.43
Sexual abuse	71.20	13.72
Physical and sexual abuse	72.48	19.98
Dysthymic		
No abuse	68.71*	23.64
Physical abuse	81.53	18.49
Sexual abuse	85.87	20.89
Physical and sexual abuse	90.00	19.08

*Significantly different than all other groups at p < .05

TABLE 9.2 • Percentage of Clients in Each Group Who Scored in the Nonclinical (less than 75) or Clinical Range (equal to or greater than 75) on the MCMI Scales

Scale Sample	Nonclinical	Clinical
*Avoidant**		
No abuse (n=148)	82.4	17.6
Physical abuse (n=36)	77.8	22.2
Sexual abuse (n=32)	53.3	46.7
Physical and sexual abuse (n=15)	46.7	53.3
*Passive-aggressive**		
No abuse	69.6	30.4
Physical abuse	41.7	58.3
Sexual abuse	33.3	66.7
Physical and sexual abuse	26.7	73.3
*Borderline**		
No abuse	68.2	31.8
Physical abuse	41.7	58.3
Sexual abuse	20.0	80.0
Physical and sexual abuse	20.0	80.0
*Anxiety**		
No abuse (n=148)	56.8	43.3
Physical abuse (n=36)	27.8	72.2
Sexual abuse (n=32)	13.3	86.7
Physical and sexual abuse (n=15)	26.7	73.3
Somatoform		
No abuse	79.1	20.9
Physical abuse	63.9	36.1
Sexual abuse	63.3	36.7
Physical and sexual abuse	66.7	33.3
*Dysthymic**		
No abuse	56.8	43.2
Physical abuse	27.8	72.2
Sexual abuse	16.7	83.3
Physical and sexual abuse	20.0	80.0

*Fisher Exact Probability Test significant at p < .01

was severe enough to result in the majority of them scoring within the clinical range on five of the seven scales under consideration.

It was interesting that the antisocial scale was not significant in this study. The possibility existed that individuals who were extreme enough to score high on the antisocial scale ended up in other treatment facilities than the clinic from which this sample was drawn. The DSM–IIIR lists some of common adult behaviors associated with the antisocial personality pattern including lying, stealing, or other forms of harassment that often involve the legal system (APA, 1987). If this were the case, the antisocial clients might be involved in treatment facilities such as prisons or inpatient units that deal with more extreme cases than the clinic from which the samples were drawn for this study.

Somatic symptoms also did not prove to be an important discriminator of physical or sexual abuse. Although the somatoform scale was statistically significant, it was not clinically relevant and was the least effective at discriminating between the abused and nonabused groups. The implication of this finding was that somatic problems were not as likely to be found in survivors of abuse as some of the other problems.

IMPLICATIONS FOR TREATMENT

The primary implication of traumatic stress theory is that victims of both physical and sexual abuse can be helped by treatment programs that address the trauma of their pasts. If the symptomology of individuals who were physically and sexually abused is similar as was found in this study, it might be possible to treat both groups of survivors in the same type of treatment program. A number of clinicians have developed programs to help victims of abuse overcome the trauma and the developmental blocking that results from it (Bass & Davis, 1988; Courtois, 1988; Engel, 1989; Scurfield, 1985; Stith, Williams, & Rosen, 1990; Williams, 1987). These programs could be very helpful for marriage and family therapists who are likely to see family members, perpetrators, and adult survivors.

There is a consensus among most professionals who study traumatized individuals that many of the aftereffects of trauma hamper an individual's ability to function in relationships (Figley, 1978, 1985; Figley & Sprenkle, 1978; Hickman, 1987; O'Connor, 1986; van der Kolk, 1987; Williams & Williams, 1987). Common problems include an inability to trust, difficulties in sharing emotions, sexual dysfunctions, poor parenting skills, explosive personalities, and aversions to members of the opposite sex.

This study lends further support to the idea that many of the marital and family problems suffered by adult survivors of abuse could be symptoms of trauma. It provides additional evidence that abused individuals suffer from problems that could seriously hamper the development and maintenance of relationships. Borderline, depressed, and avoidant individuals are not easy to relate to, and have often been difficult to work with in therapy.

Deciding that the trauma from abuse is an important problem to be addressed in therapy may greatly change the way many marriage and family therapists work with clients. The side effects of abuse, if severe enough, could contraindicate the appropriateness of marital and family therapy as a starting point for intervention, or at least indicate that individual therapy should occur simultaneously. The ability of some victims to progress in marital and family therapy could be hampered by not addressing issues stemming from their abuse. Psychologists and psychiatrists have noticed this for years when they attempted to treat the depression or borderline symptoms and failed to make progress because they did not help the clients deal with the trauma of the abuse (Herman, 1981; Gelinas, 1983). Is it any more appropriate to believe that simply addressing marital and family symptoms will remove the trauma and aftereffects of abuse and allow victims to function adequately?

Promoting trauma from abuse to the primary concern in therapy rather than an ancillary issue is in some ways contrary to pure systemic reasoning. There are at least two philosophical stances that can be taken with populations of adult survivors of abuse. First, treating the current marital and family systems as the primary concern and dealing with the "here and now" will help the survivor develop healthy relationships and thereby promote healing. This view is consistent with many traditional family therapy approaches such as the MRI approach (Watzlawick, Weakland, & Fisch, 1974), the strategic approach (Madanes, 1989), and the structural approach (Minuchin, 1974). It is also consistent with many of the brief therapy approaches (de Shazer, 1991; O'Hanlon & Weiner-Davis, 1989; Budman & Gurman, 1988).

The second view is that marital and family problems are often symptoms of the trauma. To promote healing the sources of the symptoms (the trauma) must be recognized, the emotions related to the perpetrators of the violence must be validated, and the long-term effects must be treated or the symptoms will reemerge later. This view is more consistent with approaches specifically designed to treat PTSD (Figley, 1985; Horowitz, 1986; Williams, 1987), object relations approaches (Boszormenyi-Nagy & Krasner, 1986; Gillman, 1980; Kirschner & Kirschner, 1986), feminist-informed approaches (Walters, Carter, Papp, & Silverstein, 1988), and individual approaches (Bass & Davis, 1988; Courtois, 1988; Engel, 1989; Scurfield, 1985; Silver, 1985).

It is not clear at this time which philosophical viewpoint offers the best alternative for treating adult survivors of abuse. This is an important empirical question that should be addressed in future research. Because much of the literature on adult survivors has been conducted by individually oriented therapists and researchers, there is a strong tendency to view marital and family therapy approaches as supportive rather than the treatment of choice. Still, since the family therapy approaches tend to be briefer than most individual or object relations approaches, briefer therapies are attracting research funds and are less costly, and family treatments include the individual's natural support system, it would seem to be an ideal time to investigate the relative effectiveness of marital and family therapy as the primary treatment for adult survivors of abuse.

Until such time as evidence suggests otherwise, marriage and family therapists are left in a quandary as to how to handle the common problem of their clients' abusive backgrounds. Should the more long-term individual approaches be utilized or are the marriage and family therapy approaches the treatment of choice? In our work we have chosen to utilize the pragmatic approach that is guided by the following questions:

1. Was the client abused?
2. How long and how severe was the abuse?
3. What does the client want from therapy?
4. What are the client's circumstances?
5. Does the selected approach seem to be working?

It is always important to carefully assess clients' backgrounds for the possibility of abuse. Ask questions or have clients complete self-report instruments to help determine whether abuse occurred, and if so, how extensive the abuse was. Even if very severely abused in the past but the client is seeking therapy for the amelioration of marital discord, there is an obligation to initially address the marital problem in treatment. Still, survivors of severe abuse often exhibit problems that inhibit the progress of traditional treatments for improving marital and family relationships. A passage from a classical text on marital therapy (Jacobson & Margolin, 1979, p. 149) is particularly relevant in this circumstance:

> People may tend to interpret all aspects of their spouse's behavior as evidence that they are regarded as, and therefore are, worthless. Consequently, because they view themselves as unlovable, relationship behavior delivered by the partner is likely to be viewed as rejecting or unloving. When cognitive distortions attain this level of severity, it is doubtful that an exclusively dyadic approach can remedy the situation.

This quote still is true; therefore, start initially with marital treatment if this is the request, and then, if the symptoms are too severe to allow this format, progress can often be made when the survivor is treated concurrently in group or individual therapy.

Any move to include individual and group treatment must be handled with caution. Some family therapists are reluctant to treat victims of abuse in individual therapy for fear that they might be promoting the idea that the person is sick or is responsible for the relationship problems. This is an especially relevant concern when the relationship problems include extensive blaming and punishing patterns of interaction. Certainly care must be taken to not label abused clients as sick or as the identified patient. This type of blame is the same message the perpetrator and other family members gave to the victim during childhood. Nevertheless, adult survivors of abuse are generally aware that many of their struggles are related to the aftereffects of their victimization. It is not uncommon for family members to also feel victimized by the trauma, because the abuse itself and the emergence of symptoms are both beyond their control. When therapists acknowledge the trauma as something that is significantly impacting the family that needs to be addressed in therapy, family members, including the survivor, often feel a sense of relief.

Additional complications with group treatment arise when the adult survivors have phobic or anxiety responses that make participating in group discussions difficult. An initiation of group treatment is a threatening process for most clients even though they also report it to be very helpful once they overcome their initial fears. Group therapy is an effective and useful way to approach many of the issues with which adult survivors struggle, including helping them feel they are not at fault for the abuse, providing them with models of appropriate behavior, creating additional supportive relationships, and giving them hope for improvement (Fulmer, 1990; Jelinek, 1987). These advantages outweigh the initial difficulties in starting group treatment, but the clients should be presented with the idea of group therapy in a way that respects their right to choose, provides them with ample time to adjust to the idea, and nurtures them so that they can overcome their fears.

Individual, group, and family therapy can occur concurrently or sequentially depending on the severity of the symptoms, the costs of the services, and the availability of the therapy groups. The specific financial and relationship circumstances of each client must be considered when making these important treatment decisions. Often severely abused clients are not in a financial position, or do not have the available time for the "luxury" of concurrent family, group, and individual treatment. Therapists should be aware of this problem and either reduce fees, stretch out the intervals between sessions, or have the client participate in the different modalities of therapy sequentially instead of concurrently.

The responses of each individual to trauma are very different. Some individuals seem to be more resilient while others are devastated for years (Brown & Finkelhor, 1986; Figley, 1985; Horowitz, 1986; Krugman, 1987; Laufer et al., 1985; Miller-Perrin & Wurtele, 1990; Williams, 1987). Care should be taken to not assume that each person who was abused as a child will necessarily be under extreme duress as an adult. If the client wants help with relationship problems and these seem to be successfully addressed in therapy, it should not be an automatic response to push the client to deal with past abuse. Pursue this direction only when it is apparent that there are underlying issues that are interfering with treatment, the timing seems to be right, or the client expresses a desire to deal with the abuse. In each instance, a therapist can make an informed choice only if she or he is aware of the abuse in the first place.

Some of the markers from the results in this study can provide therapists with information on whether to address the trauma from abuse. If clients exhibit high levels of anxiety, depression, or low self-esteem, it is possible that traditional approaches to marital and family problems may not be as effective as they could be with the addition of individual or group work. Anxiety and depression are problems that should be carefully monitored because they can lead to self-destructive, suicidal behaviors. In addition, low self-esteem often produces a scenario in therapy where any feedback from the therapist produces guilt. This pattern can prohibit the therapist from being effective and produce early terminations.

The avoidance, passive-aggressive, and borderline symptoms are particularly troublesome in therapy (Goodwin et al., 1990; Stone, 1981; Wheeler & Walton, 1987). These behaviors can combine to create a scenario where the client has a difficult time disclosing, the therapist becomes frustrated with this "resistance," and the client withdraws more or starts to miss sessions. The end result is that both the therapist and the client experience a negative outcome. When information about abuse is collected early on, it is possible to recognize the symptoms when they occur and to pace the therapy until the trust level is sufficient to allow the client to disclose. At other times, co-therapists, who are the same gender as the client, can be used to alleviate the aversion some clients have to disclosing to members of the opposite sex.

Another way the information from this study could be helpful in treatment is to assess the levels of depression, anxiety, avoidance, and so on, and to use these to help uncover abuse that has been repressed, dissociated, or relabeled as discipline or affection (Herman & Schatzow, 1987). Therapists should not automatically assume that clients, who present in therapy with the previously mentioned symptoms, have been sexually or physically abused. However, therapists do need to ask more questions and probe a little deeper with some clients. It is helpful to ask about the types of discipline and affection that were used in the home and to pursue details rather than to ask, "Were you sexually abused as a child?" Often perpetrators of abuse have provided very nonthreatening labels to their crimes that make it difficult for victims to recognize the behaviors as abusive. Experience and evidence confirms that certain clients who have been physically abused to the point of receiving severe bruises, or clients who have been forced to participate in sexual acts, sometimes do not consider these behaviors as maltreatment because that is not the definition they grew up with or the definition that the perpetrators used.

CONCLUSIONS

Random sample surveys of the general population indicate that between 16 to 38% of adults in the United States were sexually molested as children (Russell, 1983; Crewdson, 1988). Even if these rates are inaccurate, they only represent those individuals who were sexually abused. If those who had been physically abused individuals were added to these numbers, there are literally tens of millions of people who experienced serious trauma.

It is possible that the majority of clients seen by marriage and family therapists are dealing with one or both types of trauma in their backgrounds. In the marriage and family therapy clinic at Syracuse University, 76% of the first 60 clients who presented for therapy in 1991 reported serious physical and/or sexual abuse on a self-report instrument. Research on outpatient clinics indicates that the prevalence rates of only incest can be as high as 30% (Gelinas, 1983; Spencer, 1978). Therefore, it is important to face this problem as a profession and learn how to address it through education, training, and research.

Marriage and family therapists need to carefully assess their clients' histories for evidence of physical and sexual abuse. Some of the warning signs that could indicate abuse are high levels of depression, anxiety, avoidance, passive-aggressive, and borderline symptoms. Problems with trust, intimacy, self-esteem, and emotional expressiveness also could be indicators of past trauma. It is essential that therapists learn to recognize the symptoms of abuse and receive training in the treatment of these problems from multiple theoretical perspectives and different treatment modalities.

REFERENCES

American Psychiatric Association. (1987). *Diagnostic and statistical manual of mental disorders, Third edition—Revised*. Washington, DC: American Psychiatric Association.

Bass, E. & Davis, L. (1988). *The courage to heal*. New York: Harper & Row.

Bateson, G., Jackson, D., Haley, J., & Weakland, J. (1956). Towards a theory of schizophrenia. *Behavioral Science, 1*, 251–264.

Bolton Jr., F. G., Morris, L. A., & Maceachron, A. E. (1989). *Males at risk: The other side of child sexual abuse*. Newbury Park, CA: Sage.

Boszormenyi-Nagy, I. & Krasner, B. R. (1986). *Between give and take: A clinical guide to contextual therapy*. New York: Brunner/Mazel.

Brown, A. & Finkelhor, D. (1986). Impact of child sexual abuse: A review of the literature. *Psychological Bulletin, 99*, 66–77.

Budman, S. H. & Gurman, A. S. (1988). *Theory and practice of brief therapy*. New York: Guilford Press.

Busby, D. M., Glenn, E., Steggell, G. L., & Adamson, D. W. (1993). Treatment issues for survivors of physical and sexual abuse. *Journal of Marital and Family Therapy, 19*, 377–392.

Butcher, J. N. (1984). Personality assessment. In G. Goldstein & M. Hersen (Eds), *Handbook of psychological assessment*. New York: Pergamon Press.

Crewdson, J. (1988). *By silence betrayed*. New York: Harper & Row.

Courtois, C. A. (1988). *Healing the incest wound: Adult survivors in therapy*. New York: W. W. Norton.

de Shazer, S. (1991). *Putting difference to work*. New York: W. W. Norton.

Egley, L. C. (1991). Societal prevalence of domestic violence. *Journal of Marriage and the Family, 53*, 885–897.

Engel, B. (1989). *The right to innocents: Healing the trauma of childhood sexual abuse*. New York: Ivy Books.

Figley, C. R. (1978). *Stress disorders among Vietnam veterans.* New York: Brunner/Mazel.

Figley, C. R. (1985). *Trauma and its wake: The study and treatment of post-traumatic stress disorder.* New York: Brunner/Mazel.

Figley, C. R. & Sprenkle, D.H. (1978). Delayed stress response syndrome: Family therapy indications. *Journal of Marriage and Family Counseling, 6,* 53–59.

Finkelhor, D. (1987). The sexual abuse of children: Current research reviewed. *Psychiatric Annals, 17,* 233–237.

Finkelhor, D & Brown, A. (1985). The traumatic impact of child sexual abuse: A conceptualization. *American Journal of Orthopsychiatry, 55,* 530—541.

Finkelhor, D. & Brown, A. (1986). Initial and long-term effects: A conceptual framework. In D. Finkelhor (Ed.), *A sourcebook on child sexual abuse* (pp. 180–198). Beverly Hills: Sage.

Frederick, C. (1985). Children traumatized by catastrophic situations. In S. E. & R. S. Phynoos (Eds.), *Post-traumatic stress disorder in children.* Washington, DC: American Psychiatric Press.

Fulmer, J. F. (1990). Disguised presentation of adult survivors of incest and other child molestation. In S. M. Stith, M. B. Williams, & K. Rosen (Eds.), *Violence hits home: Comprehensive treatment approaches to domestic violence.* New York: Springer.

Gelinas, D. J. (1983). The persisting negative effects of incest. *Psychiatry, 46,* 311–332.

Gillman, S. (1980). An object relations approach to the phenomenon and treatment of battered women. *Psychiatry, 34,* 346–358.

Goodwin, J. (1985). Post-traumatic symptoms in incest victims. In S. E. & R. S. Phynoos (Eds.), *Post-traumatic stress disorder in children.* Washington, DC: American Psychiatric Press.

Goodwin, J. M., Cheeves, K., & Connell, V. (1990). Borderline and other severe symptoms in adult survivors of incestuous abuse. *Psychiatric Annals, 20,* 22–32.

Herman, J. (1981). *Father–daughter incest.* Cambridge: Harvard University Press.

Herman, J. & Schatzow, E. (1987). Recovery and verification of memories of childhood sexual trauma. *Psychoanalytic Psychology, 4,* 1–14.

Hickman, P. (1987). You weren't there. In T. Williams (Ed.), *Post-traumatic stress disorders: A handbook for clinicians.* Cincinnati: Disabled American Veterans.

Hoffman, L. (1981). *Foundations of family therapy: A conceptual framework for systems change.* New York: Basic Books.

Horowitz, M. J. (1976). *Stress response syndromes.* New York: Aronson.

Horowitz, M. J. (1986). Stress-response syndromes: A review of posttraumatic and adjustment disorders. *Hospital and Community Psychiatry, 37,* 241–249.

Hunter, M. (1990). *Abused boys: The neglected victims of sexual abuse.* Lexington, MA: Lexington Books.

Jacobson, N. S. & Margolin, G. (1979). *Marital therapy: Strategies based on social learning and behavior exchange principles.* New York: Brunner/Mazel.

Jelinek, J. M. (1987). Group therapy with Vietnam veterans and other trauma victims. In T. Williams (Ed.), *Post-traumatic stress disorders: A handbook for clinicians.* Cincinnati: Disabled American Veterans.

Kirschner, D. A. & Kirschner, S. (1986). *Comprehensive family therapy: An integration of systemic and psychodynamic treatment models.* New York: Brunner/Mazel.

Krugman, S. (1987). Trauma in the family: Perspectives on the intergenerational transmission of violence. In B. van der Kolk (Ed.), *Psychological trauma.* Washington, DC: American Psychiatric Press.

Laufer, R. S., Brett, E., & Gallops, M. S. (1985). Post-traumatic stress disorders in women who experienced childhood incest. *Child Abuse & Neglect, 9,* 329–334.

Lindberg, F. H. & Distad, L. J. (1985). Post-traumatic stress disorders in women who experienced childhood incest. *Child Abuse & Neglect, 8,* 329–334.

Madanes, C. (1989). *Strategic family therapy*. San Francisco: Jossey-Bass.

Malone, J., Tyree, A., & O'Leary, K. D. (1989). Different effects of past aggression for wives and husbands. *Journal of Marriage and the Family, 51*, 687–698.

McCabe, S. P. (1987). Millon Clinical Multiaxial Inventory. In R. C. Keyser & D. J. Sweetland (Eds), *Test critiques: Volume I*. Kansas City, MO: Test Corporation of America.

McReynolds, P. & Chelune, G. J. (1984). *Advances in psychological assessment*, Vol. 6. San Francisco: Jossey-Bass.

Meek, C. L. (1990). *Post-traumatic stress disorder: Assessment, differential diagnosis, and forensic evaluation*. Sarasota, FL: Professional Resource Exchange.

Miller-Perrin, C. L. & Wurtele, S. K. (1990). Reactions to childhood sexual abuse: Implications for post-traumatic stress disorder. In C. L. Meek (Ed.), *Post-traumatic stress disorder: Assessment differential diagnosis and forensic evaluation*. Sarasota, FL: Professional Resource Exchange.

Millon, T. (1981). *Disorders of personality: DSM-III Axis II*. New York: John Wiley.

Millon, T. (1984). *Millon clinical multiaxial inventory*. Minneapolis: National Computer Systems.

Minuchin, S. (1974). *Families and family therapy*. Cambridge: Harvard University Press.

Morrow, K. B. & Sorell, G. T. (1989). Factors affecting stress levels of sexually abused female adolescents. *Journal of Marriage and the Family, 51*, 677–687.

O'Connor, D. (1986). Later-life consequences of childhood sexual behavior. In L. Greenspoon (Ed.), *The Annual Review of Psychiatry*. Washington, DC: American Psychiatric Press.

O'Hanlon, W. H. & Weiner-Davis, M. (1989). *In search of solutions: A new direction in psychotherapy*. New York: W. W. Norton.

Russell, D. E. H. (1983). The incidence and prevalence of intrafamilial and extrafamilial sexual abuse of female children. *International Journal of Child Abuse and Neglect, 7*, 133–139.

Scurfield, R. M. (1985). Post-trauma stress assessment and treatment: Overview and formulations. In C. R. Figley (Ed.), *Trauma and its wake: The study and treatment of post-traumatic stress disorder*. New York: Brunner/Mazel.

Silver, S. M. (1985). Post-traumatic stress disorders in veterans. In P. A. Keller & L. G. Ritt (Eds.), *Innovations in clinical practice: A source book*, Vol. 4 (pp. 23–34). Sarasota, FL: Professional Resource Exchange.

Singer, M. T. (1981). Vietnam prisoners of war, stress, and personality resiliency. *American Journal of Psychiatry, 138*, 345–346.

Speigel, D. (1986). Dissociation, double binds, and posttraumatic stress in multiple personality disorder. In B. G. Braun (Ed.), *Treatment of multiple personality disorder*. Washington, DC: American Psychiatric Press.

Spencer, J. (1978). Father–daughter incest. *Child Welfare, 57* 581–590.

Stith, S. M., Williams, M. B., & Rosen, K. (1990). *Violence hits home: Comprehensive treatment approaches to domestic violence*. New York: Springer.

Stone, M. H. (1981). Borderline syndromes: A consideration of subtypes and an overview, directions for research. *Psychiatric Clinics of North America, 4*, 3–13.

Tsai, M., Feldman-Summers, S., & Edgar, M. (1979). Childhood molestation: Variables related to differential impacts on psychological functioning in adult women. *Journal of Abnormal Psychology, 88*, 407–417.

van der Kolk, B. (1987). *Psychological trauma*. Washington, DC: American Psychiatric Press.

Walters, M., Carter, B., Papp, P., & Silverstein, O. (1988). *The invisible web: Gender patterns in family relationships*. New York: Guilford Press.

Watzlawick, P., Weakland, J., & Fisch, R. (1974). *Change: Principles of problem formation and problem resolution*. New York: W. W. Norton.

Wheeler, B. R. & Walton, E. (1987). Personality disturbances of adult incest victims. *Social Casework, 68,* 597–602.

Willbach, W. (1989). Ethics and family therapy: The case management of family violence. *Journal of Marital and Family Therapy, 15,* 43–52.

Williams, T. (1987). *Post-traumatic stress disorders: A handbook for clinicians.* Cincinnati: Disabled American Veterans.

Williams, C. & Williams T. (1987). Family therapy for Vietnam veterans. In T. Williams (Ed.), *Post-traumatic stress disorders: A handbook for clinicians.* Cincinnati: Disabled American Veterans.

10

PREMARITAL PHYSICAL ABUSE OF WOMEN BY MALE PARTNERS

DEAN M. BUSBY, KYLE D. KILLIAN

In the last fifteen years, the problem of physical abuse has garnered increased attention from the media, helping professionals and educators. Although the shocking frequency and severity of the physical abuse perpetrated by men against their partners is now becoming recognized within our society, the labels of "spouse abuse" and "wife battering" perpetuate the illusion that physical abuse is a problem of only conflict-habituated, married couples. Research (Lloyd, Koval, & Cate, 1989; O'Leary et al., 1989) demonstrates that while a marriage license may be a "hitting license," it is certainly not a pre-requisite for abusive behavior. This chapter presents the scope of the problem of premarital physical violence and discusses major factors associated with the problem. A research study testing a systems perspective on premarital partners who are perpetrators and/or victims of physical abuse is then pre-sented. The results of the study carry implications for family life educators, policy makers, and therapists in regard to the early detection of physical abuse and effective intervention in violent premarital relationships.

THE SCOPE OF THE PROBLEM

Prevalence

The literature cites a great range of prevalence rates of courtship violence. Makepeace (1986) found that physical violence occurs in 16.7% of premarital couples, whereas Roscoe and Benaske (1985) reported a rate of 51%. Al-though the latter figure may appear extreme, it has been corroborated by

Note: The authors' names are listed in alphabetical order; they contributed equally to this col-laborative work.

other researchers (Roscoe & Callahan, 1985; Murphy, 1988; Rouse, Breen, & Howell, 1988; Stets & Straus, 1989) who found that one-third to one-half of college students report having initiated or experienced violence in a dating relationship. Some research suggests that the incidence of violence may be higher in cohabiting couples than in married couples (Sack, Keller, & Howard, 1982; Yllo & Straus, 1981). One might suppose that the presence of abusive behaviors during the courtship process would dissuade partners from marrying one another or even continuing the relationship, but repeated incidents of violence do not rule out the possibility of marriage (Lloyd et al., 1989; O'Leary et al., 1989).

Reciprocity of Physical Violence

Many studies report similar rates of aggression and victimization across gender (Bernard & Bernard, 1983; Meredith, Abott, & Adams, 1986; Murphy, 1988; O'Leary et al., 1989; Sigelman, Berry & Wiles, 1984; Straus & Gelles, 1986). Cate and associates (1982) report that acts of violence occur reciprocally in two-thirds of premarital relationships among college populations. Gwartney-Gibbs, Stockard, and Bohmer (1987) also found that premarital partners who inflict aggression also tend to sustain it. Therefore, a substantial segment of the literature supports the notion of reciprocity of violence between partners.

However, it is important to acknowledge how physical differences between men and women play a role in the incidence of physical violence in intimate relationships. Male aggression tends to be more serious and dangerous than that perpetrated by women due to the fact that men on average possess greater size and strength than their female counterparts. Moreover, many assaults by women against their partners may constitute acts of either self-defense and/or retaliation (Straus et al., 1980). It should also be noted that a physical attack by a male might elicit a violent response from a threatened female, which could be *construed* as an aggressive action, despite its defensive rather than offensive nature. Finally, traditional approaches to studying physical violence fail to address other social, economic, and political factors discussed later.

FACTORS ASSOCIATED WITH PREMARITAL PHYSICAL VIOLENCE

Characteristics of Perpetrators

Gender role orientation has been a major theme of research examining traits of physically abusive men. Patriarchal, traditional male attitudes and beliefs have been found to be characteristic of violent men (Avni, 1991; Ferraro, 1988; Makepeace, 1986). Violent men tend to have rigid expectations with respect to the roles of men and women in society. One such expectation is that a woman should be submissive and accept domestic responsibilities but should not participate in major economic decisions or be employed outside the home. Male perpetrators have also been described as nonexpressive, inflexible, and lacking in self-awareness (Ferraro, 1988). Thus, the stereotypical perpetrator of physical violence possesses stereotypically masculine traits. But does this mean that the only perpetrators of physically aggressive behaviors are men?

Researchers and the lay public tend to regard physical aggressiveness as a primarily "male" problem (Bernard & Bernard, 1983; Makepeace, 1981, 1986). This tendency makes sense in light of the severity of violence inflicted by men against women and the tolerance of males to female violence in a patriarchal, male-dominated culture. Nevertheless, Thompson (1991) asserts that the prevailing idea of male violence is merely a stereotype, which is supported by two phenomena: (1) a belief that only males aggress against their partners, and (2) the anticipation of "an interaction between gender and gender orientation" (p. 262). Thompson (1991) found that while gender orientation was significantly related to courtship violence, both male *and* female students who were physically aggressive in their relationships demonstrated a "more masculine and/or less feminine gender orientation" (p. 261). Thompson concludes that "physical aggression in dating relationships is not gender-specific," but that subscription to stereotypically "male" attitudes or behaviors, such as a positive valuing of being aggressive, is related to physical aggression perpetrated by men and women. This finding is supported by a study which found that measures of psychological aggression in premarital partners of both genders predicted incidents of physical aggression (Murphy & O'Leary, 1989).

Characteristics of Victims

In acknowledgment of the finding that male-to-female violence is more dangerous and severe than female-to-male violence (Makepeace, 1986), this section is devoted to female victims of physical abuse. A study of college women who had been subjected to physical violence in dating relationships found that victims of ongoing abuse were less likely to challenge controlling behaviors by their male partners and males in general (Follingstad, Rutledge, Polek, & McNeill-Hawkins, 1988). Early onset of physical abuse in the relationship was associated with women having strongly traditional attitudes toward women's roles and an increased likelihood for rationalizing the abuse and romanticizing the relationship. Walker (1983) found that many women who were victims of physical abuse came from families that inculcated "rigid traditionality." In addition, Walker (1983) also posites that in some victims' families of origin, family members wielded extensive control over them, setting the stage for learned helplessness in later relationships. In a study of courtship violence, Murphy (1988) concludes that victims (and perpetrators) of physical violence "tend to come from unhappy homes where abuse is either witnessed or experienced by the individual and where parental affection and attention is limited" (p. 294).

Situational Factors

Use of Alcohol and Drugs

With regard to the consumption of alcohol and other chemical substances, Bogal-Allbritten and Allbritten (1985) found that about half of the perpetrators of physical violence in courtship relationships were under the influence at the time of abusive incidents. In contrast, only 17% of the victims of physical abuse were under the influence. Makepeace (1981) and Makepeace (1986) also found consumption of alcohol to be a common situational factor in violent acts which result in serious injuries. Thus, although the use of alcohol and other drugs is not believed to be a prerequisite for violence, it does appear to be a facilitative factor, possibly because its influence provides victimizers with a means of rationalizing their behavior.

Duration of the Relationship

Another factor is the intimacy or length of the relationship in which the violence is perpetrated. Researchers have generally found that committed and long-standing relationships are more likely to contain violence (Cate et al., 1982; Henton et al., 1983; Makepeace, 1986). Follingstad and colleagues (1988) also found that women who sustained abuse in a relationship over a longer period of time were less likely to terminate the relationship because of the abuse. In addition, courting couples who cohabit are more likely to employ aggression to resolve conflicts than their intimately involved peers who are not living together or married couples (Yllo & Straus, 1981). However, Yllo and Straus (1981) also found that cohabitors who were over 30 years of age, divorced women, or couples who had been together over 10 years had very low rates of violence. This finding suggests a parabolic function between duration of relationship and frequency of violence in cohabiting couples, with an initially positive relationship between the two variables changing to a negative one after a number of years.

Family Factors

Family-of-Origin Violence

A major theme of research on physical violence is the positive relationship between sustaining or observing aggression within one's family of origin and sustaining or perpetrating it in one's later relationships (Kalmuss, 1984; Straus et al., 1980; Walker, 1983). Researchers of family violence have discovered that a disproportionate number of abusive adults were indeed physically abused as children (Bernard & Bernard, 1983; Gelles & Straus, 1988; Herzberger, 1983; Widom, 1989). Subsequent to these findings, a debate has ensued over whether or under what circumstances violence is transmitted intergenerationally (Egeland, Jacobvitz, & Papatola, 1987; Kaufman & Zigler, 1987; Milner, Robertson, & Rogers, 1990). Pagelow (1984) questions the validity of the "cycle of violence," pointing to numerous weaknesses in family violence research, including small, nonrepresentative samples, the lack of consensus on a precise definition of abuse, researcher bias, the unsupported generalization of findings, and the reporting of informal observations and impressions. However, Pagelow (1984) states that "research has provided some support for the claim abused children become spouse abusers" (p. 255).

Whatever the mechanism underlying this phenomenon, the families of origin appear to have a significant impact on the behavior of premarital couples. College students are twice as likely to be aggressive in their courtship relationships if they experienced or observed physical abuse in their family of origin (Billingham & Gilbert, 1987; Follingstad et al., 1988). Rouse (1983) states that "the single most important type of childhood exposure [to violence] was the observation of violence, which was associated with greater use of abusive conflict tactics" (p. 1). Murphy (1988) concludes that victims (and perpetrators) of physical violence "tend to come from unhappy homes where abuse is either witnessed or experienced by the individual" (p. 294). Gwartney-Gibbs, Stockard, and Bohmer (1987) also found that contact with aggressive parents constitutes a learning environment for inflicting and sustaining courtship aggression, but that "social learning of aggressive behavior takes place in a variety of learning environments" (p. 281). Although parents' behavior does have an impact on the later behavior of their children in their own families of procreation, Gwartney-Gibbs et al. (1987) conclude that peer groups and courtship partners also provide learning environments for aggression. Further research examining what effect family-of-origin violence may have on choices of peers and partners is needed.

Social Factors

Various social, political, and physical factors define differences between men and women and should be considered as one ponders the issue of reciprocity in cross-gender physical violence. For example, the still unequal economic positions of men and women in society perpetuate the conditions that make women vulnerable to physical abuse. Women's financial dependency on men, combined with the implicit support men receive from social and legal systems, works to maintain vast differences in power, resources, and experience (Balcom & Healey, 1990). Finally, some research (Bowker, 1983; Hall, Critcher, Jefferson, Clarke, & Roberts, 1978) suggests the possibility that male social networks may sanction men's use of violence against women in order to maintain the prevailing norm of patriarchy or male hegemony.

Consequences of Premarital Physical Violence on the Couple Relationship

Henton et al. (1983) found that approximately one-third of violent incidents in dating relationships, especially those occurring after the consumption of alcohol, resulted in physical injury, usually to the female partner (Makepeace, 1986). What was the interpretation of the violent event ex post facto? Cate et al. (1982) found that 37% of their respondents reported that "their relationship improved after the violence occurred," while another 41% indicated that "there was no change in the relationship" (pp. 84–85). Thus, persons involved in relationships where violence was perpetrated did not necessarily perceive the violence as a negative or destructive event. Moreover, as many as 45% (Makepeace, 1981) or even 53% (Cate et al., 1982) of respondents reported that they were still involved in the abusive relationship. This finding is interesting in light of the fact that dating couples in high school or college are less likely than married couples to be bound together by economic dependency or the presence of children (Carlson, 1987). A major conclusion from research on courtship violence has been that dating or courtship relationships might serve as a training ground for marital violence (Dobash & Dobash, 1979; Makepeace, 1981; Roscoe & Benaske, 1985).

THEORETICAL RATIONALE

The purpose of this chapter's study is to explore the phenomenon of premarital violence to aid clinicians in the early assessment and treatment of this problem. One framework that can facilitate the examination of couple systems is systems theory (Bertalanffy, 1962). With regard to the couple system, the authors have attempted to include interpersonal and social factors in the study's conceptualization of openness. Concepts of systems theory considered relevant to this study include the interdependence between component parts of a larger whole and the quality of the boundaries between these subsystems. *Open* boundaries allow the exchange of information and resources between systems and tend to facilitate health. *Closed* boundaries block inputs from outside of a system and tend to lead to dysfunction. Therefore, it is hypothesized that couple systems characterized by a lack of openness in partner attitudes and behaviors tend to be more dysfunctional and conflictual, and, therefore, are susceptible to incidents of physical violence. With regard to the boundary within a couple system, the degree of openness, self-disclosure, and empathy between partners may reflect the openness or permeability of the boundary between partners.

METHODOLOGY

Sample

Drawn from a nonrandom, national sample of 1,061 couples, subjects for the present study were unmarried persons who had been dating, engaged, or living with a partner. Approximately 77% of the sample were Caucasian, 4% Hispanic, 2% African American, 2% Asian, and the remainder of the sample was divided between native Americans and persons of other racial/ethnic origin. With regard to education, 52% of the sample had had some college or technical school experience, 15% had a Bachelors' degree, and 9% had an Associates' degree. Seven percent of the sample had a high school diploma or some high school education. Less than 4% had a Masters, Doctorate, or another professional degree.

Measures and Hypotheses

The Preparation for Marriage (PREP-M) is a 204-item instrument designed to measure couples' compatibility and degree of readiness for marriage (Holman, Busby, & Larson, 1989). *Premarital physical violence* was defined as acts of physical abuse between two persons who were involved in an intimate relationship but who were not married. For the purposes of this study, only more severe types of physical violence were used for the dependent variable. *Violent acts* were defined as "physical acts like kicking, hitting hard with a fist, beatings, and hitting with objects." To compensate for potential denial or minimization of violence, respondents were asked about the frequency of the incidents of violent behavior perpetrated by both themselves and their partners. Although rape and other forms of sexual abuse are implicitly violent in nature, they are usually studied as a distinct type of violence and, therefore, were not included in this study.

Some authors discuss the importance of communication and expressiveness on couple satisfaction and have found that empathic expressions of feeling and understanding of one's partner are highly correlated with couple satisfaction (Bornstein & Bornstein, 1986; Davidson, Balswick, & Halverson, 1983; Gottman & Porterfield, 1981). However, the relationship between openness of couple boundaries or communication and physical violence is not discussed in the literature. Thus, the examination of the relationship between these two variables represents a component unique to this study. It was hypothesized that couple openness would be negatively associated with the incidence of premarital violence. The variable of couple openness was operationalized through items on the scales of openness, self-disclosure, and empathy on the PREP-M. Items measured partners' perceptions of their own and their partner's openness and expressiveness. The openness scale had a standardized reliability coefficient of .79.

The variable of gender-role attitudes was also included in this study to test its effect, if any, on incidents of violence. As discussed earlier, several studies have explored the relationship between violence and gender-role attitudes (Coleman, 1980; Bernard & Bernard, 1983; Sonkin, Martin, & Walker, 1985). Past findings suggest that abusive men tend to have a more traditional gender-role orientation than nonabusive men. It was hypothesized that more traditional gender-role attitudes (role complementarity) would be positively associated with the incidents of premarital violence. Role complementarity was operationalized through scale items measuring attitudes toward gender roles (e.g., who would be in charge of money, children, housework in the marriage). The standardized reliability coefficient for the role complementarity scale was .82.

An additional hypothesis was that the degree of difference in partner attitudes regarding gender roles would also be positively associated with physical violence. Differences on role complementarity were derived from discrepancy scores between partners on gender-role attitudes. Couple religiosity was included as a potential mediating variable in this study, and items were directed toward the importance respondents placed on religion and attendance at religious functions. A standardized reliability of .85 was obtained for the religiosity scale.

The influence of family-of-origin violence was also explored in this study. The different variables of history of violence included whether partners had been witnesses to violence between their parents or caretakers, whether they had been recipients of violence at the hands of their parents, and whether they had been perpetrators of violence against their parents. It was hypothesized that experience with violence of any type in the families of origin would be positively associated with incidents of violence in current relationships.

Data Analysis

Multivariate Analysis of Variance and Discriminant Analyses were performed on the data. The MANOVA produced a multivariate F-test that determined whether incidents of violence were significantly associated with the couple factors. When the multivariate F-test was significant, a series of univariate F-tests were used to determine significant main effects for couple factors. The Discriminant Analysis was utilized to explore the ability of the independent variables (witnessing, receiving, and/or perpetrating family-of-origin violence, role complementarity, differences in role complementarity, and couple openness) to predict membership in the violent and nonviolent groups.

RESULTS

In the sample of 1,061 couples, 136 couples reported that at least one partner was violent. Within this 136 couple sample, roughly twice as many women as men engaged in physical violence against their partners according to both self-report and partner perception. In couples where female partners reported violence by their male partners, 52% of the men failed to confirm (denied) their violent behavior. In the couples in which the males reported their female partners had been violent, 41% of the women denied their violent behavior.

A Discriminant Analysis was used to determine the contributions of the five variables in determining couple membership in the violent and nonviolent groups, which classified 64.8% of the cases correctly. The standardized canonical discriminant coefficients were obtained for three of the variables: –.61 for openness, .61 for history of family violence, and .42 for difference score on role complementarity. The three coefficients were significant at the .01 level. A correlation coefficient of .73 was obtained for the factors of role complementarity and religiosity, and these two factors did not remain in the analysis due to insufficient F-level and tolerance. The interpretation of discriminant function coefficients is similar to multiple regression coefficients. With standardized variables, the larger the absolute value of the coefficient, the greater the variable's contribution to the overall function. Thus, the magnitude of the coefficients suggests that openness is the most important discriminator between the violent and nonviolent groups and that difference in role complementarity was the least important.

The MANOVA procedure was used to determine if the group to which respondents belonged (violent, nonviolent) had a significant effect on the six couple variables. Using Wilk's Lambda, a multivariate F-test was significant, $F = 3.48$, $p = .001$. The univariate F-tests (2, 450) demonstrated a significant main effect for openness with an $F = 7.13$, $p = .017$. The three forms of family-of-origin violence also demonstrated significant main effects: observing violence between parents, $F = 6.27$, $p = .002$, being the recipient of parental violence, $F = 5.93$, $p =. 003$, and perpetrating violence against one's parents, $F = 4.31$, $p = .014$. The factors of role complementarity ($F = 1.25$, $p = .289$) and difference scores on role complementarity ($F = 1.62$, $p = .20$) failed to produce significant F-values.

DISCUSSION

Men are more likely to deny abusive behavior reported by their partners, and, according to both self-report and partner report, more women than men engaged in abusive behavior. Legal and social implications may be involved in this reporting and denial phenomenon. Some portions of society are openly critical of violent behavior, especially violence perpetrated by men against women because of men's greater average size and strength. A man's admitting to having perpetrated acts of violence, even indirectly by means of a questionnaire, may be experienced as risky in light of legal sanctions and/ or social stigma. In addition, the thought of "husband abuse" or a woman physically abusive of a man is frequently viewed by lay people as not serious or dangerous (and is even viewed with misplaced humor by some) because of gender differences in physical size and strength. Women's violent behaviors may simply be acts of self-defense and/or retaliation in an already violent environment (Straus, 1980). Nevertheless, because the reports by women and their partners regarding the incidence of female-to-male violence are congruent, and the potential for physical injury connected to male reciprocity is high, this type of violence warrants further examination.

The hypothesis that couple openness would be associated with a lack of reported violence was supported by the results of both the Discriminant Analysis and the MANOVA. The magnitude of the canonical discriminant coefficient for openness indicates that partners' openness, self-disclosure, and empathy with one another is significantly related to membership in the nonviolent group. This supports the notion that more open boundaries between partners reflect healthy couple system functioning and a decreased potential for physical violence. In addition, stereotypical attitudes regarding gender roles were strongly and positively correlated with religiosity, and both variables were not important discriminators of group membership in the violent and nonviolent categories. One interpretation of this result is that high scores on religiosity may reflect strong beliefs in nonviolence, mutual respect, and the "Golden Rule" of "doing unto others as you would have them do unto you."

The hypotheses that role complementarity or differences in role complementarity would be associated with premarital violence were not supported by the results of the MANOVA. It is not clear why gender-role attitudes did not prove to be as significant in this study as in previous studies (Avni, 1991; Ferraro, 1988; Makepeace, 1986). One possible explanation is the high level of education characteristic of this sample. Further research focused on the relationship between gender-role attitudes and violence is needed. However, the hypothesis that role complementarity or differences in role complementarity would be associated with premarital violence *were* supported by the results of the Discriminant Analysis. Significant discriminant coefficients indicated that these two variables do contribute to the function of group membership in the violent category. This finding suggests that traditional gender-role attitudes are associated with violence in premarital relationships, and suggests that partner disagreement regarding expectations for one another's roles can lead to conflict, and, for some couples, physical violence.

The three forms of family-of-origin violence were significantly associated with premarital violence. This supports the finding that family-of-origin violence can be a predictor of violent behavior in later relationships, whether the subject was an observer, recipient, or perpetrator of physical violence in the family. It is interesting to note that *observation* of physical violence in the family of origin had the greatest influence on premarital violence in both the Discriminant Analysis and the MANOVA. Thus, one does not need to be the recipient or perpetrator of violence in one's family of origin but merely a witness to increase the risk of being involved in a violent relationship later in life.

In summary, the results of this chapter's study support the use of a systems approach to exploring the problem of relationship violence. The study also provides some validation of the concept of couple boundaries, through the variable of couple openness, and the notion of intergenerational transmission of violent behaviors, through the variables of family-of-origin violence.

IMPLICATIONS FOR INTERVENTION

Assessment

The initial step in treating individuals who are currently involved in a relationship in which physical violence is being perpetrated is identification of those persons requiring services. Therapists may not become aware of clients' experiences of violence in their relationships as part of the typical intake and assessment process for several reasons. First, clients may deny or minimize the abuse due to romanticism or a belief that violence denotes "love." Second, a female client may anticipate a reprisal from her partner following disclosure of physical abuse, whether it is in the form of further violence, withdrawal of affection, or threats to end their relationship. It is important for therapists to acknowledge these factors which may influence clients' willingness to disclose premarital physical abuse.

Clients may enter treatment complaining of individual problems or difficulties in their relationships. If the therapist suspects that violence has occurred in the relationship, he or she must be careful to approach the issue with sensitivity and subtlety and perform an assessment that does not place the woman at additional risk. Questionnaire items, which normalize conflict in couple relationships and then inquire about the frequency of specifically defined acts of physical violence, may identify some clients needing therapy for this problem. Individual sessions with clients for the purpose of exploring their levels of safety in their relationship and the incidence of physical abuse may also prove useful. The importance of carefully screening for premarital physical abuse cannot be overemphasized (Lloyd, 1991).

Clinical correlates of abuse and trauma of all types include high anxiety, depression, intense shame and guilt, and sexual problems (Koss, Dinero, Seibel, & Cox, 1988). Low self-esteem in either partner may be an indication of violence or potential violence. In addition, alcohol use is associated with all forms of family violence (Rosenbaum & O'Leary, 1986). Addictions to alcohol, drugs, and gambling are common problems of abusers. A common characteristic of abusive men is extreme jealousy, which is frequently manifested in attempts to socially isolate their female partners. Because physically abusive men are significantly more likely to have witnessed physical violence in their families of origin, family history of violence can prove to be a factor predictive of abusive behaviors.

In addition, the present study found that the variables of openness, history of family violence, and differences in gender-role attitudes served to discriminate between violent and nonviolent couples. The use of these identified variables as part of a clinical assessment may facilitate the early detection of couples who have been violent or who run the risk of becoming violent. Therapists can assess key problem areas in a couple's relationship that are strongly associated with the incidence of violence. First sessions with at-risk couples should include subtle but persistent probing into the area of conflict and its resolution in their relationship.

During the assessment process, it is important to begin exploring with the couple whether remediation of their relationship is a "realistic or desirable goal" (Rosenbaum & O'Leary, 1986, p. 389). Acknowledging the great emotional distress of the couple, the therapist may ask, most likely in an individual session, "Do you both wish to work on your relationship" or "Do you want to see if your relationship can continue?" When one or both partners do not wish to remain together (i.e., there is substantial doubt regarding the viability of the relationship), referral to a support group and/or individual or group counseling should be considered (Rosenbaum & O'Leary, 1986). Beavers (1985) asserts that couples therapy is contraindicated when a partner "cannot commit to an exploration of the relationship with an open mind" (p. 22). On the other hand, "if each partner can openly state that she or he wants to see if they can live together happily, there is a solid basis for treatment" (Beavers, 1985, p. 159). On completion of assessment, the therapist may elect to provide the couple conjoint therapy if and only if: (1) the partners have stated their mutual willingness to work, and (2) the therapist believes sufficient safety exists so that the victim of the abuse is in no immediate danger. For the second criterion to be fulfilled, the physically abusive partner must be willing to contract for nonviolence. If either of these two criteria are not met, the couple should be referred to individual and/or group therapy.

Therapeutic Goals

Safety of Clients

Following a determination that the partners are appropriate candidates for couple therapy, the therapist can begin with the following goals. Because violence has occurred in the couple's relationship, a major concern is the woman's safety. Therefore, the therapist's first goal is to foster an awareness of the gravity of the abuse and the implications for the woman who continues to experience abuse. She should be aware of the various services available to her (e.g., local women's shelters) should she feel endangered by her partner. The therapist should help the client formulate a plan of action, which includes a safe place to go and a list of resources for help, in the event of a crisis. A continuous priority is the provision of adequate time, space, and support to help her make a decision regarding the future of the relationship. Therapists should be willing to schedule individual sessions with clients in order to create a safe place for them to express thoughts and feelings they might be uncomfortable or afraid to discuss in front of their partners.

Contracting for Nonviolence

Elimination of physical abuse requires interventions that will change the attitudes and behaviors of both partners. In communicating the seriousness of the violence in the couple's relationship, the therapist should confront any attempts by either partner to minimize the abuse and should emphasize the high probability that it will occur again unless major changes are made in the relationship. Victims of abuse should come to view their partners' violent behaviors as something for which their partners, not themselves, are responsible. Abusers should understand their habit of "winning" in the short-term through coercion and intimidation makes everyone lose in the long-term. In addition, it is important for clinicians working with violent partners to help them differentiate between conflict, anger, and frustration, which are elements of all intimate relationships, and violence, which is an inappropriate and unacceptable behavior (Stith & Rosen, 1990). Willbach (1989) asserts the great importance of a binding nonviolent contract in effective treatment of abuse cases in the following statement:

> If the violent family member will not or cannot agree to stop the use of violence in all circumstances, or exhibits by his actions that he cannot live up to the agreement, then...[c]ouples therapy is not the appropriate modality: It will not be as effective in changing behavior as individual and/or group therapy and has negative consequences from an ethical viewpoint (p. 48).

The therapist's convictions on this subject should be clearly communicated from the inception of treatment through a contract stating that conjoint therapy will continue only as long as violence remains absent from the relationship. If the abusive partner will not agree "to stop the use of violence in all circumstances, or exhibits by his actions that he cannot live up to the agreement, then that person needs to be treated individually and/or within a group context" (Willbach, 1989, p. 48).

Confronting Denial

Breaking through partner and/or couple denial will continue to be a primary issue in treating premarital physical abuse. Denial on the levels of the individual, the relationship, and society in general is a major contributor to the perpetuation of violence. Clow, Hutchins, and Vogler (1990) describe how "[t]he erroneous thoughts of an abuser often allow him to carry out the abuse and avoid responsibility.... cognitive distortions, rationalizations, and justifications abound" (p. 69). Ganley (1981) reports that abusive men tend to maintain that their behaviors "are not seriously violent." Further, the present study also demonstrates a greater tendency on the part of men than women to minimize or altogether deny acts of physical violence. Therapists must not collude with the abuser's rationalizations (e.g., "I was abused as a child," "I am an alcoholic," "She was provoking me").

Therapists may empathize with the client's history of past abuse or neglect in his family of origin (especially when helping professionals share such a history), but they cannot allow clients' past misfortunes to cloud the work at hand. Although abusers cannot change what has already taken place, they are still accountable for their past, present, and future actions. "Being accountable means living up to expectations, taking responsibility for one's own behavior, and acting one's age" (Combrinck-Graham, 1991, p. 201).

Perpetrators who admit committing acts of violence may claim that the victim "started the whole thing" or that violence is excusable. To show that violence is dangerous, frightening, and inexcusable, therapists can create an imaginary scenario in which the abuser is the recipient of an assault similar to one he or she perpetrated. It is more difficult for perpetrators to minimize an action, say, being stabbed in the forehead with a fork by their partner, when they are on the receiving end. Another technique which avoids hypothetical scenarios is to refer the perpetrator back to an incident in their childhood in which she or he was abused by an intimate (e.g., a parent). Asking "what did you feel when that was happening to you" allows perpetrators to get in touch with the feelings of vulnerability and powerlessness they felt as victims, and again makes more difficult the minimization or dismissal of the same feelings expressed by their partners.

In addition, therapists should also keep watch for interlocking attitudes or beliefs between abuser and victim that might interfere with their perception of the abuse as a serious problem. For example, in being socialized to be responsible for events and behaviors occurring in relationships, a victim may believe that the abuse was somehow her fault, a belief which meshes well with the perpetrator's tendency to externalize all problems and difficulties and to underestimate or minimize the impact of his own behaviors on others. Subscription to various romantic beliefs and the presence of an abuse cycle with partners' attitudes toward the violence changing from phase to phase may also fuel a couple's denial of physical abuse.

Addressing Ambivalence

Another goal of therapy is facilitating the examination of the profound ambivalence that may be experienced by victims of abuse. Bograd (1992) states that the abuse victim's opposing feelings and wishes need to be clarified in treatment. The dynamic tension present in feelings of love and hate, security and panic, and in victims' wishes to continue or leave the relationship produces considerable cognitive dissonance. The confusion that ensues can immobilize abuse victims, leaving them "stuck" in an unsafe situation with the abuser. Therapists can help victims escape their paralysis by facilitating their acknowledgment, acceptance, and eventual integration of these affective polar opposites (Little, 1990). This integration permits a movement away from rigid, black/white thinking about oneself "so that the person is more balanced, centered, and can make choices (Little, 1990, p. 54).

Self-Awareness and Anger Management

Deschner (1984) elaborates on anger management skills and time-out techniques that are effective in reducing the explosive outbursts that are precursors to violence. Therapists can help abusive partners recognize the signs of rising anger and tension, and clinicians can assist clients in their discovery of pleasant memories or calming thoughts to focus on in times of stress and frustration (Stith & Rosen, 1990). Although the abuser's subjective reality may be that he is helpless and "out of control" during incidents of abuse, the therapist must be clear that violence is still a choice. A therapist's rigid adherence to a purely systemic perspective in which partners are considered equal contributors to what occurs in the relationship may not be appropriate in cases of abuse. The authors concur with others (Nichols, 1986; Willbach, 1989) that violence involves coercion and domination by one partner (the perpetrator) over the other (the victim) in a relationship that is implicitly unequal and oppressive. Although abusers may experience intense shame or guilt following acts of violence, it is not they who have been frightened and made to feel helpless.

The Enhancement of Openness

This chapter's study demonstrates the importance of openness in couple relationships, and therapists should incorporate tasks and gentle challenges that stretch partners' perspectives of one another. Broadening partners' repertoires of behaviors and constructions of one another through experiential exercises (e.g., sculpting) helps them learn new ways to see and appreciate one another. To dislodge partners who are entrenched in rigid views of one another, therapists can employ a technique known as reframing (Watzlawick, Weakland, & Fisch, 1974). A *reframe* of a situation requires the therapist to capture the emotional and conceptual flavors of the partners' viewpoints and place them in a different context that fits "the facts" of the situation but imbues a wholly different meaning to partners' thoughts and behaviors. A successful reframe permits partners to see alternative explanations for events in their relationship instead of assuming their partner is "wrong" or "bad." Of course, reframing violence as anything other than the abuse of power by the perpetrator is not helpful.

Another specific task is *role reversal*, in which each partner makes a concerted effort to capture the other's perspective in a variety of scenarios that have elicited frustration and anger in the past. Once increased empathy and understanding is achieved in the relationship, a couple is in a better position to negotiate differences such as divergent expectations of gender roles. In addition, because couple systems characterized by a closed internal boundary lack the ability to be open, empathic, and self-disclosing with one another, communication skills training can help them become more "nondefensive," "positive," and "flexible" (Bornstein & Bornstein, 1986, p. 84). Problem-solving training (Bornstein & Bornstein, 1986) can help couples learn the craft of compromise and find constructive solutions to their problems which are, unlike physical violence, mutually acceptable and appropriate.

CONCLUSIONS

Premarital physical violence is a significant problem that represents pervasive patterns in the way men and women relate to one another in our society. The prevalence of the problem demonstrates that a marriage license is not a required condition for abusive behavior in intimate relationships. Because premarital physical violence may be a precursor to marital violence, early identification of this problem through a comprehensive assessment process and effective interventions may work to stop violence before it manifests itself in marriage. There is a need to study the efficacy of couple and individual treatment modalities in order to improve the delivery of mental health services to both victims and perpetrators. Although it must be acknowledged that the systems perspective frequently ignores significant social and political factors which impact women's everyday existence, the present study supports the systems concept that open boundaries are associated with healthy system functioning. In addition, the variables of couple openness and family-of-origin violence may be used to identify couple systems at-risk for violence. The clinical implications of the study are that therapists should employ strategies aimed at increasing partners' capacity for openness, communication, self-awareness, and self-control to reduce, eliminate, and potentially prevent the occurrence of violence in couple relationships.

REFERENCES

Avni, N. (1991). Battered wives: Characteristics of their courtship days. *Journal of Interpersonal Violence, 6*(2), 232–239.

Balcom, D. A. & Healey, D. (1990). The context for couples treatment of wife abuse. In M. P. Mirkin (Ed.), *The social and political contexts of family therapy* (pp. 121–137). Boston: Allyn and Bacon.

Beavers, W. R. (1985). *Successful marriage.* New York: W. W. Norton.

Bernard, M. L. & Bernard, J. L. (1983). Violent intimacy: The family as a model for love relationships. *Family Relations, 32,* 283–286.

Bertalanffy, L. (1962). General systems theory: A critical review. *General Systems, 7,* 1–20.

Billingham, R. E. & Gilbert, K. R. (1990). Parental divorce during childhood and use of violence in dating relationships. *Psychological Reports, 66,* 1003–1009.

Bogal-Allbritten, R. B. & Allbritten, W. (1985). The hidden victims: Courtship violence among college students. *Journal of College Student Personnel, 26*(3), 201–204.

Bograd, M. (1992, February). *Domestic violence: Navigating therapy on stormy seas*. Presentation at the Annual Conference of the Central New York Chapter of the New York Association for Marriage and Family Therapy, Syracuse.

Bornstein, P. H. & Bornstein, M. T. (1986). *Marital therapy*. Elmsford, NY: Pergamon Press.

Bowker, L. H. (1983). *Beating wife-beating*. Toronto: Lexington Books.

Carlson, B. E. (1987). Dating violence: A research review and comparison with spouse abuse. *Social Casework: The Journal of Contemporary Social Work, 21*, 16–23.

Cate, R. M., Henton, J. M., Koval, J. E., Christopher, F. S., & Lloyd, S. A. (1982). Premarital abuse: A social psychological perspective. *Journal of Family Issues, 3*, 79–90.

Clow, D. R., Hutchins, D. E., & Vogler, D. E. (1990). Treatment for spouse-abusive males. In S. M. Stith, M. B. Williams, & K. Rosen (Eds.), *Violence hits home: Comprehensive treatment approaches to domestic violence* (pp. 66–82). New York: Springer.

Coleman, K. H. (1980). Conjugal violence: What 33 men report. *Journal of Marital and Family Therapy, 6*, 207–213.

Combrinck-Graham, L. (1991). Holding children accountable. *Family Therapy Networker, 15*(4), 48–52.

Davidson, B., Balswick, J., & Halverson, C. (1983). Affective self-disclosure and marital adjustment: A test of equity theory. *Journal of Marriage and the Family, 43*, 93–102.

Deschner, J. P. (1984). *The hitting habit: Anger control for battering couples*. New York: Free Press.

Dobash, R. E. & Dobash, R. (1979). *Violence against wives: A case against the patriarchy*. New York: John Wiley.

Egeland, B., Jacobvitz, D., & Papatola, K. (1987). Intergenerational continuity of abuse. In R. J. Gelles & J. Lancaster (Eds.), *Child abuse and neglect: Biosocial dimensions* (pp. 255–276). Hawthorne, NY: Aldine De Gruyter.

Ferraro, K. J. (1988). *An existential approach to battering. Family abuse and its consequences*. Newbury Park, CA: Sage.

Follingstad, D. R., Rutledge, L. L., Polek, D. S., & McNeill-Hawkins, P. C. (1988). Factors associated with patterns of dating violence toward college women. *Journal of Family Violence, 3*(3), 169–182.

Ganley, A. (1981). *Participant and trainer's manual for working with men who batter*. Washington, DC: Center for Women Policy Studies.

Gelles, R. J. & Straus, M. A. (1988). *Intimate violence*. New York: Simon & Schuster.

Gottman, J. M. & Porterfield, A. L. (1981). Communicative competence and nonverbal behavior of married couples. *Journal of Marriage and the Family, 43*, 817–824.

Gwartney-Gibbs, P. A., Stockard, J., & Bohmer, S. (1987). Learning courtship aggression: The influence of parents, peers, and personal experiences. *Family Relations, 36*, 276–282.

Hall, S., Critcher, C., Jefferson, T., Clarke, J., & Roberts, B. (1978). *Policing the crisis: Mugging, the state and law and order*. London: Macmillan.

Henton, J. M., Cate, R. M., Koval, J. E., Lloyd, S. A., & Christopher, F. S. (1983). Romance and violence in dating relationships. *Journal of Family Issues, 4*, 467–482.

Herzberger, S. D. (1983). Social cognition and the transmission of abuse. In D. Finkelhor, R. J. Gelles, G. T. Hotaling, & M. A. Straus (Eds.), *The dark side of families: Current family violence research* (pp. 317–329). Beverly Hills: Sage.

Holman, T. B., Busby, D. M., & Larson, J. H. (1989). *PREParation for marriage: The PREP-M*. Provo, UT: Marriage Study Consortium, Brigham Young University.

Kalmuss, D. (1984). The intergenerational transmission of marital aggression. *Journal of Marriage and the Family, 46*(1), 11–19.

Kaufman, J. & Zigler, E. (1987). Do abused children become abusive parents? *American Journal of Orthopsychiatry, 57*(2), 186–192.

Koss, M. P., Dinero, T. E., Seibel, C. A., & Cox, S. L. (1988). Stranger and acquaintance rape: Are there differences in the victim's experience? *Psychology of Women Quarterly, 12,* 1–24.

Little, L. F. (1990). Gestalt therapy with females involved in intimate violence. In S. Stith, M. B. Williams, & K. Rosen (Eds.), *Violence hits home* (pp. 47–65). New York: Springer.

Lloyd, S. A. (1991). The darkside of courtship: Violence and sexual exploitation. *Family Relations, 40,* 14–20.

Lloyd, S. A., Koval, J. E., & Cate, R. M. (1989). Conflict and violence in dating relationships. In M. Pirog-Good & J. Stets (Eds.), *Violence in dating relationships: Emerging social issues* (pp. 126–184). New York: Praeger.

Makepeace, J. M. (1981). Courtship violence among college students. *Family Relations, 30,* 97–102.

Makepeace, J. M. (1986). Gender differences in courtship violence victimization. *Family Relations, 35,* 383–388.

Meredith, W. H., Abott, D. A., & Adams, S. L. (1986). Family violence: Its relation to marital and parental satisfaction and family strengths. *Journal of Family Violence, 1,* 299–305.

Milner, J. S., Robertson, K. R., & Rogers, D. L. (1990). Childhood history of abuse and adult child abuse potential. *Journal of Family Violence, 5*(1), 15–34.

Murphy, J. E. (1988). Date abuse and forced intercourse among college students. In G. T. Hotaling, D. Finkelhor, J. T. Kirkpatrick, & M. A. Straus (Eds.), *Family abuse and its consequences* (pp. 285–296). Newbury Park, CA: Sage.

Murphy, C. M. & O'Leary, K. D. (1989). Psychological aggression predicts physical aggression in early marriage. *Journal of Consulting and Clinical Psychology, 57*(5), 579–582.

Nichols, M. P. (1986). *The self in the system: Expanding the limits of family therapy.* New York: Brunner/Mazel.

O'Leary, K. D., Barling, J., Arias, I., Rosenbaum, A., Malone, J., & Tyree, A. (1989). Prevalence and stability of physical aggression between spouses: A longitudinal analysis. *Journal of Consulting and Clinical Psychology, 57,* 263–268.

Pagelow, M. D. (1984). *Family violence.* New York: Praeger.

Roscoe, B. & Benaske, N. (1985). Courtship violence experienced by abused wives: Similarities in patterns of abuse. *Family Relations, 34,* 419–424.

Roscoe, B. & Callahan, J. E. (1985). Courtship violence experienced by abused wives: Similarities in patterns of abuse. *Adolescence, 20,* 545–553.

Rosenbaum, A. & O'Leary, K. D. (1986). Treatment of marital violence. In N. Jacobson & A. Gurman (Eds.), *Clinical handbook of marital therapy* (pp. 385–405). New York: Guilford Press.

Rouse, L. P., Breen, R., & Howell, M. (1988). Abuse in intimate relationships: A comparison of married and dating college students. *Journal of Interpersonal Violence, 3,* 414–429.

Sack, A. R., Keller, J. F., & Howard, R. D. (1982). Conflict tactics and violence in dating situations. *International Journal of Sociology of the Family, 12,* 89–100.

Sigelman, C. K., Berry, C. J., & Wiles, K. A. (1984). Violence in college students' dating relationships. *Journal of Applied Social Psychology, 5,* 530–548.

Sonkin, D., Martin, D., & Walker, L. (1985). *The male batterer: A treatment approach.* New York: Springer.

Stets, J. E. & Straus, M. A. (1989). The marriage license as a hitting license: A comparison of assaults in dating, cohabiting and married couples. In M. Pirog- Good & J. Stets (Eds.), *Violence in dating relationships: Emerging social issues* (pp. 33–52). New York: Praeger.

Stith, S. M. & Rosen, K. H. (1990). Family therapy for spouse abuse. In S. M. Stith, M. B. Williams, & K. Rosen (Eds.), *Violence hits home: Comprehensive treatment approaches to domestic violence* (pp. 83–101). New York: Springer.

Straus, M. & Gelles, R. (1986). Societal change and change in family violence from 1975 to 1985 as revealed by two national surveys. *Journal of Marriage and the Family, 41,* 75–88.

Straus, M., Gelles, R., & Steinmetz, S. (1980). *Behind closed doors: Violence in the American family.* Garden City, NY: Anchor Press/Doubleday.

Thompson, E. H., Jr. (1991). The maleness of violence in dating relationships: An appraisal of stereotypes. *Sex Roles, 24,* 261–278.

Walker, L. E. (1983). Victimology and the psychological perspectives of battered women. *Victimology, 8*(1-2), 82–104.

Watzlawick, P., Weakland, J., & Fisch, R. (1974). *Change: Principles of problem formation and problem resolution.* New York: W. W. Norton.

Widom, C. S. (1989). Child abuse, neglect, and adult behavior: Research design and findings on criminality, violence, and child abuse. *American Journal of Orthopsychiatry, 59*(3), 355–367.

Willbach, D. (1989). Ethics and family therapy: The case management of family violence. *Journal of Marital and Family Therapy, 15*(1), 43–52.

Yllo, K. & Straus, M. A. (1981). Interpersonal violence among married and cohabiting couples. *Family Relations, 30,* 339–347.

11

PREMARITAL SEXUAL ABUSE OF WOMEN BY MALE PARTNERS

KYLE D. KILLIAN, DEAN M. BUSBY

*All of a sudden he is on top of me, crushing me with his
weight, breathing in my ear, saying he knows that I want it.
I protest, I scream that I don't want anything, but he
doesn't listen! As he forces his way into me, I keep saying
to myself this isn't happening to me, it's not real. I mean,
I know him! I am not consenting to what he is doing to
me! After he finishes, he asks when he can see me
again, and leaves me alone. In the darkness, I begin to
wonder, "Did I lead him on, send him the wrong
signals or something? Did he really rape me?"*

Premarital sexual abuse, as depicted in the preceding example, is a serious problem in our society. While the popular media have recently acknowledged the frequency and consequences of the problem, their use of the term *date rape* is misleading to the extent that it suggests to some that a man and a woman, as two consenting adults, experience a simple "misunderstanding" in the midst of an evening of romance (Gibbs, 1991, p. 48). *Date rape* often refers to forced sexual intercourse in a dating situation, whereas the term premarital sexual abuse includes acts other than intercourse that can occur in contexts other than dating relationships. In premarital sexual abuse, a man may engage in sexual relations with a woman, and, despite hearing her protests, later insist that the act was not rape. The woman may not be certain whether she has been raped, even though she did not give her consent and was physically forced or psychologically manipulated into having sex with the man.

Note: This article is an expanded version of the following published material: Killian, K. D. & Busby, D. M. Premarital sexual coercion: Treatment issues for family therapists. Reprinted from Volume 21, Number 2, of the *Journal of Marital and Family Therapy.* Copyright 1995, American Association for Marriage and Family Therapy. Reprinted with permission.

Researchers and helping professionals have uncovered some common, if disturbing, themes of sexual violence present in cases of premarital sexual abuse. Themes include the victim's sense of shame and/or rage regarding an event out of one's control, the social restrictions and sense of isolation that are attached to an event considered taboo by one's culture, the consistent under-reporting, and typically male to female nature of the abusive acts (Leidig, 1981). However, just as the silence is beginning to break with regard to child sexual abuse, incest, marital rape, and stranger rape, premarital sexual abuse has also garnered increased attention in the media and in the field of therapy, especially since the early 1980s.

Whereas Chapter 3 in this book deals with the topic of spousal sexual abuse, this chapter describes sexual abuse between two persons who are acquainted with one another or are involved in an intimate relationship but are not married to one another. In contrast to Chapter 12, this chapter deals with sexual abuse perpetrated by persons not considered "outsiders" by virtue of the fact that the victims know them. The primary focus here is on clinical issues with regard to the systemic treatment of premarital sexual abuse.

PREMARITAL SEXUAL ABUSE AND SEXUAL COERCION DEFINED

The concepts of premarital sexual abuse and sexual coercion are inextricably intertwined. *Premarital sexual abuse* is defined as nonconsensual sexual activity between two persons who are not married to each other but through some previous experience know one another. The term *activity* is used to include acts in addition to sexual intercourse such as fondling, fellatio, and anal intercourse, which are part of the definition of rape in some states—Ohio for one (Harney & Muehlenhard, 1991). The two persons involved could be co-workers, students who share a class in high school or college, lovers, persons living together, and/or fiancees. The term *nonconsensual* refers to the absence of mutuality in the decision to engage in a sexual act and the imposition of one person's will over another. Although some men do report having had sexual intercourse they did not want with female partners because of psychological pressure from their partners (Miller & Marshall, 1987), the greater average size and strength of men and the corresponding dearth of cases in which physical force is applied by females to males has contributed to a focus in the literature on male to female forms of premarital sexual abuse.

Grauerholz and Koralewski (1991) define *sexual coercion* as "the act of being forced, tricked or pressured to engage in a sexual act or acts" (p. ix). Sexual coercion manifests itself in a variety of ways, but a common thread is the application of physical or psychological intimidation or threat as a way of controlling the victim, who is usually a woman (Kelly, 1988). Of course, intimidation or threat is most readily identified in its physical forms such as the use of deadly weapons or beatings by the perpetrator. But more subtle means of force, such as the man's use of his own body weight, are not as clearly identifiable by either victims or the legal system (Estrich, 1987, as cited by Harney & Muehlenhard, 1991). For this reason, researchers (e.g., Miller & Marshall, 1987) carefully phrase questions regarding use of physical force and employ the most inclusive categories.

Furthermore, the application of psychological pressure or manipulation, such as threatening to end the relationship, is even more difficult to classify as a use of force. Miller and Marshall (1987) found that 17% of their sample of female undergraduate students reported having intercourse with a man when they did not want to because they had felt pressured by his continuing arguments, and another 15% reported having unwanted sexual intercourse because the man became so sexually aroused that they felt it was useless to attempt to stop him. In this sample, 12% of the men admitted to having had sexual intercourse with a woman when she did not want to because she had felt pressured by their continuing arguments, and 6% said the intercourse had occurred because they had become so sexually aroused it was useless to stop themselves. Thus, subsequent to being raped, a woman may struggle to explain to law enforcement, lawyers, or even herself the experience of having felt threatened or endangered when: (1) the perpetrator was not a stranger but someone she knew or trusted, and (2) the man refrained from using physical force.

Jenkins and Dambrot (1987) demonstrate that attribution of acquaintance rape is significantly influenced by: (1) the types of dating scenarios that subjects were asked to read, and (2) subjects' subscription to rape myths. Examples of rape myths include the beliefs that women are at fault when rape occurs and that women often enjoy rape. Males who agreed more with rape myths were less likely to perceive a situation of forced intercourse as rape and were more likely to believe the woman had desired intercourse (Jenkins & Dambrot, 1987). In contrast to men, situational factors (e.g., the woman's relationship to the perpetrator) affect whether a woman acknowledges sexual assault as rape (Jenkins & Dambrot, 1987). For example, women were significantly more likely to make an attribution of rape if the date scenario involved an unplanned "pick-up" date rather than a planned date with monetary investment. Thus, personal biases concerning what constitutes rape continue to have an impact on its reporting to both law enforcement and researchers alike, making estimates of the prevalence of the problem a challenge. Researchers now avoid the use of the word "rape" in the process of collecting data to circumvent individual differences in the attribution of the crime (Harney & Muehlenhard, 1991).

SCOPE OF THE PROBLEM

As previously intimated, the accurate estimation of the prevalence of acquaintance rape is a difficult task. Victim underreporting, police failure to forward cases for prosecution, and other methodological problems have plagued researchers for years (Harney & Muehlenhard, 1991). One of the earlier surveys not suffering from some of these difficulties was conducted by Russell (1984) who found that 21% of women had been raped by acquaintances. In their study assessing the prevalence of acquaintance rape, Muehlenhard and Linton (1987) found that 14.7% of the women had been involved in rape in a dating situation, and the length of time dating partners had known one another was unrelated to risk of sexual aggression. Koss and Oros (1982) found that about 20% of the female respondents at Kent State University reported they had been physically forced to have intercourse on a date.

In terms of historical trends, Levine and Kanin (1987) claimed there has been a dramatic rise in acquaintance rape over the past three decades. Referring to data from questionnaires distributed by Kanin in the late 1950s, the researchers stated that only 3.5% of female undergraduates who were asked to anonymously report their experiences of sexual victimization identified themselves as having been the victim of date or acquaintance rape. When one compares these statistics with those of more recent studies, the prevalence of acquaintance rape does appear to have increased markedly. In a Fact Sheet on victims of rape, the U.S. House of Representatives Select Committee on Children, Youth and Families (1990) cited a survey done by Koss, Dinero, Seibel, and Cox in 1988 that found 11.4% of 3,187 college women reported having been raped by an acquaintance, casual date, or steady date. As yet another commentary on the long-standing idea that most rapists are strangers, the women in this national survey were almost as likely to have been raped by a family member (1.3%) as by a stranger (only 1.5%).

Several studies, in addition to the two discussed here, dispute the House Select Committee's estimate as being too conservative. Other estimates range from 16% (Kanin, 1985; Kiernan & Taylor, 1990) to 27% (Koss, Gidycz, & Wisniewski, 1987; Miller & Marshall, 1987) of women have experienced premarital sexual abuse. Finally, Miller and Marshall (1987) report that 15% of the men admitted having forced sexual intercourse on a woman while in a dating situation at a university. It should be noted that the data from this study lent support to past findings that few acts of coercive sex are officially reported and "most victims and victimizers do not acknowledge coercive sex (or date rape) as a rape experience" (Miller & Marshall, 1987, p. 46). Therefore, one can conclude that significant underreporting continues to be a problem in estimating the rates of sexually coercive acts today, and there is some evidence suggesting a rise in the prevalence of acquaintance rape over the past thirty years.

FACTORS ASSOCIATED WITH
PREMARITAL SEXUAL ABUSE

Characteristics of Victimizers

Researchers (Muehlenhard & Linton, 1987; Koss & Dinero, 1988) found that men who had engaged in sexually aggressive acts were more traditional in terms of gender role attitudes and more accepting of violence in relationships than other men. Muehlenhard and Linton (1987) found men and women who had been involved in acts of sexual aggression perceived relationships as more adversarial than others. Men, in general, subscribed to significantly more rape myths than women, sexually aggressive males believed rape myths significantly more than other males, and nonaggressive males believed these myths significantly more than women regardless of whether they had experienced sexual aggression. These findings of Muehlenhard and Linton (1987) are consistent with those of other researchers (Burt, 1980; Check & Malamuth, 1983; Fischer, 1986). Kanin (1985) suggests that another attitude of date rapists is the belief that one's prestige can be enhanced through the selective exploitation and degradation of women, especially those viewed as "teasers," "economic exploiters," and "loose." The use of these terms suggests intense sexism and misogyny, and Koss and Dinero (1988) confirmed that sexually aggressive men do possess more hostility toward women than nonaggressive men.

Kanin (1984) found that date rapists when compared to 227 controls obtained a significantly higher average of heterosexual orgasms and yet were "significantly more apt to evaluate their sexual achievements as unsatisfactory" (p. 99). This may account for the "predatory behavior" of date rapists (Kanin, 1984). Examining other cognitive factors, Fischer (1986) found two significant predictors of acceptance by male subjects of a male's behavior in a rape scenario were less accurate sexual knowledge, which may help perpetuate rape myths, and a self-permissive attitude toward socially unapproved sexual behaviors. Research indicates that individual psychopathology or emotional maladjustment are poor predictors of male sexual aggressiveness, and researchers are better served by concentrating on power differences along gender lines in our society and the perpetuation of rape-supportive beliefs (Koss, Leonard, Beezley, & Oros, 1985). In a riveting statement, Grauerholz and Koralewski (1991) conclude: "In many ways, rapists are 'average guys' in a sexist society. Stopping rape will require change at both the individual and societal levels" (p. 12).

Characteristics of Victims

With regard to victims of acquaintance rape, Muehlenhard and Linton (1987) found that women who had experienced male sexual aggression were less traditional than other women. This finding suggests that men erroneously interpret women as sexually available if they do not present themselves as "coy," traditional, or less "sexually accessible." Kanin (1984) claims that 68% of the cases of acquaintance rape in his sample involved consensual and reciprocal genital play. The researcher argues that if many acquaintance rapes do evolve out of consensual sexual experiences, victims may enter into the rape situation not anticipating the possibility of danger and, subsequent to the assault, may not recognize their role as a rape victim.

Supporting Kanin's (1984) finding, and employing controversial language, Miller and Marshall (1987) report that 65% of their sample of college women said they had engaged in "sexually teasing behavior" when they did not want to go as far as sexual intercourse. Of this subsample, 32% indicated that undesired intercourse had taken place; 66% of the men indicated their agreement with the women, stating that "they had experienced a woman engaging in sexually teasing behavior when she did not want sexual intercourse to occur" (p. 44). Such findings beg the question of how the respondents and society in general define sexually teasing behavior and whether the subjects' remarks reflect a socialization process which assigns to women a sense of responsibility for the sexual behavior of males.

Situational Factors

In a study of risk factors for acquaintance rape, Muehlenhard and Linton (1987) confirm Miller and Marshall's (1987) finding that both men and women report that the man had frequently felt "led on" during sexually aggressive dates. The perception of the man being teased or led on could be associated with a lack of clear, direct messages regarding limits, boundaries, or expectations of how intimate each partner wishes to become. With regard to the use of alcohol and/or drugs, Miller and Marshall (1987) found that 70% of the men who had engaged in coercive sex had done so under the influence of alcohol and other chemical substances. Other researchers (Koss & Dinero, 1988; Muehlenhard & Linton, 1987) report that a factor strongly associated with the incidence of sexual aggression is the use of alcohol at the time the assault occurred. Abbey (1991) presents several explanations for the relationship between alcohol consumption and rape, including: (1) expectancies about the effects of alcohol, (2) misperceptions of cues, and (3) the use of alcohol to justify behavior. Thus, the use of alcohol or drugs does seem to be a risk factor whether it actually decreases sexual inhibitions or provides victimizers a means of rationalizing their behavior.

The locations most closely associated with premarital sexual abuse are those in which observation by others is difficult such as a private house, an apartment, or a car parked in a relatively secluded locale (Muehlenhard & Linton, 1987; Miller and Marshall, 1987). Kanin (1984) also found that 54% of acquaintance rapes in his study occurred in the man's or his friend's residence. Muehlenhard and Linton (1987) hypothesize that the man is likely to feel greater personal control (and perceive less chance of interruption) in the environment of his apartment, and to a lesser extent, in his automobile than in the woman's apartment. Men have reported that sexually aggressive dates were more likely to have involved attendance at a movie (Muehlenhard & Linton, 1987). A final risk factor may be exposure to any media, including popular films, which depict sado-masochistic themes and portray women as becoming aroused by sexual degradation and/or violence (e.g., *Blue Velvet, 9 1/2 Weeks*). Any stimulus that supports the use of violence in relationships and perpetuates rape myths could help legitimize sexual aggression and precipitate premarital sexual abuse.

Family Factors

Conventional wisdom suggests that fathers may play an important role in socializing males to be sexually aggressive and pursue women as potential conquests. However, Kanin (1984) found that very few fathers of date rapists had been sources of sexual encouragement. In contrast, fathers tended to have the most impact on their sons' sexual behaviors through their degree of *discouragement* or disapproval. Kanin (1984) determined that 72% of the controls compared to only 28% of the date rapists had fathers whose attitude toward premarital sex was deemed "very unfavorable." With regard to modeling theory, research demonstrates a positive relationship between the observation of aggression in one's childhood and later emulation of these violent behaviors in one's adult relationships (Straus, Gelles, & Steinmetz, 1980; Walker, 1983). In addition, Bernard and Bernard (1983) found a positive relationship between aggression in one's family of origin and the inflicting or sustaining of aggression in courtship. Bernard and Bernard (1983) remark that "perhaps the most striking aspect of modeling is the extent to which students indulge in the same forms of abuse as they experienced or observed in their families of origin" (p. 286). Thus, experience or observation of sexually coercive acts in one's family of origin may be linked to later imitation of the same behaviors.

In another study using a random sample of college students, Gwartney-Gibbs, Stockard, and Bohmer (1987) found that students who witnessed parental abuse and violence were more likely to inflict courtship violence, and the witnessing of more severe forms of parental aggression was associated with more severe forms of aggression. Forty percent of males who had had physically violent and abusive parents inflicted sexual aggression on the courtship partners while only 19% of males who had experienced peaceful parental role models had been sexually aggressive in courtship. Research has been conducted to examine the possible relationship between women's experiences in their families of origin and their later chances of sexual victimization (Roth, Wayland, & Woolsey, 1990). Roth et al. (1990) found that women who had histories of sexual victimization were more likely to exhibit *denial*—an avoidant defense mechanism and a common symptom of posttraumatic

stress; they posited that "the denied effects of extensive sexual assault oper-
ate so as to increase the likelihood of revictimization" (p. 179) because past
traumatic events, whether acknowledged or denied, can continue to impact
a victim's behavior, perhaps in an unconscious manner.

Social Factors

Making a case for the existence of a dramatic increase in the rate of acquaintance rape, several researchers have addressed sociocultural changes that
might be associated with an increase in male sexually aggressive behavior.
Referring to courtship behavior, Bailey (1988) asserted that earlier in this century both parents and the community had performed a watchdog function to
protect courting couples from inappropriate behavior, but that a formal system of gatekeeping broke down over time. Lloyd (1991) states that "since
norms of sexual behavior were liberalizing and male–female relations were
becoming less formal, courting couples often were left with few rules on
appropriate courtship behavior" (p. 15).

Along these same lines, Levine and Kanin (1987) claim that today males
have dispensed with progressive stages of seduction and often "engage in
sexual intercourse at once" (p. 60) as a response to portrayals of casual sex in
the entertainment media and changes in the roles and sexual attitudes of
their female counterparts. In a study of adolescents' attitudes toward sexual
coercion, Giarusso, Johnson, Goodchilds, and Zellman (1979, as cited by
Miller and Marshall, 1987) found that 76% of boys and 56% of girls believed
it was acceptable under some circumstances for a man to use force to obtain
sex. Therefore, in the absence of clear personal and social standards proscrib-
ing sexual aggression and acquaintance rape, men may be more likely to
ignore women's resistance to their demands for intercourse (Levine & Kanin,
1987).

Using a more social/psychological approach, Kanin (1985) posits that
date rapists are products of a "hypersexual socialization process" and tend to
be both sexually very active and "successful." The finding that rapists are
more sexually experienced than other men has been confirmed by other
researchers (e.g., Koss et al., 1985). Kanin (1985) argues that past successes
may lead to high levels of aspiration for continued gratification and con-
quest, which eventually leads to a high degree of sexual frustration. Sexual
deprivation relative to the gratification the man has come to expect might be
connected to rape episodes. A more compelling notion in Kanin's (1985)
research is the "maintenance and perpetuation of group values" by date rapists and their "associates"—those peers who support their exploitive behavior. Eighty-six percent of date rapists believed that rape is justifiable under
certain conditions in contrast to 19% of a control group. In addition, Kanin
(1985) asserts that the influence of perceived peer pressure in the area of sexual behavior cannot be overestimated in the case of date rapists. Ninety-three
percent of date rapists who said they experienced moderate to great peer

pressure for sexual involvement believe rape is justifiable while only 45% of date rapists who reported little or no peer pressure for sexual activity thought rape was justifiable.

Viewing society through a nonsexist lens, a strong relationship exists between a culture's predominant attitudes toward women and the experience of women. Women living in a patriarchal society experience sexism in a variety of contexts throughout their lives. Men and women are socialized differently, with females receiving rewards for adopting traditionally feminine traits such as being dependent, nurturant, supportive, and passive. These traits act to "ensure female helplessness in the face of male aggression" (Brown & Ziefert, 1988, p. 93). Many women encounter events which serve to reinforce their socialization into a subordinate role (Brown & Ziefert, 1988). These events constitute a continuum of escalating violence against women, with some events experienced directly and others vicariously through news reports and the mass media's depictions of domestic violence, assault, and murder (p. 92); Brown and Ziefert (1988) posit that the "events along this continuum function to keep women from feeling control over their environments and/or life events" (pp. 92–93). Thus, sexual violence may reinforce the belief that women should be subordinate and submissive to men.

Finally, several social factors appear to have an influence on the underreporting of premarital sexual abuse. In addition to a sense of shame and a sense of futility, Kanin (1984) addresses an additional factor that may inhibit a victim's ability to confide in others: "The fact that these acts involved intimates [is] a significant variable in understanding both the lack of reliance on the criminal justice system and the lack of extreme resistance measures. There is something about knowing someone that makes people shy away from extreme action" (p.102). Kanin (1984) cites the work of Canavale and Falcon (1976) who found that neighbors tend to avoid serving as witnesses against one another. The status of victim and victimizer as consenting adults who "take responsibility for the consequences of consensual relationships" is another factor in victims' failure to report and/or the unfounding of cases by the police. Finally, male dominant culture may shoulder women with the burden of responsibility for and the consequences of any "misunderstandings" that occur within the sexual arena.

CONSEQUENCES OF PREMARITAL SEXUAL ABUSE

Consequences for the Victim

The devastating effects of sexual assault on women have been documented by both clinicians and researchers. Symptoms of rape include anxiety, depression, and increased incidence of sexual dysfunction (Becker, Skinner, Abel, & Treacy, 1982; Ellis, Atkeson, & Calhoun, 1981; Kilpatrick, Veronen, & Resick, 1979). A key element in understanding victims' behavior before, during, and after a crime is the relationship between victim and victimizer (Koss et al., 1988). As has been suggested previously, the victim who is acquainted with her victimizer typically does not suspect she could become a victim of rape. Victims tend to be more passive and offer less physical resistance when experiencing sexual coercion at the hands of an acquaintance rather than a stranger (Bart & O'Brien, 1981). However, the association between the victim–victimizer relationship and psychological symptoms after the rape is less clear. Several studies have failed to demonstrate that the victim's relationship with her perpetrator predicts the level of post-rape fear, depression, or social maladjustment (Kilpatrick, Veronen, & Best, 1985; Ruch & Chandler, 1983). One study done by Katz and Burt (1986), cited by Koss et al. (1988), indicates that acquaintance rape victims tend to blame themselves more and evaluate themselves as less recovered than victims of stranger rape for as long as three years after the assault. This finding suggests that a victim's level of self-blame could have a strong impact on her post-rape recovery. Victims of acquaintance rape may be "as psychologically distressed as victims of chronic childhood assault" (Roth et al., 1990, p. 178). The researchers also stress the negative impact of ambiguous assault circumstances on the victim such as consensual sexual activity immediately prior to the assault or the absence of use of physical force by the perpetrator.

Comparing stranger and acquaintance rape victims, Koss and associates (1988) analyzed the differences in victims' perceptions of the victimizer's aggressiveness, victims' resistance, the impact of the rape, and post-rape symptoms. Although stranger rapes were more likely to involve threats of bodily harm and the use of a weapon, stranger and acquaintance rapes did not differ in the reported use of arm twisting, holding down, choking, or beating. Acquaintance rapes often involved multiple assaults by the same perpetrator. With regard to resistance, women who were raped by persons they knew were less likely to scream for help.

In terms of impact of the rape, Koss et al. (1988) found that the two groups did not differ in the percentages of those who had thought of suicide following the rape, and, collectively, 27% of the victims had thought about suicide to the level of considering methods. Significantly fewer victims of acquaintance rape sought help or reported the abuse. The researchers also found that 55% of the victims abused by strangers but only 23% of those abused by acquaintances considered the experience rape. Twenty-nine percent of the women who had been raped by a stranger and 62% of the women raped by an acquaintance did not perceive their sexual abuse as any kind of crime. The likelihood of discussing the rape was negatively associated with the victim's level of intimacy with the perpetrator.

Finally, the post-rape psychological symptoms experienced by the two groups did not differ, with both groups manifesting scores on the scales of depression and anxiety that were significantly higher than the population of nonvictimized women. The finding of few differences in the psychological impact of stranger and acquaintance rape may reflect the extremely low percentages of victims who confided in someone or sought therapy. Seventy-three percent of the victims of stranger rape told someone about it, while only 44% of those victims raped by a steady boyfriend or spouse discussed the experience. The researchers note that "these levels of confiding, helpseeking, and reporting were painfully low especially in light of the potential therapeutic effect of talking" (p. 21). Koss et al. (1988) conclude by citing the work of Davis and Friedman (1985) who determined that talking about a traumatic experience is the single most therapeutic behavior victims can engage in.

Past models for explaining victims' reactions to rape, based on crisis theory and social learning theory (Kilpatrick, Veronen, & Resick, 1982), have been criticized for poorly operationalized concepts and ignoring the interpersonal processes and contexts in which sexual victimization takes place (Harney & Muehlenhard, 1991). Koss and Buckhart (1989) present an alternative framework for the long-term effects of rape that include cognitive, behavioral, and affective reactions to rape. According to Koss and Buckhart (1989), a victim's cognitive map of the abusive event has a significant effect on the chronicity of post-rape psychological effects. In addition, loss of core beliefs about the world as a result of the rape can cause severe stress and impact the victim's interpersonal relationships. A woman who has implicitly trusted most people, especially those with whom she has been acquainted, is likely to experience serious trauma after premarital sexual abuse. With a basic belief destroyed (e.g., the world is a safe place, people are trustworthy), a victim's capacity for openness and trust in her intimate relationships may be severely curtailed during the recovery process. Barrett (1982) states that "when the rapist is a friend or date, not only has her body been violated, but her trust in another human being betrayed, and her faith in her own judgment has been shaken" (p. 48). An examination of the effects of acquaintance rape on the family follows.

Consequences for the Family

There may be relatively few readily observable effects on a victim's family of origin if she chooses, like so many victims, not to disclose her experience of sexual coercion. However, clinical experience does suggest that the holding of such shameful secrets can form a boundary between the victim and her other family members. For example, in keeping the coercion secret, a victim may experience anxiety and discomfort as relevant topics are discussed within her family (e.g., date rape, her relationship with the perpetrator) and as she attempts to camouflage the problem with deception and distorted information (Karpel, 1980). Family members are also likely to experience unexplainable tension when topics related to coercion are addressed. On the other hand, disclosure of sexual coercion may upset the fragile equilibrium of the family and precipitate a "crisis." White and Rollins (1981) found that a family's degree of distress is largely contingent on the victim's agitation and distress subsequent to the assault. Family members may express emotional responses and symptoms such as anger, revenge, helplessness, and guilt—typical reactions to catastrophic events (Burge, 1983).

Consequences for Society

The high prevalence of rape in our society significantly diminishes the sense of safety and well-being experienced by women. Fear of stranger rape restricts the everyday routines and activities of many women, with cues—the setting of the sun and the prospect of crossing a parking lot alone—having profoundly different meanings for women than men. But changes in one's personal habits, such as being escorted home at night by a trusted male friend, do not address the frightening issue raised by premarital sexual abuse: A woman's chances of being raped by someone she knows far outweigh being attacked by a stranger lurking in the shadows. Who can women trust? How do they protect themselves from someone they do not consider a threat? The anxiety and fear present today in many if not most women's lives reflects an implicit inequality between genders that continues to pervade society.

Consequences for the Couple Relationship

In light of the finding that over 60% of all victims of acquaintance rape do not perceive their experience of sexual abuse to be a criminal offense of any kind (Koss et al., 1988), one may wonder how abused partners perceive acts of abuse perpetrated against them. Coercive sexual acts involving arm twisting, choking, and beating are somehow rationalized or explained away by both partners. Do premarital partners engage in a form of collusion to somehow justify an unacceptable offense?

Collusion may exist in the guise of romanticism. For both men and women, "being in love" makes courtship qualitatively different from other intimate relationships (Lloyd, 1991). In emulating a romantic ideal, a couple demonstrates the beliefs that love conquers all, that love entails both agony and ecstasy, and that love is passionate (Lloyd, 1991, p. 16, citing Waller, 1951). Cate and associates (1982) found that 33% of those who experienced violence in a courtship relationship believed that the violence meant love while only 8% thought it meant hate. Another romantic notion is that love can solve any problem. Thus, couples may believe that even destructive facets of courtship, even violence, will be resolved on marriage (Henton, Cate, Koval, Lloyd, & Christopher, 1983). But is the glossing over of serious premarital difficulties justified? Do such couples really "live happily ever after"?

The answer appears to be a resounding "no." Approximately half of all couples married today will eventually divorce (National Center for Health Statistics, 1985). The breakdown of marital relationships tends to occur early on, with the average length of marriage before separation being five years (Cherlin, 1981). With these statistics in mind, Lloyd (1991) suggests that marital difficulties start before many couples say their vows. Pursuit of the romantic ideal leads to a tendency to ignore the bad and glorify the good (Lloyd, 1991, p. 14). Researchers (Lloyd, Koval, & Cate, 1989; O'Leary et al., 1989) estimate that while nearly half of all dating relationships contain violence or sexual exploitation, such negative forms of interaction do not rule out the decision to marry. In fact, women have been known to marry their rapists (Russell, 1990, p. 246). What impact does sexual abuse have on the dynamics of premarital relationships?

Premarital sexual abuse is one expression of male dominance and female powerlessness in our society. In a courtship relationship, the man's acts of sexual coercion reinforce his sense of being in control while they erode the woman's sense of personal power. Lloyd (1991) posits that the male's use of violence and sexual exploitation could be a means by which some men regulate commitment and closeness in the relationship. "The female theme of dependence may constrain her to remain in a violent/exploitative relationship" (Lloyd, 1991, p. 16). Over time, a woman may develop a condition of learned helplessness, which has a devastating impact on self-esteem and may lead a person to take personal responsibility for any negative situations encountered (Abramson, Seligman, & Teasdale, 1978). This may account for the previously discussed findings that rape victims often blame themselves for what was done to them. A cycle of sexual abuse could develop, with the victim's self-blame and eroding sense of self-esteem and autonomy diminishing her capacity to challenge her partner's behavior and/or remove herself from the abusive situation. This cycle could lead to an escalation of unchecked abuse which increases in frequency and severity over time. Thus, in couples where the male sexually abuses the female, the therapist can expect to notice verbal and nonverbal metaphors for the power imbalance present in their relationship.

TREATMENT OF PREMARITAL SEXUAL COERCION

Many professionals who work with abused women believe the only solution to an abusive relationship is its termination. Rosenbaum and O'Leary (1986) state: "To this end, the treatment of choice is usually aimed at providing support, legal assistance, vocational counseling and/or training, child care, and advocacy through the social system" (p. 389). However, many women are unable or unwilling to exit their relationships and choose the route of therapy instead. In the Code of Ethics of the American Association for Marriage and Family Therapy (1991, pp. 1–2), two principles are relevant to clinical cases involving abuse:

> Marriage and family therapists respect the right of clients to make decisions and help them to understand the consequences of these decisions. Therapists clearly advise a client that a decision on marital status is the responsibility of the client.... Marriage and family therapists continue therapeutic relation-

ships only so long as it is reasonably clear that clients are benefiting from the relationship.

These principles are useful in drawing out complex issues in treating persons presenting with premarital sexual coercion.

The first principle relates the importance of therapists respecting the decision-making capacity of their clients, who are solely responsible for decisions regarding continuing or ending personal relationships. Considered in isolation, the first principle makes a therapist's decisions on the issue of conjoint treatment relatively simple. However, the second principle suggests that the therapist has a responsibility to determine whether therapy is benefiting the client. If the therapist is seeing a couple and the safety of the woman is clearly at risk, is couple therapy benefiting the client? In instances where the therapist believes sexual coercion is likely to occur and both partners want to continue couple therapy at the exclusion of other treatment modalities, it may be necessary to refer the couple elsewhere. Still, a conflict between the therapist's perspective and the client's perspective can usually be avoided if the client is provided adequate space to explore the positive and negative consequences of continuing the relationship without being pushed or dictated to by the therapist. Because it is often not possible to discuss such issues in a couple context, the therapist must provide individual sessions so that the client can safely discuss all the ramifications of remaining in a relationship in which she has been coerced. The assessment process for clients presenting with premarital sexual coercion is intended to follow the spirit of these ethical principles and to ensure the safety of all persons involved.

Assessment of Premarital Sexual Coercion

An essential factor affecting the therapist's approach to treating any presenting problem is the number and identity of the presenting clients. In actual practice, some of the dilemmas inherent in treating persons presenting with sexual coercion are simplified by the decisions already made by the clients. For example, many victims of premarital sexual coercion have decided to discontinue contact with the perpetrator. Hence, no ethical dilemma exists. However, there are at least two other case scenarios which are not so simple.

Victim Presents for Individual Therapy
While still involved with the perpetrator, the victim may present for treatment as an individual. The client may be seeking help around issues of empowerment and may require crisis intervention, and, although couple therapy is not appropriate at this time, it may be sought later. Therapists first must assess the client's safety. A decision tree is shown in Figure 11.1 to guide careful assessment and treatment of premarital couples who may be experiencing the problem of sexual coercion. If she is suffering from a recent

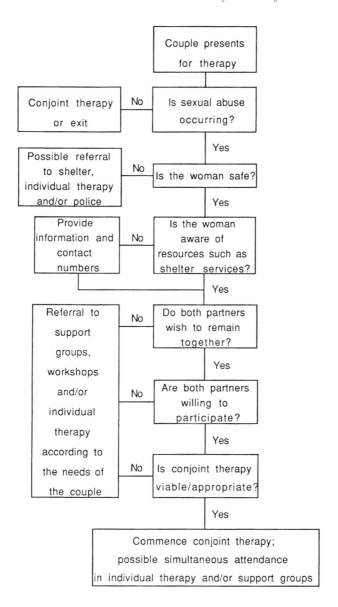

FIGURE 11.1 • Assessment and Treatment Decision Tree

Adapted from Rosenbaum and O'Leary (1986) with permission from The Guilford Press, New York.

abusive incident and has felt that her safety has been threatened, the thera-pist should provide crisis intervention.

According to the ethical principles previously discussed, the responsibil-ity for choosing to maintain the couple relationship rests with the victim. Unfortunately, in regard to the issue of safety, the quality of the relationship is determined by the *perpetrator's* actions, attitudes, and history. Most of the energy in treatment is directed toward empowering her so that she can see herself as a *survivor* with choices.

Couple Presents for Conjoint Therapy

The most complex case scenario occurs when a couple presents with issues other than premarital sexual coercion, but the coercion emerges over the course of therapy. Partners may complain about communication problems, or other issues, and therapy proceeds with its ups and downs until some-thing is said that hints at the possibility of sexual coercion. Therapists should be aware of common signs of an abusive relationship (see Koss et al., 1988; Rosenbaum & O'Leary, 1986).

Once there is any indication that sexual coercion has occurred in the cou-ple's relationship, it is essential for the therapist to provide the female partner the opportunity to communicate her inner thoughts and feelings concerning the relationship. Individual sessions within the context of couple therapy provide a safe and private space for a woman to express fears and concerns without threat of reprisal from her male partner. The frequency and severity of the coercion should be discussed with the female client, and the gravity of any abusive incident should be clarified. The possibility of the coercion hap-pening again must be clearly communicated to the client. Again, victims must be provided adequate time, space, safety, and support to begin to per-ceive themselves as survivors, people who can make choices to enhance their lives.

When one or both partners do not wish to remain together (i.e., there is substantial doubt regarding the viability of the relationship), referral to a support group and/or individual or group counseling (see Figure 11.1) should be considered (Rosenbaum & O'Leary, 1986, p. 389). Beavers (1985) states that "if each partner can openly state that s/he wants to see if they can live together happily, there is a solid basis for treatment" (p. 159). On com-pletion of assessment, the therapist may elect to provide the couple conjoint therapy if and only if: (1) the partners have stated their mutual willingness to work, and (2) the therapist believes sufficient safety exists so that the vic-tim of the abuse is in no immediate danger. For the second criterion to be fulfilled, the sexually abusive partner must be willing to contract for no vio-lence/coercion before the couple can be seen conjointly by the therapist. Willbach (1989, p. 48) asserts the critical importance of a binding nonviolent contract in the following statement:

If the violent family member will not or cannot agree to stop the use of violence in all circumstances, or exhibits by his actions that he cannot live up to the agreement, then…couples therapy is not the appropriate modality: It will not be as effective in changing behavior as individual and/or group therapy and has negative consequences from an ethical viewpoint.

Once these criteria have been fulfilled, the therapist can proceed with conjoint treatment.

Therapeutic Assessment: Detecting Premarital Sexual Coercion

The initial step in treating sexually coercive men and the recipients of their coercion is, of course, identification of those requiring services. Therapists may not become aware of clients' experiences of sexual coercion in their relationships as part of the typical intake and assessment process for several reasons. First, clients may be in denial either because of romantic beliefs or failure to recognize sexual coercion as abuse. Second, a female client may anticipate a reprisal from her partner following disclosure of sexual coercion, whether it is in the form of further violence of a physical or sexual nature, withdrawal of affection, or threats to end their relationship. It is important for therapists to acknowledge these factors that may influence clients' willingness to disclose premarital sexual coercion.

Symptoms of abuse and trauma of all types include high anxiety, depression, intense shame and guilt, and sexual problems (Koss et al., 1988). Low self-esteem in either partner may be an indication of violence or potential violence. In addition, alcohol use often is associated with all forms of family violence (Rosenbaum & O'Leary, 1986). A common characteristic of physically and sexually coercive men is pathological jealousy, which is frequently manifested in attempts to socially isolate the woman. Muehlenhard and Linton (1987) found that sexually aggressive males believed rape myths significantly more than both women and other males.

Assessment instruments are helpful in that they can obtain information in a few minutes while a therapist might require much more time to obtain the same amount of data through an interview (Stahmann & Hiebert, 1987). Descriptions of instruments that can effectively assess the variables associated with premarital sexual coercion follow. The premarital couple's strengths, weaknesses, and degree of readiness for marriage may be measured through the use of PREPARE (Olson, Fournier, & Druckman, 1986), the Caring Relationship Inventory (Shostrum, 1975), and PREParation for Marriage (PREP-M) (Holman, Busby, & Larson, 1989). In addition to providing scores of couple readiness for marriage, PREP-M provides measures of partners' self-esteem, emotional health, openness and self-disclosure, and use of addictive substances. Regarding the detection of a family history of abuse, PREP-M also includes items that inquire as to how frequently acts of physical and sexual violence occurred in clients' families of origin, as well as in their current relationships. Additional instruments that may be helpful include the Brief Symptom Inventory (BSI) (Derogatis, 1975), the Marital Satisfaction Inventory (Snyder, 1985), the Sexual Experience Survey (Koss & Oros, 1982), and the rape myth scale (Burt, 1980).

Individual Treatment of Premarital Sexual Coercion

Crisis Intervention with Victims

Brown and Ziefert (1988) cite research done by Bowker (1983) and Hanneke and Shields (1985) that documents the efficacy of crisis intervention for helping survivors of various forms of sexual assault deal with their feelings and reestablish coping capacities. This stage of intervention often involves assisting women in reexamining their beliefs about sexual assault and helping them to stop blaming themselves for the abuse. The therapist can challenge clients' subscriptions to prevalent rape myths and facilitate the differentiation between feelings of fear, terror, and revulsion associated with the sexual coercion and feelings of guilt and shame associated with an act for which they clearly were not responsible.

Women's support groups may be the next step in treatment since "Group settings provide an opportunity to decrease women's sense of isolation and powerlessness and are a vehicle to enhance competence" (Brown & Ziefert, 1988, p. 98). Although these treatment modalities function to give women permission to talk about their traumatic experiences and reconnect them to a supportive and empowering community, Brown and Ziefert (1988) concede that "it is not enough to offer crisis intervention and self-help groups" to victims of sexual violence. Therefore, once crisis intervention has been provided, victims of sexual coercion should be referred for therapy of an individual or group nature (e.g., individual psychotherapy, Women for Women support group).

Treatment Guidelines for Victims

The therapist's role is to help survivors gain sufficient confidence and understanding to make decisions that promote their safety and satisfaction in the long term. To help survivors improve the quality of their lives, therapists must: (1) help them place responsibility for the sexual coercion on the perpetrator, (2) clarify the seriousness of the coercion by investigating its frequency and severity and assessing the dangerousness of the perpetrator, and (3) help survivors understand that there are no guarantees that the perpetrator will not resort to sexual violence again. Therapy must not be seen as a guarantee that coercion will never reoccur.

Treatment for Perpetrators

For male clients with a history of sexually abusive behavior, individual therapy is complicated by client denial, a frequently violent developmental history, and the repetitive, cyclical nature of abusive behaviors. Wolf (1988) asserts that early experiences act as "potentiators" through their influence on later attitudes and behaviors. Over time, sexually aggressive behavior can become ingrained in the perpetrator's personality structure and a recurring, chronic problem. Because of perpetrators' denial or wish to conceal the full extent of their sexually aggressive behaviors, a comprehensive assessment should include "a review of all data available including victim statements, witness statements, and attendant assessments…by their therapist or by family members" (Wolf, 1988, p. 145).

Once an historical perspective on the perpetrator's problem has been procured, the therapist can begin to treat the specific patterns associated with the sexual aggression. Wolf (1988) recommends that therapists facilitate the perpetrator's recognition of distortions in his beliefs and attitudes that have worked to create and maintain sexually coercive behaviors. Therapists also need to guide the client back to childhood experiences, which contributed to the development of current attitudes and beliefs, that continue to justify abusive acts. Wolf (1988) also suggests the use of a combination of "confrontive group therapy, 'traditional' insight talk therapy, family therapy, couples therapy, and cognitive behavioral counterconditioning" (p. 146). Although still experimental, Wolf's approach has been shown to be very effective.

Conjoint Treatment of Premarital Sexual Coercion

An important issue to address in the treatment of premarital couples who have experienced sexual coercion is how they are different from marital couples struggling with the same problem. Premarital couples sometimes experience more ambiguity, romanticism, and denial than married couples.

The "good times" are often perceived as better in premarital relationships than in marriage because partners are spending more time with one another and are participating in more rewarding experiences (Stahmann & Hiebert, 1987). Premarital couples frequently have fewer stressors with which to cope such as parenting responsibilities or financial strain from house payments and other joint ventures. As a result, they may have more emotional energy available for one another. Many premarital couples may be experiencing a strong, positive attachment with a partner for the first time and may be quite impressionable. Partners may make statements such as "We have so much in common" or "This is the first time I have found someone I can really talk to." Rewarding experiences work to diminish the impact of abusive incidents and couples may view the violence as an aberration rather than as an important pattern in the relationship. This dynamic is complex, with premarital partners believing they can readily choose to end the relationship because they are not married. At the same time, rewarding behaviors contribute to the emotional bond between partners and the guilt connected to the coercion creates isolation and impedes their ability to sort out their feelings. This situation makes reality testing particularly difficult for the clients and the therapist.

The rewarding aspects of the premarital relationship and the lower level of commitment can create profound ambivalence in victims of premarital sexual coercion, especially those suffering from low self-esteem. If they simply had to choose between a rapist and a loving partner, the decision would be simple; unfortunately, the victim has experienced both persons in her partner. Because of the cognitive dissonance associated with attempts to reconcile these two extreme positions, victims often ignore the rapist and focus on the loving partner. With time the struggle between these two extremes can lead to paralysis and lower levels of self-respect. Victims ask themselves, "Why can't I make up my mind about him?" In turn the efforts exerted to maintain the facade of a happy relationship drains energy from the victim and can lead to depression. This spiral can lead to choices that are self-destructive such as unplanned pregnancy, alcoholism, or drug use. Perhaps the most intensely ambiguous scenario is the one in which the perpetrator does not coerce his partner again during the courtship. Further coercion from the male might push the victim beyond paralysis and facilitate her choice to end the relationship.

The perpetrator can experience a similar spiral if his attempts to rationalize, justify, or deny his behavior are not successful. He may struggle to maintain his self-respect knowing he has coerced and frightened his partner. Each time he experiences loving feelings for her he is reminded of what he has done, leading to an experience of love and self-hate. He feels guilty, and, as his frustration and anger increase, his resources for controlling abusive behavior may decrease. He too may resort to self-medication to escape his feelings. For both victims and perpetrators, marriage can be seen as a welcome relief because it temporarily ends the dilemma of whether to stay in or get out of a relationship so confusing in its mixture of love and hate.

Therapists can enter the system at a variety of points in this pattern. One of the most common places to enter is right before the wedding as the couple requests help in "just ironing out a few minor issues." The following case presents a sample of some of the complicated dynamics that can emerge when treating premarital couples where the woman has been sexually coerced.

> A couple who has been dating exclusively for a year and a half presented for premarital counseling at a university clinic. The man (Dan) is a 24-year-old salesman and the woman (Shari) is 20-year-old secretary. Their problems included frequent arguments and the stress the couple has been experiencing as their wedding approaches. After careful perusal of the questionnaires completed by the couple, the therapist noticed Shari had high scores on questions relating to anxiety and fear. The therapist decided to explore the content of her fears in more detail.
>
> During the initial couple session the therapist asked specific questions about Shari's fears and anxiety. She responded with vague comments about stress at

work and sometimes worrying about making Dan angry. Each time the therapist inquired about her fears in this relationship Shari shut down and looked to Dan to speak for her. As the couple session progressed, the therapist continued to feel uncomfortable with Shari's responses and asked them to come for some individual sessions the next time so that they could focus on their families of origin.

The following week, the therapist met with each of the partners and discussed their family backgrounds as well as explored Shari's fears in more depth. In individual sessions, both partners disclosed they had witnessed acts of physical violence in their families of origin. In her session, Shari also disclosed that sometimes Dan came home drunk and wanted to have sex. She said he was frightening when he had been drinking and didn't listen to her when she told him to leave her alone.

On disclosure that premarital sexual coercion was perpetrated, the therapist had several tasks to attend to, including the provision of adequate time, space, and support to help the victim make a decision regarding the future of the relationship. The therapist emphasized the gravity of the coercion, the strong possibility that such abuse could occur again, and the implications for Shari if she continued to experience coercion. The therapist informed her of the various services available (e.g., local women's shelters) should she feel endangered again by Dan. Facilitated by the therapist, Shari formulated a plan of action, which included a safe place to go and a list of resources for help, in the event of another crisis.

Once a safety plan was established, the therapist proceeded to discuss individually with Dan his perceptions of his drinking and the sexual coercion as had been presented by Shari. Dan demonstrated belief in several rape myths, including the notion that women refuse men's advances even when they desire intercourse (i.e., "she says 'no' when she really means 'yes'"). Dan also expressed confusion regarding some of the events she had referred to, conceding that his memory of those events was vague. The therapist pointed out that it was likely that his memory was impaired when he became intoxicated, as was his judgment and ability to accurately assess his partner's real wishes and comfort level with his sexual advances.

Dan said he had to think about this, but he had been aware lately that Shari had shown little or no interest in making love even when he had not been drinking. He admitted he may have forced himself on his partner, and that was something of which he was ashamed. Following Dan's concession that he might have perpetrated premarital sexual coercion, the therapist obtained a no violence/coercion contract from Dan. The therapist indicated that Dan's habit of "winning" in the short term through coercion and intimidation made him lose in the long term, and repeatedly emphasized that physical and sexual violence were unacceptable under *any* circumstances. In addition, the therapist instructed Dan to begin monitoring his drinking by counting the number of drinks he consumed per day.

After this session, the couple missed two consecutive appointments. It is common for perpetrators to avoid therapy following confrontation by the therapist. This is more likely to occur if the therapist does not strike a balance between supportive and confrontive behaviors and/or the perpetrator is extremely defensive.

Several weeks later, Shari contacted the therapist and asked for another individual session. Over the next several months the therapist saw Shari for individual work around empowerment, anxiety, and her family-of-origin issues. As Shari made some progress she started to consider changing her career and enrolling in college. Shari's movement in therapy was associated with a decrease in her tolerance of Dan's manipulation. This resulted in two episodes of her refusing to engage in intercourse on Dan's demand and her leaving the house after Dan threatened to leave her.

After another month of individual sessions, Shari requested a return to couple therapy, wanting to give the relationship one more chance. The therapist helped her recognize that Dan might coerce her again, and that he might continue to use alcohol for years. Even with these risks Shari felt that "Dan was worth it." Dan came in, although somewhat reluctantly. To facilitate Dan's empathy and understanding of Shari's experience of being coerced, the therapist guided him back to an incident in his childhood in which he himself was controlled, manipulated, and humiliated and helped him explore the feelings associated with that event. Dan was able to relate several frightening episodes when his father had beat him. The therapist was able to encourage him to express the fear he had had as a little child and how painful it was to never "get close to Dad." Several times during the next few sessions, when Dan would express a clear emotion, the therapist would ask questions to get Dan to recognize that Shari was having similar feelings toward him. Enhancing the male partner's empathy in this way over several individual sessions decreased Dan's perception of sexual coercion as a valid option in his behavioral repertoire.

At the same time, the therapist was careful not to collude with Dan by buying into his denial or rationalizations (e.g., "I was abused as a child," "I'm an alcoholic," "She was provoking me"). Although therapists may empathize with the client's history of past abuse or neglect in his family of origin, the focus must remain on accountability. "Being accountable means living up to expectations, taking responsibility for one's own behavior, and acting one's age [acting like an adult]" (Combrinck-Graham, 1991, p. 201).

From this point on, therapy consisted of individual work with Dan and Shari along with monthly couple sessions. The therapist reiterated that any violation of the contract for no violence or coercion would result in a termination of conjoint treatment. The therapist approached conjoint treatment of the premarital couple with caution. The nature of courtship, with the man traditionally possessing a disproportionate amount of control and the woman exhibiting considerable dependence (Lloyd, 1991), makes intervention into premarital relationships especially difficult. For example, in being socialized to be responsible for events and behaviors occurring in relationships, Shari believed that the coercion was somehow her fault, a belief that meshed well with Dan's tendency to underestimate or minimize the impact of his own behaviors.

While Dan's subjective reality had been that he was helpless and "out of control" during incidents of sexual coercion, the therapist made it clear that violence was still a choice. This was accomplished largely in couple sessions by helping the couple describe experiences when Dan had elected to not become violent and exploring the specific strategies Dan used to successfully avoid outbursts. These exceptions not only provided him with a sense of hope but also sent the underlying message that when he failed to use these strategies he was *choosing* to be violent.

In seeing the partners in the context of their relationship, the therapist was able to access their individual issues and see how key relationships in each partner's families of origin were being recreated (Napier, 1987). For instance, the role of the frustrated, controlling father was a part of both Dan and Shari's family scripts, and both partners while growing up had observed violent altercations between their parents. As these old scripts were explored, the couple was taught to recognize the impact of the scripts on their expectations, interactions, and the regulation of distance in their relationship.

The therapist confronted and challenged rape-supportive beliefs held by both partners (e.g., that a woman needs to be persuaded or convinced to have sex, that a woman says "no" but means "yes," that a male can be a "real" man only by "scoring"). In addition, the therapist addressed "the romantic veneer through which premarital behavior was viewed by both partners" (Lloyd, 1991, p. 18). One belief held by this couple was that with marriage and children they would no longer fight or have problems. The therapist helped them face the reality of married life with its stressors and challenges by having the clients interview several of their friends who were already married, asking these friends specific questions. Each of these experiences helped the couple realize that if anything, marriage exacerbated existing problems.

Another goal of therapy with Dan and Shari was examining the profound ambivalence which may be experienced by victims of sexual coercion. Bograd (1992) states that the victim's opposing feelings and wishes need to be clarified in treatment. The dynamic tension present in feelings of love and hate, security and panic, and in victims' wishes to continue or leave the relationship can produce considerable cognitive dissonance for victims. In the case example, the therapist attempted to help Shari escape her paralysis by facilitating her acknowledgment, acceptance, and integration of these affective polar opposites (Little, 1990).

The "up-and-down" nature of couple treatment for a problem as serious as sexual coercion must be acknowledged. During the course of therapy, Shari and Dan's perceptions of the viability of the relationship and their individual convictions with regard to staying with one another underwent sweeping changes. Couple therapy worked to challenge Dan and Shari's romanticism and to help them see beyond their relationship. By increasing clarity of the couple's issues, couple therapy may increase the likelihood that relationships will end. In this case, following several months of therapy, the two partners' commitments to a life together were no longer congruent. Although considerable progress was made with their communication, with Dan's anger/alcoholism, and with Shari's empowerment, with time, they found themselves growing apart. Couple therapy ended with a tearful session where they both acknowledged that their relationship was not working and they needed to move on.

Probably the most difficult issue to address in couple therapy when a woman has been victimized by her partner is sexual intimacy. In cases where the couple stays together, sex therapy approaches that fit the specific needs of the couple need to be used at the end of therapy. Usually a considerable amount of time and repeated demonstration of appropriate behavior by the male are necessary before the female is comfortable and capable of exploring sexual issues in a therapeutic way. Both partners must be informed that it might be some time before the sexual area of their relationship is rewarding. In addition, early in the couple sessions, the therapist should emphasize the ground rule that it is the woman's choice whether and how the couple will begin to relate sexually in the relationship again.

Primary Prevention

Across the country, a frequent response to public outcries about sexual assault is to focus on "increased security, improved lighting, emergency phones, escort services and self-defense training" (Kiernan & Taylor, 1990, p. 48). Researchers (Kiernan & Taylor, 1990; Ward et al., 1991) point out that these solutions to the problem of sexual assault fail to take into account that women are more likely to be victimized by someone they know than a stranger. While conventional policies continue to be necessary, "efforts to educate and increase awareness of this problem…may be more efficient allocations of resources" (Kiernan & Taylor, 1990, p. 48). Courses and workshops focusing on communication and problem-solving skills, alcohol awareness, rape myths, assertiveness training, and male/female socialization and its impact on relationships can help to address issues related to incidence of premarital sexual abuse (Lloyd, 1991). Community organizations should assist in the wider dissemination of the sometimes shocking but very relevant information regarding premarital sexual abuse.

In addition, Amada (1990) relates the positive impact helping professionals can have through education and activism and stressed the legal and moral responsibility of academic institutions to protect the safety of members of their communities. One avenue for facilitating consciousness raising in college communities might be health and hygiene classes that are required at many institutions of higher learning (Miller, 1988). Such courses offer the opportunity to expose students to the different perspectives of men and women on sexual experiences and situations. Educators may wish to incorporate specific in-class exercises and experiences to aid in early recognition of the assault situation since this was one factor found to be associated with women's thwarting of rape attempts. Miller (1988) suggests the use of videotapes depicting sexual situations and role-playing types of psychological coercion used to obtain sex to challenge the students' thinking about premarital sexual abuse.

It is clear that men and women should become more aware of the frequency of sexual aggression in the context of intimate relationships and how to recognize and cope with acts of sexual coercion as they occur. However, since the values and beliefs, which are correlates of male sexual violence against women, have their origins in childhood, it is recommended that elementary and secondary school systems begin the task of monitoring and enlightening the sexual attitudes of their future men and women (Amada, 1990). Through education at these different levels, the notions that a woman needs to be persuaded or convinced to have sex, that a woman says "no" but means "yes," and that only by having intercourse can a male "score" and be a "real man" may one day fall out of fashion, thereby eliminating common rationalizations for sexual assault all too often employed today.

CONCLUSIONS

Premarital sexual coercion is a pervasive, destructive problem in society. Although some may argue that couple therapy is inappropriate in cases of physical and sexual coercion, therapeutic work can be greatly enhanced by having access to relationship dynamics. Whether the couple stays together or not, as marriage and family therapists we believe that the complex issues involved in sexual coercion are more easily addressed in a combination of individual and couple sessions, if both partners wish to stay together and safety issues are continually assessed. Because sexual coercion occurs in a relationship, it is our belief that revictimization and reperpetration can be reduced if some couples work is conducted. Still, there is a serious need to study the effectiveness of couple and individual treatment modalities to determine what is most helpful for clients.

REFERENCES

Abbey, A. (1991). Acquaintance rape and alcohol consumption on college campuses: How are they linked? *Journal of American College Health, 39*, 165–169.

Abramson, L. Y., Seligman, M. E. P., & Teasdale, J. D. (1978). Learned helplessness in humans: Critique and reformulation. *Journal of Abnormal Psychology, 87*, 49–73.

Amada, G. (1990). Date rape on the college campus: The college psychotherapist as activist. *Journal of College Student Psychotherapy, 4* (2), 89–93.

American Association for Marriage and Family Therapy. (1991). *Code of Ethics.* Washington DC: AAMFT.

Bailey, B. L. (1988). *From front porch to back seat: The history of courtship in America.* Baltimore: The Johns Hopkins University Press.

Barrett, K. (1982, September). Date rape: A campus epidemic? *Ms.*, pp. 48–51, 130.

Bart, P. B. & O'Brien, P. H. (1981). A study of women who both were raped and avoided rape. *Journal of Social Issues, 37*, 123–137.

Beavers, W. R. (1985). *Successful marriage.* New York: W. W. Norton.

Becker, J. V., Skinner, L. J., Abel, M. D., & Treacy, E. C. (1982). Incidence and types of sexual dysfunction in rape and incest victims. *Journal of Sex and Marital Therapy, 8*, 65–74.

Bernard, M. L. & Bernard, J. L. (1983). Violent intimacy: The family as a model for love relationships. *Family Relations, 32*, 283–286.

Bograd, M. (1992). *Domestic violence: Navigating therapy on stormy seas.* Presentation at the Annual Conference of the Central New York Chapter of the New York Association for Marriage and Family Therapy, Syracuse, February 7.

Brown, K. S. & Ziefert, M. (1988). Crisis resolution, competence, and empowerment: A service model for women. *Journal of Primary Prevention, 9*(1–2), 92–103.

Burge, S. K. (1983). Rape: Individual and family reactions. In C. R. Figley and H. I. McCubbin (Eds.), *Stress and the family, Volume II: Coping with catastrophe* (pp. 103–119). New York: Brunner/Mazel.

Burt, M. (1980). Cultural myths and supports for rape. *Journal of Personality and Social Psychology, 38,* 217–230.

Cate, R. M., Henton, J. M., Koval, J. E., Christopher, F. S., & Lloyd, S. A. (1982). Premarital abuse: A social psychological perspective. *Journal of Family Issues, 3,* 79–90.

Check, J. P. & Malamuth, N. M. (1983). Sex role stereotyping and reactions to depictions of stranger versus acquaintance rape. *Journal of Personality and Social Psychology, 45,* 344–356.

Cherlin, A. (1981). *Marriage, divorce, remarriage.* Cambridge: Harvard University Press.

Combrinck-Graham, L. (1991). Holding children accountable. *Family Therapy Networker, 15*(4), 48–52.

Derogatis, L. R. (1975). *Brief Symptom Inventory.* Baltimore: Clinical Psychometric Research.

Ellis, E. M., Atkeson, B. M., & Calhoun, K. S. (1981). An assessment of long-term reaction to rape. *Journal of Abnormal Psychology, 90,* 263–266.

Fischer, G. J. (1986). College student attitudes toward forcible date rape: I. Cognitive-predictors. *Archives of Sexual Behavior, 15*(6), 457–466.

Grauerholz, E. & Koralewski, M. A. (1991). *Sexual coercion.* Lexington, MA: D. C. Heath.

Gwartney-Gibbs, P.A., Stockard, J., & Bohmer, S. (1987). Learning courtship aggression: The influence of parents, peers, and personal experiences. *Family Relations, 36,* 276–282.

Hanneke, C. R. & Shields, N. M. (1985). Marital rape: Implications for the helping professions. *Social Casework, 6,* 451–458.

Harney, P. A. & Muehlenhard, C. L. (1991). Rape. In E. Grauerholz & M. Koralewski (Eds.), *Sexual coercion* (pp. 3–15). Lexington, MA: D. C. Heath.

Henton, J. M., Cate, R. M., Koval, J. E., Lloyd, S. A., & Christopher, F. S. (1983). Romance and violence in dating relationships. *Journal of Family Issues, 4,* 467–482.

Holman, T. B., Busby, D. M., & Larson, J. H. (1989). *PREParation for Marriage.* Provo, UT: Marriage Study Consortium, Brigham Young University.

Jenkins, M. J. & Dambrot, F. H. (1987). The attribution of date rape: Observer's attitudes and sexual experiences and the dating situation. *Journal of Applied Social Psychology, 17*(10), 875–895.

Kanin, E. J. (1984). Date rape: Unofficial criminals and victims. *Victimology: An International Journal, 9*(1), 95–108.

Kanin, E. J. (1985). Date rapists: Differential sexual socialization and relative deprivation. *Archives of Sexual Behavior, 14*(3), 219–231.

Karpel, M. A. (1980). Family secrets: I. Conceptual and ethical issues in the relational context: II. Ethical and practical considerations in therapeutic management. *Family Process, 19,* 295–306.

Kelly, L. (1988). *Surviving sexual violence.* Minneapolis: University of Minnesota Press.

Kiernan, J. E. & Taylor, V. L. (1990). Coercive sexual behavior among Mexican-American college students. *Journal of Sex & Marital Therapy, 16*(1), 44–50.

Kilpatrick, D. G., Veronen, L. J., & Best, C. L. (1985). Factors predicting psychological distress among rape victims. In C. R. Figley (Ed.), *Trauma and its wake: The study and treatment of post-traumatic stress disorder* (pp. 113–141). New York: Brunner/Mazel.

Kilpatrick, D. G., Veronen, L. J., & Resick, P. A. (1979). The aftermath of rape: Recent empirical findings. *American Journal of Orthopsychiatry, 49,* 658–669.

Kilpatrick, D. G., Veronen, L. J., & Resick, P. A. (1982). Psychological sequelae to rape: Assessment and treatment strategies. In D. M. Doleys, R. L. Meredith, & A. R.

Ciminero (Eds.), *Behavioral medicine: Assessment and treatment strategies* (pp. 473–498). New York: Plenum.

Koss, M. P. & Buckhart, B. R. (1989). A conceptual analysis of rape victimization: Long-term effects and implications for treatment. *Psychology of Women Quarterly, 13*, 27–40.

Koss, M. P. & Dinero, T. E. (1988). Predictors of sexual aggression among a national sample of male college students. In R. A. Prentsky & V. L. Quinsky (Eds.), *Human sexual aggression: Current perspectives* (pp. 133–147). New York: New York Academy of Sciences.

Koss, M. P., Dinero, T. E., Seibel, C. A., & Cox, S. L. (1988). Stranger and acquaintance rape: Are there differences in the victim's experience? *Psychology of Women Quarterly, 12*, 1–24.

Koss, M. P., Gidycz, C. A., & Wisniewski, N. (1987). The scope of rape: Incidence and prevalence of sexual aggression and victimization in a national sample of higher education students. *Journal of Consulting and Clinical Psychology, 55*, 162–170.

Koss, M. P., Leonard, K. E., Beezley, D. A., & Oros, C. J. (1985). Nonstranger sexual aggression: A discriminant analysis of the psychological characteristics of undetected offenders. *Sex Roles, 12*, 981–992.

Koss, M. P. & Oros, C. J. (1982). Sexual Experiences Survey: A research instrument investigating sexual aggression and victimization. *Journal of Consulting and Clinical Psychology, 50*, 455–457.

Leidig, M. (1981). Violence against women: A feminist-psychological analysis. In S. Cox (Ed.), *Female psychology* (pp. 190–205). New York: St. Martin's Press.

Levine, E. M. & Kanin, E. J. (1987). Sexual violence among dates and their acquaintances: Trends and their implications for marriage and family. *Journal of Family Violence, 2*(1), 55–65.

Little, L. F. (1990). Gestalt therapy with females involved in intimate violence. In S. Stith, M. B. Williams, & K. Rosen (Eds.), *Violence hits home* (pp. 47–65). New York: Springer.

Lloyd, S. A. (1991). The darkside of courtship: Violence and sexual exploitation. *Family Relations, 40*, 14–20.

Lloyd, S. A. & Cate, R. M. (1985). The developmental course of conflict in dissolution of premarital relationships. *Journal of Social and Personal Relationships, 2*, 179–194.

Lloyd, S. A., Koval, J. E., & Cate, R. M. (1989). Conflict and violence in dating relationships. In M. Pirog-Good & J. Stets (Eds.), *Violence in dating relationships: Emerging social issues* (pp. 126–184). New York: Praeger.

Miller, B. (1988). Date rape: Time for a new look at prevention. *Journal of College Student Development, 29*, 553–555.

Miller, B. & Marshall, J. C. (1987). Coercive sex on to the university campus. *Journal of College Student Personnel, 28*, 38–48.

Muehlenhard, C. L. & Linton, M. (1987). Date rape and sexual aggression in dating situations: Incidence and risk factors. *Journal of Counseling Psychology, 34*, 186–196.

Napier, A. Y. (1987). Early stages in experiential marital therapy. *Contemporary Family Therapy, 9*(1–2), 23–41.

National Center for Health Statistics. (1985). Annual summary if births, marriages, divorces, and deaths, United States, 1984. *Monthly Vital Statistics Report, 33*(13).

O'Leary, K. D., Barling, J., Arias, I., Rosenbaum, A., Malone, J., & Tyree, A. (1989). Prevalence and stability of physical aggression between spouses: A longitudinal analysis. *Journal of Consulting and Clinical Psychology, 57*, 263–268.

Olson, D. H., Fournier, D. G., & Druckman, J. M. (1986). *Prepare/Enrich counselor's manual*. Minneapolis: Prepare/Enrich, Inc.

Rosenbaum, A. & O'Leary, K. D. (1986). Treatment of marital violence. In N. Jacobson & A. Gurman (Eds.), *Clinical handbook of marital therapy* (pp. 385–405). New York: Guilford.

Roth, S., Wayland, K., & Woolsey, M. (1990). Victimization history and victim–assailant relationship as factors in recovery from sexual assault. *Journal of Traumatic Stress*, 3(1), 169–180.

Ruch, L. O. & Chandler, S. M. (1983). Sexual assault trauma during the acute phase: An exploratory model and multivariate analysis. *Journal of Health and Social Behavior*, 24, 174–185.

Russell, D. E. H. (1984). *Sexual exploitation: Rape, child sexual abuse, and workplace harassment*. Beverly Hills: Sage.

Russell, D. E. H. (1990). *Rape in marriage*. Bloomington: Indiana University Press.

Shostrum, E. L. (1975). *Manual, Caring Relationship Inventory*. San Diego: Educational and Industrial Testing Service (EDITS).

Snyder, D. (1985). *The Marital Satisfaction Inventory: Manual*. Los Angeles: Western Psychological Services.

Stahmann, R. F. & Hiebert, W. J. (1987). *Premarital counseling: The professional's handbook*. Lexington, MA: Lexington Books.

Straus, M., Gelles, R., & Steinmetz, S. (1980). *Behind closed doors: Violence in the American family*. Garden City, NY: Anchor Press/Doubleday.

Walker, L. (1983). Victimology and the psychological perspectives of battered women. *Victimology*, 8(1–2), 82–104.

Ward, S. K., Chapman, K., Cohn, E., White, S. & Williams, K. (1991). Acquaintance rape and the college social scene. *Family Relations*, 40, 65–71.

White, P. N. & Rollins, J. C. (1981). Rape: A family crisis. *Family Relations*, 30, 103–109.

Willbach, D. (1989). Ethics and family therapy: The case management of family violence. *Journal of Marital and Family Therapy*, 15(1), 43–52.

Wolf, S. (1988). A model of sexual aggression/addiction. *Journal of Social Work and Human Sexuality*, 7(1), 131–148.

12

PREMARITAL SEXUAL ABUSE OF MALES BY FEMALE PARTNERS

SUSAN V. COMPTON, DEAN M. BUSBY

When does sexual persuasion constitute sexual coercion? Never, in the case of an adult female persuading an adult male? In other words, can an adult male be raped or in some other way forced to engage in sexual behaviors against his will by a female partner? This study is a preliminary investigation of data pertaining to adult males who self-report having been pressured by their female partners to participate in intimate behaviors, against their wills.

In recent decades coercive sex has been studied within a variety of relationship contexts. Sexual abuse perpetrated against women by men—especially rape by strangers—has been recognized and investigated (Kilpatrick, Veronen, & Resick, 1979; Koss & Buckhart, 1989). More recently, date and acquaintance rape of women has also been a subject of increased awareness and investigation (Kanin, 1984, 1985; Koss, Dinero, Seibel, & Cox, 1988; Levine & Kanin, 1987; Miller & Marshall, 1987). In addition, marital rape—historically treated as somewhat of a legal oxymoron—has become a focus of study (Finkelhor & Yllo, 1985; Russell, 1990; Shields, Resick, & Hanneke, 1990).

Furthermore, coercive sex perpetrated on children by adults, including family members, has been well documented and the subject of considerable investigation within the child sexual abuse literature (Becker & Kaplan, 1990; Conte, 1990). Recent developments include growing recognition of sexual abuse perpetrated against children by children, even by young children (Gil & Johnson, 1993; Ryan & Lane, 1991). Finally, sexual coercion of adults by same-sex offenders—either strangers, acquaintances, or partners in a gay or lesbian relationship—has gained some recognition as a problem deserving of study (Anderson, 1982; Frazier, 1993; Waterman, Dawson, & Bologna, 1989). In summary, historical trends indicate increased attention to the suffering and needs of the victims of sexual coercion.

Victims, however, are, by definition, relatively powerless. As a consequence, perceptions of women and children are congruent with stereotypical portraits of victims, particularly victims of coercive sex, as women and children are relatively lacking in physical and socioeconomic power in our adult-male dominated society. Male adults, especially homosexual men, on the other hand, appear to be reduced to the status of sexual victims only in relation to other, more powerful males. Consequently, a serious consideration of the possible plight of male victims in instances of coercive sex perpetrated by women may seem unnecessary, at best. At worst, it may seem to diminish appreciation of the suffering of women and children who clearly comprise the overwhelming majority of victims of coercive sex.

Assuming that exceptional cases of adult male sexual victimization by women may exist, one can still reasonably question the commitment of resources to the study of such exceptions in the face of the obvious needs of other, more numerous victims. Traditions of scientific exploration, however, include recognition of benefits that may result from the study of unusual data, or outliers. Thus, from a pragmatic standpoint, examination of the exceptional case may lead to insights, for example, about the underlying processes of the phenomenon under study (Pedhazur & Schmelkin, 1991). From an ethical point of view, one could persuasively argue that any victimization deserves recognition and attention. Moral consistency—in this case, a willingness to confront sexual coercion in any form—would seem to speak most powerfully to the needs of all victims.

RELEVANT RESEARCH

To date, little attention has been directed toward the investigation of sexual victimization of adult males by women. Historically, as Sarrel and Masters (1982) attest, studies of sexual behavior have not included questions that might reveal adult male victimization in heterosexual relationships. According to Smith, Pine, and Hawley (1988), prior to a report of eleven case studies by Sarrel and Masters (1982), accounts of adult male sexual victimization by women were rare and primarily anecdotal. Sarrel and Masters interviewed male subjects who had been molested by women at some time in their lives. Three had been victims, during their adulthood, of forced sexual assault by women; the assault involved physical constraint and fear for their safety. Two other subjects experienced a single episode of overt female sexual aggression as adults. All eleven subjects were identified as a consequence of seeking professional help for sexual dysfunction; only one had consciously associated the dysfunction with the prior molestation.

More recently, several studies have explicitly investigated the prevalence and, to a limited degree, the nature of male sexual victimization by women (Stets & Pirog-Good, 1989; Struckman-Johnson, 1988). Stets and Pirog-Good specifically asked a sample of 118 male and 169 female college students to indicate if—against their will and during the past year—they had sustained any of the following sexual activities: necking, chest fondling, genital fondling, oral sex, attempted intercourse, intercourse without violence, and intercourse with violence. Stets and Pirog-Good found that 22% of the men, in comparison with 36% of the women, reported sexual victimization by one or more partners.

Struckman-Johnson (1988), in a survey of 268 male and 355 female college students, asked, on the other hand, how many times each respondent had been "forced to engage in sexual intercourse while on a date" (p. 236); no other sexual behaviors were investigated. Nine percent of the men, in comparison with 13% of the women, reported an episode of forced sex while at the university. One percent of the women, in comparison with 3% of the men reported forcing sex on a campus date.

Struckman-Johnson (1988) also found significant differences between the types of coercion most often experienced by men versus women. Whereas 52% of the men reported experiencing coercion in the form of psychological pressure, 55% of the women reported having been coerced through physical force. That is not to say, however, that men did not report experiencing physical force. Twenty-eight percent of the men reported having been coerced through a combination of psychological pressure and physical restraint or force, and 10% reported experiencing coercion primarily through physical force. Both the Struckman-Johnson (1988) and the Stets and Pirog-Good (1989) studies were limited to samples of college students; thus, they beg the question of the extent and nature of the sexual victimization of men by women among members of the general populace.

Researchers commonly note the reluctance of men to disclose experiences of victimization (Frazier, 1993; Sarrel & Masters, 1982; Stets & Pirog-Good, 1989). In fact, men who overcome their reluctance are likely to be met with skepticism, if not stigmatization; for example, three subjects in the study by Sarrel and Masters (1982) had disclosed to a therapist, and only one had been believed. As a consequence of reluctance to disclose and the lack of public awareness, let alone acceptance, of the idea that adult men can be sexually victimized by women, current estimates of prevalence are likely to reflect significant underreporting. Several studies have investigated popular myths and attitudes concerning male victimization in heterosexual relationships (Bethke & DeJoy, 1993; Smith, Pine, & Hawley, 1988; Struckman-Johnson & Struckman-Johnson, 1992). Their results dramatize the largely untenable position of males sexually victimized by women.

Although the study by Bethke and DeJoy (1993) did not focus on attitudes toward violence in connection specifically with sexual coercion, several of their findings appear, nonetheless, to be relevant. In an investigation of male and female attitudes regarding the use of violent tactics—slapping and pushing—in a typical dating situation, Bethke and DeJoy found that subjects were more tolerant of such behavior if the perpetrators were female. Secondly, perceptions of both physical and emotional harm to the victim were lower if the perpetrators were female, despite the fact that the violence scenarios were identical. Furthermore, male victims were perceived as "needing relatively little recourse. Telling a friend, contacting the police, seeking counseling, ending the relationship, and even responding with physical violence were all rated as more appropriate for the female than male victims" (Bethke & DeJoy, p. 47).

Smith et al. (1988) report similar findings for their investigation of social cognitions with respect to sexual assault scenarios. In comparison with other victim–assailant gender configurations, male victims of female assailants were viewed as more likely to have encouraged or initiated the incident, to have gained more pleasure from it, and to have suffered less consequent stress. Smith et al. note that these views were held more strongly by male subjects, and the researchers characterized these perceptions as consistent with common sex-role stereotypes and myths about rape.

Smith et al. (1988) argue that, stereotypically, men are believed to be more sexually oriented, more sexually assertive, and more interested in sex for the sake of sex than women. In addition, they note that, despite evidence to the contrary, the myth persists that men are incapable of functioning sexually unless they are sexually aroused and arousal is viewed as indicative of consent; thus, for example, a man with an erection during an assault must be a willing participant, rather than a victim. Struckman-Johnson and Struckman-Johnson (1992) also cite myths suggesting that men should be able to protect themselves from sexual assault and that men do not suffer significant emotional effects from coercive sexual experiences. Evidence that stereotypical beliefs about male sexuality affect behavior can be seen, for example, in Muehlenhard and Cook's (1988) findings: Among 507 men and 486 women on a college campus, more men (62.6%) than women (46.3%) reported engaging in unwanted intercourse. Many of the reasons given for doing so were related to sex-role expectations.

Struckman-Johnson and Struckman-Johnson (1992), in a study of attitudes among college students, were surprised by the degree to which the subjects in their particular sample did not subscribe to common myths about male sexual victimization. Even so, they found that, when the offender was a woman, the myths operated more strongly, particularly the myth that the male victim was to blame. According to Smith et al. (1988, p. 111), in essence, male rape mythology suggests that:

> The passivity and loss of control over the sexual interaction that occurs in sexual assault of men by women is so inconsistent with stereotypical beliefs concerning male sexual motivation and behavior that male victims are viewed as more likely to have encouraged the act and to have derived pleasure from it.

In other words, to be a man and to be victimized sexually by a woman are essentially mutually exclusive ideas. Given that male victims are, themselves, affected by gender stereotypes and myths, they are likely to assume blame or weakness, to experience confusion and shame, and to remain silent (Smith et al., 1988; Struckman-Johnson & Struckman-Johnson, 1992).

In conclusion, initial studies suggest that sexual coercion of men by women does in fact exist and that prevailing attitudes about masculinity mitigate strongly against the recognition, study, and treatment of such abuse. The focus of this study is a preliminary investigation of a subset of data collected through the administration of the PREParation for Marriage (PREP-M) instrument (Holman, Busby, & Larson, 1989). The data pertain to adult males who self-report having been pressured against their wills to participate in intimate behaviors by their female partners. Given prevailing stereotypes of male and female sexual roles, the main question regarding these exceptional cases is: How is it, then, that in some cases an adult male reports participating in sexual behaviors, with a current partner, against his will? More specifically, what distinguishes these males and their partners from other couple relationships? The latter question was addressed through comparing couple relationships involving the sexual victimization of males with couple relationships involving the sexual victimization of females, of both males and females, or of neither the males nor the females.

Consistent with the theoretical framework of contextual therapy (Boszormenyi-Nagy & Krasner, 1986), sexual coercion of one partner by another was viewed by the researcher as evidence of relational failure. The fact that partners would report having been pressured to engage in behavior(s) against their wills suggested that genuine dialogue about relational fairness was severely constricted for such couples. It was hypothesized that subjects with family-of-origin experiences conducive to the development of "destructive entitlement," as defined by Boszormenyi-Nagy and Krasner (1986), were more likely to be members of current relationships involving some form of sexual coercion, rather than no coercion.

Dynamically, destructive entitlement arises from historical failures of the adult world to meet the legitimate needs of a child for nurturance and protection; consequently the child develops a sense of overentitlement, or feelings of justification in seeking redress for past wrongs. In the child's adult life, such feelings of overentitlement may manifest themselves, through either overt or covert behaviors, in substitutive vindication of the child's rights; thus new relational failures and injustice result. In other words, subjects who had limited experience with trustworthy relationships while growing up—who had not received adequate nurturance and fair consideration of their needs as children—were predicted to comprise the coercive couples.

With respect to the coercive couples, it was also predicted that they would be characterized by fewer relational resources and lower levels of commitment to reciprocal, responsible care than the noncoercive couples.

Finally, the three different manifestations of destructive entitlement under consideration (i.e., sexual victimization of the male, the female, or both) were predicted to be related to gender patterns among the family-of-origin factors. In addition, the relational consequences of the three patterns of sexual coercion were expected to vary in ways reflecting vulnerability to gender socialization.

In summary, previous studies have surveyed individual men and women; no information about their relationship partners was collected. The purpose of this study was to identify and describe a population of men sexually victimized in heterosexual relationships. In so doing, the study was designed to conduct a preliminary exploration of the men's—and their partner's—historical, family-of-origin variables for sources of destructive entitlement. Furthermore, the study involved a preliminary investigation of current individual characteristics and couple relationship dynamics for evidence of deficiencies in relational trust and commitment to reciprocal care. For all investigations, the sexually pressured males and their partners were examined in comparison with partners constituting the following three relationship patterns: sexual victimization of the female, sexual victimization of both partners, or sexual victimization of neither partner.

METHOD

Subjects

Data were analyzed for 3,032 couples who completed the PREParation for Marriage instrument. Members of the couples group described themselves as single and going with one person (65%), engaged (22%), living with one person (5%), or married (8%). More than half of the couples (63%) were reporting about relationships that had endured for at least six months; of these, many (45%) were of a year's duration or more.

The subjects were predominantly white (91%); subjects comprising the next two largest groups were Hispanic (4%) and black (2%). Also, the majority of the subjects were educated beyond high school—65% had attended some college or technical school; others had earned associates (10%), bachelors (14%), masters (2%), or doctorate or professional (1%) degrees. Geographically, they were primarily from the West (47%) and the South (33%). With respect to religion, the majority identified themselves as Latter Day Saint (44%), Protestant (27%), or Catholic (20%).

Measures

The PREP-M is a comprehensive premarital assessment instrument consisting of 206 items; these items were designed to measure significant background characteristics, personality variables, and interactional processes of premarital couples. Consequently, the PREP-M lends itself to investigations of relational issues involving historical and current factors. A thorough description of the development of the PREP-M, along with discussion of reliability and validity issues, is provided by Holman, Larson, and Harmer (1994).

Three classes of data from the PREP-M were centrally relevant to the purposes of this study. First, a single, paired item was used to categorize couples according to patterns of sexual pressure or coercion in their current relationships. Second, four subscales and two single items were used—for both members of a couple—in order to measure six individual, historical (or family-of-origin) variables relevant to the concept of destructive entitlement. With respect to when the respondents "grew up," the subscales measured the following four variables: (1) experiences of physical abuse, (2) experiences of sexual abuse, (3) satisfaction in their relationships with their mothers, and (4) satisfaction in their relationships with their fathers. The two single items measured the following, final two family-of-origin variables: the respondents' perceptions of (1) how satisfied their fathers were in their marriages and (2) how satisfied their mothers were in their marriages. With respect to entitlement, subjects who experienced physical abuse, sexual abuse, poor relationships with one or both parents, and/or poor parental marital relations were conceptualized as at greater risk for accruing destructive entitlement.

Third, two subscales and one single item were used to measure current individual and couple variables relevant to current relational resources. The two subscales assessed each partner's self-reported levels of openness and self-esteem. With regard to relational resources, subjects in coercive relationships were hypothesized to have deficiencies in relational trust. Consequently, they would demonstrate restricted abilities, in comparison with subjects in noncoercive relationships, to validate themselves and their partners through trust-building interactions such as offering the sharing of feelings (openness) to the partner. Also, in light of both past and current deficits in self-validation, partners in coercive relationships would evidence lower levels of self-esteem than partners in noncoercive relationships.

In addition, a related subscale was used to assess for couple incongruity with respect to how dissimilarly partners viewed each other's levels of self-esteem. Assuming the failure of genuine dialogue and the presence of dynamics related to destructive entitlement, coercive couples were hypothesized to be characterized by greater incongruity in their perceptions of one another.

Finally, the remaining current variable was related to the viability or vitality of the relationship. This single item determined each respondent's reported level of satisfaction with his or her current relationship. Partners in coercive relationships were hypothesized to experience fewer opportunities for self-validation in the relationship and thus less satisfaction than partners in noncoercive couples.

Data Analysis

To investigate the individual and couple characteristics of males who reported having experienced some degree of sexual coercion in their current heterosexual relationships—in comparison with males who report other patterns of sexual relating—the Multivariate Analysis of Variance (MANOVA) procedure was chosen. The design of the MANOVA procedure was appropriate for use with multiple measures that were correlated (the subscales) and with groups comprised of unequal numbers of subjects.

Prior to employing the MANOVA procedure, a preliminary analysis of paired data from the PREP-M was conducted to determine subjects' group memberships. On the basis of an item for which male respondents and their partners were asked to report on the frequency of having been "pressured to participate in intimate behavior (such as petting or intercourse) against your will" (Holman et al., 1989, p. 9), the following four subsamples, or groups, were identified. They were composed of couples in which: (1) the male reported having been sexually pressured in his current relationship and the female did not, (2) the female reported having been sexually pressured in her current relationship and the male did not, (3) both the male and the female reported having been sexually pressured in their current relationship, and (4) the male and the female both reported never having been sexually pressured in their current relationship.

The MANOVA procedure was conducted separately for two classes of data. One analysis involved the measures related to historical, family-of-origin factors for both members of each couple; they were comprised of the following measures:

1. Physical abuse of male
2. Sexual abuse of male
3. Male's satisfaction in relationship with father
4. Male's satisfaction in relationship with mother
5. Male's perception of father's marital satisfaction
6. Male's perception of mother's marital satisfaction
7. Physical abuse of female
8. Sexual abuse of female
9. Female's satisfaction in relationship with father
10. Female's satisfaction in relationship with mother
11. Female's perception of father's marital satisfaction
12. Female's perception of mother's marital satisfaction

The second analysis involved the measures related to current individual and couple factors. The current variables were comprised of the following measures:

1. Male's self-report of openness
2. Male's self-report of esteem

3. Female's self-report of openness
4. Female's self-report of esteem
5. Couple esteem incongruity
6. Male's satisfaction with current relationship
7. Female's satisfaction with current relationship

Both MANOVA procedures produced multivariate F-tests that indicated whether group membership had a significant relationship to the measures. When a multivariate F-test was significant, a series of univariate F-tests was used to determine which of the measures were significantly related to group membership.

Subsequent to the identification of significant measures, a series of step-down F-tests were used to determine which of the groups were significantly different from one another with reference to each historical and current variable of interest. Thus, the analysis of variance (ANOVA) procedure was used to test the means for departure from chance occurrence.

RESULTS

Family-of-Origin Analysis

The MANOVA procedure was first used to determine if the group the subjects belonged to (male sexually pressured, female sexually pressured, both male and female sexually pressured, and neither male nor female sexually pressured) had a significant relationship with the historical, family-of-origin measures by calculating a multivariate F-test. The multivariate F-test was significant—$F (3.07) = .04$, $p < .0005$ (Pillai's Trace).

The univariate F-tests revealed significant group main effects for all six family-of-origin measures for the male subjects (all degrees of freedom = 3, 2644): physical abuse of male, $F = 4.82$; sexual abuse of male, $F = 4.21$; relationship with father, $F = 8.58$; relationship with mother, $F = 12.25$; father's marital satisfaction, $F = 7.95$; and, mother's marital satisfaction, $F = 8.80$ (all $p < .01$). In contrast, the univariate F-tests revealed significant group main effects for just three of the six family-of-origin measures for the female subjects (all degrees of freedom = 3, 2644): physical abuse of female, $F = 4.97$; relationship with father, $F = 12.38$; and, relationship with mother, $F = 9.11$ (all $p < .01$). The univariate F-tests failed to reveal significant group main effects for the following measures for the female subjects: sexual abuse of female, $F = .38$ ($p < .77$); father's marital satisfaction, $F = 2.34$ ($p < .07$); mother's marital satisfaction, $F = 2.47$ ($p < .06$).

Subsequent to the identification of significant family-of-origin variables, planned comparisons with step-down F-tests were used to investigate significant differences among the groups. Table 12.1 summarizes the means and standard deviations for each group on the six variables for the males and the three variables for the females that were significant. In general, whereas group membership for the males was significantly related to historical experiences of abuse, relationships with parents and parental marriage satisfaction, group membership for females was only significantly related to experiences of physical abuse and relationships with parents while growing up. However, that is not to suggest, of course, that females experienced less sexual abuse or perceived their parents' marriage as more or less satisfying than the male subjects; for example, the entire sample means for males for sexual abuse, father's marital satisfaction and mother's marital satisfaction respectively were 0.18, 2.84, and 2.78, while for females they were 0.46, 2.83, and 2.70.

Examination of the planned comparisons of the family-of-origin measures with step-down F-tests for males revealed several patterns. First, the sexually victimized males were most like the males in the other two coercive relationships and most unlike the males in relationships involving no coercion. In other words, the sexually pressured males—or current male victims—were most like both the current male offenders and the males involved in a current relationship as both a victim and an offender. The only departure from this pattern involved the measure of sexual abuse while growing up. Specifically, current male victims, along with males in noncoercive relationships and male offenders, reported significantly less sexual abuse while growing up than the males in relationships involving the coercion of both partners.

For females, planned comparisons were conducted only for the measures of physical abuse while growing up and of satisfaction with relationships with both parents; no significant main group effects were found for the other family-of-origin measures. First, the planned comparisons revealed that females involved in sexually pressuring their partners (i.e., current female offenders) and female victims reported significantly more physical abuse while growing up than females in noncoercive relationships. No significant effect was found for females involved in a relationship as both a victim and an offender; however, the means in Table 12.1 suggest that small sample size may be implicated, for the mean for "both sexually pressured" is proximal to the mean for "female sexually pressured." It appears that females with a history of having been physically abused are more likely to be in relationships involving some pattern of coercion as adults.

Second, the planned comparisons with respect to the female subjects' satisfaction in their relationships with their fathers and their mothers revealed a pattern identical to the findings for the male subjects. The female offenders reported the lowest level of satisfaction in their relationships with their fathers and their mothers than all other groups.

Current Individual and Couple Analysis

Second, the MANOVA procedure was used to determine whether subjects' group membership had a significant relationship with the current individual

TABLE 12.1 • Means and Standard Deviations of the Four Groups on the Family-of-Origin Measures

Sample	Mean	Standard Deviation
Male: Victim of Physical Abuse		
Male Sexually Pressured (n = 166)	2.04	2.80
Female Sexually Pressured (n = 336)	2.07	2.71
Both Sexually Pressured (n = 81)	2.12	2.69
Neither Sexually Pressured (n = 2,065)	1.63	2.40
Male: Victim of Sexual Abuse		
Male Sexually Pressured	0.27	1.10
Female Sexually Pressured	0.23	1.29
Both Sexually Pressured	0.54	2.51
Neither Sexually Pressured	0.16	0.90
Male: Satisfaction with Father		
Male Sexually Pressured	16.26	4.80
Female Sexually Pressured	16.66	4.69
Both Sexually Pressured	15.95	4.16
Neither Sexually Pressured	17.56	4.89
Male: Satisfaction with Mother		
Male Sexually Pressured	18.89	4.02
Female Sexually Pressured	18.87	3.85
Both Sexually Pressured	18.36	3.97
Neither Sexually Pressured	19.88	3.82
Male: Father's Marital Satisfaction		
Male Sexually Pressured	2.63	1.23
Female Sexually Pressured	2.67	1.31
Both Sexually Pressured	2.46	1.34
Neither Sexually Pressured	2.90	1.23
Male: Mother's Marital Satisfaction		
Male Sexually Pressured	2.52	1.23
Female Sexually Pressured	2.59	1.37
Both Sexually Pressured	2.47	1.31
Neither Sexually Pressured	2.85	1.23
Female: Victim of Physical Abuse		
Male Sexually Pressured	2.10	2.71
Female Sexually Pressured	1.89	2.58
Both Sexually Pressured	1.86	2.79
Neither Sexually Pressured	1.52	2.40
Female: Relationship with Father		
Male Sexually Pressured	16.10	5.32
Female Sexually Pressured	16.92	5.09
Both Sexually Pressured	16.43	5.58
Neither Sexually Pressured	18.06	5.26
Female: Relationship with Mother		
Male Sexually Pressured	19.05	4.40
Female Sexually Pressured	19.69	4.43
Both Sexually Pressured	19.41	4.13
Neither Sexually Pressured	20.49	4.38

and couple measures by calculating a multivariate F-test. The multivariate F-test was significant—F (10.89) = .09, p < .0005 (Pillai's Trace). This MANOVA included one measure of couple incongruity concerning the degree to which partner's perceptions of each other were dissimilar with respect to esteem. A preliminary MANOVA had determined an absence of significant group main effects for couple incongruity with respect to perceptions of openness.

The univariate F-tests revealed significant group main effects for all of the current variables for both the male subjects and the female subjects (all degrees of freedom = 3, 2346).

For the four variables—two for males and two for females—related to the validation of the self and the partner, all univariate F-tests revealed significant group main effects: male openness, F = 8.57; male esteem, F = 11.73; female openness, F = 16.10; female esteem, F = 19.87 (all p < .01). For the incongruity measure, the univariate F-test was also significant: couple esteem incongruity, F = 4.75 (p < .01). Finally, for the remaining two variables, those related to evidence of the viability of the couple relationship, both univariate F-tests were significant: male relationship satisfaction, F = 22.65 (p < .01); and female relationship satisfaction, F = 44.10 (p < .01).

As with the MANOVA for the family-of-origin variables, once the significant current variables were determined, it was appropriate to conduct planned comparisons with step-down F-tests to investigate for significant differences among groups. Table 12.2 summarizes the means and standard deviations for each group on the measures that were significant. Given the fact that the planned comparisons involved seven measures and four groups, the revealed relationships were complex; however, several overall patterns emerged.

First, with respect to the individual current variables, female offenders and male offenders differed in that female offenders appeared most similar to females in relationships involving no coercion and most dissimilar to female victims and females in mutually coercive relationships. In contrast, the findings for male offenders resulted in a more mixed picture; male offenders were, in some respects, similar to each of the other groups. In addition, female victims appeared similar to females in mutually coercive relationships but not to female offenders. Male victims, on the other hand, appeared similar to both males in mutually coercive relationships and to male offenders.

More specifically, with regard to the measures related to the validation of the self and the partner—openness and self-esteem—both female offenders and females in relationships with no coercion rated themselves as significantly more open than did female victims, and as higher in self-esteem than female victims or females in mutually coercive relationships. In contrast, all male subjects in coercive relationships rated themselves as lower in self-esteem than did males in relationships with no coercion. Additionally, male offenders were simultaneously lower in self-esteem than the males in noncoercive relationships and significantly higher in self-esteem than victims or

TABLE 12.2 • **Means and Standard Deviations of the Four Groups on the Current Individual and Couple Measures**

Sample	Mean	Standard Deviation
Male: Openness		
Male Sexually Pressured (n = 143)	7.26	1.76
Female Sexually Pressured (n = 307)	7.81	1.88
Both Sexually Pressured (n= 82)	7.45	1.46
Neither Sexually Pressured (n = 1,818)	7.96	1.81
Male: Self-Esteem		
Male Sexually Pressured	19.08	3.27
Female Sexually Pressured	19.79	3.03
Both Sexually Pressured	19.09	3.17
Neither Sexually Pressured	20.28	3.01
Female: Openness		
Male Sexually Pressured	8.82	1.60
Female Sexually Pressured	7.98	2.09
Both Sexually Pressured	8.31	1.94
Neither Sexually Pressured	8.73	1.77
Female: Self-Esteem		
Male Sexually Pressured	19.15	3.32
Female Sexually Pressured	18.56	3.41
Both Sexually Pressured	17.85	3.65
Neither Sexually Pressured	19.74	3.15
Couple: Esteem Incongruency		
Male Sexually Pressured	5.59	3.65
Female Sexually Pressured	5.47	3.59
Both Sexually Pressured	5.65	3.38
Neither Sexually Pressured	4.91	3.31
Male: Current Relationship Satisfaction		
Male Sexually Pressured	3.27	0.83
Female Sexually Pressured	3.28	0.98
Both Sexually Pressured	3.22	0.79
Neither Sexually Pressured	3.57	0.68
Female: Current Relationship Satisfaction		
Male Sexually Pressured	3.47	0.75
Female Sexually Pressured	3.13	0.98
Both Sexually Pressured	3.06	0.96
Neither Sexually Pressured	3.60	0.70

males involved as both victims and offenders. For openness, male victims rated themselves as significantly less open than both males in relationships with no coercion and male offenders.

In summary, males and females in relationships with no coercion reported significantly higher self-perceptions of openness and self-esteem than most of the other groups. Second, both male and female victims and males and females in mutually coercive relationships all reported lower self-perceptions of self-esteem than one or more other groups. Male and female victims reported lower perceptions of openness as well. Finally, whereas male offenders reported lower self-esteem than did males in relationships with no coercion, female offenders did not. Both male and female offenders reported higher perceptions of openness, respectively, than male and female victims.

With respect to the measure of couple esteem incongruity, the results necessarily depart from the overall pattern noted thus far in that the measures yield composite means for males and females. Essentially, all of the offenders' couple relationships were most like those of the subjects in the other coercive relationships and most unlike the subjects in the noncoercive relationships. The esteem incongruity mean was highest for the mutually coercive couples and lowest for the noncoercive couples.

Finally, for the measures conceptualized as indicators of the vitality of the relationship—both of which revealed significant main group effects—the overall pattern was, for the most part, again replicated. The measure of the female subjects' satisfaction with the relationship portrayed female offenders as most like the females in noncoercive relationships and most unlike the females in the other coercive relationships. Female offenders and females in noncoercive relationships indicated significantly higher satisfaction with their relationship than did female victims and females in mutually coercive relationships. In contrast, for the measure of relationship satisfaction, the male offenders were most like the other males in coercive relationships and most unlike the males in noncoercive relationships. Male subjects in coercive relationships indicated significantly lower levels of satisfaction with their relationships than did the male subjects in the noncoercive relationships.

DISCUSSION

The purpose of this study was to investigate the sexual coercion of adult males by females in heterosexual relationships in comparison with subjects identified as members of relationships involving either the sexual coercion of females, of both males and females, or of neither. The results from this study demonstrate that the majority of both the family-of-origin variables and the current individual and couple variables under consideration were significantly related to group membership for both the male and female subjects. Thus, it was possible to consider the researcher's major hypotheses in light of the results.

Previous studies of sexually coerced males have not included data on the offenders or on the couple relationships of the subjects. Not uncommonly even the sex of the offender was not known; therefore, males sexually coerced by either females or other males were considered as one group. In addition, males who experienced sexual coercion by a mere acquaintance, or even a stranger, were grouped with males coerced in relationships of longer duration. A significant strength of this study was the richness of the data for the male victims, the female offenders, and the couple relationships, as well as the comparatively large sample size. Unfortunately, the sample lacked diversity. Although the sample was drawn from various regions of the country, the lack of representation of certain cultural and religious groups was a distinct disadvantage. Future studies should investigate sexually coerced males from a more diverse group.

An additional weakness of the study involved the lack of information regarding the nature of the pressure—to participate in intimate behaviors (e. g. petting, intercourse) against their wills—that sexually coerced subjects experienced. Future investigations should explore the ways in which methods and patterns of coercion are similar and dissimilar among groups.

With respect to the first major hypothesis under investigation, the results provide strong support to the hypothesis that subjects with family-of-origin experiences conducive to the development of destructive entitlement were more likely to be members of current relationships involving some form of sexual coercion, rather than no coercion. Essentially all of the males in heterosexual relationships involving the sexual coercion of one or both partners reported significantly more physical abuse while growing up, less satisfaction in their relationships with both parents, and less marital satisfaction for both parents than males in relationships involving no coercion. In addition, most of the females in sexually coercive relationships reported significantly more physical abuse while growing up and all the females in sexually coercive relationships reported less satisfaction in their relationships with both parents.

Contrary to expectation, neither sexually coerced males nor male offenders reported more sexual abuse while growing up than males in noncoercive relationships. A striking finding was that males in relationships involving the sexual coercion of both partners reported significantly more sexual abuse while growing up than any other group. Also surprising was the finding that females in sexually coercive relationships did not report significantly more sexual abuse while growing up than females in noncoercive relationships. Thus, for females only, a history of sexual abuse while growing up was apparently unrelated to increased likelihood for involvement in a sexually coercive adult relationship. This difference was observed despite at least comparable entire sample means for sexual abuse for females as for males. Each finding, for males and for females, and the related gender effect appear to merit exploration in future studies.

Also contrary to expectation was the finding that parental marital satisfaction demonstrated a significant main effect for group membership for males but not for females. These findings suggest a sensitivity to the quality of their parents' marriage on the part of males while growing up that is somehow different from that of females. This difference, along with those noted for the sexual abuse variable, suggest gender differences among the dynamic origins of destructive entitlement with respect to sexual coercion. In future investigations these gender effects should be considered in depth, relative to gender socialization patterns in the subjects' cultures.

Concerning the failure to find significant main group effects for females for the sexual abuse and parental marital satisfaction variables, one possible explanation is that the results were confounded by inadequate sensitivity on the part of the measures to the extent and nature of the abuse and marital dissatisfaction. Johnson (1993), in a review of two studies of child offenders, suggests that "it appears that it may require a more severe history to push girls into the role of an abuser than boys" (p. 76).

Also noteworthy was the observation that gender of the subject in combination with the different genders of the parents did not yield different effects. In other words, satisfaction with father versus mother, or the marital satisfaction of father versus mother, did not interact with the gender of the subject. This observation suggests the critical roles of both parents with respect to relational outcomes in the adult lives of their offspring.

With respect to the second major hypothesis, the results also provide strong support for the proposal that coercive couples would be characterized by fewer relational resources than noncoercive couples. An examination of the current individual and couple variables revealed, for the most part, that coercive couples reported lower levels of openness, self-esteem, and satisfaction with their relationship, as well as higher levels of incongruity with respect to their perceptions of each other's self-esteem. An unexpected finding, however, was that female offenders were in many ways similar to females in noncoercive relationships, whereas male offenders were similar to males in other coercive relationships. One possible explanation is that this finding reflects the operation of stereotypical beliefs and myths about sexual coercion. Both partners, the female offender and the male victim, may fail to take the sexual coercion of the male partner seriously. As a consequence the female offender, for example, may be less impacted by her role as an abuser and may therefore resemble females in noncoercive relationships.

Finally, a survey of the means for both sets of variables suggests that the mutually coercive relationships were notably problematic. This population appears to warrant more recognition and attention.

In summary, the overall results suggest a profile of males who report having been sexually coerced by a female partner. While growing up, they were likely to have experienced more physical abuse, less satisfaction in their relationships with both parents, and lower perceptions of both parents' marital satisfaction than males in adult relationships with no coercion. Also, they were less likely to have experienced sexual abuse than males in adult relationships involving the coercion of both partners. As adults, in their current, heterosexual relationships, they are likely to be less open, to have lower self-esteem, and to report less satisfaction with their relationship than males in relationships with no coercion.

Furthermore, the sexually coerced males are more likely to have female partners who, while growing up, experienced more physical abuse and less satisfaction in their relationships with both parents than females in relationships with no coercion. However, the female partners appear likely to be as open, as high in self-esteem, and nearly as satisfied with their current relationship as females in relationships involving no coercion. Finally, as a couple, sexually coerced males and their partners are likely to evidence greater esteem incongruity than couples in relationships involving no coercion.

CONCLUSIONS/THERAPEUTIC IMPLICATIONS

The findings with respect to the family-of-origin measures suggest that involvement in some type of adult, sexually coercive, heterosexual relationship on the part of both males and females, but especially of males, appears related to problematic patterns of relating in the subjects' families of origin. The apparent vulnerability of subjects with less satisfying family-of-origin relationships and physically abusive—and for males, sexually abusive—experiences while growing up argues for therapeutic attention to, or at least exploration of, these family-of-origin variables in adults presenting with coercive sexual relationships. Furthermore, these findings provide support to the contention, on the part of proponents of contextual therapy, that the concept of destructive entitlement may be helpful in conceptualizing the dynamics of relationships involving some type of victimization.

With respect to therapeutic efforts in prevention, the findings also appear to argue for the importance of including both parents and of addressing marital issues during work with children. In addition, the examination of current individual and couple variables reveals deficiencies in relational resources for coercive couples.

Several therapeutic implications can be implied from the results of this study. It appears that a significant amount of education is important in dispelling the myth that males cannot be sexually coerced by females. Work on this myth would help couples more effectively deal with the destructive patterns in their relationship, help prevent sexual coercion in the first place, and reduce the tendency of helping professionals to deny this problem.

The results suggest that male victims shut down or become more closed in a similar way to female victims. Therapists may need to probe more thoroughly for patterns of coercion when a male seems particularly closed or defended, not just for the possibility that the male is a perpetrator, but for the possibility that the male may be a victim.

In contrast, female perpetrators exhibit higher levels of self-esteem, openness, and relationship satisfaction than females who are victims or who are both victims and perpetrators. This finding is fascinating to consider in light of feminist ideology. It is possible that the accumulation of female experiences in relationships that are experienced as powerless or demeaning creates a scenario where the female actually demonstrates a boost in self-esteem and openness when she perpetrates sexually coercive behaviors. Maybe it is a short-lived boost, or one that has other costs in the relationship over time, but this is not clear. Without the social guilt or blame that is associated with male perpetration, it is possible that the female perpetrator will experience very few intrapsychic costs of perpetration on male partners.

An additional interpretation from a feminist ideology is that the measures of self-esteem and openness are simply defined in a way that values a males' perspective. This would suggest that female perpetrators are not necessarily more happy or experiencing higher levels of self-esteem, they are simply acting more like traditional males.

Regardless of the interpretation, the therapist may need to explore, with the female and the male, the meaning of coercion in their relationship and the costs it has over time. It also would be crucial for the therapist to coach the victims, whether male or female, to express when they are feeling pressured against their wills to be sexual. Issues of safety and protection will need to be primary concerns for the therapist as they are in all coercive relationships. Helping the couple find more acceptable ways of getting emotional and sexual needs met will benefit both parties.

REFERENCES

Anderson, C. L. (1982). Males as sexual assault victims: Multiple levels of trauma. *Journal of Homosexuality, 7*(2–3), 145–162.

Becker, J. V. & Kaplan, M. S. (1990). Perpetrators of child sexual abuse. In T. Ammerman & M. Hersen (Eds.), *Treatment of family violence* (pp. 266–279). New York: John Wiley.

Bethke, T. M. & DeJoy, D. M. (1993). An experimental study of factors influencing the acceptability of dating violence. *Journal of Interpersonal Violence, 8*(1), 36–51.

Boszormenyi-Nagy, I. & Krasner, B. R. (1986). *Between give and take: A clinical guide to contextual therapy.* New York: Brunner/Mazel.

Conte, J. R. (1990). Victims of child sexual abuse. In T. Ammerman & M. Hersen (Eds.), *Treatment of family violence* (pp. 50–76). New York: John Wiley.

Finkelhor, D. & Yllo, K. (1985). *License to rape: Sexual abuse of wives.* New York: Holt, Rinehart, & Winston.

Frazier, P. A. (1993). A comparative study of male and female rape victims seen at a hospital-based rape crisis program. *Journal of Interpersonal Violence, 8*(1), 64–76.

Gil, E. & Johnson, T. C. (Eds.). (1993). *Sexualized children: Assessment and treatment of sexualized children and children who molest.* Rockville, MD: Launch Press.

Holman, T. B., Busby, D. M., & Larson, J. H. (1989). *PREParation for Marriage.* Provo, UT: Marriage Study Consortium, Brigham Young University.

Holman, T. B., Larson, J. H., & Harmer, S. L. (1994). The development and predictive validity of a new premarital assessment instrument: The Preparation for Marriage Questionnaire. *Family Relations, 43*(1), 46–52.

Johnson, T. C. (1993). Preliminary findings. In E. Gil & T. C. Johnson (Eds.), *Sexualized children: Assessment and treatment of sexualized children and children who molest* (pp 67–89). Rockville, MD: Launch Press.

Kanin, E. J. (1984). Date rape: Unofficial criminals and victims. *Victimology: An International Journal, 9*(1), 95–108.

Kanin, E. J. (1985). Date rapists: Differential sexual socialization and relative deprivation. *Archives of Sexual Behavior, 14*(3), 219–231.

Kilpatrick, D. G., Veronen, L. J., & Resick, P. A. (1979). The aftermath of rape: Recent empirical findings. *American Journal of Orthopsychiatry, 49*, 658–669.

Koss, M. P. & Buckhart, B. R. (1989). A conceptual analysis of rape victimization: Long-term effects and implications for treatment. *Psychology of Women Quarterly, 13*, 27–40.

Koss, M. P., Dinero, T. E., Seibel, C. A., & Cox, S. L. (1988). Stranger and acquaintance rape: Are there differences in the victim's experience? *Psychology of Women Quarterly, 12*, 1–24.

Levine, E. M. & Kanin, E. J. (1987). Sexual violence among dates and their acquaintances: Trends and their implications for marriage and family. *Journal of Family Violence, 2*(1), 55–65.

Miller, B. & Marshall, J. C. (1987). Coercive sex on the university campus. *Journal of College Student Personnel, 28*, 38–48.

Muehlenhard, C. L. & Cook, S. W. (1988). Men's self-reports of unwanted sexual activity. *The Journal of Sex Research, 24*, 58–72.

Pedhazur, E. J. & Schmelkin, L. P. (1991). *Measurement, design, and analysis: An integrated approach.* Hillsdale, NJ: Erlbaum.

Russell, D. E. H. (1990). *Rape in marriage.* Bloomington: Indiana University Press.

Ryan, G. D. & Lane, S. L. (Eds.). (1991). *Juvenile sexual offending: Causes, consequences, and correction.* Lexington, MA: Lexington Books.

Sarrel, P. M. & Masters, W. H. (1982). Sexual molestation of men by women. *Archives of Sexual Behavior, 11*(2), 117–131.

Shields, N. M., Resick, P. A., & Hanneke, C. R. (1990). Victims of marital rape. In R. T. Ammerman & M. Hersen (Eds.), *Treatment of family violence: A sourcebook.* New York: John Wiley.

Smith, R. E., Pine, C. J., & Hawley, M. E. (1988). Social cognitions about adult male victims of female sexual assault. *The Journal of Sex Research, 24*, 101–112.

Stets, J. E. & Pirog-Good, M. A. (1989). Patterns of physical and sexual abuse for men and women in dating relationships: A descriptive analysis. *Journal of Family Violence, 4*(1), 63–76.

Struckman-Johnson, C. (1988). Forced sex on dates: It happens to men too. *The Journal of Sex Research, 24*, 234–241.

Struckman-Johnson, C. & Struckman-Johnson, D. (1992). Acceptance of male rape myths among college men and women. *Sex Roles, 27*, 85–100.

Waterman, C. K., Dawson, L. J., & Bologna, M. J. (1989). Sexual coercion in gay male and lesbian relationships: Predictors and implications for support services. *Journal of Sex Research, 26*(1), 118–124.

13

SEXUAL ASSAULT AND SEXUAL HARASSMENT OF FAMILY MEMBERS

STEVEN M. HARRIS

This chapter focuses on the treatment of families who have experienced sexual abuse at the hands of someone outside of the family. In these cases the perpetrator is not related to the family in any biological or legal way; for the purpose of this chapter, this includes live-in partners. Extrafamilial sexual abuse occurs when a child is sexually molested; when a daughter, son, or parent is raped; and when a breadwinner of the family is sexually harassed on the job. Childhood sexual abuse, rape, and sexual harassment are the topics most widely addressed in the literature. The consequences for the individual, the family, and the involvement of larger systems affected by the types of abuse identified are discussed here. Implications for treatment are then presented.

Many variables need to be accounted for when dealing with extrafamilial sexual abuse. Variables, such as the gender of the victim, developmental stage of the victim, family life-cycle stage, nature of the abuse, and the time at which the abuse becomes problematic, may influence the severity with which the family experiences the abuse. In an attempt to provide accurate and concise information, the treatment portion of this chapter is limited to discussing how to help the family soon after the abuse has occurred. The very nature of sexual abuse is such that many, if not most, of the effects are felt years after the initial abuse occurs. Because the scope here is limited to how to treat abuse soon after its occurrence, this chapter has a crisis intervention flavor.

WHAT IS KNOWN ABOUT EXTRAFAMILIAL SEXUAL ABUSE?

There is a paucity of current information regarding extrafamilial sexual abuse. Most of the family systems literature focuses on treating the individual and the family after father–daughter incest. The titles of books and articles are generic with reference to childhood sexual abuse, or sexual abuse and the family, and automatically seem to assume a father–daughter/perpetrator–victim relationship (Adams-Tucker & Adams, 1984; Crewdson, 1988; Faller, 1988; Finkelhor, 1984; Kaye & Winefield, 1988; MacFarlane, 1986; Valentich & Anderson, 1990). Perhaps because of the psychotherapy community's fairly recent acceptance of the incidence of intrafamilial sexual abuse, the issue of extrafamilial sexual abuse has not yet received attention (DeFrancis, 1969; Finkelhor, 1979).

It is hard to obtain accurate data on the incidence of sexual abuse (Finkelhor, 1984). A literature review reveals a lack of attention dedicated specifically to extrafamilial sexual abuse in comparison to the literature on intrafamilial abuse. This may be a reflection of a belief that extrafamilial sexual abuse does not occur frequently. Perhaps this suggests that families are not presenting to clinicians with extrafamilial sexual abuse as an identified problem. The research of Finkelhor (1984) and Russell (1983) suggests that extrafamilial sexual abuse is more prevalent than intrafamilial. Considering the many different ways a family can be victimized sexually by "outsiders," it is highly probable that extrafamilial sexual abuse is the most prevalent type of sexual victimization in our society.

LITERATURE REVIEW

In 1979, a study of college students reported that one in five girls and one in eleven boys had some kind of sexual experience with an older person (Finkelhor, 1979). Other reports suggest that 5 to 9% of all boys and 8 to 38% of all girls have been sexually abused (Finkelhor, 1984). Statistics regarding the incidence of extrafamilial sexual abuse, as defined in the introduction, have never been compiled.

Childhood Sexual Abuse

Consequences for the Individual Victim

Professionals are still somewhat confused about the effects of sexual abuse on children. Clarke and Hornick (1988) report that some researchers believe sexual abuse does not necessarily have harmful effects on children. Others believe that using a child to fulfill adult sexual desire is always destructive (Finkelhor, 1984; Russell, 1983). The latter opinion seems to be the most accepted.

Adams-Tucker (1982) outline the following "clusters" of pathology discovered in children as a result of sexual abuse: Self-destructive behavior, aggressive/sex-related problems, school problems, anxiety, somatic complaints, and sleep-related symptoms. Other research has uncovered depression, guilt, learning difficulties, sexual promiscuity, runaway behaviors, somatization, and significant change in expected behavior, as indicators of sexual abuse (Kolko, Moser, & Weldy, 1988). Victims of extrafamilial sexual abuse seem to display less "pathological affective responsivity and affective involvement with their family" (p. 143) than children who have been victims of incest (Hoagwood & Stewart, 1989). This suggests that the prognosis for a successful resolution of the traumatic experience is better for victims of extrafamilial sexual abuse compared to victims of intrafamilial sexual abuse.

Some children present with symptoms consistent with the DSM III–R Post-Traumatic Stress Disorder (PTSD) diagnosis (American Psychiatric Association, 1987; Conte, 1990). Looking at the effects of child sexual abuse using a posttraumatic stress disorder lens is being challenged. Finkelhor (1988) argues that many of the symptoms exhibited by sexual abuse survivors are not congruent with the categories used in the DSM III–R to warrant a diagnosis of PTSD. He also suggests that PTSD symptoms are not evident in all survivors of sexual abuse. Clearly this is an area that needs further research.

Other research (Kempe & Kempe, 1984; MacFarlane, 1986) suggests that the type of victimization and the duration of the abuse can be contributing factors to the way the child responds to abuse. Other contributing factors are the developmental stage of the child, the relationship the child has with the perpetrator, and the relationship the perpetrator has with the child's family.

Consequences for the Family System

Conte (1990) refers to the sexual abuse of a child as "an assault on the adults who care for and love the child" (p. 62). The family is also victimized as a result of extrafamilial sexual abuse. One of the system's members has been violated and the boundaries of the system have been invaded. Parents' reactions can be anger, shame, and a wish for retribution (MacFarlane, 1986; Rogers & Tremaine, 1984). Parents also may feel a sense of guilt for not being able to protect their child. This is compounded if the perpetrator is someone who is a close friend of the parents or a trusted individual such as a baby-sitter. Parents may blame themselves for putting the child in a harmful situation. They may think that they should have known better than to hire a certain caregiver, or let the child spend time at a certain friend's home. On discovery of the abuse, parents may worry about the safety of their child and possibly smother him or her with overprotectiveness which may hinder the child's resolution of the abuse. MacFarlane (1986) suggests that there is a tendency for parents to feel embarrassed. This embarrassment contributes to denying that the abuse ever occurred (Everstine & Everstine, 1989).

The sexual abuse of a child can also put considerable stress on the marital relationship. There is a tendency for one of the partners to blame the other for the abuse (MacFarlane, 1986). This becomes a therapeutic issue to be discussed with the marital dyad and possibly the whole family. If a child is abused by someone outside of the family it does not necessarily mean that the parents have been neglectful (Kempe & Kempe, 1984).

Consequences for the Larger Systems

A review of the literature most often reveals the impact and involvement of the legal system where extrafamilial childhood sexual abuse is concerned. This may be attributed to the fact that pressing charges would usually involve a unified family against an outside perpetrator. In contrast, intrafamilial sexual abuse might involve the splitting of nuclear and extended family loyalties and relationships when legal action is taken. Charges are three times more likely to be filed against the perpetrator of extrafamilial sexual abuse than against perpetrators of intrafamilial sexual abuse (Russell, 1983). The legal system is involved more quickly and more often in cases of extrafamilial abuse (Hartman, Finn, & Leon, 1987). Religious, educational, and other social systems would also be affected by extrafamilial sexual abuse.

Some states have recognized that the sexual abuse of children is a serious social problem requiring government intervention. Many states provide funds to assist the treatment of sexually abused children. However, the majority of states that provide funds will only do so in cases of intrafamilial sexual abuse (Conte, 1990). In some cases, departments of social services may not be mandated to investigate cases of extrafamilial abuse (MacFarlane, 1986). Families looking for government intervention may be surprised at the government's inability to provide help in cases of extrafamilial sexual abuse.

Rape

Rape is largely perceived as a problem that only affects women. In fact, recent studies suggest that 15 to 22% of women have been raped at some time in their lives (Koss, Gidycz, & Wisniewski, 1987; Koss & Oros, 1982; Russell, 1983). Women are most likely to be raped by someone they know well or someone they have recently met (Levine & Kanin, 1987). Other studies show that men are victims of sexual assault as well (Freeman-Longo, 1986; Myers, 1989; Struckman-Johnson, 1988) with 12 to 15% of all men having experienced rape (Kempe & Kempe, 1984). Men are generally more likely than women to be violently assaulted by perpetrators, and more likely to be subjected to multiple assaults by multiple assailants (Kaufman, 1984). Regardless of who experiences the traumatic experience of a rape, rape is an acute form of stress that pushes the individual and the family into crisis.

Rape is often looked at as a deviant sex crime. Frequently, feminist thinking has looked at the issue of rape as a crime of power. Feminist theory suggests that rape is the oppression of the female class by a more "entitled" male class (Burt & Katz, 1987). In this regard, rape has less to do with sex than it does with gender and the political implications of oppression. Kempe and Kempe (1984) outline four possible reasons why rape occurs: (1) a general hostility toward women, (2) alcohol or drugs lower inhibitions, (3) psychological pathology in the perpetrator, and (4) use of the sex act as a defense against homosexuality or sexual inadequacy. Although rape has been considered in the literature, a systemic look at the phenomenon can help the clinician understand how rape can be equally traumatic to the family as is the sexual abuse of a child.

Consequences for the Individual

"Rape is an act of aggressive sexual domination which the victim feels powerless to prevent" (Kempe & Kempe, 1984, p. 39). Researchers identify the following long-term consequences of rape: persistent anxiety, depression, difficulty trusting in interpersonal relationships, drug abuse, sexual dysfunction, poor self-esteem, increased sense of dependency, and a significant struggle with compulsive behavior (Feinauer, 1982; Feinauer & Hippolite, 1987; Gise & Paddison, 1988). Rape is considered by victims to be a life-threatening experience for both themselves and their children (Emm & McKenry, 1988). According to Rowan and Rowan (1986, pp. 239–240):

> The victim experiences a loss of control, helplessness, and especially, fear. Anxiety symptoms may take the form of free-floating anxiety, phobias, sleep disturbances, mood swings, recurrent thoughts of rape, depression, nonspecific physical complaints such as headaches or gastrointestinal disturbances, or trauma-specific symptoms such as inability to swallow or pelvic pain.

At all developmental levels, "rape makes women worry about their independence, their autonomy, and their ability to take care of themselves" (Gise & Paddison, 1988, p. 637). Men experience reactions to being raped similar to women's. Some of the more gender-specific issues male rape victims deal with are the following: isolation, a feeling of being the only man who has been raped, questioning one's masculinity, fear of being called a coward if people knew of the rape, minimization of the actual event, and uncertainty about one's own sexuality (Struckman-Johnson, 1988).

Both male and female victims deal with being exposed to sexually transmitted diseases and women risk an unwanted pregnancy. Victims of rape also deal with a phenomenon referred to as "Rape Trauma Syndrome." This term, coined by Burgess, and Holstrom (1976), has two phases that require clinical attention. The first phase is an acute, or crisis phase. Symptoms here include shock and disbelief that the event occurred. Feelings of humiliation, guilt, shame, embarrassment, self-blame, and fear are characteristic of the acute phase (Gise & Paddison, 1988). The second phase is called the resolution phase. During this stage, life-style changes are made as a result of the rape. Rowan and Rowan (1986) suggest that if the crisis intervention work is done well, it is possible that psychotherapy in the resolution phase will be easier on the individual.

Finally, several researchers (Burt & Katz, 1987; Feinauer, 1982; Rowan & Rowan, 1986) identify loss as a major issue to be dealt with when treating rape victims. Research suggests that this loss is the result of a culmination of several losses: a loss of control, safety, integrity, and part of the victim's being (Feinauer, 1982). Loss, as a therapeutic issue, is addressed later in the treatment section.

Consequences for the Family

Partners of rape victims describe the rape as a shared experience (Emm & McKenry, 1988). Common reactions of significant others are: helplessness, anger, frustration about not knowing how to help the victim, and rage toward the perpetrator. Male partners will sometimes exhibit protective behaviors toward victims. When asked, male partners reported that they were curious about the assault but were not sure it was appropriate for them to ask the victim questions about the rape (Emm & McKenry, 1988). At times, supportive men will not view their actions as being supportive enough.

Other family members might feel a sense of anger toward the victim for humiliating them, frightening them, or shaming the family. If the shame is too great, there may be a tendency for significant others to deny that the abuse took place and consequently push for a return to normalcy. The victimization of the family through a rape experience is an invasion of the family's boundaries. Refusal to acknowledge the rape experience of a family member prevents the family from admitting and understanding that the family's boundaries were compromised and violated.

It is the author's experience that after the discovery of the rape, parents or loved ones tend to ask questions that might imply that the victim was responsible for the rape. It would not be uncommon for a rape victim to be asked these questions: "What were you doing at that bar that late?" "How much did you have to drink?" "Why would you choose to walk home?" "Why didn't you call me for a ride?"

Consequences for the Larger Systems Involved

Some of the larger systems involved when a rape occurs are the police, a rape crisis center, the medical system, and the judicial system. Because a large number of acquaintance rapes occur on college campuses, other systems, such as college judicial boards, or residence hall staff, may be involved. With the involvement of many systems, victims may feel as though "everyone" knows about the rape and all hope for anonymity is gone. Some research suggests that involvement with other systems, particularly the justice system, could result in further victimization (Emm & McKenry, 1988; Gise & Paddison, 1988).

Because of the high incidence of rape and the focus on the victimization of women, rape centers act as advocates for the victim's rights. Rape center staff believe their effectiveness in fighting the social phenomenon of rape is enhanced when they educate their patrons about rape. Their responsibility is to the community as well as the individual. Because of this, their services include individual/group therapy for survivors, as well as making an effort to educate victims about the judicial process and the social aspects of rape. Emm and McKenry (1988) found that some rape centers seemed more interested in helping women seek retribution against their attacker than joining with the client and supporting her. Most rape centers have in the past catered only to women. More and more community rape centers, however, are opening their doors to male survivors of rape. Community rape centers generally have access to organizations such as The United Way which may subsidize the costs involved in running the center. Because of this, fees are not collected from patrons. All victims of sexual assault qualify and are accepted as suitable clients regardless of income or social status.

Sexual Harassment

During the early 1990s the issue of sexual harassment received increased attention. As a result of Anita Hill's testimony in the much-publicized Judge Thomas Supreme Court Confirmation Hearings, many women have spoken out about harassment they experience on the job. In a study conducted by Loy and Stewart (1984), more women than men found harassment a serious problem; 50% of the women in their sample reported having been direct recipients of sexual harassment. It has also been reported that 45% of all working women and only 2% of working men have experienced sexual harassment (Salisbury, Remick, Ginorio, & Stringer, 1986). According to the U.S. Equal Employment Opportunity Commission, *sexual harassment* is defined as "...sexual attention which is 1) unwelcome (defined by the recipient), or 2) unreasonably interferes with an individual's work performance, or 3) is a condition of employment, or 4) forms the basis of an employment decision, or 5) creates an intimidating, hostile, or offensive working environment" (Salisbury, 1992, p. 13).

Salisbury (1992) explains that "sexual harassment attacks the intimate self, the career self-esteem, and one's economic survival" (p. 13). The effects this can have on an individual and her family can be devastating. Issues that women deal with in addition to the work-related ones are: "self-blame, embarrassment, humiliation, depression, anger, paranoia, helplessness, fear, headaches, severe sleep disturbance, gastrointestinal difficulties, and sexual desire disorders" (p. 13). Women feel pressure to forget or deny the harassment and are often scorned for levying charges against the perpetrator.

Many women report that harassment is like rape (Salisbury et al., 1986). There is a similar loss of control over one's situation, in this case one's work environment. Major costs associated with sexual harassment, in addition to the emotional costs to the victim, are decreased work performance and increased employee turnover in the workplace (Loy & Stewart, 1984). The invasion of one's boundaries, and the power differential that exist in childhood sexual abuse and rape seem to be similar with sexual harassment.

TREATMENT AND ASSESSMENT OF EXTRAFAMILIAL SEXUAL ABUSE

The treatment of sexual abuse is often a difficult area for family therapists to negotiate. Difficulty comes in the form of balancing the rights of the clients, which may at times compete against one another within a single family. Although most clinicians believe their interventions and theories to be acceptable and beneficial to the client, some clients can be hurt by certain misguided interventions (Conte, 1990). This is one of the reasons why helping professionals need to have an understanding of the sexual abuse dynamics associated with personal, family, and societal systems.

Goals of Therapy

Recovering from extrafamilial sexual abuse is a difficult, sometimes time-consuming process. It might be too much to expect a clinician to remember the exact specifics of all three areas identified as "extrafamilial" sexual abuse. After all, some therapists have made life-long work out of studying and treating child abuse, others have focused on rape, and still others concentrate on sexual harassment. There are, however, some common themes that seem to be found in all the areas identified. It is important to remember, as Emm and McKenry (1988) state, that strong social support is the "single most important factor in recovery…" (p. 273). This social support can be the family. The following paragraphs discuss some of the familial reactions to extrafamilial sexual abuse; all these reactions could be encountered in therapy sessions. Therapists are encouraged to identify familial responses and normalize the feelings and emotions of family members.

Denial seems to be the first reaction of all significant others when they hear about the abuse. Sometimes denial is so powerful that the victim does not get heard. The abuse is ignored and forgotten when it is not discussed. This can have a dramatic affect on the victim. What kind of message does the victim receive when telling family members about the abuse fails to provide an audience? Denial manifests itself in a number of ways. Parents may minimize the effects of the abuse on their children. Children may encourage mothers to forget about the harassment and "just deal with it." Spouses may push for a return to normalcy in the sexual relationship before adequate resolution of the abuse trauma. Sometimes family members may be punished for asking questions about the abuse. Consequently, the impact of the abusive event becomes tabled and is never addressed in the future.

Another reaction of parents and family is anger. Often a combination of anger and denial is conveyed to the victim. If family members keep their anger at the perpetrator locked up inside themselves, and are not provided an outlet, it can become destructive; anger can quickly grow into resentment, and it inhibits communication. Anger is a natural reaction of family members and the individual. It is often beneficial to connect other strong emotions, such as feeling hurt, frightened, scared, or worried, to the anger expressed in the family. Connecting these feelings with the anger helps the family tune into their full affective experience about the traumatic event. When family members can share these feelings with each other, a solid base of understanding is created and healing can begin.

When a family accepts that something traumatic has occurred, two common reactions are guilt and shame. *Guilt* is an internally generated state that exists within the individual as well as within the family system. It can be a positive thing and can push a family into resolution of conflicts associated with the abuse. For example, parents may make changes in their parenting behaviors to compensate for any deficits they believe may have contributed to the event. Shame is different than guilt and is externally generated. *Shame* is the feeling that the individual and the family get when they believe others are judging them for the victimization in their family. Somehow the family members view themselves as damaged—a common reaction observed in individuals who are survivors of sexual abuse. Shame and guilt are issues that have a tremendous impact on the family's functioning. Without giving some attention to shame and guilt, there may be a tendency to hide the abuse from each other; when the abuse is hidden, it becomes a secret that inhibits intimacy in the family.

In most instances there is a tendency for family members to blame both themselves and the victim. Blaming is not healthy, and it prevents the system from making the necessary changes toward healthy functioning. Taking responsibility is the other side of the "victim blaming" coin. When an individual takes responsibility for his or her actions in conjunction with the abuse, there is a greater ability to understand the position of others in the family. For example, taking responsibility for being in a compromising situation may actually become a resource and prevent future victimization (Boss, 1988).

A multisystemic outlook should be incorporated into treatment. The therapist can easily become a liaison for the other systems involved in the case. Legal, medical, educational, and vocational systems are all affected in extrafamilial sexual abuse (Conte 1990). It may be necessary for the therapist to talk with other people in the community who are involved with the family. The therapist needs to be open and discuss exactly what information will be released after obtaining the family's proper authorization.

Assessment

It should be remembered that when dealing with a family system that has recently been sexually abused, the abuse may be an "out-in-the-open" phenomenon. There may be very little need to do any assessment. Assessment comes in the form of verification of one person's story about the abuse or probing for other areas of family life being affected by the abuse. Clarke and Hornick (1988) explain that it is difficult for the therapist to find a balance between obtaining correct information and being careful not to alienate the client by being too intrusive. Assessment is a sensitive issue because there is increased potential for the therapist's own issues to be brought up while interviewing someone who has undergone a traumatic experience. If the therapist tries to protect the client from retelling the abuse and does not assess it, the client may be just as harmed as when the therapist conducts the assessment in an abrasive way. During assessment, it is easy to participate in the denial of the abuse that may be projected by the family. This can make joining with the client/family difficult.

Research shows that most assessment devices pertain only to child sexual abuse. The literature available on child abuse is mixed and suggests that some children will easily disclose the abuse and related facts and other children will not want to talk about it at all (Conte, 1990).

According to Clarke and Hornick (1988), the treatment of childhood sexual abuse should include a formalized assessment procedure. Assessment devices should be used to monitor treatment success and treatment should be altered depending on the findings of the assessment. They suggest using the Achenbach Child Behavior Checklist (1983). This instrument provides a profile of the child's behavior. Another area of assessment is the developmental level of the child. Age- and stage-appropriate behaviors may not be observed in some sexually abused children. For example, a child who displays sexual knowledge beyond the norm for his or her age group may have been exposed to some type of inappropriate sexual behavior. Regression—a child reverts to past "normal" developmental behaviors—may also be observed. Curling up in a fetal position, talking in baby talk, or sucking fingers are some signs that might indicate something traumatic has happened in the child's life.

Conte (1990) suggests that "it is too early in the development of this [child sexual abuse] research to determine the usefulness of existing measures" (p. 70). Current measures at best identify what the child might be experiencing, but they do not point to interventions or strategies for treatment. This is also the case for sexual harassment, where no assessment devices exist other than standard devices which assess mood, depression, or demographics.

When considering assessment, it is important to remember the systemic nature of families. Hoagwood and Stewart (1989) suggest that it might not be enough to look only at the individual. "A group (or family) pathology may exist where an individual pathology does not. Thus the family assessment approach may point out dysfunctional elements that might not be noted through individual assessments of perpetrators or victims solely" (p. 146). The McMaster Family Assessment Device (FAD) (Epstein, Baldwin, & Bishop, 1983) has been used in assessment procedures (Hoagwood & Stewart, 1989). The FAD measures "healthy" family functioning along six dimensions: problem-solving, communication, roles, affective responsivity, affective involvement, and behavior control. These dimensions are regularly monitored in family therapy sessions by the therapist. The FAD provides a "self-report" of family functioning from the client's perspective. It may be beneficial for all family members to complete it and then compare answers.

Assessment of the victim's developmental and family's life-cycle stages should also be considered. A traumatic experience may be the type of event that prevents a college student from a successful launching into adulthood. The launching period becomes extended and possibly put on hold so that the child stays at a postadolescent/preadult level. Sexual abuse has a profound effect on the developing sexuality of any individual. Any issues that pertain to sexuality should be discussed and parents should be supported in discussing sexuality with their children. After sexual abuse has occurred, parents can use the unfortunate circumstance to educate other family members about sexual abuse. This further reduces the potential for future harmful extrafamilial sexual experiences.

At times of crisis, the therapist must remember that some family members can become so focused on their own pain that they will become less attentive to the needs of others in the family. This is the biggest strength of the systems model in treating extrafamilial sexual abuse. Assessing the whole family together or including the family in all phases of the treatment may actually raise the level of postcrisis functioning (Boss, 1988).

In the assessment of extrafamilial sexual abuse, the final component to assess is the strengths and resources of the family. As Hill (1958) describes in his crisis model, all families have strengths and resources before the crisis event. The resources to be evaluated are the psychological, economic, and physical assets from which the family can draw (Boss, 1988). A routine "family strengths" assessment may help the family begin to define themselves as survivors and not merely as victims.

TREATMENT ISSUES SPECIFIC TO THE AREAS IDENTIFIED

Treatment of Childhood Sexual Abuse and the Family

Most of the literature available that addresses treatment issues for families focuses on those who have experienced incest. Research suggests that the prognosis for recovery is better for victims of extrafamilial sexual abuse than intrafamilial abuse (Hartman et al., 1987). Conte (1990) suggests that a child's relationship with supportive adults and siblings is a powerful factor associated with successful recovery work. Faller (1988), who advocates seeing only the child in therapy, suggests that for extrafamilial sexual abuse "...caretakers can be part of the therapy sessions but more to act as supportive persons or surrogate therapists than as recipients of treatment for themselves" (p. 56).

Working with a family that has experienced extrafamilial sexual abuse presents a dilemma. Families may present with the understanding that the child is the only one getting or needing help. Some therapists have experienced parents dropping children off for therapy accompanied by an expressed, "fix my kid" attitude. Some education on family systems during an initial meeting with the whole family helps them see how different members of the family are experiencing the abuse. This is easily facilitated through the use of circular questioning, where family members are encouraged to talk for one another in an attempt to promote discussion about significant family relationships and experiences (Selvini-Palazzoli, Boscolo, Cecchin, & Prata, 1980). As family members' experiences are shared, understanding is fostered and intimacy can grow.

Some of the work that needs to be done may include individual sessions with the child who has been victimized. When this happens, the therapist can be in a difficult position. Conte (1990, p. 67) explains the dilemma this way:

> The therapist walks a fine line between encouraging expression and trying to force a child to reveal information that the child is reluctant to talk about. The therapist must be aware that being coercive may cause considerable distress in the child. Indeed, it is unlikely that a child will be forthcoming under conditions of force. On the other hand, it also is unlikely that the child will express anxiety-causing material unless the therapist encourages such revelations.

Given this position, it is important to join with the child in an attempt to build response potential. The joining should be a genuine effort to connect with the child, not a manipulative or contrived effort to trick the child into disclosure. The therapist needs to follow the child's cues before delving into disclosure of the abuse.

If an individual interview with the child is held, the therapist might want to be clear with the family that they will be involved soon. This helps parents and other family members look at the victimization as a family issue and not one limited to the "identified patient."

When trying to involve parents who are reluctant to enter family counseling, a therapist might consider telling them that at a very basic level the abuse was a learning experience for their child. Regardless of the specific experience, the child must have learned something about human nature (Conte, 1990). Framing the event this way, the therapist acts as a moderator in a session where the parents interview the child about what was learned. If it is discovered that the child doesn't share the same opinions about human nature, the parents can offer their own beliefs and help share their values with the child. Some of the lessons learned from an abusive experience will affect the way the child regards sexuality, relationships, power, and self-worth. Family members need to accept the abuse, convey a feeling of acceptance to the child, and help instill hope that the future will somehow be normal again for both the child and the family (Conte, 1990).

Everstine and Everstine (1989) recommend that the therapist tell the parents that the abuse will not just go away. This can be a powerful way to confront parents in denial about the abuse and its effects on their child. Some parents may underestimate the significance of what happened to their child (Conte, 1990). This may result in parents conveying the message of "get over it and quit dwelling on it," which may be damaging to the child. Parents, as the leaders of the family, need to confront the issue and deal with their feelings around the abuse. If they do not, it is more difficult for the rest of the family to do so. The therapist's position becomes one of encouraging a dialogue between the child and the parents. Parents need to remember, and sometimes have to be told, their child is seeking approval and acceptance even though there might be a tendency for the parents to think of the child as injured, dirty, or damaged (Feinauer & Hippolite, 1987). The child can pick up cues from the parents and other family members about the shame that surrounds the abuse. Because parents may have a hard time connecting with the child, a new kind of "joining" needs to happen. The therapist needs to encourage parents' efforts in joining with their child. As important as it is for the therapist to join with the child and the family, it is more important for the family to be joined to one another.

Cohen-Esquilin (1987) outlines five areas that need attention when helping a family deal with the sexual victimization of a child. The family must first believe the child; this sends a message of caring and understanding. If the perpetrator is a close family friend, this may mean altering the way the perpetrator is viewed by the family. The second adaptive response is to protect the child. The family needs to be able to protect the child from the perpetrator, which may mean prosecution, geographically moving the family, or changing schools for the child. The family must then focus on the child. The shame the family feels cannot overshadow the child/victim. Family issues cannot be pushed aside either. The family needs to accept the child's feelings. This is not to be confused with producing a cure. Parents might feel the need to come up with solutions in an attempt to both protect the child and reduce their own anxiety concerning the abuse. The family's role is to be one of availability and not intrusion. The fifth response is to help the child see himself or herself as a survivor. Past accomplishments, awards, or special things the child has done that have held meaning for the family (parents in particular) need to be discussed. This helps the child see his or her own worth in the family and the lives of others.

Families need to be consistently polled on their activities. They need to be aware of when they are being either too helpful or not supportive enough. Patience will be a necessary attribute for all the family to learn. Often, the child will have short-term reactions to the abuse. For example, it is not uncommon for a child to have sleep disturbances, anxiety, or psychosomatic symptoms. Working through these symptoms becomes an essential part of the overall treatment (Cohen-Esquilin, 1987).

As mentioned earlier, anger is a common reaction of family members when they hear about abuse. This can be compounded if the perpetrator was someone trusted by the family. It is important to acknowledge the anger and help the family find an acceptable way to express it. Experiential work with soft bats (batacas) may be helpful within a family session. The child's anger needs to be monitored. The child may perceive the abuse as a result of being left in the care of an abusive person, or the manifestation of parental inadequacy (Conte, 1990). This might result in the victim thinking that the abusive act was not nearly as destructive as the fall-out that occurs when she or he has to confront parents with questions of neglect or betrayal. Rage is another part of this process. Rage, however, can be destructive when the family becomes preoccupied with it. It is acceptable for family members to have rage fantasies that involve revenge, but they need to understand they must remain fantasies.

By keeping a systemic framework, parents need to understand that other children in the family should not be neglected just because one has been victimized. The abusive experience can be used as a teaching moment for the other children. Many children witness the pain of their sibling and only know that they do not wish a similar experience on themselves. Parents need to take the time to educate themselves and other family members about abuse and techniques for reducing the likelihood of revictimization (Kolko, 1987). Parents need to monitor the other children's behaviors and be sure they are not in contact with the same abusive person.

This systemic framework should also be applied to the marital dyad. MacFarlane (1986) states that the discovery that a child has been abused can put a significant strain on any marriage. There may be a tendency for one partner to blame the other or indulge in self-blame. The couple issues that need to be considered are denial of the abuse, the possibility that the parent was also abused as a child, sexuality, and parenting skills.

Treatment of Rape and the Family

A review of the literature shows that the preferred treatment modality for rape victims usually happens in a one-on-one format. Soon after the rape occurs, the therapy takes on a crisis intervention nature. There is nothing in the literature that suggests that the family be included in the initial treatment of the victim. In fact, some suggest that the friends and family may actually hinder the recovery process (Gise & Paddison, 1988). Rape usually is viewed as an individual phenomenon. Goals for individual therapy include symptom reduction, helping the victim return to normal functioning, and the utilization of new coping skills (Rowan & Rowan, 1986). This section concentrates more on treatment for the family after a rape.

Even though the preferred method for the treatment of rape is group therapy, it is surprising that professionals continue to neglect the most important group, the family. There are many advantages to treating rape in a family context when compared to individual or group treatment. Individuals in the family can feel less awkward, a greater understanding of family suffering can be shared, and the family's unity increases the chances that familial strengths will be utilized. Above all, therapists must realize that the family is related—they have always been together and will continue to be together in the future. Connections that are created in a family help equalize the trauma inflicted on the family from external abuse. Crisis intervention techniques, which focus on the individual, may be inadequate at providing for the needs of survivors or significant others. Feinauer (1982) suggests that when a rape occurs the whole family feels victimized. She suggests that the family is a "silent" victim because it is often overlooked with regard to treatment. Any treatment plan must take the family system into consideration (Miller, 1987; Rowan & Rowan, 1986; Silverman, 1978). According to Emm and McKenry (1988), survivors need time to mourn the loss of their old life and be supported in creating a new identity as a victim and then as a survivor. Part of this process is providing family members with information about rape. In fact, survivors of rape request this (Emm & McKenry, 1988).

Family members may feel helpless after a rape has occurred. Helplessness is a natural reaction to the violation of a family's boundaries. Because of this helpless feeling, many family members will express a need to do "something" for the victim. Survivors indicated that they thought just having someone to "listen to them, accept them, and comfort them in some verbal or physical way" was helpful (Emm & McKenry, 1988, p. 277).

A second normal reaction to the violation of a family's boundaries is anger. In individual treatment, rape victims need to get to a place where they can recognize they have been victimized; they need to be able to feel the intense anger, aggression, hostility, and rage before a resolution can be made. This applies to the family as well (Feinauer & Hippolite, 1987). Attempts to deny the violence or sweep the incident "under the rug" can prevent the victim from being heard, and the family from supporting the victim.

Families need to be encouraged to express their feelings about the rape. Each family member needs to work toward understanding what the rape experience means to the victim, and each other. Therapy may also include an educational or didactic component. This will help prepare the family for the possible ramifications of the rape (Silverman, 1978). Everstine and Everstine (1989) comment on education in treatment and suggest that communication should be directed to the parents. Their views on rape and how to involve other siblings in discussions about the rape become cues for the therapist to assess the leadership abilities of the parents. If the parents can begin to control therapeutic disclosure outside of therapy, they can be the people in the family who the children look to for answers. Parents are also encouraged to discuss their own feelings of helplessness and model this behavior for their children. The therapist needs to be available to other family members who are having a harder time coping with the crisis. These interventions help give the family direction in the recovery process.

For couples who have experienced the rape of a spouse, there are four characteristics that often become treatment issues (Miller, 1987). The first is that partners often lack an empathic understanding of each other. Males typically move to rage before their female counterparts and are ready to seek revenge while the female is only concerned with safety and protection. While the male brainstorms different ways revenge can be attained, in terms of seeking legal retribution or direct confrontation, the woman is concentrating on survival responses such as withdrawing, avoiding, or denying issues around the rape (Miller, 1987). The second area affected by the rape is the couple's communication. The third is the victim's feelings of dependence which, over time, may be viewed by the partner as burdensome or draining. Finally, the couple's sexual relationship needs to be a topic of discussion in therapy. Although rape is considered a crime of power, there is little room to dispute the fact that the victim's core sexuality is violated and the effects of this violation impact the couple's sex life (Miller, 1987). It may be necessary to refer the couple to a competent sex therapist or conduct sex therapy techniques designed to restore comfort levels within the couple's sexual relationship. One way of creating safety in the couple's sexual relationship is to discourage sexual contact for a while until the victim feels comfortable initiating it.

Miller (1987, p. 177) describes the position the therapist needs to take in treating rape:

> The therapist needs to address the problems with what can be referred to as "informed eclecticism." That is, the therapist needs to make a careful assessment of the needs of each couple and then to apply any of a wide variety of treatment approaches, techniques, and modalities to the issues at hand.

This may include a treatment plan consisting of both individual and couple sessions designed to assess understanding of the rape experience as well as the couple's functioning and level of desired intimacy.

Feinauer and Hippolite (1987, p. 252) offer an experiential technique to help the family cope with the after-effects of the rape. They advocate the use of ritual in treatment:

> Through the use of a short metaphorical story and symbolic ritual, each individual member and the family as a whole can experience, reexperience, and redecide how they will respond to this traumatic event through open expression of their emotions and responses.

Feinauer and Hippolite encourage the family to meet at a specified location. The rape victim is given an envelope that she is to open when the family is assembled. Inside, the instructions tell the family to sit in a semicircle in front of the rape victim. Another sealed envelope contains a metaphorical story. The rape victim is instructed to read the story while the other family members are instructed to keep quiet.

The story is titled, "Once a Princess, Always a Princess?" The story tells of a King and Queen who had a daughter. At her birth, a mysterious crown was found beside her bed. The crown was too big for the princess to wear, so the King and Queen decided that in time the princess would wear the crown. The night before the princess was to receive the crown, a man broke into the castle and stole the crown. The next day the princess was ashamed that her crown had been taken from her and pled with her father to call off the coronation ball. When the story ends, the family is left to discuss the meanings they understood from the tale. In the next therapy session, with the victim's family, the experience is processed. This ritual experience is one way of helping the victim gain some more control of her environment. She is helping herself and her family. This experience may open up doors of communication that were previously closed during a formal therapy session, and quite possibly conclude therapy.

Rape presents a unique working experience for the therapist because rape cannot be "cured." Rape more accurately resembles a loss; it must be mourned (Gise & Paddison, 1988). Going through a mourning process helps the victim obtain a sense of control over his or her life (Gise & Paddison, 1988). Therapists are encouraged to help family members understand the characteristics of rape trauma syndrome and posttraumatic stress disorder. It is important to normalize the phases that the individual might go through in the future (Everstine & Everstine, 1989). This not only prepares the victim of rape for the flashbacks, shortness of breath, possible catatonia, or other dissociative experiences, but it also gives the family a context in which to experience these symptoms. The therapist must be supportive and nonimposing (Everstine & Everstine, 1989). This is done through following the client's lead and pacing the client (victim and family) when it comes to disclosure of facts about the rape. If the therapist is sensitive to the client's lead, rapport will begin to build. This shows respect for the client's already violated boundaries.

Treatment of Sexual Harassment and the Family

Clients who present with issues of sexual harassment usually will be women. Current marriage and family therapy literature on sexual harassment involves scenarios in which women are the victims. These clients are reluctant to seek treatment because of denial that the harassment even occurred or is occurring (Salisbury, 1992).

Therapists who work with a client who has been sexually harassed need to be prepared to be crisis-focused. The harassment has disrupted (and may be disrupting) the client's daily routine. Often there is pressure from other employees to drop the charges against the perpetrator who might be their boss. There may be a tendency for co-workers to make excuses for the perpetrator by suggesting, "that's just the way he is." Therapists need to be informed about the legal process. If the client does not have proper legal counsel with the appropriate experience, it is recommended that the therapist help find one. This is a crucial part of the therapeutic relationship because it demonstrates from the onset of therapy that the therapist is someone who can be trusted and believes the client's story (Salisbury, 1992). This is also an important step because it is possible for the therapist to be subpoenaed.

After joining with the client, the first phase of treatment should include letting the client tell her side of the story. She needs to be able to feel comfortable enough with the therapist so that every detail can be told. A therapist might find that the sexual harassment has been going on for some time but has taken the form of subtle passes, or comments that the client just ignored in hopes the comments would stop. It is beneficial for the client if the therapist reinterprets the client's self-blame and acknowledges the effects of the harassment. The therapist must try to normalize the client's use of humor, ignoring, and joking with the perpetrator as common defense mechanisms (Salisbury et al., 1986). At the same time, the therapist needs to encourage the client to be aware of the defense mechanisms and challenge the client to be consistent in refuting the unwanted sexual advances.

When the client is at a point where she is not blaming herself as much, it is important for the therapist to help her identify resources in the workforce. Human resource departments and trusted upper/middle management employees can be sources of validation and security. These people may be more in touch with reactions or experiences other employees have had in relation to the perpetrator. Clients need to be prepared to accept that the corporation may take action against the perpetrator. If this happens, the client needs to know that she may not have control of the events. The offending employee may be fired as a result of her complaint. This may be an area of great conflict and emotional fall-out. If this occurs, it can help the client get a sense of taking charge of her life; she has refused to be a victim and has taken action.

Getting the perpetrator fired is not necessarily a part of the overall focus of the treatment. This is not in the therapist's or client's control. It is important, however, for the therapist to encourage a confrontation between the client and the perpetrator. This can take place either in person or through a letter. This demands courage on the part of the client and helps her move out of the victim role. The therapist and client must remember that some types of confrontations may have legal ramifications. The purpose of a confrontation is to work on the client's anger associated with harassment, not to exacerbate conditions in the problematic system.

The effects of the abuse on the family system are very real. Family and spousal subsystems are often unsympathetic to the client's emotional distress (Salisbury, 1992). There is a tendency for them to either think that the victim is taking the harassment too seriously, or to blame the victim for having asked for it. In cases of harassment, there is a great propensity to blame the victim. Victim blaming may be a coping mechanism for the husband with guilt feelings about not being able to protect "his" woman. The family obviously suffers from the loss of income in the event the client quits her job or is fired. They may even be upset with her for having "rocked the boat" at work. The therapist must be an advocate for the client and support her in explaining her story in a way the family can understand how she experienced the harassment. This is important because, over time, family members tend to lose the empathy they originally felt for the victim (Salisbury et al., 1986).

There is also a possibility that sexual relations between husband and wife may become strained in this process. It might be beneficial to consider possible sexual dysfunctions. The therapist might suggest that the couple focus less on sexual contact and more on being supportive of one another for a period of time until the woman feels comfortable initiating sexual contact. Therapists are encouraged to pay close attention to this and be flexible enough to follow the client's lead in talking about her sexual relationship. There is also a good chance that no disturbance in sexual functioning has occurred.

Therapists are cautioned to keep a focus on the family system but not to the exclusion of the larger work and legal systems that interface on a social and employment level. The therapist must remember that the workplace system strives for homeostasis. Therefore, turbulence is created for women who decide to take action against sexual harassment. The system's need for homeostasis, combined with the long-lasting effects of sexual harassment, make ignoring or stopping the fight against it a tempting option at times. A brief explanation of systems theory and the concept of homeostasis may help a survivor gather the strength to stay in treatment and at work.

TREATMENT STRATEGIES

Whenever a person in the family is victimized, the whole family is victimized. Boss and Sheppard (1988) highlight the need for a model of family victimization. They suggest that the victimization experience brings a feeling of shame on the whole family. They further suggest that the whole family can suffer from a type of PTSD, where an implicit message is sent to numb themselves from the feelings they are experiencing.

Clinicians should help the family recognize or take an inventory of their behavior "before and during their victimizing situation" (Boss & Sheppard, 1988, p. 212). The therapist can assist the family by concentrating on behaviors and not on characterological deficits. This helps the family realize their capacity to strengthen weaker areas of coping. Bentovim (1987) calls for a systemic outlook on family violence and suggests that, "violence does not belong to the individual, the family, or to society, but to all three. As family systems thinkers, we have to see violent interaction as being related to all three systems, even though we choose to make our first priority for action the family domain" (p. 384).

ROLE OF THE THERAPIST

If good rapport is established, the therapist can have a powerful effect on how the family perceives the abuse. For example, when working with families of childhood sexual abuse, the therapist needs to reinforce the parents' acceptance of the abuse and support the good parenting efforts they have made (Cohen-Esquilin, 1987). The parents can then be congratulated for coming into therapy. This can be viewed as a sign of strength that suggests the parents want what is best for the child and the family.

The phenomenon of victimization as described in this chapter is an area of "tricky" negotiation for any therapist. The therapist needs to be able to support the client by understanding the victimization and also to support the family in redefining themselves as survivors. Many therapists consider themselves advocates for the client/family. Advocacy is an important part of showing clients understanding, but therapists need to be aware that doing things for the client, such as arranging resources, may be a way of siding with the family's belief that they are victims. If the therapist is too removed, the family may feel that they are "in this thing alone" and may not see the value of coming back to therapy. With a premature withdrawal from family therapy, the chances are increased that the experience will not be discussed and intimate relationships will be strained unnecessarily.

Structure of Therapy

The very nature of sexual abuse is such that the family must go through some grieving (Feinauer, 1982). If comparing the grieving that takes place within families who have experienced sexual abuse to other types of grieving, it should be noted that no one can force the family to move through the steps of grieving outlined by authors such as Kübler-Ross (1969) and Rosen (1990). Families have to move through these steps at their own pace. This reaffirms the need for the therapist to establish rapport. Without rapport, the family may not feel comfortable coming back to the therapist when they come to a new area of their life affected by the abuse. Recovery may take a long time; however, the same is not necessarily so for treatment.

If recovery is a long process, it might be beneficial for therapists to realize that clients may come and go. When rapport is established, clients who have left therapy without a complete resolution of the effects of the abuse will feel more at ease coming back to therapy in the future. This allows for plateau stages in recovery. These need to be framed positively for the family. For example, a family may have resolved the initial trauma but become "stuck" when approaching a new family life-cycle stage. The therapist can be instrumental in normalizing their "stuck" experience and reflect to the family their past successful negotiations of "new" developmental ground.

The therapist needs to know where his or her own anxiety is regarding the symptoms presented by clients. If clients are not ready to pursue the issues brought up by sexual abuse, therapists need to support them in this decision. Being wed to the idea that a complete cathartic experience needs to happen can inhibit therapy. An offer to come back whenever the family "needs to" is an invitation that conveys respect and empathy for the difficulties in coping with the abuse. The therapist cannot pressure them to deal with the abuse if the family reports not being ready. If the therapist does push, it will not be the family's treatment, as much as it will be the therapist's.

Effectiveness of the Various Approaches

One of the commentaries on the condition of the helping profession in dealing with sexual abuse is the profession's reluctance to conduct long-term research on treatment outcomes. Conte (1990) states: "To date there are no evaluations of alternative treatment approaches with sexually abused children. There exist no treatment outcome studies…. Therefore it is premature to describe what forms of treatment are most effective for sexually abused children" (p. 61).

There are many questions that still need to be asked regarding extrafamilial sexual abuse. One of the main questions is whether the treatment methods employed by helping professionals are effective for treating families. There is a need for more research to determine the differences between the victimization of men and women. It has also been discovered that some people are not as severely affected by extrafamilial sexual abuse as others. The reasons why this is so are not yet known. This points to the need for more resiliency studies. In looking at abuse as a systemic phenomenon, there is a need to determine what role significant others must play in treatment that might contribute to coping with the victimization. As this chapter attempts to do, the term *extrafamilial sexual abuse* needs to be broadened to include rape and sexual harassment, as well as childhood sexual abuse. Research that incorporates both genders is needed. More studies that compare differences between men and women might help clinics construct gender-specific programs for treatment. Additional research needs to be done on nonclinical samples; this makes data collection more difficult but may also lead to more generalizable findings. Finally, longitudinal studies should be conducted by those offering treatment programs to show effectiveness over time.

Recommendations/Suggestions for the Therapist

One of the most critical issues therapists will confront is that of their own comfort level with sexuality and sexual abuse. Therapists need to recognize their anxiety levels around sexuality and sexual victimization. Extrafamilial abuse can occur in any family. Because sexual abuse is so prevalent, it is possible that any therapist helping a client deal with sexual abuse could have had a similar experience. It is imperative for the therapist to know personal boundaries. No research has been conducted on self-disclosure of therapist's sexual victimization so therapists might want to avoid bringing in personal experiences, or closely monitor clients' reactions when they do discuss their own abuse. This may help the client know the therapeutic boundaries and limits of the therapist/family relationship.

Several legal and ethical issues are confronted when working with families of extrafamilial sexual abuse. Duty to warn is still in effect. If the therapist believes that a child molester is "out there," it has to be reported. Duty to warn is not necessarily an issue for rape or sexual harassment. Another issue is the interface of the therapist with the legal system. Therapists should keep accurate notes and avoid personalized thoughts that lawyers might be able to question in the event of a court case (Everstine & Everstine, 1989). Some therapists suggest that notes should be kept purposely ambiguous so that investigators might be dissuaded from calling the therapist as a witness. There is always the possibility of being called as an expert witness. If this happens, the therapist might have to educate the jury on the dynamics associated with extrafamilial sexual abuse. This includes systemic issues. The role of expert witness should not necessarily be filled by the same therapist treating the family. It might be beneficial for two therapists to testify, one to discuss the generalities and one to discuss the specifics of the abuse (Everstine & Everstine, 1989).

Another legal and ethical issue that arises as a result of childhood sexual abuse is reporting the perpetrator to the authorities. Brock and Coufal (1989) surveyed marital and family therapists and discovered that up to 17 percent of their sample rarely or never reported an incidence of childhood sexual abuse. These therapists felt they had a better chance of helping the family if the department of social services was not involved. Regardless of theoretical orientation, therapists are required by law to report any incidence of child sexual abuse and mistreatment. The way in which the report is made can vary (i.e., therapist makes the call with family present, therapists calls, family makes the call in therapist's presence, family calls on their own). Each way the call is made necessitates some involvement on the therapist's part to assess the impact of making the call.

Systemic Issues

The therapy modality of choice for most therapists will be individual therapy. There is a tendency to acknowledge only the victim's suffering and forget the family and other systems. Indeed it will be a struggle for any clinician trained as an individual psychotherapist to see extrafamilial sexual abuse as a family issue. While intrafamilial sexual abuse is recognized as belonging to a dysfunctional family system, it may be too easy to dismiss extrafamilial sexual abuse as an unfortunate isolated event that happened to one of the family members.

In a recent case, the effects of extrafamilial sexual abuse on the family were underscored for the author when a client, who had been raped, went home from college to escape the continued trauma only to find a family that was unwilling to admit that the abuse had occurred. There is a need for family therapists, historically pioneers in systems thinking, to recognize the other systems involved in extrafamilial sexual abuse. For example, a therapist working with a family where a daughter has been raped might think system-ically by considering the religious system in which the family operates. This may be best dealt with by employing the counsel of clergy (Cohen-Esquilin, 1987).

One of the largest systemic issues is too large to address in this chapter: The societal context that contributes to the occurrence of extrafamilial sexual abuse. A significant power differential between men and women, and between adults and children, exists in society and seems to be perpetuated by our beliefs and norms. As long as one person is physically stronger than another, or one person is given power or authority over another, there will be a tendency to abuse that strength, power, or authority. Policy, educational, and social reforms are still necessary to educate people about abuse and improve prevention efforts.

Case Example

The following example illustrates some of the dynamics associated with treating extrafamilial sexual abuse. Not every family exhibits the same responses to the abuse. This chapter attempts to highlight those reactions most often experienced by individuals and families who live through a sex-ual invasion of their family boundaries.

Sharon was a first-year student at a large university. On weekends, she and her friends would go barhopping. Throughout the evening, she would meet new people. As one fall evening drew to a close, Sharon was invited to go to Bill's room to watch TV. Although Sharon had just met Bill for the first time an hour ago, she believed he was a decent, attractive man. She also knew Bill was well liked by his fraternity brothers and was involved in student government. Sharon agreed to go.

When they arrived at his room they began to makeout. Their passionate activities increased in intensity and both agreed to have oral sex. Soon into the sexual experience, Sharon became uncomfortable and expressed her desire to quit. Bill took exception to her plea and continued to engage in the now unwanted sexual activity. Sharon opened the door and made an attempt to leave the room. Sharon managed to yell, "Rape!'" and Bill pulled her back into the room. Bill continued to initiate sex with Sharon and in so doing ripped her under-clothing. People in the hall responded to her call for help, intervened between Bill and Sharon, and escorted her to a different room. From there, campus security and local police were notified.

Sharon had experienced a form of extrafamilial sexual abuse commonly known as acquaintance rape. In discussing her dilemma, it became clear that Sharon had been humiliated by the experience. Sharon reported feeling torn between believing she was at fault to being infuriated with her attacker.

Throughout the next week, Sharon's story was publicized in the local news-paper. Reporters obtained both her and her roommate's name from police reports open to the public. As I spoke with her in her residence hall room, a newspaper reporter called to confirm the story. This added to the shame that Sharon already felt. Sharon was feeling exposed, vulnerable, and stupid about what had happened. She was not easily reassured by my insistence that the abusive incident was not her fault. Throughout the week after the attack, some editorials in the newspaper called for Sharon to leave school, while others offered support. Still, another article exclaimed that any woman who would engage in oral sex with a perfect stranger deserves anything she gets.

As a crisis counselor, I met with Sharon. After assessing Sharon's individual emotional experience, I continued to explore the systemic ramifications of the recent events. The assessment included asking questions to determine how Sharon's family was taking the news. Sharon told me that the student newspaper story, which outlined the events of the evening, was picked up by her hometown newspaper and was printed in its entirety. Sharon began to feel her world getting smaller as more and more people knew about the rape. When questioned about the support she received from home, Sharon admitted that her mother wanted her to "stay in school, ignore it, and just get over it."

I discussed Sharon's affective state with her mother: Sharon was tearful, scared, angry, ashamed, and feeling exposed. I also shared with her mother some of Sharon's suicidal ideation. Although not suicidal at the time, Sharon's emotional stability was constantly being compromised by things people said or other events related to her rape experience. When I first talked with her mom, it seemed as though Sharon did not have support from her family. Her mother reported being incredibly embarrassed by the story in the newspaper. She told me that all of her friends knew about Sharon's behavior and that their social standing was in jeopardy because of her daughter's actions.

Because Sharon's parents lived in another state it was not possible to schedule an appointment with them. My job consisted of acting as both an advocate for Sharon and a mediator between her and her mother. I explained the nature of Sharon's experience and her need for support. I suggested that she try to just understand how Sharon might have been feeling. As our discussion progressed, her mother began to soften and to see Sharon's pain. To my surprise, she revealed that she too had experienced unwanted sexual contact in college. She revealed the fact that no one had really known about that experience, not even her husband. She admitted that hearing about Sharon's victimization triggered thoughts and feelings associated with her own victimization.

Her mother's demeanor changed as she heard the pain Sharon was experiencing. Her understanding of the pain was underscored by her own experience of sexual victimization. I recommended that Sharon go home for at least a weekend to decide if she wanted to finish out the semester. I further recommended that her mother arrange for a family therapy session with a local therapist. After ending the conversation with Sharon's mother, I turned to Sharon and encouraged her to be open and honest with her mother, and told her that her mother had something important to share with her.

This crisis presented an opportunity for Sharon to increase her awareness of acquaintance rape and its prevalence. It also offered Sharon and her mother a chance to connect with each other in a different way. Sharon completed the semester but then continued her education at another university. She continued to feel overwhelmed by things that reminded her of the attack (i.e., the residence hall, the bar scene, his fraternity, judicial hearings at the university). Her idea to transfer to another university was supported by her parents.

Before leaving school, Sharon reported to me that she had never known her mother was attacked as a college student. She also said her mother and father were continuing in couples counseling to fully process the feelings associated with her mother's sexual victimization. Although Sharon's experience was unwanted and unfortunate, she and her family grew closer as they opened up to and supported each other.

This scenario shows that therapists need to be flexible in their orientation. Both family and individual assessment are necessary. Sharon was treated as an individual in need of crisis intervention. However, the assessment phase of her treatment included a systemic dimension. Had the therapist in this situation not offered himself to the family or suggested the family's involvement in Sharon's treatment, mother and daughter might not have connected the way they did. The family was further strengthened by the parent's continued investment in counseling to thoroughly discuss the mother's victimization and its impact on the relationship. Early intervention helped Sharon. Although intervention for her mother came at a later date than her victimization, relationships were strengthened because of the intervention.

CONCLUSIONS

Conte (1990) refers to sexual abuse as an area that is filled with "ambiguity" but also a great deal of "potential." This chapter summarizes some of the initial reactions of individuals and families soon after they experience a sexual assault. There are many other issues that may arise for the individual and the family years after the abusive incident has occurred. Unfortunately, this chapter cannot come close to providing a voice for the thousands who have suffered.

It is important for the therapist to remember the use of collegial consultation and supervision. Extrafamilial sexual abuse is complex. The origin of the problem is societal. Family therapists can contribute to helping victimized families become survivors and, hopefully, healers of the future. It is the author's hope that family therapists will recognize the powerful impact they can have on helping families realize their own healing potential. Strength comes from support. Support cannot happen without connection, and families have the greatest potential for fostering lasting connections with individuals who have suffered the trauma of sexual abuse.

REFERENCES

American Psychiatric Association (1987). *Diagnostic and statistical manual of mental disorders*, III, revised. Washington DC: American Psychiatric Association.
Adams-Tucker, C. (1982). Proximate effects of sexual abuse in childhood: A report on 28 children. *American Journal of Psychiatry, 139*, 1252–1265.

Adams-Tucker, C. & Adams, P. L. (1984). Treatment of sexually abused children. In I. R. Stuart & J. G. Greer (Eds.), *Victims of sexual aggression: Treatment of children, women, and men* (pp. 57–74). New York: Van Nostrand Reinhold.

Bentovim, A. (1987). Physical and sexual abuse of children—The role of the family therapist. *Journal of Family Therapy, 9,* 383–388.

Boss, P. (1988). *Family stress management.* Newbury Park, CA: Sage.

Boss, P. & Sheppard, R. (1988). Family victimization and recovery. *Contemporary Family Therapy, 10,* 202–215.

Brock, G. W. & Coufal, J. D. (1989). Ethics in practice. *The Family Therapy Networker,* (March/April), 27.

Burgess, A. W. & Holstrom, L. L. (1976). Rape trauma syndrome. *American Journal of Psychiatry, 131,* 981–986.

Burt, M. R. & Katz, B. L. (1987). Dimensions of recovery from rape: Focus on growth outcomes. *Journal of Interpersonal Violence, 2,* 57–81.

Clarke, M. E. & Hornick, J. P. (1988). The child sexual abuse victim: Assessment and treatment issues and solutions. *Contemporary Family Therapy, 10,* 235–242.

Cohen-Esquilin, S. (1987). Family responses to the identification of extra-familial child sexual abuse. *Psychotherapy in Private Practice, 5,* 105–113.

Conte, J. R. (1990). Victims of child sexual abuse. In R. T. Ammerman & M. Hersen (Eds.) *Treatment of family violence: A sourcebook* (pp. 50–76). New York: John Wiley.

Crewdson, J. (1988). *By silence betrayed: Sexual abuse of children in America.* Boston: Little, Brown.

DeFrancis, V. (1969). *Protecting the child victim of sex crimes committed by adults.* Denver: American Humane Association.

Emm, D. & McKenry, P. C. (1988). Coping with victimization: The impact of rape on female survivors, male significant others, and parents. *Contemporary Family Therapy, 10,* 272–279.

Epstein, N. B., Baldwin, L. M., & Bishop, D. S. (1983). The McMaster Family Assessment Device. *Journal of Marital and Family Therapy, 9,* 171–180.

Everstine, S. E. & Everstine, L., (1989). *Sexual trauma in children and adolescents: Dynamics and treatment.* New York: Brunner/Mazel.

Faller, K. C. (1988). *Child sexual abuse: An interdisciplinary manual for diagnosis, case management, and treatment.* New York: Columbia University Press.

Feinauer, L. L. (1982). Rape: a family crisis. *The American Journal of Family Therapy, 10,* 35–39.

Feinauer, L. L. & Hippolite, D. L. (1987). Once a princess, always a princess: A strategy for therapy with families of rape victims. *Contemporary Family Therapy, 9,* 252–262.

Finkelhor, D. (1979). *Sexually victimized children.* New York: The Free Press.

Finkelhor, D. (1984). *Child sexual abuse: New theory and research.* New York: The Free Press.

Finkelhor, D. (1988). The trauma of child sexual abuse: Two models. In G. E. Wyatt & G. J. Powell (Eds.), *Lasting effects of child sexual abuse* (pp. 171–191). Newbury Park, CA: Sage.

Freeman-Longo, R. E. (1986). The impact of sexual victimization on males. *Child Abuse & Neglect, 10,* 411–414.

Gise, L. H. & Paddison, P. (1988). Rape, sexual abuse, and its victims. *Psychiatric Clinics of North America, 11,* 629–648.

Hartman, M., Finn, S. E., & Leon, G. R. (1987). Sexual-abuse experiences in a clinical population: Comparisons of familial and nonfamilial abuse. *Psychotherapy, 24,* 154–159.

Hill, R. (1958). Generic features of families under stress. *Social Casework, 49,* 139–150.

Hoagwood, K. & Stewart, J. M. (1989). Sexually abused children's perceptions of family functioning. *Child and Adolescent Social Work, 6,* 139–149.

Kaufman, A. (1984). Rape of men in the community. In I. R. Stuart & J. G. Greer (Eds.), *Victims of sexual aggression: Treatment of children, women, and men.* (pp. 156–179). New York: Van Nostrand Reinhold.

Kaye, M. & Winefield, H. R. (1988). Child sexual abuse: A cybernetic description and its implications for professionals. *The Australian and New Zealand Journal of Family Therapy, 9,* 131–138.

Kempe, R. S. & Kempe, C. H. (1984). *The common secret: Sexual abuse of children and adolescents.* New York: W. H. Freeman.

Kolko, D. J. (1987). Treatment of child sexual abuse: Programs, progress, and prospects. *Journal of Family Violence, 2,* 303–318.

Kolko, D. J., Moser, J. T., & Weldy, S. R. (1988). Behavioral/emotional indicators of sexual abuse in child psychiatric inpatients: A controlled comparison with physical abuse. *Child Abuse & Neglect, 12,* 529–541.

Koss, M. P., Gidycz, C. J., & Wisniewski, N. (1987). The scope of rape: Incidence and prevalence of sexual aggression and victimization in a national sample of higher education students. *Journal of Consulting and Clinical Psychology, 55,* 162–170.

Koss, M. P. & Oros, C. J. (1982). The sexual experiences survey: A research instrument investigating sexual aggression and victimization. *Journal of Consulting and Clinical Psychology, 50,* 455–457.

Kübler-Ross, E. (1969). *On death and dying.* New York: Macmillian.

Levine, E. M. & Kanin, E. J. (1987). Sexual violence among dates and acquaintances: Trends and the implications for marriage and family. *Journal of Family Violence, 2,* 55–65.

Loy, P. H. & Stewart, L. P. (1984). The extent and effects of the sexual harassment of working women. *Sociological Focus, 17,* 31–43.

MacFarlane, K. (1986). Helping parents cope with extrafamilial molestation. In K. MacFarlane, J. Waterman, S. Conerly, L. Damon, M. Durfee, & S. Long (Eds.), *Sexual abuse of young children: Evaluation and treatment* (pp. 299–311). New York: Guilford Press.

Miller, W. R. (1987). Effects of rape on the marital relationship. In G. R. Weeks & L. Hof (Eds.), *Integrating sex and marital therapy: A clinical guide* (pp. 171–182). New York: Brunner/Mazel.

Myers, M. F. (1989). Men sexually assaulted as adults and sexually abused as boys. *Archives of Sexual Behavior, 18,* 203–215.

Rogers, C. M. & Tremaine, T. (1984). Clinical intervention with boy victims of sexual abuse. In I. R. Stuart & J. G. Greer (Eds.), *Victims of sexual aggression: Treatment of children, women, and men* (pp. 75–91). New York: Van Nostrand Reinhold.

Rosen, E. J. (1990). *Families facing death: Family dynamics of terminal illness.* New York: Lexington Books.

Rowan, E. L. & Rowan, J. B. (1986). Rape and the college student: Multiple crises in late adolescence. In I. R. Stuart & J. G. Greer (Eds.), *Victims of sexual aggression: Treatment of children, women, and men* (pp. 234–250). New York: Van Nostrand Reinhold.

Russell, D. E. H. (1983). The incidence and prevalence of intrafamilial and extrafamilial sexual abuse of female children. *Child Abuse & Neglect, 7,* 133–146.

Salisbury, J. (1992). Helping victims of sexual harassment. *Family Therapy News, 23,* 13, 26.

Salisbury, J., Remick, H., Ginorio, A., & Stringer, D. (1986). Counseling victims of sexual harassment. *Psychotherapy, 23,* 316–324.

Selvini-Palazzoli, M., Boscolo, L., Cecchin, G., & Prata, G. (1980). Hypothesizing-circularity-neutrality: Three guidelines for the conductor of the session. *Family Process, 19,* 3–12.

Silverman, D. l. (1978). Sharing the crisis of rape. *American Journal of Orthopsychiatry,* *48,* 166–173.

Struckman-Johnson, C. (1988). Forced sex on dates: It happens to men, too. *Journal of Sex Research, 24,* 234–241.

Valentich, M. & Anderson, C. (1990). The rights of individuals in family treatment of child sexual abuse. *Journal of Feminist Family Therapy, 1,* 51–65.

14

THERAPISTS AND MANDATED REPORTING

DEAN M. BUSBY, JOSEPH R. NORTON

It is almost certain all marriage and family therapists will come into contact with the issues of child abuse and maltreatment during their careers. According to Besharov and Younes (1988), the reporting of suspected cases of child abuse and maltreatment is a procedure found in all fifty states, the District of Columbia, American Somoa, Guam, Puerto Rico, and the Virgin Islands, comprising fifty-five jurisdictions. In addition, they report that therapists and counselors are required to make reports of suspected child abuse and maltreatment in thirty-six states. Every therapist needs to be aware of the appropriate procedure for reporting suspected cases of child abuse and maltreatment in his or her respective state. Besharov and Younes found that some twenty-six states require that the mandated reporter complete and send a written report to the local child protective agency after the oral report to the child abuse and maltreatment hotline has been made.

This chapter addresses conceptual issues of what to consider when making a child abuse report. It explores the Child Protective Services (CPS) process and how casework decisions are typically made. Most important, it underscores the fact that therapists have been and are an integral part of the team effort in reaching solutions of child abuse and maltreatment.

The current philosophy with regard to child abuse reporting laws is that "the state" has the responsibility to protect the rights of children and to intervene with appropriate action as necessary. Part of the state's authority includes actions taken by CPS agencies, law enforcement officials, and the courts, which could supersede parental rights if needed in order to protect the child's health and safety. It is important to understand that the state (country) has not always held this view. Historically, in 1874, a young child from New York City named Mary Ellen was repeatedly abused to the consternation of her community. The "state" had no authority to intervene at that time. Finally, community leaders were able to remove her from the home in a very creative and interesting manner—Mary Ellen was declared "an animal" and removed under the auspices of the Association for the Prevention of Cruelty to Animals (ASPCA). Much has been accomplished by individual states to address the concerns of child abuse and maltreatment since that time. National legislation on child abuse, maltreatment laws, and mandated reporting were not in effect until 1974. Since 1974, every state has had to develop child abuse and maltreatment legislation to be in compliance with the national laws.

The ability to supersede parental authority could be viewed as a most invasive policy for a country built on the principles of freedom and personal liberty. In part the rationale of the state's intervention is that the child may be unable to protect herself or himself and hence needs the protection of the state.

An abused or maltreated child typically is a young person who is less than eighteen years of age and has been physically, mentally, or emotionally impaired, or is at risk of being impaired, by parent(s) or other person(s) legally responsible for the child's (children's) care and well-being (Family Court Act, 1970).

DECIDING WHEN TO REPORT

Making a call to the child abuse hotline can create a dilemma for the reporting therapist. On one hand the therapist believes that the child (children) may be at risk of harm and affirmative action (making a child abuse report) may need to be taken to protect the child from that harm and to facilitate the therapeutic process. On the other hand, the therapist might believe calling the child abuse hotline without sufficient cause or evidence may harm the therapeutic alliance. Either decision has consequences for the therapist and the family. Choosing to not make the child abuse report could place the child (children) at further risk of harm and might also be giving the parents an implicit message that abusive behavior toward children is condoned. The therapist could face civil and/or criminal charges if it could be shown that the decision not to report resulted in the child (children) being maltreated or abused. On the other hand, choosing to make the child abuse report could be a reason for the family to decide to exit from therapy completely because they believe that they have been betrayed and/or therapy is not a safe environment.

The most typical question that all mandated reporters ask is how to know when they have reasonable suspicion that a child has been abused or maltreated. Should a hotline call be made to the Child Abuse and Maltreatment Register? At this point, each therapist needs to review the child abuse reporting guidelines in his or her respective state and consult with the local CPS agency regarding these concerns. Therapists are also encouraged to attend mandated reporter training in their local county or district. Mandated reporter training assists the therapist with the identification of the physical and behavioral indicators of abuse and maltreatment, as well as the specific reporting procedures for the locale.

Space does not permit a full listing of all the nationwide child abuse reporting statutes here. Generally speaking, however, when a child's physical and/or emotional health has been impaired or is at risk of being impaired by an act of omission or commission by a parent or other person legally responsible, a CPS report should be made. Erring on the side of making a report to the child abuse hotline is the cautious and prudent action to take.

The making of a child abuse report to any of the various states' registries is an important function in the professional capacity of therapists. The mandated reporting procedure, however, is often accompanied by a great deal of trepidation for reporting therapists. Some questions therapists might be thinking are:

Do I have enough evidence to make a report?

Will the family ever trust me again if I call them into the hotline?

Is the child protective caseworker really going to accomplish something that I as their therapist cannot?

Will the CPS unit take this report seriously and really do what is needed?

I wonder if the child protective caseworker will make the situation worse by scaring and strong-arming the family?

Therapists may face tremendous anxiety as they consider their responsibility to the child (children), the family, and their professional role in sorting out their thoughts regarding these issues.

The therapist needs to assess how the parent's behavior has had a negative impact on the child (children). Are there concerns for the child (children) receiving adequate supervision, food, clothing, shelter? Have they been struck to the point of causing injury, leaving marks and bruises? What could the parent have done but didn't to prevent injury or risk of harm to the child (children)? This is a particularly difficult question because many childhood accidents occur regardless of parental vigilance. What must be considered is whether the parent's action or lack of action placed the child (children) at risk of harm. The child's age is often of great importance in assessing risk of harm. For example, a child under school age who is regularly left home alone unsupervised is categorically at greater risk of harm than an older child given the same circumstances.

Some therapists have the opinion that if they can stop or control the maltreating and abusive behavior while the family is engaged in therapy, a child abuse report need not be made. This premise should be examined closely. A therapist's responsibility includes taking appropriate action when clients disclose that they are a danger to themselves or others. A component of this responsibility includes reporting incidents of suspected child abuse and maltreatment. Therapists are urged to inform their clients at the onset of therapy of a therapist's responsibility to report concerns when it appears clients represent a danger to themselves or others.

After the CPS report has been made, therapists need to understand that they have performed a social control function. The therapeutic process has now taken a shift from the dyadic therapist/client(s) course of therapy to a direction where a third party (CPS agency) has entered the system, resulting in a change in the interrelationships and the therapeutic process. The impact of the change may be relatively small but more likely it will have a profound affect on it. For example, if a therapist were to receive a disclosure of sexual abuse from a ten-year-old girl in a session, in addition to making the CPS report, she or he may then be asked to give a notarized statement and be subpoenaed to testify in court by the local CPS caseworker and/or law enforcement official. How do therapists find themselves testifying in a family or criminal court proceeding when all they had in mind was to make the required hotline report and then let CPS take care of the rest?

COPING WITH THE SYSTEM

Social service systems often can be baffling to most therapists and at least difficult to understand. Figure 14.1 is a flow chart of what could happen after a hotline call is made to the child abuse and maltreatment register, some of the agencies and their processes, along with the potential effects on the therapist and client. The figure shows a series of stages that could occur after making a report. The left side of the figure incorporates the changing roles the therapist may play with respect to the system (e.g., CPS, law enforcement, the courts). The middle of the figure describes the agencies and their possible actions or responses to a child abuse report. The right side of the figure describes the potential effects on the family.

The CPS agency is by law, statute, and regulation responsible for the investigation of alleged incidents of child abuse and maltreatment. CPS is required to assess the degree of risk and/or impairment to the child named in the report. The investigation typically includes interviews with the child in a neutral setting (such as the school), a home visit to assess the child's environment, interview(s) with the parents regarding the allegations of the report, and collateral contacts with other involved agencies and professionals in the community.

As the top middle portion of the figure illustrates, a joint investigation with law enforcement may be initiated if the impairment or risk to the child is serious and involves a penal code (e.g., physical and/or sexual abuse). CPS and law enforcement will be working together on the case yet each are conducting investigations in accordance with their respective legal statutes. To prove a criminal court case, many of the same steps would be followed, however, some of the investigation procedures will be more rigorous because the standard of evidence is higher (e.g., beyond a reasonable doubt). In many states, CPS carries out their responsibilities pursuant to Social Services Law and Family Court Acts, while law enforcement follows their line of investigation pursuant to the Penal Code and Criminal Procedure Law.

A CPS caseworker will consider filing a petition of neglect or abuse in family court in response to reports of children who are at substantial risk of or are being physically, sexually, and emotionally impaired. There are occasions when the parents have not cooperated with services offered and the children continue to be harmed which may require intervention by the family court.

The premise of family court is to first assess the culpability of the parents' behavior toward the children and then rehabilitate the family by directing them to comply with specific terms and conditions in a dispositional court order. A family court proceeding and a criminal court proceeding can be filed concurrently, however, the criminal court proceeding will almost always take precedence over a family court petition, which would be tried after the criminal court proceeding had taken its course.

Figure 14.1 attempts to represent a flow of how a report of suspected child abuse and maltreatment could progress through the legal system. It is important to consider that there are points in time when both CPS and law enforcement could end their case investigation without progressing to family or criminal court. A criminal court proceeding that progresses through to trial can be a very time-consuming process. A year or more may pass between the time criminal charges are filed and a verdict is reached. The verdict (if found guilty) could include a period of probation, a jail sentence, and an order of protection to safeguard the children and, possibly, the spouse.

CASE SCENARIOS

This section includes three scenarios in which the therapist is involved at different phases of the child protective, court, and treatment process.

First Scenario

The therapist makes a child abuse and maltreatment report:

> The therapist, Steve, has been working with this family for several weeks. The presenting concern was that their son Johnny (age 13) has been acting out in school. Johnny has been picking fights with his peers, distracting his classmates in each period, and has been damaging school property. A referral was made by the guidance counselor because all in-school efforts to change his behavior failed.
>
> Steve had the entire family come for therapy sessions. He thought that Johnny's behavior may be due in part to the [punitive] manner in which he was being parented. On at least one occasion the father said to Steve that he had struck Johnny with his hands or belt for misbehavior. Johnny disclosed to Steve

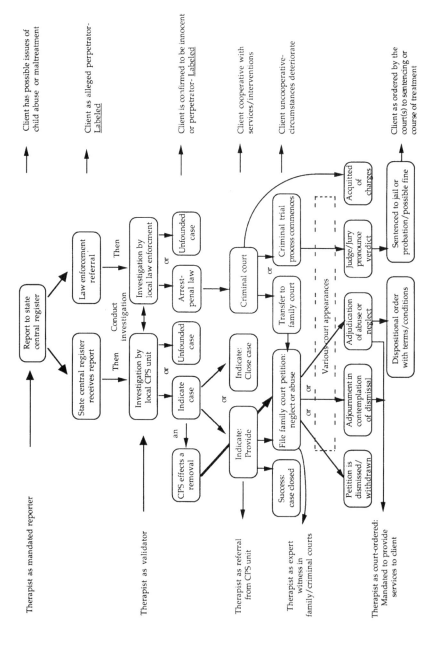

FIGURE 14.1   •   The Interface of Therapists in the Child Protective and Legal Systems

in the fourth session that he had received a number of welts and bruises after being disciplined by his father and that he currently had bruises.

Decision point—therapist decides to initiate a child abuse report (see Figure 14.1) and chooses to inform the family of his obligation to report these concerns to the state child abuse and maltreatment hotline. Johnny's parents may have felt stigmatized by being reported and labeled "child abusers," as well as confused because they came into counseling to address "their son's issues" and not explore their parenting and discipline practices.

Typically, a course of therapy includes the therapist advising the family that any statements or acts that represent a danger to themselves or others would be reported to the appropriate authorities (e.g., child abuse hotline). The therapist may choose to inform the family regarding the decision to report in order to give the family an explicit message of what is not acceptable in parental behavior. Disclosing the therapist's obligation to report may help maintain the family's trust and confidence. On the other hand, the family may feel betrayed by the therapist at this point because they believed that their sessions were "confidential" and nothing would be revealed to others.

The therapist could decide to discuss concerns of child maltreatment and/or abuse with the family in session. The family could then be encouraged to self-report these events to the child abuse hotline to signal their willingness to change and accept responsibility for their behavior. One point to remember is that it is the mandated reporter's responsibility to see that a call is made to the child abuse hotline if the parents decline to self-report. The therapist should give consideration to the appropriateness of who will make the call and when a call to the hotline is to be initiated. There are circumstances where the question of the child's safety dictates that the therapist report the concerns to the hotline with as much speed as possible.

Incidents of alleged sexual abuse require special attention because such abuse often exists in an environment of denial, fear, collusion, and secrecy. These circumstances usually would preclude the therapist from permitting the family to self-report to the child abuse hotline. An investigation of child sexual abuse will almost always involve a law enforcement agency, therefore, if the allegations are true, criminal as well as family court could be in the families' future.

Allisan (1992) states: "Reporting child abuse is considered a distasteful job, and generally the world is not delighted by people who do it. Certainly, you receive no thanks from the victim's family." Allisan suggests attempting to have an emergency meeting with the family. During this meeting the parents are educated as to why the child abuse report needs to be made and are encouraged to self-report. If they refuse to self-report, Allisan (1992) says the therapist should initiate the hotline call.

For therapists who provide their clients the opportunity to self-report, we recommend that they consider these three avenues in how the report could be made to the child abuse hotline:

1. The family is given the opportunity to self-report and call the hotline but only in the therapist's presence.
2. The family declines to self-report but is willing to be present while therapist calls the hotline.
3. The family is unwilling to self-report or to be present for the hotline call. Therapist calls the hotline out of session.

If the therapist allows the parents to leave the session and call the hotline on their own, the therapist will have no control over when and how accurately the facts are represented. In one recent incident a therapist allowed the parents to call the hotline out of session regarding a clear incident of maltreatment. The parents subsequently stated to the therapist that the person on the hotline did not accept the information as sufficient to make a report. The therapist was then faced with a dilemma. The mandated responsibility to call in an incident of suspected child abuse or maltreatment still existed. Should the therapist now call the information in and risk seeming to betray the family? Should the therapist trust that the parents represented the facts accurately to the hotline and let the matter drop? Further questions and debate could continue as to the therapist's next move. All of these issues are preventable by utilizing the steps mentioned previously.

The therapist should report all incidents of child maltreatment and abuse immediately in order to maximize the child's (children's) emotional and physical safety. Networking with a clinical supervisor and the local CPS unit are important first tasks to consider when making a mandated report of any kind.

The therapist is advised to have clients sign informed consent releases at the onset of counseling. These releases should help the client understand explicitly that the therapist will be required to report to the appropriate authorities when any member of the family is suspected to be a danger to themselves or others, including reporting incidents of child abuse and maltreatment.

Once the report has been called into the appropriate state child abuse hotline, it is forwarded to the local social services district where the CPS worker will begin investigating the allegations. The first task of the CPS caseworker is to make an assessment of risk to the children in the home. The assessment of risk should not only substantiate whether the allegations are true, it also needs to determine the risk of physical and emotional impairment to the children in a broader context. This would include an assessment of the children's home environment as well as interviews with parents and children. In addition, the caseworker may obtain the children's school and medical information to understand their functioning on a more global level.

Secondly, the caseworker formulates a service plan to address the identified family issues. The service plan could include a number of services such as a family aide and/or family counseling. The CPS caseworker may need to initiate a neglect or abuse proceeding in family court if the risk or impairment to the child (children) is great enough. As discussed in other portions of this chapter, the goal of utilizing the family court process is to help rehabilitate the family.

The caseworker may ask the therapist, or source of the report, to provide an assessment of risk to the young person(s) and share relevant details about the family's background. As stated earlier, the therapist could then be asked by the CPS caseworker and/or law enforcement official to provide a written statement and testify in a family or criminal court proceeding regarding the disclosed abusive intrafamilial incidents. Many therapists are contacted subsequent to a report by the CPS caseworker for just this purpose because they are qualified by training and experience to complete a sexual abuse assessment of the child and provide testimony in court as an expert witness.

Therapists should consider consulting with their agency or (in private practice) their attorney to decide whether to accept or decline requests by CPS/law enforcement to complete depositions or testify in court unless they have been subpoenaed to do so. In some states local law enforcement officials could be contacted by the Child Abuse and Maltreatment Register, the local county district attorney's office, and/or the CPS caseworker to conduct a parallel and probably joint investigation anytime during the CPS investigatory period when a crime appears to have been committed (see Figure 14.1).

Furniss (1983) states that the CPS worker is coming from the perspective of a "better-parent" and is by law and regulation compelled to make an assessment of whether the reported child abuse allegations are true or not. Caseworkers and law enforcement may need to resort to the use of statutory authority and remove the child (children) from the parents and family environment if imminent risk of danger to life or health is present. Removal in itself may compound the problems for the child and the family. The decision to remove the child from the home environment is almost always carried out as a last resort. In the next section the therapist is asked to address and ameliorate the consequences of child abuse and maltreatment after CPS has become involved.

Second Scenario

The therapist receives a counseling referral from the local department of social services:

> A CPS caseworker has completed a case investigation and has indicated (i.e., allegations to be true) the parents for lack of supervision and excessive corporal punishment of their two children, ages eight and five. The caseworker wants to make sure that the family receives the therapeutic assistance it needs and refers them to a local counseling agency for treatment. The therapist receiving the referral

from the CPS caseworker needs to address the identified concerns and be ready to overcome the family's potential barriers to engaging in a fruitful course of therapy.

The therapist should be aware that many referrals from CPS or Department of Social Services (DSS) will be accompanied by requests for follow-up information regarding how cooperative the family has been in therapy and their pattern of attendance. Molin & Herskowitz (1986, p. 204) state that:

> The referral to a clinician generates the trilateral system...where both the caseworker and the family are looking for services from the clinician. At the same time, the clinician is looking for collaborative help with the family from the caseworker. The interests of the family and the caseworker may be convergent or divergent; their family may agree with the caseworker's wish for therapeutic intervention, or prefer both intervenors to disappear. Clinicians are trained to assess the overt and covert agendas of clients in two-party systems. A similar analysis of the caseworker's various needs is essential in determining the course of action in this three-party system. The agendas of the caseworker may be categorized as task-related and anxiety- or stress-related. The former refers to the recognized needs of the family for services and the caseworker's need for diagnostic input to be used in his/her own assessment and intervention with the family. The latter refers to the pressures to use the clinician in various ways to diffuse and defend against the anxiety and role-related stresses stemming from protective service work.

Therapists will have much to contend with in meeting the needs of the abused child (children), their families, and the various social agencies involved. A frequent expectation of CPS, law enforcement, the courts, and the family is that the therapist should be able to single-handedly impede further incidents of child abuse while effecting lasting solutions for the family's issues! In reality, close teamwork by the therapists and other social agencies will be needed to address the complex dynamics of abuse.

Baglow (1990) discusses two intervention responsibilities. The first responsibility is the therapeutic resolution of child and family issues. The second is containment of the family so that the abuse does not recur and they continue to participate in counseling sessions. In abuse cases, responsibilities are shared by several agencies because no one agency can or should perform both functions alone. Baglow (1990, p. 392) states:

> Because containment and therapy are interlocking concepts, confusion can arise during the allocation of treatment tasks if one agency is seen to be solely therapeutic, while another is seen to be solely responsible for containment....Therapeutic personnel need to alert the appropriate authorities if reabuse occurs. Similarly, those principally responsible for containment need to conduct themselves in a therapeutically sound manner.

If the course of the therapeutic intervention is successful in ending the abusive behavior because of the combined efforts of the family, therapist, and caseworker, the case may be closed following the conclusion of therapy and casework interventions. If the treatment intervention is unsuccessful—the parents fail to cooperate with the therapist yet no further abuse occurs, the therapist and caseworker may decide to close the family's case without further action. If, however, the parents have not only been unresponsive to therapy but have continued to abuse the child, perhaps escalating the abuse, the therapist or CPS caseworker will be in the position of reporting those subsequent abusive incidents to the child abuse hotline. The CPS caseworker will then need to consider seeking relief on behalf of the child by filing a neglect or abuse petition against the parents in family court (see Figure 14.1).

The reason for pursuing court action is to bring the consequences of the parent(s) abusive behavior to the attention of the family court so that it can decide on the appropriate use of its authority in establishing the facts regarding the abusive issues, establishing the onus of responsibility (if any) for those abusive acts, and finally to order terms and conditions to ameliorate the problem. At the time the neglect or abuse petition is filed in family court by the CPS caseworker from the local DSS office, the therapist may be asked by that agency to submit a written report to the court regarding the course of therapy. The therapist also may be subpoenaed to give testimony at a family court appearance. The submission of critical treatment reports, and/or offering testimony at a family court appearance, can certainly be anxiety provoking for the therapist. Having to officially disclose sensitive information about the family in a potentially negative vein is rarely easy to do.

It is critical that the therapist establish clear expectations for what the responsibilities of client and therapist will be from the beginning of a course of counseling. Several guidelines concerning some expectations that should be considered by the therapist are presented later in this chapter.

The most important fact to remember is that the CPS caseworker has everything to gain by helping to keep the client–therapist relationship intact. This includes not having therapists routinely testify at family court hearings unless it is absolutely necessary. Treatment summaries and/or periodic progress reports are more routinely requested of therapists than is their testimony in family court.

Third Scenario

In this last case scenario, the therapist will receive a referral subsequent to a dispositional court order requiring the parents to comply with a course of therapy. Referral to a therapist from a criminal or family court dispositional order:

> At the point at which a court-ordered referral is made to the therapist, the family has probably been exposed to a great number of "official people" and agencies. The "handling" the family has received from these various personages may have left the family with an overall sense of diminished trust which a therapeutic experience is now going to attempt to build on.

As Haley states (1987, p. 44):

> When a judge tells someone to go to therapy or suffer something worse, like going to jail, the therapist faces the difficult task of doing therapy with people who do not wish to be there and often are reluctant to concede they have a problem. Such clients can look upon the therapist as an agent of the state and not on their side. This kind of "involuntary therapy" requires special interviewing techniques. One goal is to change the therapy to a voluntary one in the sense that the clients realize they can resolve their problems and get out of such situations.

The challenge to the therapist is to engage the resistant family into a meaningful course of treatment. If the task of engaging the family was not difficult enough already, the therapist may also be required to submit periodic reports to the court regarding the treatment progress of the family. This scenario is especially pertinent for the treatment of perpetrators of intrafamilial or extrafamilial child sexual abuse. Perpetrators need the mandate and consequences of the criminal justice system in order to successfully engage and complete a course of treatment. Other families will also need the structure provided them by a court-ordered referral to therapy. Kagan and Schlosberg (1989, p. 160) have found that:

> Court orders are often effective in providing the necessary leverage for families with chronic and severe problems to make difficult transitions. Someone needs to play the "heavy" in making firm orders that will stick. Someone also needs to monitor the family to ensure compliance. This is the mandate of departments of social services, mental health, and mental retardation. Otherwise the family will continue to revolve in cycles of perpetual crisis and trauma.

Providing treatment to parents and children ordered by a family or criminal court can be both a rewarding and frustrating experience for therapists. It is a rewarding experience to see positive changes in the family dynamics that result in the reduction and/or elimination of abusive behavior. It can be a frustrating experience to cope with a multitude of agency representatives and court stipulations on the way to that positive change. Careful steps are required on the part of the therapist to engage the family in a meaningful treatment experience as well as keep the court and/or monitoring agencies apprised of the family's progress in therapy. In part, these steps include the following:

1. Understanding the problem(s) from the family's perspective, including evaluating whether the parents have taken responsibility for the problem (abuse) or whether they have externalized it to the intervening agencies?
2. Establish the parent's knowledge of the court order and what tasks they are responsible for.

3. Inquire as to previous therapy (if any) the family has had; what was and was not successful for them?
4. Explore with the family what they hope to gain from this therapy experience and how they believe the therapist can help them.
5. Discuss the parameters of the therapeutic process, including informed consent issues; expectations of attendance (cancellations, no shows); signing appropriate information releases to communicate with other involved agencies; responsibility for payment; and if applicable, the therapists obligation to submit periodic progress reports to the court or monitoring agency.

The therapist is by design blending administrative and therapeutic elements from the first session. A sense of trust in the therapeutic process will be most appropriately engendered once clear administrative expectations and boundaries exist. Finally, effective communication and the establishment of clear expectations with the family and all involved agencies will go a long way toward creating a firm basis for the therapeutic experience.

ISSUES AND CONCERNS

Zellman and Antler (1990) conducted a study in which 1,196 mandated professionals from 15 states responded to a questionnaire. The questions asked included whether they had ever reported child abuse or neglect, how recently they had reported it, and finally if they had ever suspected child abuse or neglect and decided not to report it. The study also included field visits to six states to examine their CPS policies and reveal its impact on mandated reporting. The authors found that there were significant problems in the ability of the current child protective system to respond to the overwhelming demands of increased numbers of reports with limited agency resources. Mandated reporters experienced commensurate difficulty in gaining timely access to child abuse hotlines and the effectiveness of subsequent CPS interventions. As Zellman and Antler (1990, pp. 34–35) state:

> CPS workers and administrators know about the situation; many brought up some of these problems without prompting. But while some agreed that mandated reporters are increasingly disaffected, not a single respondent believed that it was important to try to increase report rates from mandated reporters. Indeed, any attempt to increase the number of reports was seen as absurd, given the high caseloads and intense efforts to reduce the numbers of investigations in most agencies. Nor was failure to report a concern. When queried, protective officials usually acknowledged occasional failures to report. Most conceded, however, that they could not, in good conscience, promote increased reporting when they knew their own systems were already overcommitted.

There are many unresolved issues regarding the child protective system as noted previously here. Mandated reporters in general and therapists specifically need to know that by reporting suspected child abuse they are intervening in family situations to try to ensure the safety of the child (children) and promote positive change and healing. A sense of teamwork should exist between the local CPS agency and therapists as mandated reporters. One barrier to team building that is especially pernicious is when agencies/therapists have to repeatedly justify and defend their actions.

As an illustration of frustration:

> A therapist reported a suspected case of child abuse. In the process of reviewing the family situation, the therapist had some thoughts as to how this situation should be resolved by CPS in the best interest of the family. The investigation was initiated and completed by CPS; the results were not what the therapist believed should have happened. The therapist thought the CPS caseworker should have consulted with her regarding the progress of the case, and that the parents needed milder consequences for the harmful acts committed toward the child. On the other hand, the caseworker believed the therapist had fulfilled her responsibility by reporting the incident and that no further communication with the therapist was necessary during the investigation. Besides, the caseworker perceived the therapist as being too soft regarding what the family really needed.

It would be easy to infer from this stereotyped example that the therapist and caseworker had significant frustrations as to what did or did not occur after the child abuse report was made. Tragically, neither party in this scenario believed the best outcome had been achieved and a willingness to work with the other party on future occasions may have been compromised.

Communication of the therapist's expectations to the CPS caseworker at the beginning of the report investigation and vica versa could have made the perception of the case outcome quite different for the family, the therapist, and caseworker. Indeed one or more contacts between the caseworker and therapist during an investigation should be the norm and not just the exception. Zellman and Antler (1990) found that the most productive CPS climate was where regular communication existed between mandated reporters and local CPS staff.

If therapists choose not to report suspected child abuse it places them and their clients in a precarious and potentially harmful position. According to Hutchison (1993, p. 60):

> As long as there are mandatory reporting laws, professionals outside the CPS system are diminished in the eyes of clients and the state when they do not report known cases—even if they are correct that there is no benefit to reporting. Choosing to be out of compliance with state mandates and to have clients aware of that choice is an untenable ethical position for any professional.

Therapists who believe that existing reporting statutes need changing are encouraged to advocate for those changes in their respective state legislatures. If a therapist chooses to ignore reporting laws as a way of protesting an ineffective system, it is questionable whether using clients to further one's political interests is in the best interest of clients or the therapist.

With the crushing burden of large numbers of child abuse reports, understaffed CPS and DSS units, and rapid caseworker turnover, it is of little wonder that therapists as mandated reporters have not always received adequate and/or timely feedback from CPS caseworkers. The burden on the CPS system to effect "solutions" and "significant change" with multiproblem families is very evident with regard to the issue of removing and placing children in foster care.

In the 1970s, New York State experienced a tremendous influx of children into the foster care system with little plan or provision for their return home. Many children remained in foster care for years without the placing agency being held accountable for an adequate plan of action for their return home. Many professionals in the child welfare field realized this problem and advocated that children need to have "permanence" in their lives. This idea gained momentum in the late 1970s and legislation, entitled the Child Welfare Reform Act, was passed in 1979. This Act, in part, provided for a course of Preventive Services to be provided by the local DSS to families in which children were assessed to be "at risk of placement." It also stipulated that the placing agency had to adhere to clear guidelines for permanency planning regarding children entering or being discharged from foster care. An integral component of Preventive Services to families with children at risk is the provision of therapy.

Therapists have contributed important clinical information regarding the high potential for emotional trauma to children (and families) by their removal and subsequent placement in out-of-home settings. It is becoming increasingly clear that children can and do suffer emotionally when separated from their families of origin. It is imperative that the children and family receive support services, including family therapy, to help preclude the need for placement. It also is critical to promote emotional healing if placement into foster care has occurred and to work with the family toward the child's return home.

There are two treatment responsibilities when working with families where the children have been abused and/or neglected, are at risk of foster care placement, or are moving toward a return to their family. Baglow (1990) describes these as containment and therapy. In the first, the abusive acts are contained so that they do not reoccur; second, therapy addresses the clinical issues of the family and works on their resolution. Both must occur together for an intervention to be successful. Neither task is exclusively the responsibility of CPS or the therapist alone. As Baglow (1990, p. 392) remarks:

> Because containment and therapy are interlocking concepts, confusion can arise during the allocation of treatment tasks if one agency is seen to be solely therapeutic, while another is seen to be solely responsible for containment.

The truth is that each agency is involved in both, uncomfortable as this may be. In reality, if this were not so, the treatment process would quickly break down. Therapeutic personnel need to alert the appropriate authorities if abuse reoccurs. Similarly, those principally responsible for containment need to conduct themselves in a therapeutically sound manner.

Therapists can contribute to the solutions of child abuse and maltreatment by conceptualizing the therapeutic intervention as part of a team endeavor. The identification and reporting of suspected child abuse is an integral component of team building and the desired solutions. Research needs to be conducted on how therapists, CPS agencies, law enforcement, and the courts can coordinate their efforts most effectively. Essentially, the solutions of child abuse and maltreatment are systemic in nature. More than one person in the family needs to change their behavior and/or beliefs through the efforts of the team intervention. It is critical to realize that increased reporting of suspected child abuse and subsequent CPS investigations alone will not produce solutions to child abuse. Hutchison (1993, p. 59) states:

> Once the costs of services to children and families are factored in, it is not clear that a categorical CPS system is more efficient than an improved general social services system would be under a broad definition. Insufficient economic resources are an enduring characteristic of families in the CPS system, and the provision of effective services would have to address this problem. The state has managed to contain the economic costs of reporting laws only by decreasing the level of funding programs that affect children.

It has been our experience with training marriage and family therapists that many of them have a distorted view of CPS even when they have had no prior experience with the system. It appears that many therapists believe that CPS is not interested in maintaining family unity and that all children are going to be placed in foster care. While these assumptions are inaccurate, the larger question is, why do therapists choose to believe them? The child protective worker is often in an impossible position between several systems. On the one hand, one system wants CPS to stop the abuse and keep if from reoccurring, but, on the other hand, CPS is seen as too intrusive and as violating the rights of families. Therapists are often coming from both perspectives— they would like extra clout to keep the abuse from happening, but they do not want someone to intrude on their work.

Additional issues of elitism seem to pervade therapists' views of CPS. Most caseworkers deal with bachelor's level class issues regarding level of training, education, and expertise. It has been our experience that both the therapists and CPS workers want to help families and that there is much in common between these fields. To be effective, therapists need the CPS system and caseworkers need the therapeutic system.

CONCLUSIONS

During its course, this chapter has traversed over several complex and inter-connected issues. We have discussed that mandated reporting is required across the nation; reviewed the major elements that define child abuse and maltreatment; presented three case scenarios in which therapist's are involved in the making of a report or responding to the consequences of the abuse; and, finally, given an overview of the various agencies that typically become involved in the child abuse investigation/litigation process. We have, however, merely touched on some of the challenges facing the therapist in coping with mandated reporting requirements and some of the treatment concerns of families who present with child abuse and maltreatment issues.

A critical issue arises in the reporting process regarding the support that therapists need to receive from their supervisors or colleagues when fulfilling their obligation to report suspected child abuse incidents. It is of tremendous benefit to talk to a fellow professional when fine-tuning one's perception of the problem and to be affirmed for taking a risk in order to promote change in a family system.

The watchword for today's professionals working in the human services field is networking. No one therapist, police officer, judge, caseworker, or clergyperson can hope to solve the broad issues related to violence in the family. However, there are many human service agencies embroiled in con-flicts regarding budget constraints, personnel shortages, jurisdiction, policy, procedures, differing agendas, personality clashes, culpability, liability, and so on. Many professionals have to contend with this climate while attempting to promote healing and growth in the families they serve. The current and future challenge then becomes one of how do the involved professionals and agencies compliment and augment each other in moving toward solutions for overwhelming familial and societal problems.

REFERENCES

Allisan, M. R. (1992). When you suspect child abuse. *The Family Therapy Networker, May/June,* 54–57.

Baglow, L. J. (1990). A multidimensional model for treatment of child abuse: A frame-work for cooperation. *Child Abuse & Neglect, 14,* 387–395.

Besharov, D. J. & Younes, L. A. (1988). Appendix: State child abuse and neglect laws: A comparative analysis. In D. J. Besharov (Ed.), *Protecting children from abuse and neglect: Policy and practice* (pp. 463–480). Springfield, IL: Charles C Thomas.

Family Court Act of 1970, Article 10, Sec. 1012. New York.

Furniss, T. (1983). Mutual influence and interlocking professional-family process in the treatment of child sexual abuse and incest. *Child Abuse & Neglect. 7,* 209–220.

Haley, J. (1987). *Problem solving therapy* (2nd ed.). San Francisco: Jossey-Bass.

Hutchison, E. D. (1993). Mandatory reporting laws: Child protective case finding gone awry? *Social Work, 38,* 56–63.

Kagan, R. & Schlosberg, S. (1989). *Families in perpetual crisis*. New York: W. W. Norton.

Molin, R. & Herskowitz, S. (1986). Clinicians and caseworkers: Issues in consultation and collaboration regarding protective service clients. *Child Abuse & Neglect, 10*, 201–210.

Zellman, G. L. & Antler, S. (1990). Mandated reporters and CPS: A study in frustration. *Public Welfare, Winter*, 30–37.

AUTHOR INDEX

SUBJECT INDEX